In Praise of Veg

the ultimate cookbook for vegetable lovers

alice zaslavsky

appetite

Dedicated
to The Nut

With praise from:

José Andrés

Matt Stone

May Chow

Mark Best

Jeremy Chan

George Calombaris

Coskun Uysal

Philippe Mouchel

Christine Manfield

Selassie Atadika

David Thompson

Palisa Anderson

Darren Robertson

Prateek Sadhu

Amanda Cohen

Monica Galetti

Simon Bryant

Ben Shewry

Guy Grossi

Ana Roš

Mauro Colagreco

Ivan Brehm

Jo Barrett

Rosio Sanchez

Sat Bains

Joan Roca

Ciccio Sultano

Karen Martini

Albert Adrià

Clare Smyth

Phil Wood

Jp McMahon

Alla Wolf-Tasker

Josh Niland

Tobie Puttock

Michael Hunter

Niki Nakayama

Danielle Alvarez

Alanna Sapwell

Luka Nachkebia

Dan Barber

Matt Wilkinson

Skye Gyngell

Monique Fiso

Tetsuya Wakuda

Nicky Riemer

Saransh Goila

Ray Adriansyah

Rick Stein

Ashley Palmer-Watts

Guillaume Brahimi

Matt Moran

Andrew Wong

Andrew McConnell

Garima Arora

Jack Stein

Bill Granger

Contents

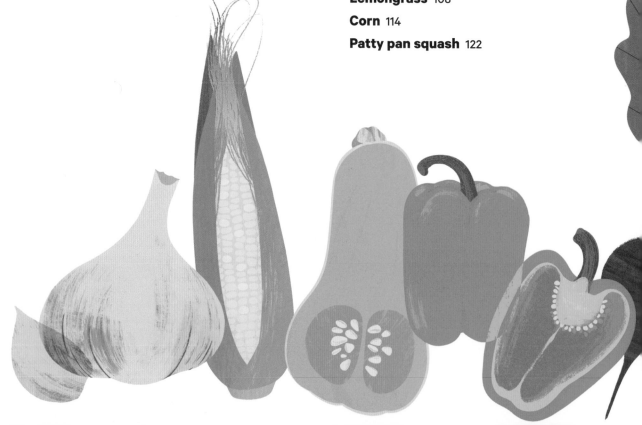

Well, hello there ...

You might have flipped here from the fancy front cover, or cavorted back through a kaleidoscope of color-coded recipe pages to land at this one, with its big bold greeting. Let's hang out!

This hefty tome is my tribute to the wonderful world of veg. I've chosen 50 of my all-time favorites and delved a little deeper into what makes them special for cooks and eaters alike, offering ways to bring the best out of them in the kitchen, no matter what your skill level. Once you leaf (ha!) through these pages, you'll be able to pick up a root, a tuber, a bulb, a stalk, and have ideas and inspiration bubble forth, so that you're never short of a meal or a menu. You'll be able to use the other books you already have, with a better understanding of *why* a recipe does what it does, and what you can do to adapt or play with it.

This is not a purely plant-based book, because that is not reflective of how my family – my husband Nick and our daughter Hazel (a.k.a. The Nut) – and I eat. We are, however, plant-forward, in that we start with the veg and build the dishes around them. I wanted to write a book with that principle at its heart, because I believe many of us have a desire to flex our 'flexitarian' muscle – to grab more greens, reduce the load we put on the environment, and take more care with the proteins we choose. But often, we just don't know where to start, and aren't at the point of going cold tofu quite yet. That's why these recipes are all vegetable-driven, first and foremost, and if there's some flaked fish or a bit of bacon, it's there as a secondary element because it *makes* the dish – with substitutions for anyone who's up for the full veg.

Growing up in Georgia in the former Soviet Union, my diet was vegetable-heavy by both culture and necessity – a Caucasus cuisine with an abundance of fresh produce, bartered behind the Iron Curtain. On emigrating, my appreciation for cuisine became informed and enriched by the melting pot of Australia; a place where splashing soy sauce onto spaghetti bolognese seems like a perfectly sensible thing to do. The recipes in this book are reflective of both tradition and modernity, like all good cooking should be.

Bucking further from tradition, this book is not alphabetical or seasonal – rather, it is tonal. Vegetables are grouped by color, with comprehensive entries for more commonly found forms, crib notes for CSA surprises, and recipes for the more unusual varieties smattered throughout for when you're feeling adventurous, or you've been handed a home-grown heirloom something-or-other. I want you to be able to flick through and find what you're looking for, through the squinty eyes of someone who's spent too long staring into the fridge, trying to figure out what to do with the dregs at the bottom of the crisper. And, better yet, to open your mind to the fabulous forms and flavors that are right at your fingertips.

Loving your leftovers

There has never been a better time for accessing, storing, using and *reusing* fresh food as there is today. It's no surprise that the more readily available fresh produce has become, the less love we give to the stuff left over – yet somehow, I missed that memo. I'm a leftovers-lover from way back! And vegetables are easier to reincarnate than any other food group, thanks to their long shelf life and chameleonic capabilities. When I was young, Mum's Big Batch Borsch was the after-school snack of dreams for this latch-key kid. And once I figured out that I could put bonus stuff in the borsch, like croutons and luncheon meat, the culinary world was cracked wide open to me forever more. These days, I purposely make *more* of stuff than I need, because the only thing better than a home-cooked dinner is knowing that you've still got a perfectly packed portion to reinvigorate for lunch the next day.

One of the biggest secrets you may not realize about restaurant food is that much of it could easily be classified as 'reinvigorated leftovers'. Unless it's something cooked *à la minute*, most of the work's been done well before you place your order – hours, if not days, in advance. That's why prices can seem so steep: it's not just the cost of ingredients that you're paying for, but the prep hours too. If you've got a choice between eating last night's spag bol or ordering takeaway, consider the fact that either way, you're eating leftovers.

At what point do 'leftovers' simply become 'meal prep'? Well, that's entirely up to you. I'm an unapologetically lazy cook, so I consciously load up my fridge with extra stuff to help speed up the journey from hangry to happy. Hard cheese rinds, frozen stock (cooked down to fit into an ice-cube tray, to pop out a cube or two as needed), frozen peas and corn ready for tossing into a pot when dishes need bonus bits, and half an onion in the door (why is there *always* half an onion in every fridge?) are but some of the delights that you will always find in my arsenal. Extra servings of roasted/steamed/boiled/fermented/pickled vegetables are the gifts that keep on giving, ready to become soup, salad, sauce or a dip at the blitz of a button or the flick of a fork.

Shortcuts to the 5 S's

Cooking doesn't have to be difficult or elaborate – in fact, I glean the most gratification from the simplest things: a caramelized crust on just about anything (easier to do when it's already been cooked the day before); butter melting into the cracks of something steaming away; or flipping out a precariously-yet-perfectly formed omelet full of wilty arugula and cheese. The kitchen is where fun can be had, creativity flexed and risks taken.

Most importantly, it's a place where you should feel safe enough to break away from convention, take control of your dining destiny and find better and easier ways to make the food you love. Nobody polishes off a delicious meal and says, 'Gee, I wish that recipe was harder!'.

Wherever I can, I've included shortcuts that take advantage of bits and pieces you might have at your disposal, as well as suggesting how you can give dishes another spin of the turntable (a 'double duty' so to speak), which usually takes the form of one of the 5 S's: Soup, Sauce, Stew, Salad or Sandwich.

The simplest **soup** is really just a runny purée, so blitzing left-over roast veg or any form of stew to a finer consistency with a bit of extra liquid (such as stock or even water) is a great way to feel like you're eating a new meal with minimal effort.

The same goes for **sauces**, which I'm especially enamored with during the summer months, when barbecue marinades become dipping sauces (be sure to heat and eat here), or juices in the bottom of the pan are transformed into pasta-sauce perfection. Sometimes it's as simple as letting a pan that has had something caramelizing in it hang out on the stove for the afternoon, only to reheat it to become the flavor base for that evening's dinner.

Stews, casseroles, curries and rich pasta sauces always taste better the next day. I like to give them a new lease on life by adding extra fresh veggies that are capable of cooking through by the time the dish is reheated – baby spinach works well here, as do corn kernels, mushrooms and cherry tomatoes.

As for **salads**, anything from curry to kebabs to quark to cans of fish or beans from the pantry can be added to fresh (or even left-over!) vegetables and become inexpensive, delicious and nutritious hot-weather dinners or lunch at your desk. Have fun with textures and temperatures by roasting, steaming or crumbing and deep-frying (bonus points if you've made your own crumbs from left-over bread!). You can boost flavor with some form of onion, use nuts and seeds for texture, and shake things up with different oils, vinegars and fats (such as cheese or avocado).

When in doubt, turn it into a **sandwich** filling. I'm using the term 'sandwich' here very loosely, because who says it's gotta be bread? Anything from pita to tortilla wraps to rice paper to lettuce leaves … if you can pick it up and eat it with your hands, it's a sandwich, people! Try to pack your choice of wrapping separately from the leftovers in question, and assemble just before you eat for max crunch, and the smug satisfaction of showing your co-workers how organized and industrious you are.

In living color

Part of what makes vegetables one of nature's wonders is the available palette of colors to tantalize the palate. Colors are evocative, and have a natural effect on our sense of flavor expectation. Why else does a smattering of herbs suddenly make a lackluster salad look infinitely fresher? Team juicy crimson tomatoes with torn basil leaves and serve them up with but a splash of olive oil, a blob of buffalo mozzarella and a sprinkling of flaked sea salt and people will gaze at you like maybe you're a wizard, transporting them to a sun-dappled Italian piazza, complete with *il Tricolore* flag flapping overhead. Similarly, an absence – or uniformity – of color can have an impact of its own, both for the better (*à la* cheffy monochrome marvels), and not so much, when food gets decidedly greige.

The expression 'eat the rainbow' isn't just a throwaway line, either. Colors also signify what phytochemicals (protective compounds) each vegetable contains as a natural defense mechanism – something that we, too, can harness for our own wellbeing. The deeper or darker the color, the more antioxidants and functional benefits within. Our tastebuds are the best indicator of what we need at any given time, and we have evolved to crave the foods that give us the nutrients we're lacking. Once we tap into these natural desires with the skills to bring out the best in our base ingredients, we can't help but see and appreciate the spectrum of flavors that the natural world is bursting forth with – Mother Nature's medium, a palette of colors ready for the canvas that is your plate.

At its heart, this book is organized by shades of color for a very simple reason: because a love of vegetables is universal, and whether it's a courgette or a zucchini, an aubergine or eggplant, it's still green, or purple (or … aubergine). So whatever language you speak, it's time to get praising.

The vegetable matrix

If you'd rather freestyle than follow a recipe, here's a reference chart for fool-proof, people-pleasing plant-fiddling. Some vegetables prefer low and slow, others like getting hot and heavy, and some are best with just a lick of heat and a flick of the pan.

No matter the cooking method, or the veg, chop it into similarly sized pieces to prevent uneven cooking. The less cooking time you have, the smaller you should cut – even a grater on its largest teeth might be a good option if you're planning a purée, building a sauce or blitzing a soup. A shorter cooking time is also a way of minimising nutrient loss, as is avoiding too much time bobbing about in water that is to be discarded.
A note on ovens: My oven is fan-forced (and super hot!) so you may need to adjust cooking times to suit your own oven.

VEG	IN A HURRY	LIGHT & BRIGHT	SET & FORGET	FLAVOR BOMB
Cauliflower	**Raw** Blitz into cauli rice, *à la* Purple cauli tabouleh (page 83)	**Florets + Steam** 4–6 minutes, until fork-tender	**Florets + Roast** Toss with salt + oil, 450°F, 15–20 minutes	**Florets + Batter** KFC: Keralan fried cauliflower with coconut chutney (page 86)
Parsnip 	**Raw** Grate through a salad or slaw	**Cubes + Boil** Just enough liquid to cover, 10–15 minutes until fork-tender, then purée	**Sticks + Roast** Toss with salt + oil, 425°F, 25–30 minutes	**Grate + Bake** Four-ginger parsnip sticky date pudding (page 60)
Fennel 	**Raw + Shredded (or finely sliced)** Toss through a salad or slaw	**Wedges + Braise** Color in a pan, then add stock, orange juice or tomato passata to cover, simmer for 10–15 minutes	**Chunks + Roast** Toss with salt, oil + parmesan, 400°F, 40–45 minutes	**Wedges + Crumb** Crispy fennel wedges with sour cream & sweet chili sauce (page 74)

VEG	IN A HURRY	LIGHT & BRIGHT	SET & FORGET	FLAVOR BOMB
Corn 	**Raw** Fresh corn, shaved off the cob and straight into your salad	**Cobs + Boil** 5–7 minutes	**Kernels + Simmer** 2:1 Corn:Stock, 20–25 minutes; blitz half to purée, stir in cream or crème fraîche	**In husk + BBQ** Cheese-cloud corn cobs with apple chipotle barbecue sauce (page 120)
Carrot 	**Grate + Raw** Salad or slaw	**Chunks + Steam** 5–10 minutes, depending on thickness	**Halves + Roast** Toss with salt + oil; preheat tray along with oven, 400°F, 25–30 minutes	**Grate + Bake** Zesty gluten-free carrot cake (page 134)
Sweet potato 	**Cubes + Simmer** Darl's dal (page 146)	**Shredded + Fry** Bind with egg, then fry as fritters, 4–5 minutes each side	**Whole (small) + Roast** Prick with fork or paring knife, then toss with salt + oil, 400°F, 30–40 minutes	**Slice + Bake** Sweet & savory sweet potato galettes (pages 152–153)
Pumpkin, butternut squash 	**Chunks + Roast** Pumpkin soup (page 165)	**Halves + Roast** Buttered Butternut Squash (page 158)	**Cubes + Roast** Toss with salt + oil; preheat tray along with oven, 400°F, 30 minutes	**Cubes/grate + Braise** Seven-spice butternut tagine (page 160)
Bell pepper 	**Raw** Slice raw through salad (especially Greek!)	**Whole + Char** Roasted bell peppers (page 200)	**Chunks + Roast + Blitz** One-pan romesco soup (page 198)	**Stuff + Bake** Samosa-mix stuffed peppers (page 202)
Beet 	**Thinly sliced + Raw** No-bake beet salad (page 246)	**Grate + Simmer** Grate borsch (page 238)	**Whole + Roast** Toss with salt + oil, then wrap in foil, 425°F, 45–60 minutes	**Boil + Blitz + Bake** Blender beet brownie (BBB) (page 248)

Eggplant

Cubes + Sauté
Salt for 15 minutes, squeeze out moisture. Heat oil in pan, toss eggplant over medium heat until tender; 10–15 minutes

Slice + Roast
Badrijani: walnut eggplant rolls (page 266)

Halve, Score + Roast
Brush with oil + salt, cut side down, 425°F, 35–40 minutes. Scoop out + blitz for a baba ghanoush dip OR glaze with teriyaki, miso or tahini

Sticks + Fry
Sichuan sticky eggplant (page 270)

Mushroom

Buttons + Raw
Salads, crudités

Buttons/cups/exotics Slice + Sauté
Sweat in minimal oil/butter to start, then add more fat + flavorings, 5–8 minutes until golden

Portobello/field Whole + Roast
400°F without oil, 15–20 minutes, then stuff with cheese and/or herbs + drizzle with oil; then grill for an extra 3–5 minutes, until topping melts and burnishes

Slice + Fry
Forest floor fry-up (page 322)

Potato

Peel + Quarter + Steam
10–12 minutes, until fork-tender, then toss with oil or butter + herbs

Whole + Boil
Cover with cold well-salted water, bring to a boil, then simmer 20–25 minutes OR All-seasons potato salad (pages 302–303)

Peel + Half/Quarter + Parboil + Roast
Cover with cold well-salted water, bring to a boil, then simmer vigorously 2 minutes. Preheat tray along with oven, 425°F. Drain spuds, shake, toss with oil + salt, roast 40–50 minutes

Boil + Mash + Fry
Mash, crackle & pop (page 298)

Broccolini, broccoli

Florets + Blanch
1–2 minutes, then refresh in iced water to stay bright
Thinly slice/shred + Raw
Dress with zesty vinaigrette

Florets + Steam
3–6 minutes OR Broccolini caesar salad (page 366)

Chunky/Florets + Roast
Toss with salt + oil; preheat tray along with oven, 425°F, 20–25 minutes for broccoli; 10–15 minutes for broccolini

Char + Roast
Broccoli steaks with tkemali (page 368)

VEG	IN A HURRY	LIGHT & BRIGHT	SET & FORGET	FLAVOR BOMB
Zucchini 	**Raw + Shaved** Dress with zesty vinaigrette/pesto	**Chunky slices + Grill** Rub with salt, leave for 15 minutes, then grill in hot pan for 2–3 minutes each side and dress	**Grate + Bake** Summer slice (page 378)	**Spiralize** Mid-week bolognese (page 380)
Green beans 	**Top + Blanch** 3–4 minutes **Top + Steam** 5–7 minutes	**Split + Blanch** Jalapeño four bean salad (page 392)	**Top + Braise** Sweat some onion or shallot, stir in beans + stock or tomato passata; simmer for 30–40 minutes, until tender	**Top + Sauté** Georgian green beans with caramelized onion (page 390)
Brussels sprouts	**Raw + Shredded** Brussels sprout slaw with chives, parmesan & chardonnay vinegar (page 438)	**Shred + Sauté** 4–5 minutes until tender	**Halves + Roast** Preheat tray along with oven, 425°F; roast for 10–20 minutes cut side down, depending on marinade	**Halves + Roast** Seventies dinner party sprouts (page 440)
Asparagus	**Snap ends + Blanch** 2–4 minutes	**Split + Soften** Three-ingredient puffy asparagus & Persian feta omelet (page 414)	**Snap ends + Roast** On a foiled tray, 425°F for 8–10 minutes	**Split + Roast** Asparagus crumb & soldiers (page 412)
Bok choy	**Chunks + Stir-fry** Lau's vegetables with fresh ginger (page 104)	**Leaves + Soften** Miso soup with bok choy, potato & radish (page 432)	**Halves + Steam** 5–7 minutes, until stalks are tender	**Halves + Grill** Grilled bok choy with peanut sauce (page 434)
Onion 	**Red/white/salad: Thinly sliced + Raw** In every salad!	**Brown: Dice + Sweat** Low heat, oil/ghee/butter, 2 minutes lid off, 5 minutes lid on, then 2 minutes lid off	**Brown: Slice + Caramelize** Sweat on low heat, oil/ghee/butter, 40–60 minutes; sprinkle with sugar to help it along	**Slice + Bake** The 'any kind of onion' tarte tatin (page 286)

The heat spectrum

Most vegetables need little in the way of cooking before they're safe to eat, so applying heat is more about bringing out the best in each. These methods sit on a spectrum from gentle and indirect through to point-blank and searing hot.

Boiling

With direct wet heat, the golden rule is that veg growing in the ground starts in just enough cold water to cover, while above-ground veg goes straight into boiling water (in your biggest pot), to stop the temperature dropping too drastically. This helps stop fibrous root veg from falling apart, and keeps leafy greens happy. Once brought to the boil, drop the heat to more of a rumbling simmer, so as not to push the veg around too much in the pot – which leads to cracks and unevenly cooked bits. Good seasoning starts with the water, so whatever the veg, add a good pinch or two of salt before boiling. A squirt of lemon juice or vinegar in the water will help keep oranges, reds and purples bright – but lay off the acid for anything green.

Blanching

This method is especially handy when cooking delicate greens that have a precarious point between 'cooked' and *cooked*. Have a big bowl of iced water on hand, and lift the veggies straight out of boiling water into cold, to shock them into keeping their color just-so and stop the cooking process. This is especially helpful when blanching to peel – such as for tomatoes, or for peaches in fuzz-free desserts. However, for green beans and the like, particularly when it's just for a quick mid-week meal, I'll halve the blanching time and drain them directly into a colander, ready for blasting with cold water straight from the tap.

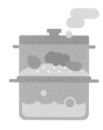

Steaming

Indirect wet heat is best for vegetables with fine skins and delicate flavor. Unlike boiling, which can be quite aggressive, and where much of the nutrients and taste can leach out into the water, steaming gently heats from outside in, retaining moisture during cooking. It's also easy to keep an eye on your veg by lifting the lid of your steaming vessel – be it a bamboo stack or a special insert. You can also 'steam roast' by covering vegetables cooking in the oven with foil (or in a parchment paper pouch) and ensuring they're plenty juiced up (even, literally, with orange juice) until they soften, then crank up the heat and pull off the covers to give them a chance to crisp up a little.

Braising

Once but an afterthought to meaty mains, veg-driven braises such as stews and tagines are hearty one-pot wonders. Putting your veg front-and-center in a casserole with some form of braising liquid – such as stock and aromatics, or tomato passata (strained tomatoes) – and maybe some beans or pulses to cook down for an extended period of time is a surefire road to rustic wholesomeness. All vegetables braise well, from beans all the way to cabbage and root veg. There's no need to 'check for doneness' – even the most fibrous ones soften within an hour. And the best part? They taste even better the next day.

Confit

Technically, confit is supposed to refer to a protein – such as duck – slowly cooked in its own fat, or in oil and butter. However, the trick can be translated to vegetables, using a neutral-flavored oil or ghee, and then keeping the heat of the stovetop or oven at a reasonably low temperature. While traditional confit requires that the ingredient be submerged, veg is far more forgiving, so this method just requires using far more oil than you normally would, which helps to conduct heat, while sealing in moisture. The oil absorbs the flavor of the vegetables, while the veg itself, intensified in color on the outside, takes on a silky unctuousness (and the flavors of your chosen aromatics) through to the center.

Deep-frying

If you've considered skipping this bit, because, 'fat', I have news for you: since this is such an efficient way to cook, deep-fried veggies actually absorb less oil than shallow-fried. Also, fat = flavor, people! The key to an efficient deep-fry is to use the right oil. Look for a neutral-flavored oil with a high smoke-point, such as grapeseed or peanut oil, and – especially if you're just using it to fry veg – let it cool, then strain, rebottle and reuse the oil a couple of times until the color turns dark, or it starts to smell whiffy. Drain your deep-fried delights on paper towel or a clean cloth to absorb any excess oil, and season generously with flaked sea salt and spices while still hot, so everything gets a chance to mingle.

Stir-frying

The biggest pitfall when stir-frying is a wok that is too cold, or loaded up with too many ingredients that sweat into an unhappy slop at the bottom. If you have a big enough wok, then you can do everything together; otherwise, try the following trick. Heat the wok until smoking, then batch-cook the veggies, starting with the most fibrous, in plenty of neutral-flavored oil with a high smoke-point (I like peanut oil best). If you're using meat or any other protein – even tempeh – fry this off first. Keep a big bowl nearby to keep adding the cooked ingredients on top of each other to stay warm, then whack it all back in, add garlic and chili (these two burn very easily) and stir your sauce combo through.

Grilling

Softer vegetables that don't take much to heat through benefit from being lightly oiled and grilled in a hot pan. I like to use a grill pan or the grill grates on a barbecue, so the veggies get those familiar char lines that make everything taste better. The heat you get from grilling is hot and heavy – especially if you've allowed your cooking surface to warm up properly; a dry pan, close to smoking, is what you're after. Some level of supervision is required, but don't be afraid to leave your veg sizzling on each side for longer than you think, to ensure that char marks are forthcoming. Moisture bubbling to the surface and evaporating on your first side is a good indicator that it's time to flip.

Sautéing

This method of high heat, less oil is terrific if you're pressed for time and ready to fry. No lid required. Loosely translated, sauté means 'to jump', because the key here is to keep everything moving, through either stirring or tossing. Heat your pan and your oil and have a spatula or wooden spoon on hand to stir regularly, so that everything has a chance to make happy with the heat source. If you're worried that something looks like it's burning, turn the heat down and don't panic: you control the heat, the heat does not control you.

Searing

Usually reserved for meat-talk, searing your veg on a high heat before roasting is especially beneficial for naturally sweeter vegetables such as corn, sweet potato and pumpkin, where it encourages caramelization – both pleasing to the eye, and more complex on the palate. Caramelization also has the added benefit of mitigating bitter flavors in broccoli and kale. It also makes vegetables that are rich in amino acids, such as eggplant and mushrooms, taste even more 'meaty'. Use a hot pan to brown your veg on all sides, then whack it in a moderate oven to roast, as you might a large cut of beef. You can even skip this step but gain a similar result by leaving the roasting tray in the oven (I'm talkin' 500°F) while it heats up, then carefully arranging the oiled-up/marinated roast veg on this 'searing hot' tray and dropping the oven temperature to 400°F to finish cooking.

Sweating

For no-sweat sweating, especially where high-risk-of-burns veg such as onions are in play, I have one tip for you: keep a lid on it. You want the moisture to get trapped in the pan, keeping everything safe from burning. I like to start a sweat unlidded, just to build up a little heat first, then drop the heat, pop the lid on and go about my business, checking intermittently. Leave the lid off for the last 3 minutes to help absorb any excess moisture and give a golden glow. For a deeper flavor, leave the lid off for 8–10 minutes on a low heat, stirring every now and then, and watching like a hawk. Most people are impossibly impatient when it comes to sweating – so however long you're sweating your onions now, double it. The texture and flavor of your dish will come alive once you let onions reach their full potential.

Caramelizing

While we're talking 'caramelization', the most commonly caramelized veg is onion, best done in a wide-based shallow pan. Onions are rich in amino acids and sugar, which is why they become such a savory–sweet flavor bomb as they brown. Good caramelization happens slowly – you want to 'brown' not 'burn' – and can take as long as an hour if you're doing a big batch (which stores well in the fridge or freezer, mind you). To game the system, scrunch a pinch of salt through the onions before they go in the pan, to help accelerate cell breakdown, then add a pinch of brown sugar to the pan with the onions to remind them to 'dream big, think sweet', as my mate Kylie would say. Keep the heat on medium–low and stir often.

Roasting

The dry, radiating heat of an oven does wonders for veggies, crisping the outside and tanning the edges in the most appealing way. You can give starchy veg a speedy headstart by parboiling first until they just start to soften; softer veg and leaves can go straight into the oven. Toss the veg in plenty of olive oil and seasoning, then arrange on a baking tray lined with parchment paper, with some space between each piece to ensure they get a chance to cop some heat. I usually roast at 400°F, but like to start the oven hotter (as though roasting a chicken) at 500°F, just to shock the outside into burnishing up a bit more.

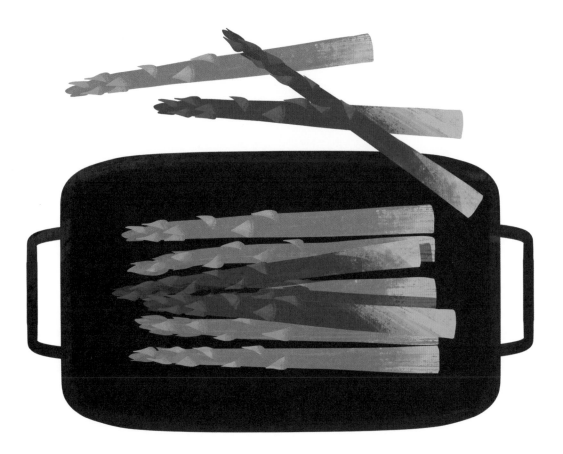

The power pantry

If you're in awe of people who always manage to just 'whip things up' and wonder how they do it, you'll be pleased to know that 90 per cent of it is in the shopping. And that doesn't mean buying ready-meals or packets of stuff constantly – nor should it conjure up romantic scenes of wicker baskets and daily trips to the market. It mostly means loading up your pantry with dried goods and condiments – pulses, grains, nuts, seeds, oils, vinegars and other specialty ingredients – to adorn and complement fresh and frozen ingredients, for extra oomph with minimal mucking about.

Where to start really depends on what you like to eat. If you're into pasta, your perfect pantry will look different from someone who is more of a curry nut, and so on. The basics remain the same, though. It will require some initial outlay, but the key is to look at cost-per-wear. Do you plan on cooking dishes like these often? If so, invest. If it's a one-off thing, or you're just dipping your toe in, quell the impulse to splurge, and find a substitution instead. It's a far more sustainable way to shop, in more ways than one.

As a starting point, I've included my 'must-haves' for every cook, as well as 'lust-haves' that you can pick and choose from. The bigger and bolder the font, the stronger the want, if you catch my drift. These are top-line stock lists – kind of like a fake-it-til-you-make-it collection, and there will always be far more nuance once you really immerse yourself in any cuisine. If you feel like geeking out way more specifically, be sure to check out the very uncomprehensive list of Books You'll Love on page 472.

Storage & sustainability

A lot of the dried goods that we're used to buying in little packets are available from bulk wholefoods stores, sold by weight. Bring your own containers – which might be fancy stackables, or trusty old jam and passata jars, or even paper lunch bags – and label them clearly (including the purchase date). You'll find this is not only more cost-effective, and reduces your rubbish load, but it also tends to be fresher stock – particularly where nuts and spices are involved.

Thankfully, there are more nifty, reusable storage solutions than ever. Stylish, long-wearing and budget-friendly glass, steel, ceramic and fabric options are all becoming more readily available and affordable for those who are keen to go plastic-free. Speaking of 'plastic', when researching this book, it became very apparent that much of the advice on storing vegetables had been written before single-use plastics fell out of favor. If you're wondering why the emphasis is on bagging things for storage in the first place, it is to do with retaining moisture (particularly where the addition of damp cloth or paper towel is concerned), and the way in which various gases in fresh produce interact – kind of like separating the naughty kids in the class (or in this case the crisper).

If I do use plastic, it'll tend to be in the form of reusable shopping bags, which fit everything that needs to be kept damp, separated with dampened paper towel. (I'll often reuse this paper towel if I can get away with it, too.) These days there are even various calico and fabric swags that fit the bill. The outlay may seem expensive, but you'll find yourself thanking your lucky stars when your veggies seem to last twice as long as they did before. Beeswax is great for wrapping stuff, as is foil, which can be carefully repurposed.

Herbs & spices

When buying spices, buy less but better, and purchase whole seeds rather than ground if you're not sure when you'll use them again; this retains their integrity and intensity longer. I do love a spice mix, particularly when I'm in a hurry, but it is especially important to buy these in smaller quantities, as ground spices and dried herbs have a shorter shelf life and are particularly susceptible to fizzing out when exposed to heat or sunlight.

Store them in a cool, dry place, preferably in dark-colored glass. To test whether your spices or herbs are past it, rub a little between your fingertips and take a whiff – if the fragrance is only faint, or even slightly moth-bally, don't ruin your efforts at the pot with some below-par sprinkles.

Special mention

These spices will give you the secret ingredient you didn't know you needed, and suddenly everything tastes better.

* **Smoked and sweet paprika** – the good stuff in a tin
* Ground white pepper – offers a distinctively floral heat to dishes
* Ground fenugreek – I use this a lot, to turn dishes a bit Georgian and exotic
* **Curry powder** – gives a beautiful golden color and great all-round flavor
* Celery and fennel seeds – for instant earthiness
* Cayenne pepper – for instant kick
* **Garlic powder** – try to find the powder, rather than the granules

Nuts, seeds, oils & fats

I've popped nuts and seeds here because they're full of natural oils, and are therefore a solid place to start when talking about storage of fats. Nuts always store – and taste – better when bought in-shell and cracked as you need them, and some fats are always better kept in the fridge. The oils within certain nuts – especially richer ones such as walnuts – are wont to go rancid and start to taste bitter, so storing them properly makes a big difference. It may seem a tedious ask, but nut-crackers are worth the squeeze, so to speak – and technology has moved far beyond the ones that used to pinch your phalanges. Store shelled nuts in the fridge – and if you only ever use them toasted, you can even double their shelf life by keeping ones such as pine nuts in the freezer. Almond meal should always go in the fridge.

Other oils such as extra virgin olive oil and sesame oil have a much shorter shelf life than you think, so if you only use a little of these for flavoring, you're better off buying smaller bottles and using them up quickly. Less is more. Mind you, when they're on special, picking up a drum of olive oil for cooking and one of sunflower, rice bran or peanut oil for deep-frying always makes me feel smug. Decant into smaller bottles and store any remainder in your coolest, darkest place – probably near the potatoes.

Pantry

* Olive oil (cheaper, for cooking)
* **Extra virgin olive oil** (dressings)
* **Vegetable/canola oil** (stir-frying and deep-frying)
* Butter (stored in a butter bell, for spreading)
* Coconut oil (curries or South-East Asian desserts)
* Chili oil (finishing, preserves, dressings)
* **Sesame oil**
* Grapeseed oil (for mayonnaise)
* Mustard oil (for Indian/ subcontinental curry bases)
* Walnuts (unshelled)

Fridge

* **Butter** (salted, cultured butter has the best flavor to shelf-life ratio)
* Ghee (curries/high-temp cooking alternative to butter)
* Half and half cream
* Heavy cream
* Sour cream
* Crème fraîche
* **Marinated feta** (keep the oil)
* Almonds
* Almond meal
* Hazelnuts (shelled)
* Macadamias (shelled)
* Sesame seeds

Freezer

* Pine nuts

Acids & vinegars

Whenever you taste a sauce or soup and think, 'Hmmm … it needs something,' that something is most likely acid. It's what helps to stimulate your saliva, cuts through rich or creamy flavors (which can otherwise be quite cloying if left unbridled), and lifts something out of the one-note doldrums into a polyphonic palate philharmonic.

You might find yourself reaching for a squirt of citrus, a splash of vinegar (which is really dictated by the cuisine you're cooking, and whatever fruit or grain they had handy for fermenting) or even a combination of the two.

Some alcohols have acidic properties, so these can be used for tang. That's what the splash of red wine is about in a pasta sauce, or mirin through a ponzu dipping sauce. A splash of sake into a buttery sauce, or Shaoxing rice wine into a saucy stir-fry, helps to build dimension and makes everything taste rounded out.

You don't need all of these – just pick a couple based on the cuisine you cook the most.

Pantry

* **Balsamic vinegar** (dressings, caramelizing)
* Aged balsamic vinegar (finishing, dipping)
* Red wine vinegar (dressings, adding zip to Mediterranean/Middle Eastern sauces)
* **White wine vinegar** (chardonnay is pricey, but exceptional)
* Sherry vinegar (Pedro Ximénez is my fave)
* Rice vinegar (Japanese vinegar for dipping sauces and light curing)
* Chinese black vinegar (saucing and balancing)
* Coconut vinegar (neutral acid for dressings)
* Apple cider vinegar (dressings and drinking)
* Malt vinegar (great for tomatoes on toast)
* Shaoxing rice wine (Chinese cooking wine)
* Mirin (for flavoring Japanese cooking)
* **Lemons & limes** (these can be so expensive at the shops ... grow a tree, or make friends with green-thumbed neighbors)

Pulses & grains

This is one area of the pantry that's almost always an afterthought, but stocking up on pulses and grains from different cuisines can make your life so much easier – particularly during the mad midweek scramble. I like to keep things simple and ask myself, 'What would this traditionally be served with?', and then go from there.

Pantry

* Dehydrated potato
* **Basmati rice**
* **Jasmine rice**
* Brown rice (nuttier texture)
* Arborio rice (risotto)
* Bomba rice (paella)
* Puy lentils
* **Chickpeas**
* Split peas
* Polenta
* Couscous
* Israeli couscous
* **Pasta** (spaghetti, macaroni, farfalle, orecchiette, orzo, risoni, lasagna sheets)
* **All-purpose flour**
* **Gluten-free flour**
* Self-rising flour (to make your own, mix 1 cup all-purpose flour with 1 1/2 tsp baking powder)
* Semolina
* Tapioca
* Tortilla shells
* **Corn chips**
* Vietnamese rice papers
* **Vermicelli noodles** (the mung bean ones are my favorite)

Preserves & pickles

This is probably my favorite section of the pantry, because it's the one where most of the hard work has already been done for me. It's like being handed a half-filled-in crossword, and all I have to do is bring it home with a few more clues. Less is more with the ingredients on the labels – the closer it is to how you'd make it at home, the better it'll taste, and the better you'll feel for eating it. That's why the price of preserves is often inversely proportional to the amount of ingredients – because what you're paying for is labor and fresh produce, rather than additional chemicals and preservatives. All killer, no filler. Buy less of the best you can afford, then bulk it out with cheaper pulses, grains and seasonal fruit and veg.

This section lives across my pantry and fridge, because some of the best preserves – the fermented ones – are still living and bubbling away. Sauerkraut, kimchi and pickles of all kinds are not only delicious (dill-icious?) alongside meals as an added burst of color, flavor and texture, but can also be incorporated into them, too – just think of thinner ones as condiments, and chunkier ones as bonus boosters for fry-ups and tray-bakes.

Ferments are also much easier to make at home than you think. The best one to start with is probably sauerkraut, which the 'fermentation revivalist' Sandor Katz likes to describe as 'The Gateway'. If you're not ready to commit, look for live ferments in the fridge section at the shops rather than in a can in the central aisles, and look for labels that include words like 'live cultures' and 'active' warnings. There's little else more satisfying than opening a jar of kraut and seeing it start to erupt like a geyser ... and I'd recommend doing so with the jar perched atop a saucer to catch the juice, as it's too good to waste!

Pantry

* **Tomato passata** (strained tomatoes)
* Tomato paste
* **Canned whole tomatoes**
* Ketchup
* Canned tuna
* Smoky barbecue sauce
* Chipotle chilis (canned)
* Jarred chilis
* Onion jam
* Cornichons
* **Capers**
* Anchovies
* Mango chutney (Indian)
* Lime pickle (Indian)
* Tomato chutney
* Preserved lemon
* Jarred artichokes
* **Olives** (black Kalamata and green Sicilian are my faves)
* Jam (for glazing – as well as grazing)
* Coconut cream
* Coconut milk
* Maraschino cherries
* Apple sauce

Fridge

* **Sour pickles**
* **Kimchi**
* **Sauerkraut**
* Pickled ginger
* Pickled turnips
* Pickled onions/ shallots
* Chili paste/jam
* Sweet chili sauce
* Sambal oelek

Seasonings & sauces

The salt you use makes a big difference to a dish, and many serious cooks have several different kinds on standby. I still remember chef Neil Perry telling me the golden rule of his kitchens: pink for veg, white for steak, and it's still something I stick to. I use pink flaked sea salt for salads, and for garnishy seasoning in general; have kosher salt by the stove for seasoning water, or when actually following a recipe (it's the accuracy of weight and salinity that makes this one so coveted for consistency by cooks globally); and flaked sea salt for seasoning hot pans for searing, or making fancy salts when I'm feeling extra bougie. I also cannot go past a smoked salt – it makes anything remotely charred taste like it has come straight off a barbecue.

Other seasonings such as worcestershire sauce, fish sauce, anchovy sauce and soy sauce are very cuisine dependent, and offer an extra dimension of funk through the alchemy of fermentation.

In general, I prefer to under-season a dish, and offer the corresponding seasoning on the table for people to help themselves. It's also my way of comfortably serving The Nut everything we eat.

On the sweet end of the spectrum, granulated sugar is a natural place to start, as its fine texture and refined flavor make it the default for most dessert recipes. A sprinkle of brown sugar into a savory sauce, or across the face of a root veg before roasting, can provide that *je ne sais quoi*. Honey, maple syrup, molasses (including pomegranate molasses) all have a place in my pantry, for both savories and desserts. Palm sugar (jaggery) is a must for South-East Asian cooking, but I'm also a big fan of coconut sugar syrup, which adds a bonus layering when making coconut-based curries and desserts.

Pantry

* **Pink flaked sea salt** (for sprinkling)
* Flaked sea salt
* **Kosher salt** (for the pot)
* Pink, white and black peppercorns
* Ground white pepper
* Hot English mustard
* Worcestershire sauce
* Sriracha sauce (or hot chili sauce)
* **Fish sauce**
* **Soy sauce** (light and dark)
* Pomegranate molasses
* Vanilla extract/ **vanilla bean paste**
* Palm sugar (jaggery)
* Palm sugar syrup
* Maple syrup
* **Honey**

Fridge

* **Oyster sauce**
* Hoisin sauce
* Miso paste (red and white)
* **Parmigiano Reggiano** (keep the rinds in the freezer)
* Pecorino
* Dijon mustard
* Wholegrain mustard
* **Kewpie mayo**

White

* **GARLIC**
* **HORSERADISH**
  + Wasabi
* **DAIKON**
* **PARSNIP**
* **KOHLRABI**

* **FENNEL**
* **CELERIAC**
* **CAULIFLOWER**
  + Caulilini
* **NAPA CABBAGE**

Garlic

Any self-respecting cook will tell you that when a recipe calls for two garlic cloves, they'll triple it and add six. Garlic's pungent, heady aroma is a welcome addition to any savory dish, and has even been known to rear its head in desserts on the odd occasion ... the operative word here being 'odd' – I'm not about to suggest you grate garlic into your chai instead of nutmeg or anything crazy like that. I *am*, however, going to recommend that even when a savory soup or stew recipe doesn't have garlic listed, it may pay to add a clove or two or three, because the author probably just forgot.

'Garlic is deep in the DNA of human cooking; it can be found in amazing dishes all around the world. To me, it is one of the most humble yet profound ingredients, and can swing from spicy to sweet, pungent to delicate and savory to fruity. Garlic is like that cool friend you can bring to every party – it always gets along with everybody!' – JOSÉ ANDRÉS, SPAIN

BUYING & STORING

Buying locally grown bulbs whenever possible is very important when it comes to garlic, as this will guarantee a longer shelf life, better flavor, and the need for fewer chemicals or irradiation – an unfortunate but necessary step when the garlic is imported. An early summer perennial, freshly picked garlic is so juicy that it needs 3–4 weeks of curing (drying down) before being stored or sold – though you can occasionally find young garlic on the shelf, which should be treated more like green onion or leek. Give the bulb a squeeze, and if the skin is well attached and slightly brittle, and the flesh feels firm underneath, you'll get a while out of it. Any rattling means that the cloves have started to dry out inside their skins – treat this as you would the rattle of a snake and avoid if you can. If you've ever found yourself muttering 'Shoot!' under your breath when pulling out a mushy garlic bulb, it's probably because the cloves have started going to seed, or quite literally, 'shooting'. The green shoots of garlic may look sweet and fresh, but they quickly turn bitter when cooked, so are best removed by simply squeezing the clove and pulling out the green bit, then proceeding as usual. You can stave off accelerated ageing by storing your garlic in a cool dark place, with some level of airflow and minimal moisture.

PREPPING

Unless you own a large chain of takeaway shops, don't get suckered into buying pre-peeled garlic, because the skin is your clove's protection against the elements, so you want it to stay on for as long as possible. Sometimes, particularly in French cookery, you'll be asked to leave the skin on the garlic and/or onion, which they rather poetically describe as *l'ail en chemise*, or 'in its shirt'. That's because the skin, as well as containing flavor, also has a decent hit of pectin – the compound responsible for thickening jams, jellies and sauces. In fact, don't worry about peeling garlic unless you're planning on crushing or slicing it. If roasting a whole bulb, slice off the top to unleash some pungent potency, but keep the skin on. For speed-peeling, when you do need to peel garlic, use the heel of your hand, the bottom of a jar or any heavy item to help create some force to break the skin, and the clove should pop right out. If you're looking to peel a bunch of garlic cloves at once, popping them into a jar with a lid and giving it all a good shake for half a minute or so should do it.

COOKING WITH

Garlic is full of sugars that burn quickly at high temperatures, so the key to getting the most from it is to keep the cooking low and slow. Wait until the other ingredients such as onion or celery soften before adding the garlic, to keep it from burning. If you're a movie buff like me, you may have spent far too long trying to slice your garlic paper-thin and then flicking it into the shimmering oil like some gangster from *Goodfellas*. But unless you are indeed a gangster from *Goodfellas*, your efforts would best be spent elsewhere as far as I'm concerned. Roughly chopping with a knife or a good-quality garlic crusher is really all you need if the dish is going to be on the heat for a while.

Wrapping a whole bulb in foil with a glug of olive oil and roasting it in a moderate oven is a great option for mellowing out the flavor for use in dips and dressings. For other dishes, below is a decision-tree for how to process your garlic for cooking.

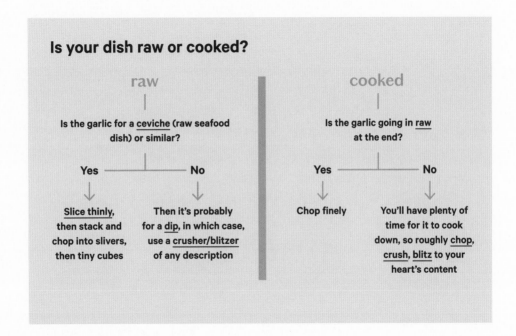

Is your dish raw or cooked?

raw

Is the garlic for a ceviche (raw seafood dish) or similar?

Yes — No

Slice thinly, then stack and chop into slivers, then tiny cubes

Then it's probably for a dip, in which case, use a crusher/blitzer of any description

cooked

Is the garlic going in raw at the end?

Yes — No

Chop finely

You'll have plenty of time for it to cook down, so roughly chop, crush, blitz to your heart's content

DIY garlic paste

Making your own garlic paste is about as easy as schlepping down to the shops to buy a jar, but the result is far more satisfying. Use your chef's knife to grind garlic down to a paste by sprinkling some salt on your peeled and roughly chopped cloves, then using your knife on a 35-degree angle, with the friction of the salt, to break up the garlic until it turns to magical mush. The salt also helps mellow out the bitterness of older garlic, so this is a good option if your cloves are starting to look a little sad. Some people store their paste with olive oil in an airtight jar, but I find that the flavor does turn and dissipate. If you decide to make a big batch, try freezing it in a 5 mm (¼ inch) layer on a lined plate or tray, then breaking it up into 2 cm (¾ inch) squares to whip out for use in all your cooking – often without the need to defrost.

FUNCTIONAL FOOD

If you grew up with an overzealous nonna/baba/nana, you've no doubt experienced garlic's sickness-fighting properties first-hand at the first sign of cold season, be it in a poultice or punching up a broth. Indeed, garlic's antimicrobial properties have long been lauded as a natural antibiotic, helping to stave off infection and relieving toothaches for centuries. Chomping a clove down against an aching molar releases allicin, a chemical that acts as an anti-inflammatory, while also potentially targeting any underlying bacterial infection. Garlic's pungency also acts as a great insect repellent, masking the scent of human blood like a deodorant; it's not just your breath that smells garlicky, after all. This natural potency is also what lands garlic into vampire-repelling folklore, because if the smell doesn't keep blood suckers (mosquitoes, ticks, vampires) at bay, then perhaps its antibiotic properties might help heal the blood infection reputed to cause vampirism in the first place.

Rid the reek

If garlic breath is a bug-bear, consider adding some fresh flat-leaf or curly parsley to your dishes, as it is a natural breath freshener. For garlicky fingertips, rubbing your hands on something stainless steel is the cure – be it a specialty stainless steel 'soap', or just the back of a saucepan or other kitchen utensil.

WITH COMPLEMENTS

Garlic is the white T-shirt of savory ingredients: it goes with everything.

SCRAP MEDAL

Before you start peeling your garlic on auto-pilot, ask yourself: do I want the flavor of garlic to be background or foreground? If it's background you're after, leaving the garlic in its skin to roast with your other veggies is a no-fuss solution that means less scraps and, let's face it, less work. If you do indeed have a heap of garlic scraps left over, you can put them to good use against garden pests. Steep your skins and offcuts in boiling hot water, allow to cool, then transfer to a spray bottle to keep bugs at bay.

AJO BLANCO FRUIT SALAD

I'm sure the photo is doing enough to capture your attention and push you past the 'huh?' factor, but stay with me. My favorite part of the traditional soupy version of ajo blanco is the garnish – some people use cucumber, others prefer fruit, be it melon or grapes. I've combined the two, upped the garnish, and now it's up to you what ratio of soup to salad you're into. You'll note I've also skipped the bread bit, which is usually what thickens the soup, choosing instead to whip yogurt and cucumber flesh into a frenzy. You can make this fully plant-based by subbing out the yogurt and adding more cucumber, too. If you can get your hands on some black garlic, it will elevate the dish even further, creating texture, interest and extra funk – like an ersatz black truffle.

SERVES 4

2 black garlic cloves
   (mildly optional)
100 g (1 cup) blanched
   almond meal
1 cup (250 ml)
   vegetable stock
3 Lebanese cucumbers
3–4 garlic cloves, peeled
50 g (1¾ oz) plain yogurt
1 tablespoon
   sherry vinegar
1 teaspoon flaked sea salt
100 ml (3½ fl oz) extra
   virgin olive oil, plus
   extra for drizzling

½ honeydew or
   Piel de Sapo melon
1 cup (180 g) green
   grapes, larger ones
   cut in half lengthwise
1 cup (150 g) fresh
   currants (if available)
1–2 star fruit, sliced – very
   optional, but very wow!
amaranth or micro-herb
   leaves, to garnish
   (optional)

If using the whole black garlic cloves, pop them in a preheated oven at 225°F for 45 minutes. When cool enough to handle, peel off the skins and set aside.

Toast the almond meal in a dry frying pan over medium heat until fragrant but not colored, giving the pan a shake every now and then – about 5–10 minutes. Pour in the stock and stand off the heat.

Peel and quarter one of the cucumbers. Chop the others into interesting oblong-ish shapes by rolling across the chopping board and cutting into fork-sized, uneven pieces; set aside for the salad.

Add the quartered cucumber to a blender or food processor with the plain garlic cloves, yogurt, vinegar and salt. Whiz for a minute or so, until the garlic is fully blitzed. Add the almond meal and stock mixture, blitz again for 10 seconds or so to combine, then with the motor running, pour in the olive oil in a steady stream. Taste for seasoning, transfer your ajo blanco to a container and chill in the fridge for at least 1 hour before serving.

Scoop the seeds out of the melon with a spoon. Slice the melon in half lengthwise, then cut each half into four thin wedges. Turn skin side down and peel off the skin as you might a fish fillet, edging a sharp chef's or paring knife along between the flesh and the skin.

Create a moat of chilled ajo blanco in the bottom of a shallow bowl or platter. Arrange the melon and cucumber jauntily along the bowl, then let the grapes, currants and star fruit fall where they might. Pour over more ajo blanco. If using the black garlic, grate the dehydrated cloves over the top. Finish with your chosen garnish and an extra drizzle of olive oil and serve.

Shortcut **Turn the ajo blanco into a quick tzatziki dressing. Leave out the almond meal, stock and olive oil, then simply bump up the yogurt factor.**

Double duty **Serve as a simple chilled soup the next day, *sans* all the fruity trimmings. Top with sliced cucumber, flaked almonds and a drizzle of olive oil.**

ONE-PAN ROASTED GARLIC HUMMUS PLATE

A love of hummus appears pretty universal. Every now and then, however, the raw garlic can get people into a bit of a tizz. Also, how do you make hummus more substantial? Cue the deep-voiced trailer guy: 'One pan!' By crisping up some of the chickpeas and softening the garlic in both texture and heat, you're buffing out the edges and turning a dip into a dish.

SERVES 4

1 garlic bulb
400 g (14 oz) can chickpeas, drained and rinsed
½ teaspoon smoked paprika, plus extra to serve
90 ml (3 fl oz) olive oil, plus extra for drizzling

juice of ½ lemon
2 tablespoons tahini (hulled or unhulled – you choose)
½ teaspoon ground coriander
½ teaspoon ground cumin
1 teaspoon flaked sea salt

Preheat the oven to 425°F.

Lop the head off the garlic bulb so that the tops of the cloves are exposed. Place a tray-sized sheet of foil on a baking tray, pop the lopped garlic bulb and about 50 g (1¾ oz) of the chickpeas in the middle, sprinkle with the paprika and 2 tablespoons of the olive oil, then fold the foil into a parcel. Give everything a shake to get familiar, then pop into the oven for 25 minutes.

Meanwhile, place the remaining chickpeas in a food processor, along with the lemon juice, tahini, spices and salt. Add the remaining 50 ml (1¾ fl oz) olive oil and blitz until smooth and combined.

When the roasting time is up, remove the foil parcel from the oven. Reserve the roasted chickpeas. Allow the roasted garlic to cool slightly, then use a teaspoon or your fingers to ease each clove out of its sheath, into the food processor. Blitz for another 20 seconds, or until fully incorporated into the hummus.

To serve, spoon the hummus into a shallow bowl, top with a mountain of the roasted chickpeas, then drizzle with a little extra olive oil and sprinkle with a little extra paprika.

Shortcut If you've no time to muck about with pans and ovens, cut back on the garlic – to maybe 3–4 cloves – keep it raw and blitz the whole tin's worth of chickpeas along with the rest of the ingredients into a quick and easy stand-alone hummus. Carrot sticks and celery sticks might be nice for dipping ... but so are teaspoons and fingers!

Extra Soft-boil or poach an egg or two (see page 330) while the garlic and chickpeas bake, then pop the eggs and crispy chickpeas on top of the hummus and serve alongside a simple Israeli salad (tomatoes, cucumbers, maybe a little onion) for a quick and nutritious brunch or lunch.

GARLIC AIOLI

Is it a dipping sauce? A spread? A dish in and of itself? (Probably not.) Purists might wonder at the inclusion of egg in what is traditionally an emulsion of just garlic and olive oil, mixed by hand, in a mortar and pestle, under the hot Mediterranean sun … but these days, any maxed-up mayonnaise is deemed an aioli, so who am I to judge? Using salt to create friction for your garlic paste has the added benefit of mellowing out the heat and bitterness, while whisking in the olive oil separately adds to its aioli credentials, without clumping into a cloying mess.

MAKES ABOUT 1 CUP (250 ML)

4–5 garlic cloves, peeled	1 egg
1 teaspoon flaked sea salt	⅔ cup (170 ml)
1 teaspoon warm water	grapeseed oil
juice of ½ lemon	⅓ cup (80 ml) olive oil

On a wooden board, roughly chop the garlic cloves, then sprinkle the flaked sea salt on top. Use the flat face of your knife blade on a 35-degree angle to press against the garlic, as though you're buttering bread, until the garlic mound becomes minced.

Immersion blender method: Add the water, lemon juice, egg, minced garlic and grapeseed oil to the cup attachment of your immersion blender. Pop the immersion blender in so that the blades are at the bottom of the cup, then blitz until an emulsion forms.

Food processor method: Add the water, lemon juice, egg and minced garlic to the food processor, then with the blades running, pour in the grapeseed oil in a gentle, steady stream.

Use a flexible spatula to transfer your mixture into a clean bowl, creating a ring with a dampened tea towel to nestle the bowl into and stabilize it if needed. Whisk in the olive oil in a gentle, steady stream by hand. Season to taste with salt and pepper if desired.

The garlic aioli will keep covered in the fridge for up to 1 week.

Tips If the mixture looks grainy, it might have split. Whisk in 2 teaspoons of boiling water to bring it back together again.

You can also make the aioli by hand, using a bowl stabilized on your work surface by the tea towel trick. Crush or mince the garlic into a paste. Mix together all the ingredients except the oils, then slowly drizzle the oils from one hand as you whisk with the other.

Extra Jazz up your aioli with whatever flavorings tickle your fancy, from fresh shaved truffle to tarragon, paprika, parsley …

Shortcut Make an even quicker aioli by grating a garlic clove or two through some Japanese Kewpie mayonnaise. You might even like it better.

ULTIMATE CHEESY GARLIC BREAD BAKE

I know you might scan this recipe and baulk at the thought of 16 cloves of garlic in just one dish, particularly as it looks like a good one to take to parties. BUT if you were to break this down per person, it's only two garlic cloves – which is quite manageable, and a good rule of thumb, if you ask me. And anyway, I've popped the parsley in there as a natural breath-freshener, so you'll be right. Begin this recipe 1 day ahead.

SERVES 8

150 g (5½ oz) unsalted
   butter, roughly diced
16 garlic cloves, peeled
1 cup parsley leaves,
   plus extra to garnish
1 tablespoon olive oil,
   plus extra for drizzling
1 tablespoon flaked sea
   salt, plus extra for
   sprinkling
1 teaspoon freshly cracked
   black pepper

1 x 600 g (1 lb 5 oz)
   ciabatta loaf,
   halved lengthwise
125 g (4½ oz) grated
   raclette cheese (or
   gruyère or cheddar)
1½ cups (375 ml)
   vegetable stock
1 egg, lightly beaten
2 teaspoons white
   sesame seeds

Heat the butter in a small saucepan until partially melted, or in a microwave for 30 seconds. Transfer to a small food processor with the garlic, parsley, olive oil, salt and pepper. Whiz until the parsley is finely chopped and the butter is green.

Smear the garlic butter over the bread halves and sprinkle with the cheese. Sandwich the halves back together, then use a serrated knife to cut the loaf into 3 cm (1¼ inch) thick slices. Arrange the slices snugly in a large roasting pan, so that the green butter oozes out a bit. Pour the stock over, making sure to coat each piece of bread. Soak overnight.

The next day, preheat the oven to 400°F. Brush the bread tops with the egg and sprinkle with the sesame seeds. Bake for 20–25 minutes, or until the crust is golden and crunchy to your liking.

Sprinkle with parsley and salt, drizzle with more olive oil and serve as you might a pudding. Only savory.

Tips Once you're confident with the dish, feel free to play with the flavors. Try salty stuff such as anchovies or olives – or go hot and spicy with chili sauce, or just straight-up chili in the food processor.

If you have some pan juices left over from roasting a chicken, loosen them off with a little boiling water and use instead of the stock. This method also works with baked-on roast veggie pan juices, particularly where onion or pumpkin are concerned.

Shortcut Slash through a whole soft loaf or baguette with a bread knife like a hasselback (see page 56), then smear a spoonful of the garlic butter between each slice. Drizzle with olive oil and bake until golden.

Double duty This is also good cold, so slide leftovers into your lunchbox with a handful of cherry tomatoes in summer, or a flask of hot soup for dipping in winter.

Coarsely blitz any left-over bits and use for stuffing a roast chicken or butternut squash cavity.

Horseradish

With its spicy bite and spindly looks, it's hard to believe that horseradish is actually part of the Brassica family, along with the cabbages, cauliflowers and mustard greens of this world. Unlike the aforementioned, however, it is most often the root of the plant that is eaten – grated over vegetables, meat and seafood, or blitzed into mustard-like condiments with vinegar or cream. The leaves can also be torn into salads, used as a wrapping for parcels of ceviche or tartare, and popped into jars of pickled gherkins to enhance their flavor and preserve their crunch. You might be surprised – nay, shocked! – to discover that horseradish is also the secret stand-in for wasabi in many commercially available wasabi tubes, with a verdant tinge in the form of either the chlorophyll from spinach or, more commonly, artificial food coloring.

'Horseradish and beets are a fantastic combination – the sweetness of the beets with the heat of the horseradish play against each other beautifully.' – MATT STONE, AUSTRALIA

BUYING & STORING

Though you're most likely to find it in the colder months, access to fresh horseradish can be challenging. Even then you might find yourself looking at a long, rooty spindle and wondering what to do with it all – but the flavor of fresh horseradish, along with the theater of grating it across a plate, is worth investing in. If you'll only be using a little at a time, pick a thicker, stumpier root, and freeze the bit you don't need; you can use it straight from the freezer. Otherwise, store your horseradish root in a little water on the kitchen counter, peeling and grating as needed. Just keep an eye on the tip of your horseradish, as it'll dry out if left too long.

FUNCTIONAL FOOD

It's no surprise that horseradish, which grows during cold and flu season, is beneficial for respiratory health. If you've ever copped a chunk of fresh horseradish on the tongue, you will have felt its potent nose-clearing and eye-flushing effects! The intrepid explorers who brought it west from south-eastern Europe actually regarded it as a medicine, and it wasn't commonly eaten in England until the 16th century – and only then by 'country people and laboring men'. The Germans, on the other hand, were right into it, and still are to this day.

Horseradish chrain

Serve this chrain (pronounced '*khhhhrain*') as a condiment with anything that needs some extra punch, turn it into a dip by stirring in grated raw carrot or beet, or smear across a platter and sprinkle veggie crudités across the top. Simply combine 1 tablespoon fresh grated horseradish, 200 g (7 oz) crème fraîche, 1 heaped tablespoon cream, 1 teaspoon chardonnay vinegar, ¼ teaspoon salt and ¼ teaspoon ground white pepper. Store in the fridge. If fresh horseradish isn't available, use the best-quality jarred stuff you can find – or even fresh wasabi.

BEYOND HORSERADISH: WASABI

Fresh wasabi has far more dimension than the artificially greened, reconstituted horseradish version of wasabi paste commonly sold with sushi. The most prized wasabi varieties are grown in water, with broad, peppery leaves used as you might betel leaves, while the main root looks like a cross between a broccoli stalk and a barnacled jetty post. Wasabi is also available in powdered form, but I prefer the fresh stuff. Store any bits you don't use in the freezer, and if you're a true fan, consider investing in a specialty wasabi grater.

WASABI LEAF CEVICHE

Although 'wasabi' and 'ceviche' may seem an incongruous combination, the Japanese influence on Peruvian food – particularly the way fish is prepared – is well documented. In fact, the combo-cuisine even has a name: Nikkei, which utilizes Peruvian ingredients through a Japanese cook's lens. Even the timing of ceviche as we know it was tweaked, from hours on end to just long enough to let the acid (in this case, yuzu juice) 'cook' the outside of the fish. If you'd prefer to cook it through longer, leave the dressing on the fish for half an hour before serving. And don't let the flavorful sour liquid at the bottom of the bowl go to waste – it is often spiked with a little pisco and drunk as an aphrodisiac that has its own name, too: *leche de tigre* ... tiger's milk. Raar!

In a bowl, mash the avocado flesh with a fork, mixing in 2 teaspoons of the yuzu juice and 1 teaspoon of the wasabi paste.

Put the remaining yuzu juice and wasabi paste in a bowl big enough to fit all the fish. Add the soy sauce, sesame oil and pickling juice, if using, and whisk together into a dressing.

Just before serving, gently toss the fish, cucumber and radish through the soy sauce mixture. You can let this stand for a maximum of 5 minutes, but I prefer to serve immediately.

Spread a little avocado mixture on the wasabi leaves. Add a squirt of mayonnaise, then about ½ tablespoon of ceviche. Garnish with ginger and a sprinkling of sesame seeds and furikake, if using. Serve immediately.

SERVES 4 AS A STARTER

1 avocado, stone removed
⅓ cup (80 ml) yuzu juice (see tips)
2 teaspoons wasabi paste
2 tablespoons light soy sauce
1 teaspoon sesame oil
2 tablespoons pickled ginger juice (optional)
100 g (3½ oz) sashimi-grade ocean trout or salmon, cut into 1.5–2 cm (⅝–¾ inch) cubes (see tips)
100 g (3½ oz) sashimi-grade kingfish, cut into 1.5–2 cm (⅝–¾ inch) cubes

1 cucumber, cubed
6 radishes, thinly sliced
10–12 fresh wasabi leaves (see tips)

To serve
Kewpie mayonnaise
grated fresh ginger, chopped pickled ginger or pickled daikon (page 48)
sesame seeds
Daikon leaf furikake (page 52), optional

Tips Yuzu is a Japanese citrus with the flavor of clementine, but with more sweetness and more sourness. It is available from specialty grocers in various different forms, but if you can't find it, use lemon or lime juice and add a tiny pinch of sugar.

You can get your butcher to sashimi slice your fish for you, then cut it into cubes at home – or even ask them to cube it, if you plan on making the ceviche that night. Otherwise, use a very sharp knife, gliding it against the natural grain of the fish.

If you can't find fresh wasabi leaves, use nori sheets – the kind you'd use for sushi hand rolls, chopped into quarters.

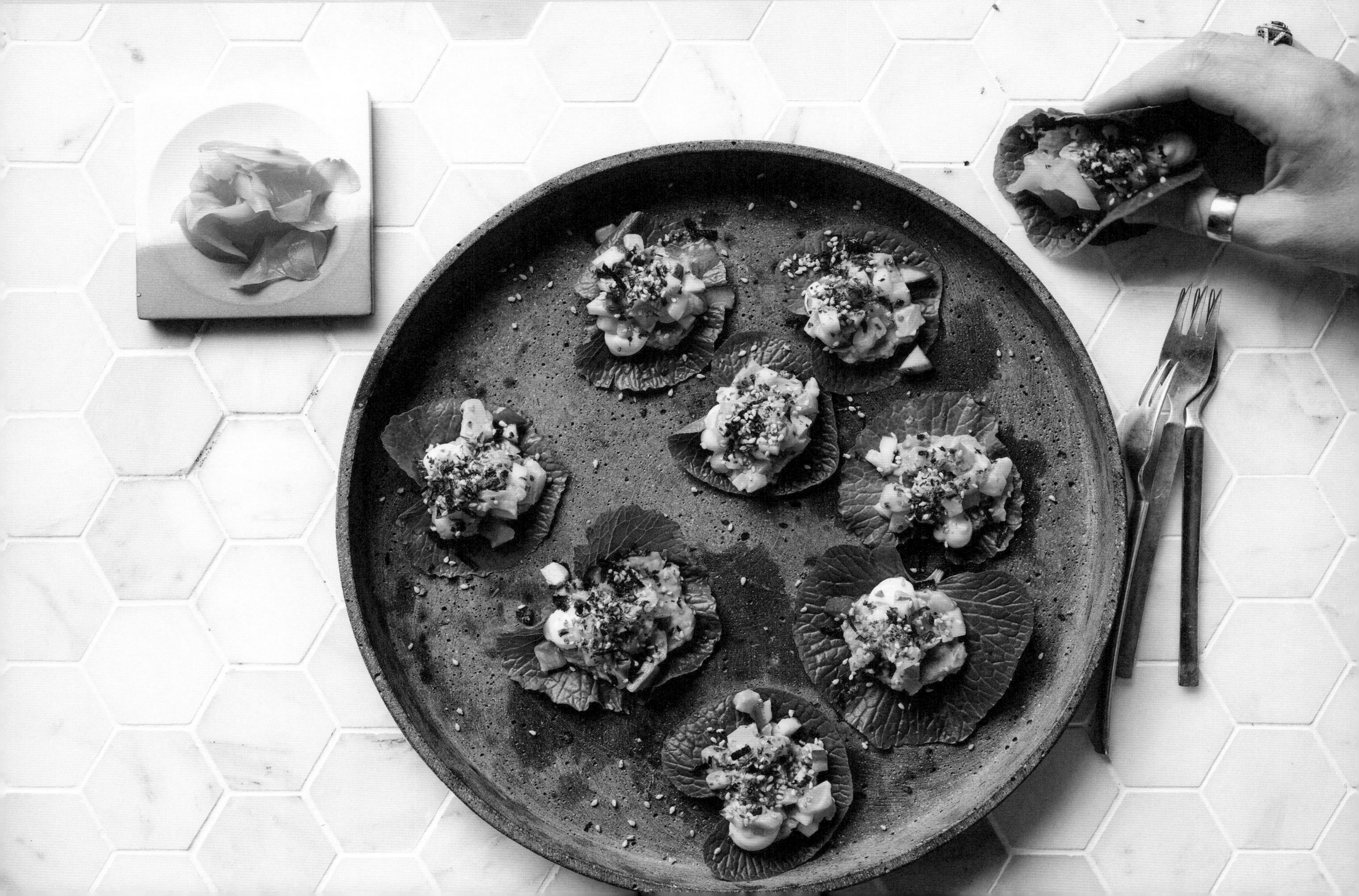

Daikon

With a Latin varietal name that makes me giggle every time I see it – *Longipinnatus* – and a common name loosely translating to 'big root' in Japanese, the daikon packs a relatively gentle punch in the heat stakes. When eaten raw, it's a bit like drinking a tall glass of water as you chomp into a pink radish, which isn't surprising given it's a member of the radish family. Its mild flavor yet fresh and crunchy texture is what makes daikon an easy addition to funky ferments such as Korean kimchi, Japanese pickles, and more subtle Japanese dishes such as *nimono*, in which thick veggie discs are slow-braised in soy-splashed dashi broth. When grated fresh into salads, daikon sucks up the dressing like nobody's business, which is also why you'll find it finely grated into many ponzu dressings for dipping your tempura veg into. Incidentally, daikon can be battered and tempura-fried, too.

'I'll julienne it, add a bit of salt and sugar and cook slowly until soft and sweet, maybe adding a dollop of butter to make it creamy. I like to stuff this in pastries, put it on burgers, or chill it, roll into balls, panko-crumb and deep-fry – or mix it in with mushrooms as a veggie side. It's such a great pairing with anything earthy.'
– MAY CHOW, CANADA

BUYING & STORING

Daikon is a cold season vegetable. Seek out ones with their leaves still intact, as their presence is the clearest marker of freshness – especially if they look like the fronds of a well-maintained indoor plant in someone's California beach house. When bringing one of these befronded daikons home, slice the leaves off at the base and store them separately in damp paper towel or cloth, lest the leaves suck all the moisture out of the root. If the leaves are no longer with us, feel for a firm radish, where the skin is still luminous and taut across its face, without yet having started to lose any slack from too many days between drinks. Some radishes – especially the larger ones – will have a green tinge across their top, because they've managed to work themselves above the surface of the soil and cop some sun, thereby commencing photosynthesis. These specimens are usually older and drier in texture, with an extra bit of bite to them – which I suppose is to be expected, seeing as it takes time and experience to build up the tenacity to push beyond the dirt ceiling, so to speak.

FUNCTIONAL FOOD

There's a very good reason why daikon is such a staple food in many Asian cuisines: its digestive do-gooding. It's the sulfur in radishes that gives your guts a good going-over. Daikon (and the rarer black radish) contains more of these compounds than the regular squat red radish, making it a processing powerhouse. Within complementary medicine circles, daikon is believed to have the same enzymatic profile as the human digestive tract, and its juice is prescribed to help ease indigestion and heartburn. A word of warning, though: these highly effective enzymes can also cause a bit of gassiness on the way out, too!

WITH COMPLEMENTS

Carrot, ginger, miso, sesame, soy sauce, green onion (scallion).

Daikon oroshi

Ponzu, the traditional Japanese dipping sauce for dishes such as tempura and gyoza, is decidedly duller without the addition of grated daikon, or *daikon oroshi*. Loosely translating to 'down-wind daikon' in reference to the hit of fresh spicy air it brings, grated daikon is either stirred through the ponzu sauce before (or sometimes after) serving, piled on top of noodles or next to a plate of fish or meat, and eaten as a condiment as you would wasabi. Many Japanese soups and hotpot dishes are also beneficiaries of a blob of grated daikon, bobbing on top of the broth like a piece of melting snow, earning itself the name *mizore*, or 'mixed rain and snow'. To make it at home, start with the base half of a daikon, which has a milder flavor, slice it in half lengthwise, then grate finely or blitz in a food processor until slushy-like in appearance. Drain of excess liquid through a clean cloth or fine sieve and use immediately, or freeze in a thin layer for future use.

SCRAP MEDAL

If you think of daikon as an enormously stretched breakfast radish with all the color sucked out of it, you can easily deduce that the leaves are fit for the same purpose as any other peppery leaf. In Japan, the leaves are often fried into *furikake* along with sesame oil, sesame seeds, soy sauce and mirin – perfect for tossing through salads for extra clusters of flavor, or for zhuzhing up steamed rice. A lot of daikon's bite is in the skin, so if you're looking for extra heat, keep the skin on. For delicate dishes, peel the skin and reserve this for adding to kimchi, or whiz it up in a blender for a very gentle version of horseradish.

TICKLED PINK PICKLED DAIKON

If you're a fan of pickled ginger, say *konichiwa* to pickled daikon – its crunchier, hotter, sweeter and more bang-for-buck sibling. I adore the way the red radishes and young ginger turn the lily-white daikon a ballerina pink, and how the finely sliced discs billow and curl like the frothy layers of a tutu. Serve alongside sushi and sashimi, slip into sandwiches for a little extra zing, or just eat off a fork, as I do far too often. This pickle is also especially good in a poké bowl, such as the one on page 52.

MAKES 1 X 850 ML (30 FL OZ) JAR

550 g (1 lb 4 oz) daikon, peeled and thinly sliced into rounds

40 g (1½ oz) fresh young ginger, peeled and shredded

2 red radishes, thinly shredded

3 teaspoons flaked sea salt

¼ cup (55 g) granulated sugar

¼ cup (60 ml) rice wine vinegar

¼ cup (60 ml) mirin

Wash an 850 ml (30 fl oz) glass jar in hot, soapy water, rinse well and stand upside down to dry on a rack.

Combine the daikon, ginger and radish in a colander set over a bowl. Sprinkle with 1 teaspoon of the salt and leave for 2 hours to draw out the moisture.

Squeeze the excess moisture from the daikon mixture and place the mix into the dry jar.

Place the sugar, vinegar, mirin and remaining 2 teaspoons salt in a small saucepan. Add ½ cup (125 ml) water and bring to the boil. Pour the hot liquid into the jar, making sure all your slices are submerged.

Seal the lid and leave to cool, then store in a cool dark place; I like to keep this pickle in the fridge, because the coolness of the first bite belies the heat coming up from the second.

The pickle is perfectly pink and usable after 3–4 days, and will keep in the sealed jar for 2 months. Once opened, store in the fridge and use within 1 month, making sure the vegetables are always covered with the pickling liquid.

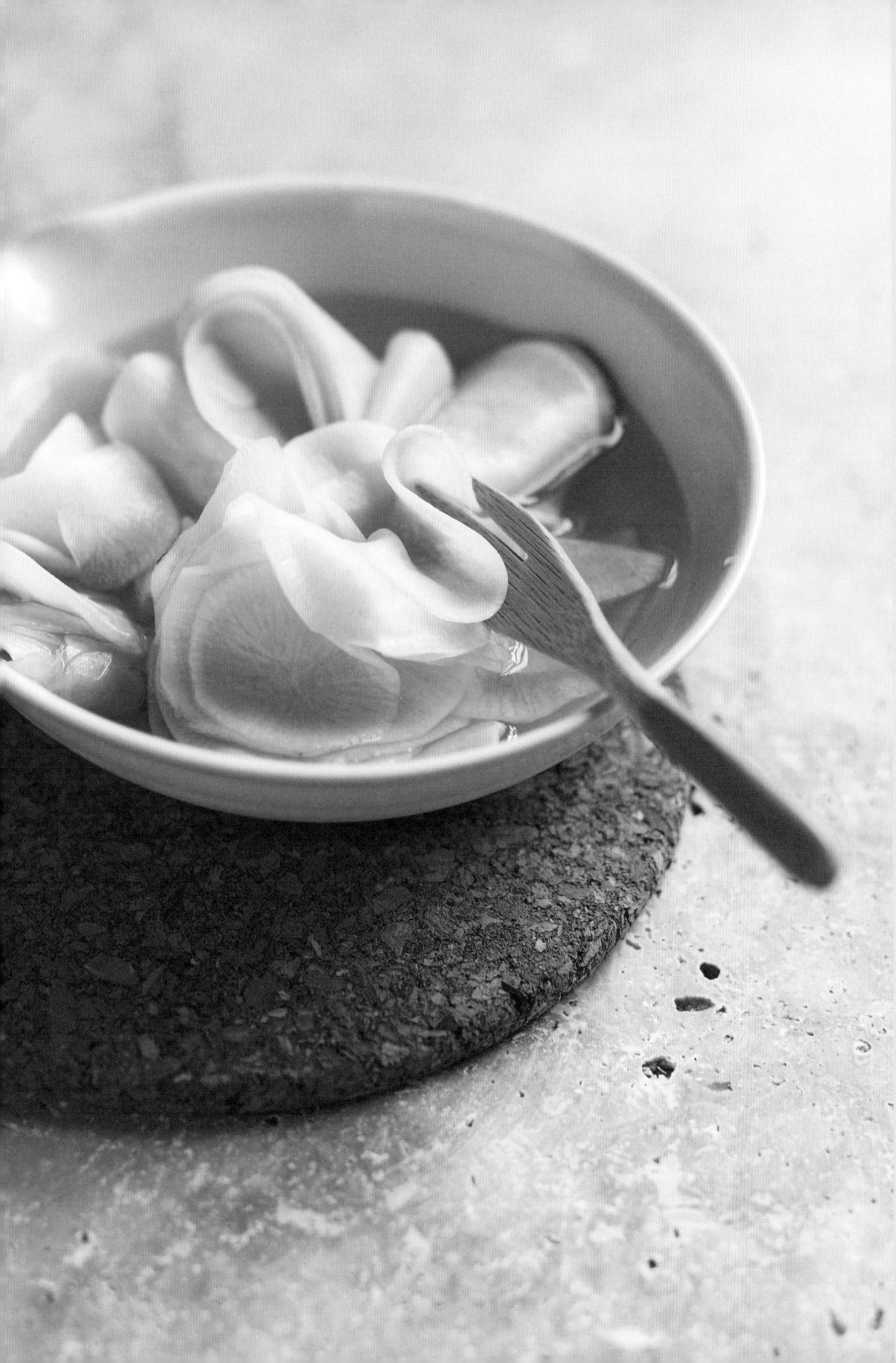

DAIKON TURNIP CAKE WITH VEGO XO

The recipe here is not as important as the ratio you need to remember – 10:4:2 daikon:water:flour. This golden ratio is what keeps the texture of this savory 'cake' the perfect balance, fluffy on the inside, crispy on the outside, playing off the gentle heat and natural meatiness of cooked daikon, held together with just enough batter to bind. Begin this recipe 1 day ahead.

SERVES 4

2 green onions (scallions)
1 medium daikon, about
    400 g (14 oz)
¼ cup (60 ml) peanut oil,
    plus extra for greasing
½ teaspoon ground
    white pepper
½ teaspoon flaked sea salt
½ teaspoon granulated
    sugar
1 teaspoon sesame oil

80 g (2¾ oz) gluten-free
    all-purpose flour
1 handful of fresh shiitake
    mushrooms
1 cup (250 ml) Honkignese
    Vego XO (page 221),
    or crispy chili oil from
    Asian grocers

Tip This is traditionally steamed in a deep pan or dish, then cut into cubes before frying; the golden ratio still stands.

Extra Sometimes, Chinese lap cheong sausage is added to the mix. If using, chop it into fine dice and fry it off with the green onion whites.

Thinly slice the green onions, reserving the green bits in the fridge for garnishing. Peel and coarsely grate the daikon and set aside.

Heat 1 tablespoon of the peanut oil in a frying pan. Add the green onion whites and leave to soften for 1–2 minutes. Add the daikon, pepper, salt, sugar and sesame oil, then cook away for 10 minutes, or until the daikon is softened, glossy and turning translucent.

Drain the mixture through a sieve, into a measuring jug, then allow to cool.

Check how much liquid has drained out of the daikon mixture, giving it an extra squeeze with your hands or a wooden spoon, then add enough water to make up 160 ml (5½ fl oz) in the jug. Pour the liquid into a large bowl, then whisk in the flour until quite gluey. Stir in the cooled daikon mixture with a flexible spatula.

Line two heatproof plates with parchment paper; I use earthenware plates with a diameter of 18 cm (7 inches) and higher sides. Shape the batter into two flat discs 5 mm (¼ inch) thick and place one on each plate.

Set a large bamboo steamer (that fits the plates comfortably) over a saucepan or wok of simmering water. Steam for 45–50 minutes. The 'cakes' will be set, but the tops may still be a little sticky; don't worry, the stickiness will dissipate on cooling. Leave to cool, then refrigerate for at least 2 hours, but preferably overnight.

Just before serving, heat the remaining 2 tablespoons peanut oil in a frying pan over high heat. Stir-fry the mushrooms for about 3 minutes, or until just golden, then remove with a slotted spoon and set aside to drain.

Cook one cake in the pan at a time for 4 minutes on one side, or until golden, then flip it over and repeat on the other side. Repeat with the remaining cake.

Return the pan to the heat, add the XO sauce and stir to warm through. Transfer to a serving dish.

Serve the cakes hot, sprinkled with the mushrooms and reserved green onion greens, with the XO sauce on the side.

TUNA POKÉ BOWLS WITH DAIKON LEAF FURIKAKE

These bowls are packed to the brim with different fun textures and colors that turn into an absolute mouth party. As with any good party, if one of the elements can't make it, invite a B-lister that serves the same purpose – say, frozen peas instead of edamame, and marinated tempeh instead of tuna, if that's more your jam. The home-made furikake is an absolute revelation. It uses up some daikon leaves that normally end up in compost, and tastes freaking great. If you don't have the time to make it, any store-bought Japanese rice seasoning will be sufficient – but you know we'll both be mildly disappointed you didn't go the full furikake.

SERVES 4

1⅔ cups (335 g)
   jasmine rice
1 x 300 g (10½ oz)
   daikon, peeled
2 carrots, peeled
¼ cup (50 g) pickled
   ginger (or the pickled
   daikon from page 48),
   plus 2 tablespoons of
   the pickling juice
2 teaspoons sesame oil
2 x 170 g (6 oz) cans tuna
   in spring water, drained
⅓ cup (100 g) Kewpie
   mayonnaise
3 teaspoons soy sauce
avocado slices, to serve
blanched edamame
   beans, to serve
lemon wedges, to serve

**Daikon leaf furikake
(Makes 1 cup)**
3 nori sheets, finely
   shredded using scissors
2 teaspoons black and
   white sesame seeds
1 tablespoon brown sugar
2 teaspoons onion powder
50 g (1¾ oz) daikon leaves
   (say 10–12 bits), washed
   and thoroughly dried
¼ cup (6 g) bonito flakes
2 teaspoons Korean
   chili powder
2 teaspoons garlic powder
2 teaspoons
   flaked sea salt

Place the rice and 2 cups (500 ml) cold water in a saucepan over medium–high heat and bring to the boil. Reduce the heat to low, cover and simmer for 12–15 minutes, or until the rice is cooked. Remove from the heat and keep a lid on it until required.

Meanwhile, make the furikake. Preheat the oven to 400°F and line a baking tray with parchment paper. In a bowl, mix together the nori, sesame seeds, sugar and onion powder, then spread onto the baking tray. Bake for 5 minutes, or until bubbling. Remove from the oven and stand to cool. Reduce the oven temperature to 250°F, place the daikon leaves on a rack and bake for 20 minutes, or until completely dried.

Tip the toasted nori mixture into a bowl. Mix in the bonito flakes, spices and salt, using your fingertips to crumble and break up the mixture into a rough powder. Add the dried daikon leaves and crumble them a little with your fingers, tossing to combine. Set aside.

Use a vegetable peeler to create thin shavings of daikon and carrot. Toss in a bowl with the ginger, pickling juice and sesame oil.

Divide the tuna, rice and salad among serving bowls. Squirt in the mayo and splash on some soy sauce. Top with avocado slices and edamame beans, sprinkle with the furikake and serve with lemon wedges.

Shortcut So yes, I'm bummed you're checking this, because it probably means you're not making your own furikake, but you can also just grate some carrot and daikon together and dress with sesame oil, pickling juice (or vinegar) and salt. I know you'll be hooked, and will try the proper poké next time …

Double duty This furikake also makes for an incredible garnish on everything from plain rice to corn. I love it with the Radish quickle on page 188.

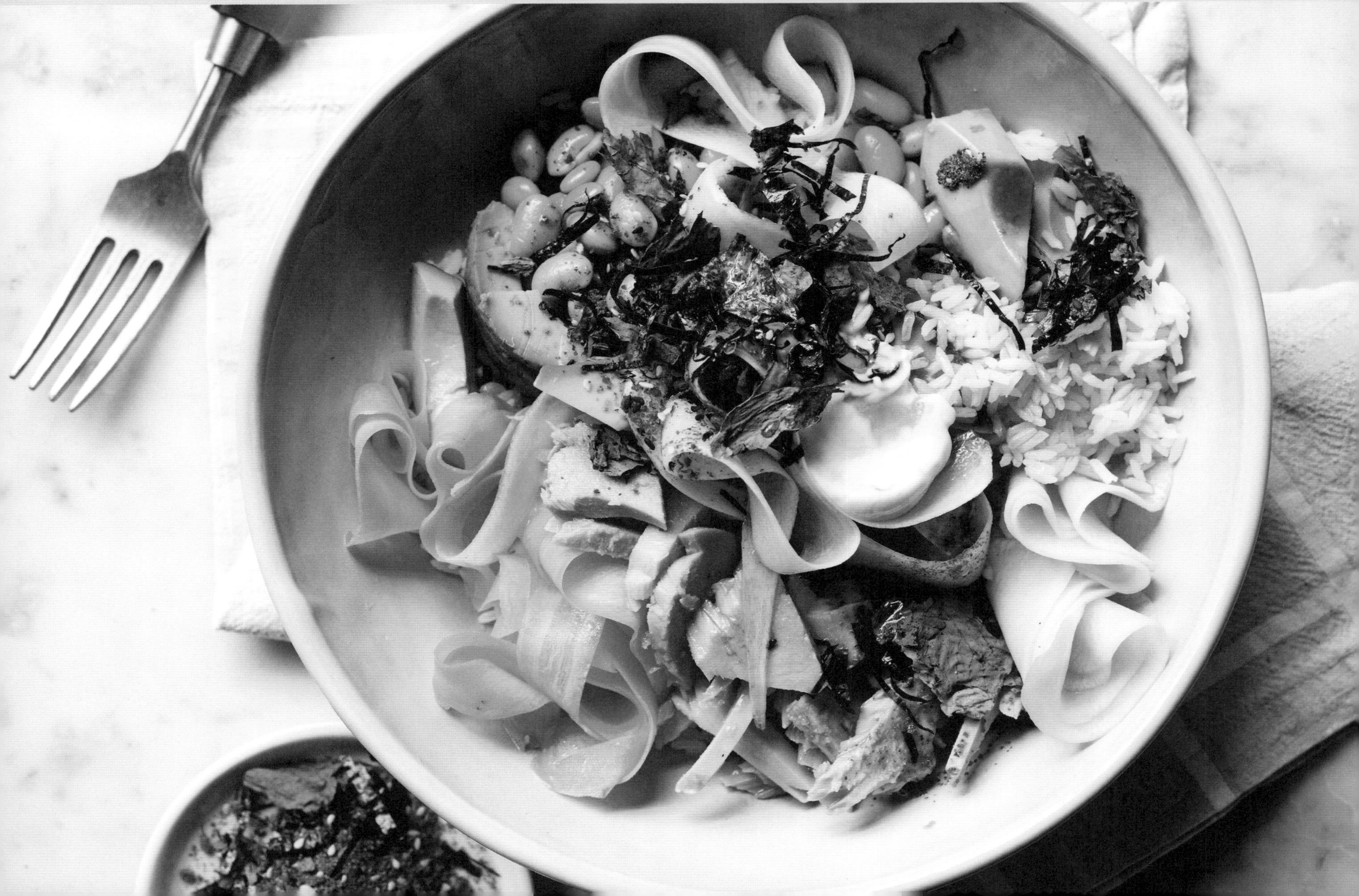

Parsnip

You'll likely be able to find it all year round, but much like its compadre cousins, carrot and parsley, parsnip finds itself at its best in cooler weather – late autumn into the depths of winter, when it is at its syrupy tenderest. Colloquially referred to as 'the white carrot', it would be wise to seek parsnip's freshness cues from carrots, too. Look for parsnips that are firm to the touch, with a decent amount of girth (because they shrink preposterously upon roasting). Small to medium-sized parsnips are less fibrous and make for the best fries – keep small ones whole, and cut medium ones in half or quarters. Large ones, having had a chance to mature and let some of their natural starches break down into sugars, are better for deep-fried parsnip chips and grating into cakes.

'The parsnip is a revelation in terms of its sweet, moist nuttiness. And, counterintuitively, the delicateness it can bring to a dish. I would have a parsnip ice-cream over a strawberry one any day.'

–MARK BEST, AUSTRALIA

BUYING & STORING

Like carrots, the longer parsnips are out of the ground and on the shelf, the more they soften up and then dry out, so avoid buying when they're starting to look a little limp or droopy. Any withering at the base is an extra big no-no. It's rare to find parsnips sold with their parsley-like tops attached, but if you do, grab them, because that's a great big green beacon that the roots have only recently been pulled. Seek out the smoothest you can find, as any baby hairs are indicative of having been grown in dry soils, so they may be woody to taste, too. If you're planning on keeping the skin on your parsnips, consider buying organic. Store them in your crisper, where they can keep for several weeks, or chop and freeze to use in stews and braises.

COOKING WITH

Parsnips are so versatile, happily grated raw into salads, boiled in salted water, or simply steamed until soft. For a quick one-pan parsnip purée or soup, splash olive oil over 2 cm (¾ inch) pieces of parsnip and a sliced leek and roast at 190°C (375°F) for 30 minutes, then blitz with enough stock or water to your desired viscosity and season. Peeling is not necessary when roasting parsnips, as the skin will help them hold their shape. Speaking of golden brown, parsnip also lends itself gorgeously to cakes, offering a sweet nuttiness that was used to much advantage in medieval times before cane sugar made its way to Europe.

WITH COMPLEMENTS

Brown sugar, butter, carrots, cream, garlic, ginger, honey, maple syrup, parsley, spices (especially cumin, curry powder, nutmeg, pepper), thyme.

SCRAP MEDAL

Save any peels and ends in a freezer bag for making stock. Alternatively, heat some rice bran oil to 350°F and fry the peeled bits (and maybe some thinly peeled strips of flesh as well) until golden, drain on paper towel and they'll cool into crunchy, crinkly chips. Yum! If you've scored the parsnip tops, treat them as you might parsley – or even carrot tops – by using them to garnish your parsnip creation or blitzing into pesto.

HASSELBACK PARSNIPS WITH ROSEMARY OIL & SALT

Though parsnips behave quite like carrots when grated or chopped, roasting them whole yields a decidedly drier result. By the time the fibers of the thick end relax enough to serve, the tips are toast. Slashing into them using this classic hasselback technique, which allows heat to permeate the parsnip's thickest points through the accordion-like layers, means a much more even – and strikingly beautiful – result. To make it extra special, we're infusing the oil with fresh rosemary, then turning the same rosemary into a herbaceous salt garnish, so diners will be sure to appreciate how extra special they must be to you, too!

SERVES 4

⅓ cup (80 ml) olive oil
4 rosemary sprigs
6–8 medium-sized
    parsnips, washed (and
    any fuzzy bits removed)
1 teaspoon flaked sea salt

Preheat the oven to 400°F.

Add the olive oil and rosemary sprigs to the roasting pan you're going to roast the parsnips in. Place in the oven and heat for 5 minutes.

Meanwhile, place a whole, unpeeled parsnip on a chopping board, take two chopsticks and lay one down on each side of the parsnip. Use a sharp knife to slash into the top of the parsnip, down to the top of the chopsticks, taking care to cut more slashes through the thicker base of the parsnip than the thinner tip. Repeat with each parsnip.

Remove the rosemary sprigs from the roasting pan and drain on paper towel. Carefully tip the pan so that the rosemary-infused oil pools along one side and, one by one, gently place the hasselbacked parsnips in, coating well with the oil.

Roast for 40–45 minutes, or until the thickest part of the parsnips is soft, turning every 15 minutes or so to ensure even coloring.

Pull the leaves off the cooled rosemary sprigs and grind them into a rough powder using a food processor or mortar and pestle. Add half the salt, grind together and taste. Add more salt if needed.

Pile the roasted parsnips onto a serving dish, drizzle with the oil from the roasting pan, then sprinkle with the rosemary salt and serve.

Tips I like to use the 'tip of the nip' (tip of the parsnip) to roll the root slightly from side to side and keep the knife still against one of the chopsticks. If this doesn't suit your style, hold on by the base end instead.

Now that you've got the hasselbacking down pat, try it out on any other round or conical veg, such as carrots, sweet potatoes, and especially potatoes.

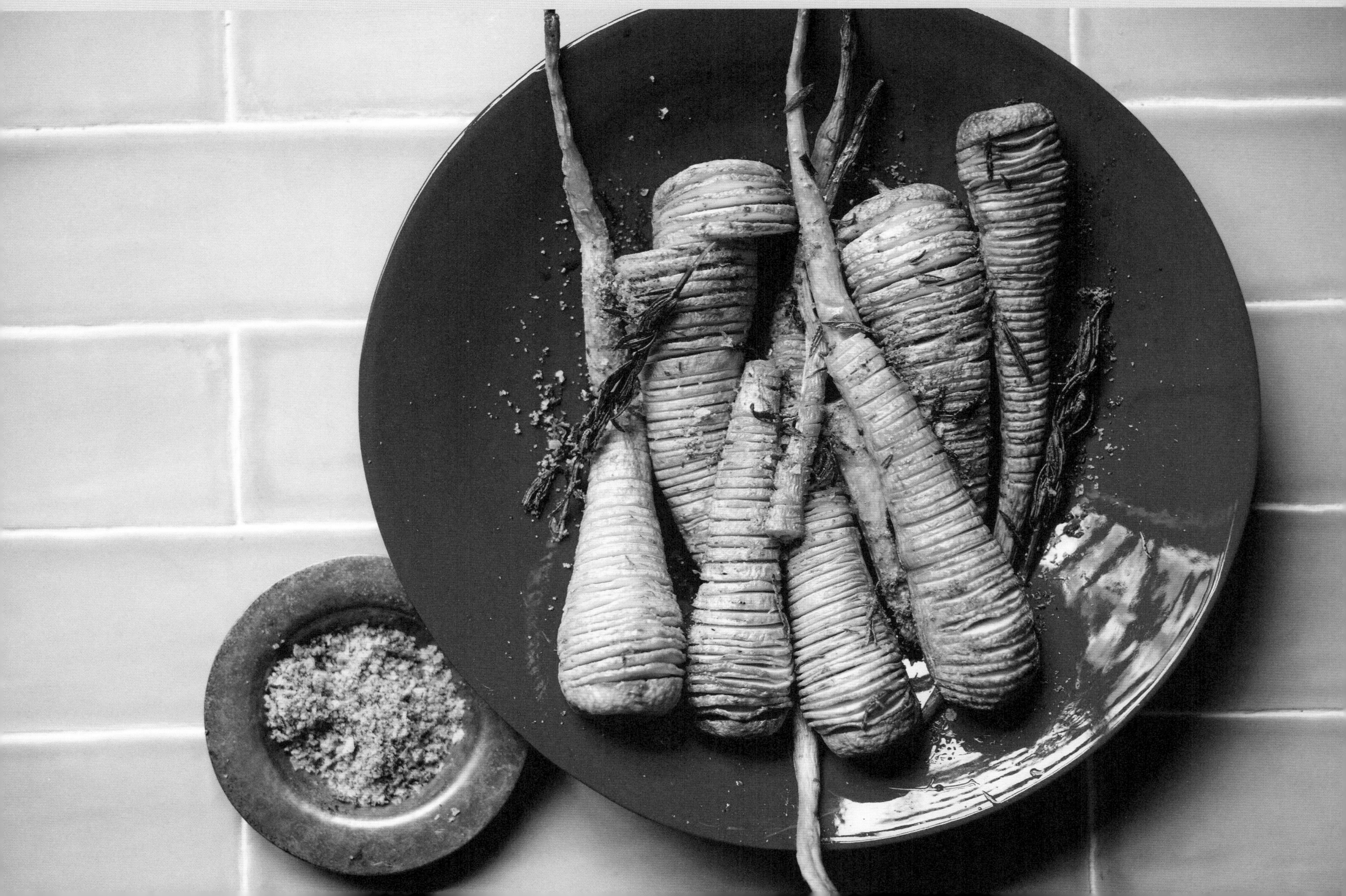

PARSNIP LATKES

Latkes are a staple food of one of Judaism's most popular holidays, Hannukah. The 'Festival of Lights', as it is otherwise known, celebrates the lighting of a one-day supply of oil that lasted for eight days instead of one night – kind of like your smartphone sitting on 1 per cent for a whole week. Clearly a miracle. This miracle is marked by yet another one – eating your weight in oily food, from doughnuts to fried fish, to my personal favorite, fried starchy veg. These latkes, which are essentially rösti by another name, are most often made with potato, which is absolutely delicious if that's all you have, but if you're packin' parsnips, add some in and you'll end up with a remarkably lighter, sweeter, miraculous canapé – no matter what you're celebrating.

MAKES 16–18 (DEPENDING ON SIZE)

1 roasting or baking potato (160 g/5½ oz), washed and scrubbed (no need to peel)

2 medium-large parsnips (360 g/13 oz), washed and scrubbed (no need to peel)

1 French shallot (or small yellow onion), peeled

½ teaspoon flaked sea salt, plus extra for sprinkling

½ lemon

2 eggs

¼ cup (35 g) plain gluten-free flour (or matzo meal)

¼ teaspoon ground white pepper

½ cup (125 ml) vegetable or canola oil

Serving suggestions
Salmon roe
Smoked salmon
Crème fraîche
Dill or chervil sprigs
Lemon wedges

Line a bowl with cheesecloth. Coarsely grate the potato, parsnip and shallot into the bowl. Add the salt and squeeze in the lemon juice. Pop the used lemon half in a small bowl of water and reserve.

Combine the mixture with your hands, squeezing out any excess moisture. Twist the cloth into a swag, using a wooden spoon as a tourniquet, and hang this over the bowl to catch the liquid; you can also use a sieve or colander to keep it elevated. Let the liquid stand undisturbed for at least 5 minutes to let the starch settle.

Beat the eggs in another bowl using a fork. Add the potato mixture, along with the flour and pepper. Scoop out the starch that has settled on the bottom of the first bowl (it'll feel like runny glue) and add this to the bowl as well. Use your hands or a wooden spoon to combine all the ingredients very well, almost as you would a meat patty.

Heat the oil over medium heat in a large, high-sided frying pan. Test that it's ready by adding a little of the mixture – it should sizzle and color almost immediately.

Line a baking tray with paper towel. Using a ¼ cup (60 ml) measuring cup, scoop out equal portions of the latke mix and shape into flat patties, dipping your hands in your bowl of reserved lemon water every now and then to stop the mixture sticking to your hands.

Working in batches, fry the latkes for 3–4 minutes on each side, until golden. Drain on paper towel, sprinkling with extra flaked sea salt as soon as they come out of the oil. (If you like, you can pop them on a wire rack over a baking tray and keep in a 250°F oven until all the latkes are ready.)

Serve warm, as the base for all manner of schmears and toppings – my favorite is the classic crème fraîche (or sour cream) and smoked salmon (or salmon roe), garnished with dill or chervil.

Tip Cold latkes are quite delightful in a lunchbox. You can also re-fry them for bonus crispy bits if need be.

Extra If you happen to have some *schmaltz* (chicken fat) or duck fat in the fridge, add a tablespoon or so to the frying oil, for extra flavor.

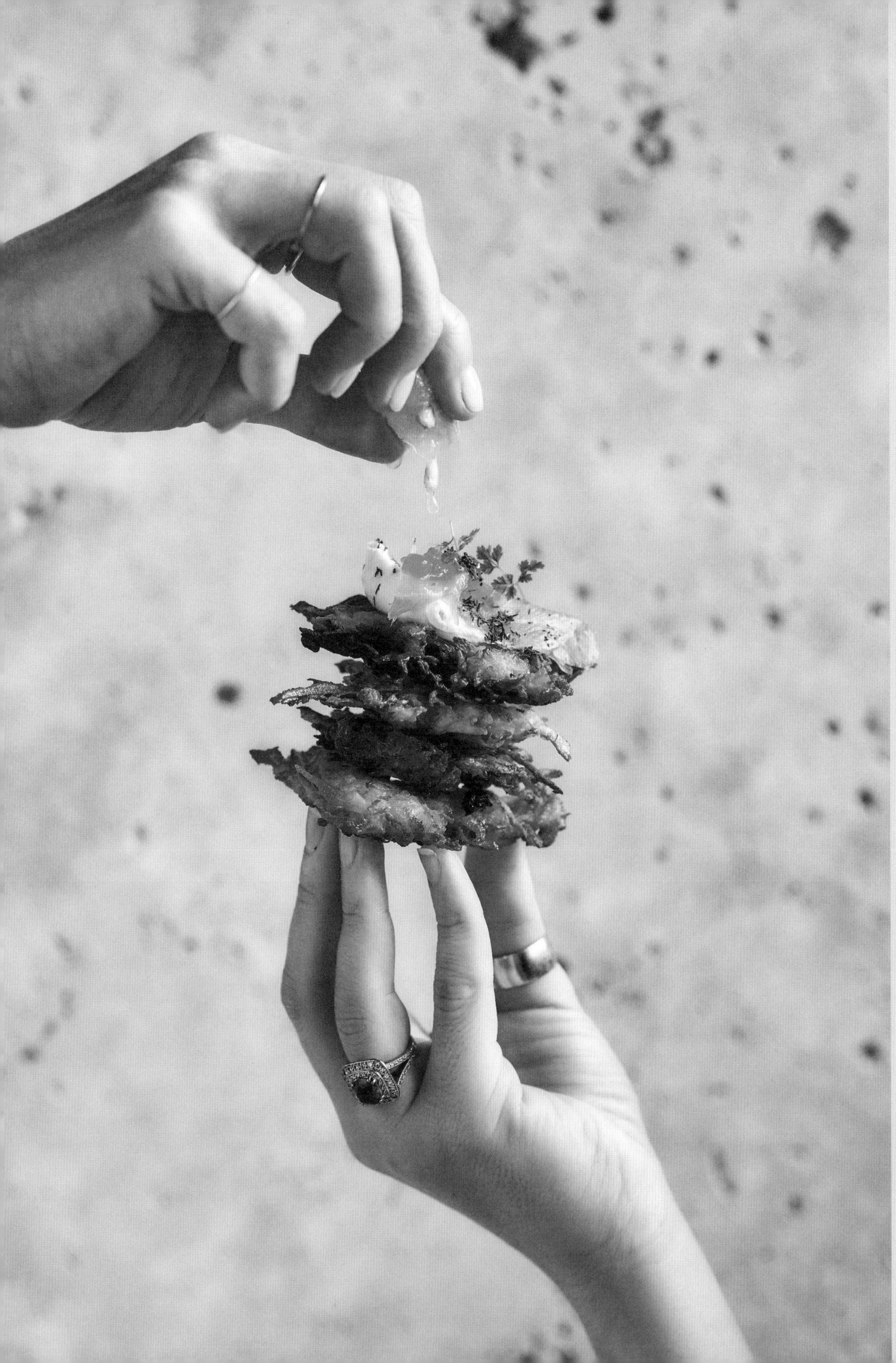

FOUR-GINGER PARSNIP STICKY DATE PUDDING

Sticky date pudding is my go-to winter dessert, and the four-way layering of warming ginger only serves to solidify it as a seasonal stayer. But it's the addition of parsnip that really makes this a show-stopper. This pud is extremely moreish, which is why this recipe is designed for when you have a large group of friends around – or to leave you with plenty of leftovers. Feel free to halve. Serve with a syrupy moat of salted caramel, plus cream and ice cream, thanks! Any left-over salted caramel sauce makes the BEST topping for ice cream … or any dessert, really.

SERVES 12

300 g (10½ oz) medjool dates (see tip), pitted and roughly chopped

400 g (14 oz) grated parsnip (3–4 grated parsnips), plus 1 peeled and thinly sliced parsnip to garnish

2 tablespoons freshly grated ginger

1 cup (190 g) crystallized ginger, sliced

2 teaspoons ground ginger

2 teaspoons baking soda

1 cup (250 ml) ginger ale, boiling hot

250 g (9 oz) butter, melted

2 cups (370 g) loosely packed dark brown or demerara sugar

2 teaspoons natural vanilla extract

4 eggs

3 cups (450 g) self-rising flour (page 23)

¼ teaspoon flaked sea salt

Salted caramel sauce

1 cup (185 g) loosely packed dark brown or demerara sugar

300 ml (10½ fl oz) heavy cream

1 teaspoon natural vanilla extract

50 g (1¾ oz) butter

½ teaspoon flaked sea salt

Preheat the oven to 400°F. Grease and line the base and sides of a 12-cup (3 liter) cake pan or high-sided baking dish.

Pop the dates and grated parsnip into a mixing bowl, along with the grated, crystallized and ground ginger and the baking soda. Pour the boiling ginger ale over. Leave for 20 minutes to soften and cool.

In a large mixing bowl, introduce the melted butter, sugar and vanilla to each other using a wooden spoon. Add the eggs, one at a time, mixing well after each addition. Mix in the parsnip and ginger mixture, then fold in the flour and salt until just combined.

Spoon the mixture into the cake pan. Arrange the parsnip slices over the top of the pudding with some artistic flair. Bake for about 1 hour, or until a skewer inserted into the center of the pudding comes out clean. If the top looks like it's coloring up too quickly, cover with foil for the last 15 minutes or so. Leave to cool in the cake pan on a wire rack.

Combine all the sauce ingredients in a saucepan over medium heat. Cook, stirring often, until the sauce comes to the boil. Reduce the heat and simmer for a few minutes until it thickens and turns from blonde to bronde.

Spoon the warm pudding into serving bowls, then pour a generous ladleful of warm sauce over the top.

Tip **Medjool dates are bigger and softer than the regular dates found in the baking section. Look for them in the baking aisle at your local grocery store or the fresh food aisle at your local deli.**

Shortcut **If you can't wait for the whole pudding to bake, you can zap a bit of the batter in a mug in the microwave at 30-second increments until cooked through. Scoop a blob of vanilla ice cream on top and get back to whatever show you're binge-watching on the couch. No judgement.**

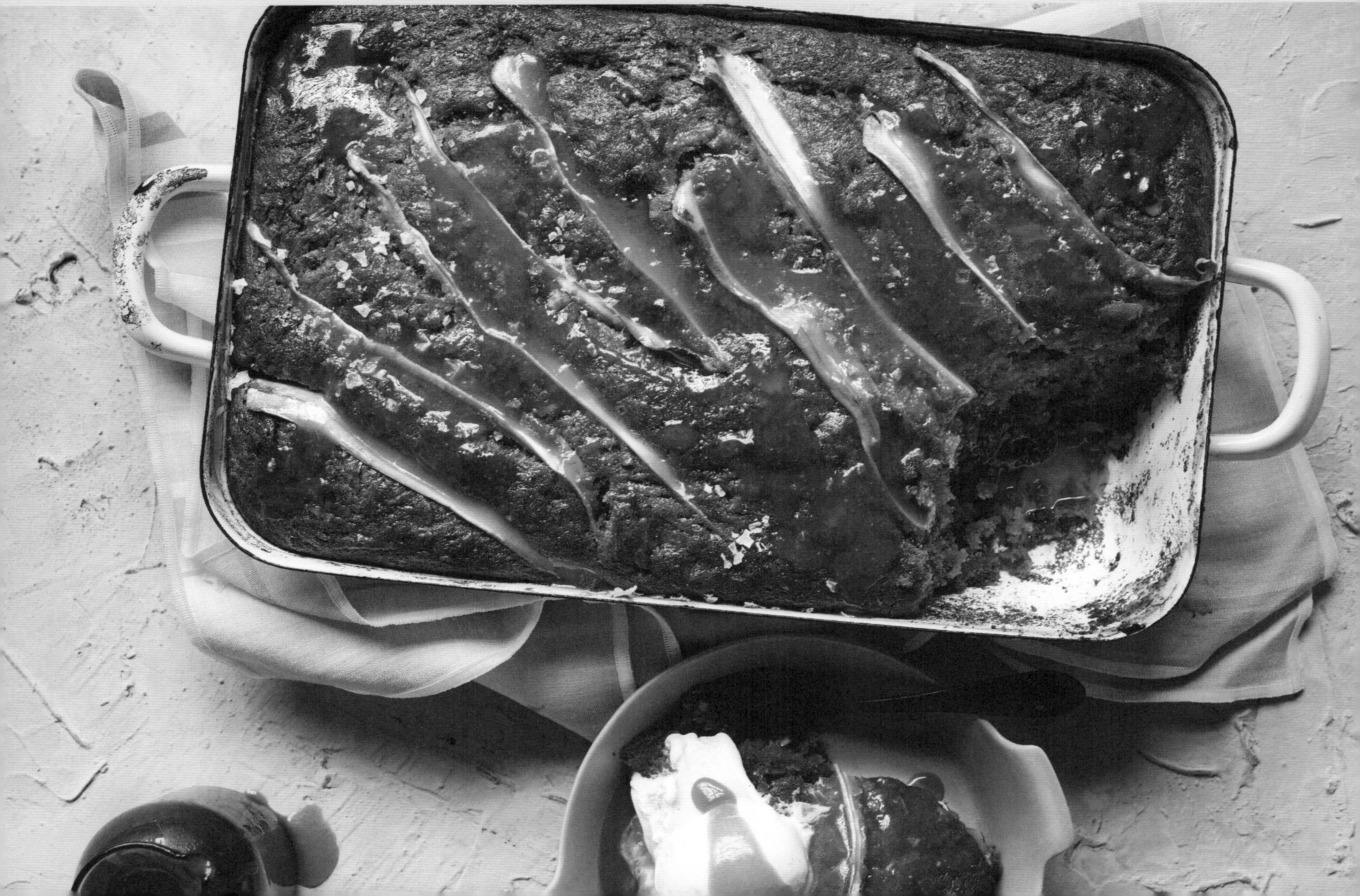

Kohlrabi

Kohlrabi is to the Brassica family what Kim is to the Kardashians: more extra than its relations, and best known for its lower end. Indeed, if you're a fan of slicing into a broccoli or cabbage heart to get at its sweet, sweet center, the kohlrabi offers a far more rewarding result. Once you peel away the woody outer skin, its swollen stem is all your Brassica-heart hopes realized – ready to be stir-fried, thinly sliced, or chomped into like an apple as you cook (my personal favorite). Like its cabbage-y counterparts, the white variety is tinged slightly green on the outside, and is quite white inside. Rarer still is the purple rendition, which is still white inside once the pretty purple skin is peeled, so is best capitalized upon as a fine julienne, where the skin is present enough to be a feature without the woodiness getting in the way.

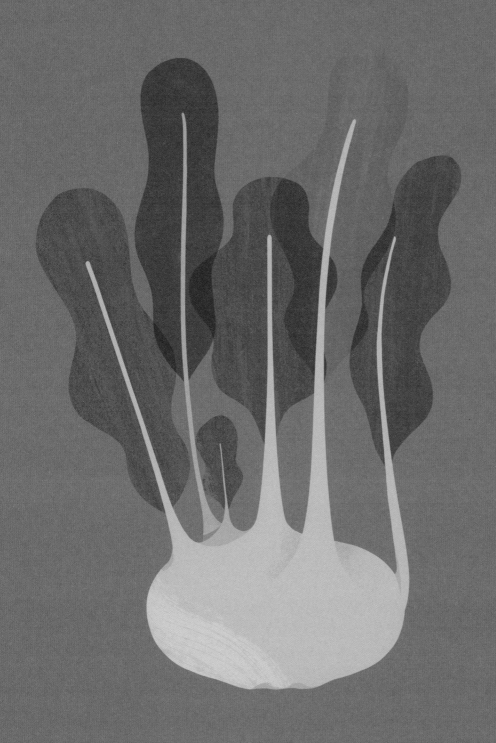

'I like to cook kohlrabi with gentle heat as this brings out its potential for sensational sweetness and a warm nutty flavor. The most tremendous thing about a slowly cooked kohlrabi is its texture: firm but melt-in-the-mouth; a sharp knife can carve distinctly clear lines through the vegetable without it falling apart.' – JEREMY CHAN, UK

BUYING & STORING

Once again, it's the leaves that indicate whether to love it or leave it, so look for kohlrabi with cruciferous curls attached where possible, from early autumn through spring. If you're left with nothing but the bare stem and a few alien-looking antennae, think back to the Kardashian analogy and seek out ones that are weighty for their size and kinda glowy, with the odd contoured corner. Medium-sized orbs will serve you best in terms of flavor – the older and bigger kohlrabi gets, the woodier it becomes (clearly, this is where the Kardashian analogy screeches to a halt, because Kris is kween). Kohlrabi prefers cold, moist environments, so store loosely wrapped in the crisper. Separating stem from leaf could gain you *heaps* of storage time, too.

PREPPING

If you've won the leafy lottery, trim these off and save them (see 'scrap medal' for ideas), then get to work on the swollen stem (more appetizing than it sounds, I promise). Trim off any 'antennae' until you're left with what appears to be an unfuzzy tennis ball, then taste an antenna – if it's quite woody, you'll have to peel the kohlrabi. If it's quite tender to the tooth, no peeling for you! Just slice thinly using a sharp knife or a mandoline, if using for salads. If steaming or boiling, consider chopping it into cubes and cooking for a lot less time than you think. But I'm getting ahead of myself ... read on!

COOKING WITH

Though traditional recipes recommend steaming or boiling, I think this does kohlrabi an injustice, turning it more cabbage-y than it deserves to be. I like slicing it thinly and sautéing with butter, mustard seeds and a dash of white wine, where the texture relaxes slightly, and the flavor stays sweet with a touch of Brassica bitterness that dances with the creamy butter. I also love kohlrabi raw, julienned, perhaps softened slightly with a splash of cider vinegar and salt, and then put through a bright salad of some description.

WITH COMPLEMENTS

Butter, cheese (especially hard cheeses), caraway seeds, cider vinegar, citrus (especially oranges, lemons), crème fraîche, dill, garlic, mustard (sauce and seeds), parsley, sesame oil, sour cream, soy sauce.

SCRAP MEDAL

Don't even think about turfing the leaves of your kohlrabi – they are just perfect roasted as you would kale or broccolini. The skin could end up in your veggie stock, too, if you're that way inclined (though it will give off a slightly sulfuric funk, so use responsibly).

KOHLRABI WALDORF SALAD

The man widely credited for this iconic salad – Oscar Tschirky, the Waldorf Astoria's long-time *maître d'hôtel* at the turn of the 20th century – deemed it necessary to include the following extremely specific instruction in the original recipe, which is only three sentences long: 'Be very careful not to let any seeds of the apple be mixed with it.' I've gone one better and scrapped the apple entirely. Kohlrabi's apple-y shape and sweetness makes it an obvious addition to Oscar's classic combo, which was originally apple–celery–mayo, but has since had a squillion iterations (probably because the recipe is indeed so vague, besides the bit about the seeds) – including the addition of walnuts, which I deem entirely mandatory, seeing as both celery and kohlrabi love this nut.

SERVES 4 AS A SIDE DISH

2 tablespoons currants
1 French shallot,
    finely chopped
¼ cup (60 ml)
    chardonnay vinegar
¼ cup (60 ml) olive oil
1 cup (115 g) walnuts,
    toasted and
    finely chopped
1 purple kohlrabi, small
    leaves reserved
1 celery heart, small
    leaves reserved

1 Bartlett pear,
    thinly sliced
100 g (3½ oz) red
    or green grapes
    or fresh currants,
    bigger ones halved
1 bunch of chives, cut into
    3 cm (1¼ inch) lengths
½ cup (125 g) mayonnaise
juice of 1 lemon

Place the currants and shallot in a bowl, pour the vinegar over and set aside for 5 minutes to macerate and pickle. Stir in the olive oil and half the walnuts and season to taste with salt and pepper.

Meanwhile, shred the kohlrabi into matchsticks, thinly slice the celery and soak them in a bowl of iced water until ready to serve.

Drain the kohlrabi and celery, then gently mix the pear through. Stir some of the walnut vinaigrette through, then arrange on a serving plate.

Drizzle the remaining vinaigrette over, then sprinkle with the grapes, chives, reserved celery and kohlrabi leaves and remaining walnuts.

Mix the mayonnaise and lemon juice until well combined, drizzle over the salad and serve immediately.

Tip Kohlrabi is seasonal, so if you have a hankering for this salad but no kohlrabi is forthcoming, sub in some extra celery and pear, or green apple if you must.

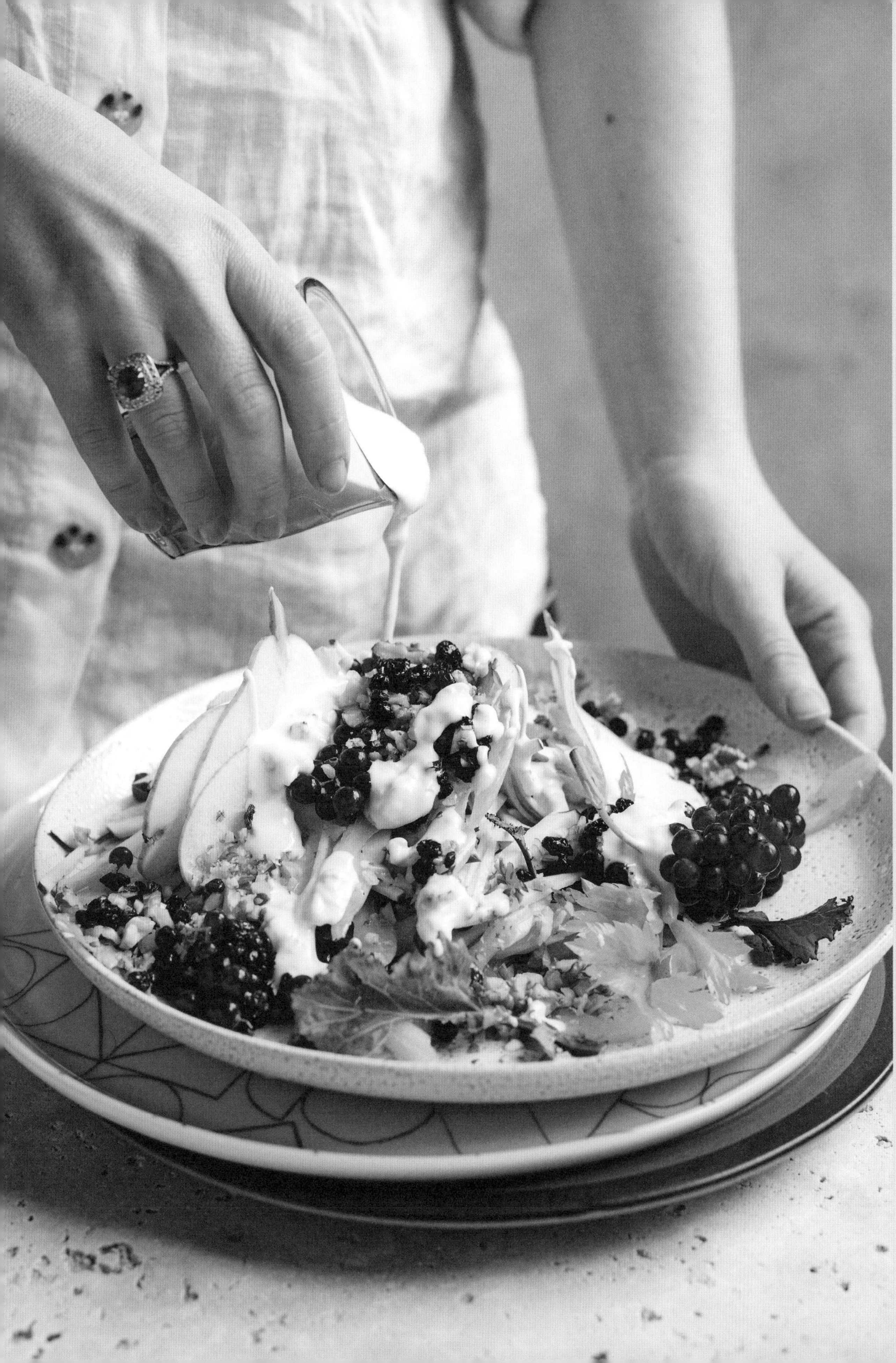

Fennel

Even though fennel is most abundant in the autumn and winter months, it's in summer that its refreshing, liquorice-y flavor really comes alive. I love it finely sliced (using a mandoline or a good sharp knife), seasoned generously and dressed with lemon juice and olive oil as a simple side to fish dishes; in warmer weather, whack in some chopped ripe tomatoes and maybe some fresh cheese such as ricotta, if you have some handy. Braised fennel is just heavenly in the colder months, with lemon zest to really make it sing. In fact, any time you serve fennel, think about adding some lemon – the two have been fast friends ever since lemons arrived on the shores of the Mediterranean via the Roman empire. And whatever you do, don't forget about the fronds. Use them as you would dill – fennel and dill are cousins, after all.

Fennel is one of the most incredible vegetables, full of the most delicious flavors. You can braise it, fry it, bake it, make a salad out of it. Just get fennel with it, because it's freaking awesome!'
GEORGE CALOMBARIS, AUSTRALIA

BUYING & STORING

Fennel is a bit like celery in that it starts to lose moisture and look quite haggard when it has been sitting on the shelf for too long. Avoid bulbs with any woody brown bits, or slimy spots that show it's had a tough time in cold storage. If the fronds are intact, protect them by wrapping in damp paper towel or cloth and storing in the fridge. Try to use your fennel within a couple of days, as the fridge will continue to sap it of life. If you're using a little at a time, wrap the remainder with beeswax to stop the edges drying out.

COOKING WITH

Fennel quickly starts to oxidize and discolor once you chop into it, so have some acidulated iced water on hand to dunk your bits into. Recipes will often call for fennel to be shaved, which is best done using a mandoline. Try to slice with the shape of the fennel, rather than working against the grain as you would with meat, utilizing the stem end like a handle. If using a knife, halve the fennel lengthwise, then rest on its flat edge and cut into half-moons.

FUNCTIONAL FOOD

Fennel seeds are often a key ingredient in lactation aids such as teas and cookies, because the seeds (and the plant itself) contain estrogen-like properties, handy for boosting breastmilk production, as well as helping to alleviate menstrual symptoms. Some mothers have even reported success with treating colicky babies by upping their fennel intake while nursing.

WITH COMPLEMENTS

Apple, butter, cheese (parmesan, fresh, blue), fish, lemon, olive oil, olives, orange, pepper, tomato.

SCRAP MEDAL

If your fennel is looking a little worse for wear, trim off any bruises or dried-out dents before finely slicing and refreshing in iced water; don't leave it in the water for longer than an hour, however, as its flavor will leach out. Any scraps belong in your 'stock-up' bag in the freezer.

FENNEL & TOMATO PANZANELLA WITH HOME-MADE RICOTTA

It may seem fairly extreme to be asking you to make your own ricotta, but here's the thing: it's so quick and easy that you'll likely want to start making it all the time. Traditionally, a panzanella uses up stale bread, allowing tomato juices to soak in and soften it back up. This version is all about the crunch of the bread and fennel against the creaminess of the ricotta, cut through with sweet, sweet summer tomatoes. I love the way the seed mix takes me right to the bagel shops of Brooklyn or Balaclava ... at which point I realize I've basically just made an 'everything bagel' in a bowl.

SERVES 4 AS A SIDE OR STARTER

1 small fennel bulb, fronds picked and reserved
1 red onion, thinly sliced into rounds
500 g (1 lb 2 oz) heirloom tomatoes, cut into chunks
¼ cup (60 ml) red wine vinegar
¼ cup (60 ml) extra virgin olive oil, plus extra for drizzling
150 g (5½ oz) sourdough bread, torn
3 tablespoons crispy fried shallots, roughly chopped

1 teaspoon caraway seeds
1 teaspoon sesame seeds
1 teaspoon nigella seeds
holy basil or green or purple basil, to serve (optional)

Ricotta (makes 2 cups)
2 teaspoons fennel seeds (or 1 teaspoon ground fennel, if you can find it)
1 liter (4 cups) milk (see tip)
2 tablespoons lemon juice

To make the ricotta, use a mortar and pestle to grind the fennel seeds into a fairly fine powder. Add to a saucepan along with the milk. Place over medium heat and bring to the boil. Stir in the lemon juice, then as soon as you see the mixture begin to split, remove from the heat and set aside for 30 minutes to curdle.

Line a sieve or colander with cheesecloth or a clean cloth. Strain the mixture through the sieve to separate the curds from the whey. Reserve the whey for your next batch of pancakes or vegetable soup!

Place the sieve over a large bowl and leave in the fridge for 1 hour to drain and cool completely.

Meanwhile, cut the fennel bulb in half lengthwise, then use a mandoline to thinly slice the fennel halves on the cut side. Place in a bowl of iced water.

Toss the onion, tomatoes and vinegar in a bowl.

Heat the olive oil in a frying pan over high heat. Add the bread chunks and cook, stirring, for 4–5 minutes, or until golden. Add the shallot flakes and the caraway, sesame and nigella seeds, and cook for 1–2 minutes, or until fragrant.

To serve, drain the fennel and toss with the tomato mixture. Arrange on a platter and crumble the ricotta over. Sprinkle with the crispy spiced bread mixture, fennel fronds and basil, and finish with a final drizzle of olive oil.

Tip **You'll find that the richer and creamier your milk, the better flavor and texture your ricotta will have. Since you're going to the effort of making it, seek out the best-quality milk you can find.**

Shortcut **Of course I'm going to say 'buy the ricotta' ... so when you do, look for one that's made from buffalo milk if you can, for the best flavor and texture. The next best option would be a pure-whey ricotta – the way it used to be made.**

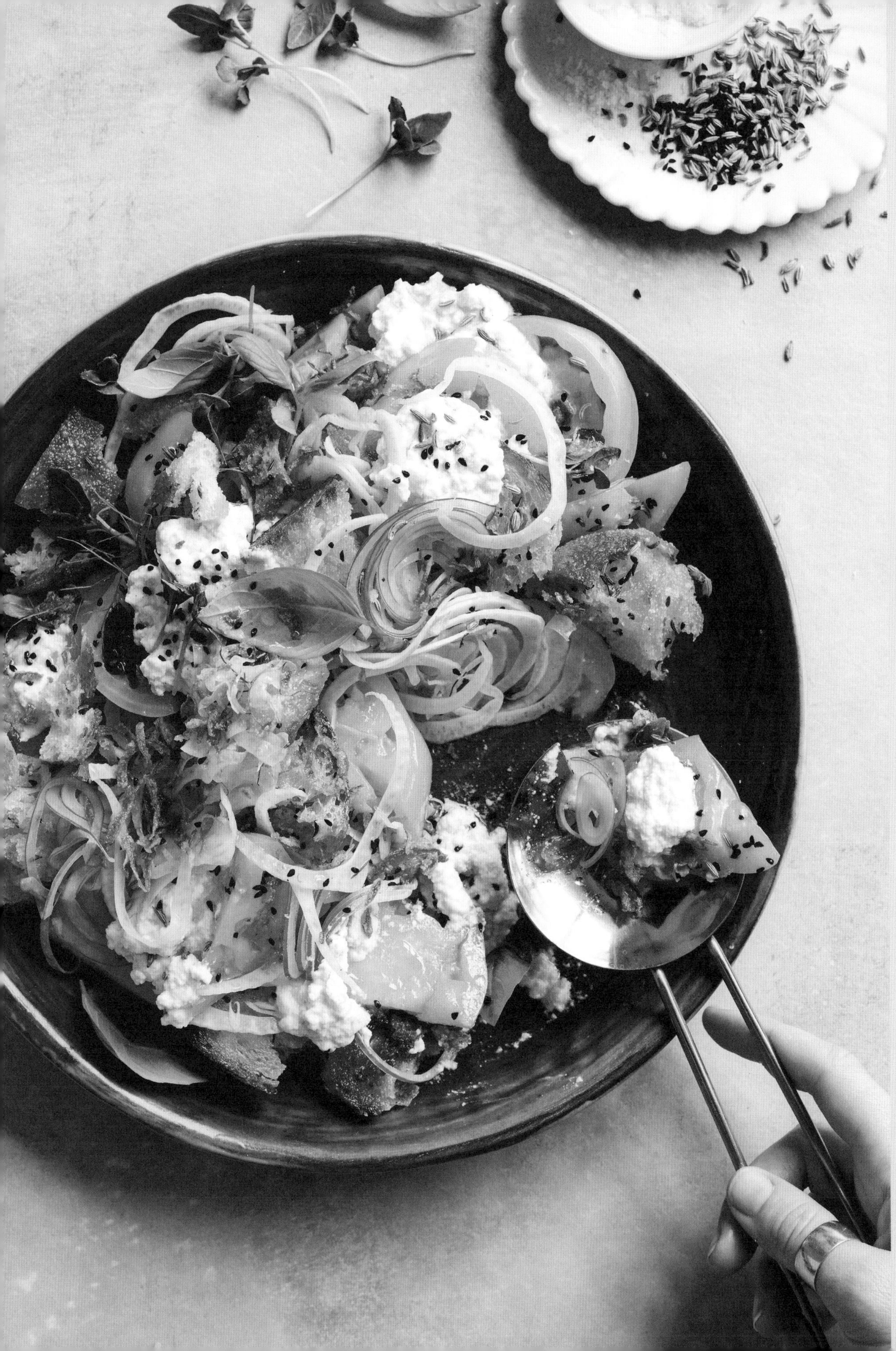

White Fennel

FENNEL CACCIATORE WITH FREE-FORM POLENTA DUMPLINGS

Chicken cacciatore is classically a 'hunter's stew', but I've borrowed the general idea and stalked the produce aisle for fennel instead of fowl. I've flipped polenta on its head, too, turning it into free-form dumplings that add body and texture to the stew from above, rather than remaining hidden and hushed underneath. Braising fennel softens its fibrous, woolly edges and brings out even more floral notes. I love the idea of burnishing them a little before letting them bubble away in the oven. It's also interesting to taste the interplay between tomato and fennel when they're both cooked, compared to the preceding salad.

SERVES 4–6

1 cup (190 g) polenta

3–4 medium fennel bulbs, stalks trimmed (see tips), fronds reserved

2 tablespoons olive oil, plus extra for drizzling

¾ cup (140 g) kalamata olives, pitted (see tips)

2–3 garlic cloves, roughly chopped

400 g (14 oz) can whole peeled tomatoes

1 teaspoon brown sugar

1 teaspoon salt

2 rosemary sprigs

grated parmesan, to garnish

Preheat the oven to 400°F, with an ovenproof casserole dish inside. Soak the polenta in 1 cup (250 ml) cold water while preparing the remaining ingredients.

Meanwhile, cut the fennel bulbs vertically in half at their widest point, then cut again into quarters. Coat generously in the olive oil.

When the casserole dish is hot, carefully extract it from the oven wearing oven mitts and arrange the fennel in a single layer, then sear on each side over medium–high heat for 5–10 minutes.

Reduce the heat to medium–low, add the olives and garlic, and stir until glossy. Break the tomatoes up a little as you pour them out of the can, into the pan. Half-fill the empty can with water, give it a swirl, then add to the pan. Sprinkle in the sugar and salt. Simmer for 10 minutes.

Use two tablespoons to shape the soaked polenta into blobs, arranging them on top of the sauce. Cover the dish with foil, or a tightly fitting lid. Transfer to the oven and bake for 40 minutes, or until the fennel is softened and the sauce has reduced.

Remove from the oven and take the foil or lid off. Turn the oven up to 450°F. Add the rosemary sprigs to the dish and sprinkle with parmesan. Bake, uncovered, for a further 5 minutes.

Check for seasoning, then garnish with more parmesan and the reserved fennel fronds. Serve as a rich side dish, or a hearty main for vegetarian pals.

Tips Don't forget to add the fennel stalks to your 'stock-up' freezer bag.

To pit the olives, press together with your fingers at the fleshiest point and pop the stones out.

Shortcut If you've no inclination to brown the fennel, whack all the ingredients (except the dumplings) into a baking dish and bake in a preheated 500°F oven for 45 minutes. Serve with instant polenta.

Extra Squeeze some pork and fennel sausages out of their casings to use as 'meatballs', brown on all sides, then add them to the simmering sauce. Easier still, add some chicken thighs and drumsticks for a chicken and fennel cacciatore.

Double duty Turn any leftovers into a gratin by tossing some parmesan and fennel fronds with panko crumbs and sprinkling the mixture on top before baking.

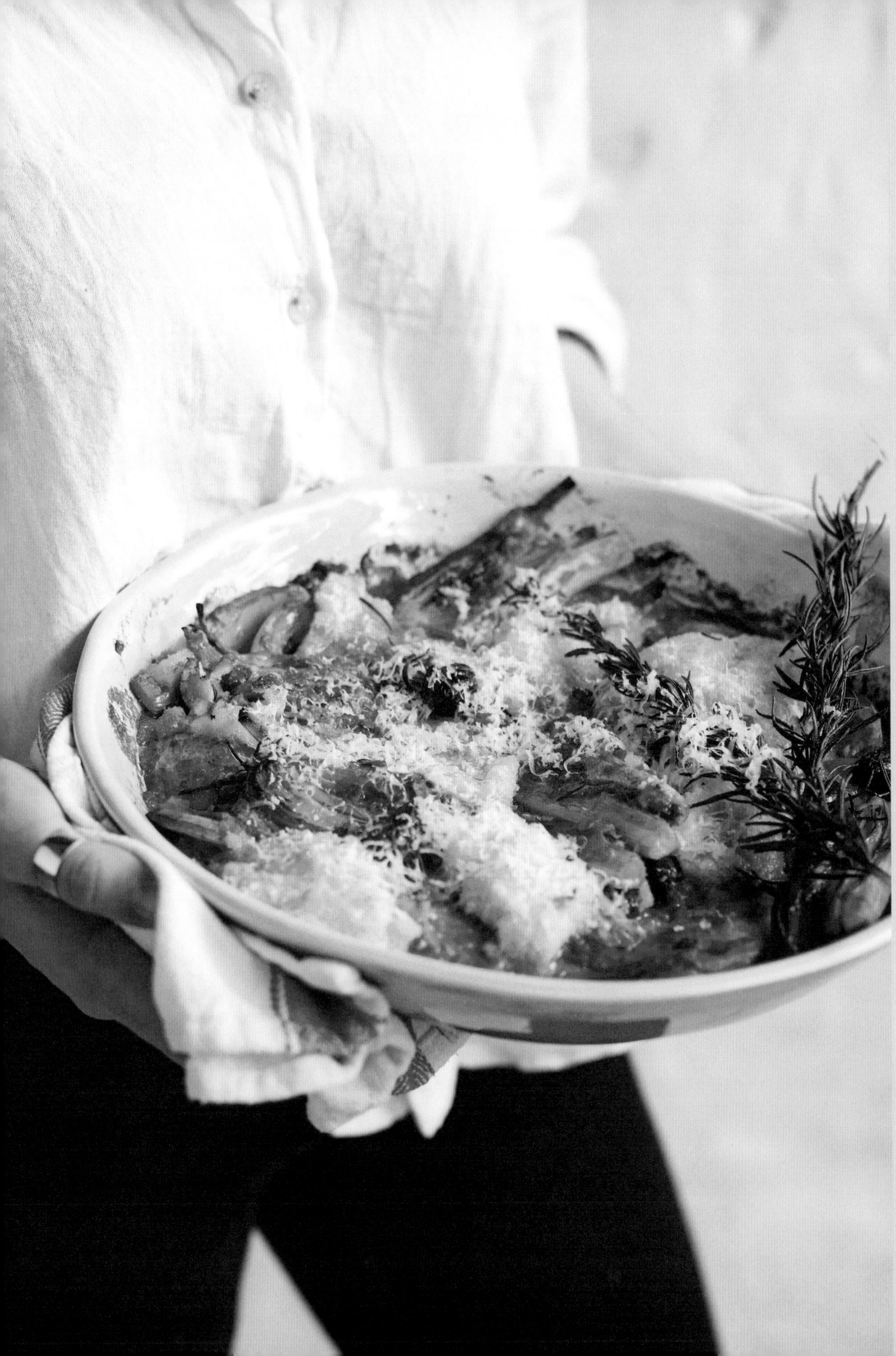

White Fennel

CRISPY FENNEL WEDGES WITH SOUR CREAM & SWEET CHILI SAUCE

If you grew up in the 1980s and 1990s like yours truly, you'll have had your fair share of wedges with sour cream and sweet chili. At the time, this combination – the crunch of the wedges, the gentle heat and aggressive syrupiness of the sweet chili, teamed with the coolness of sour cream against your lips – was about as close as a teen could get to 'gourmet'. Here's my grown-up version, where fennel takes the place of potato wedges, adding a bonus bout of herbaceousness, and lightening up the whole proposition to a point where you might find yourself wowed by wedges once more.

SERVES 4–6 AS A SIDE DISH

2 fennel bulbs,
    fronds reserved
1 garlic clove, bruised
1 tablespoon reduced
    vinegar (from the
    hollandaise, page 330),
    or white wine vinegar
1½ tablespoons flaked
    sea salt
2 cups (100 g) panko
    breadcrumbs
1 cup (150 g) all-purpose
    flour

1 teaspoon ground
    white pepper
2 eggs
vegetable or canola oil,
    for deep-frying
4 tablespoons Indonesian
    Sambal with pineapple
    (page 220), or use
    store-bought
2 tablespoons honey
sour cream, to serve

Cut the fennel bulbs in half lengthwise, then cut into 2 cm (¾ inch) thick wedges, following the length of the fennel. Place in a large heatproof bowl with the garlic clove, vinegar and 1 tablespoon of the flaked sea salt. Cover with boiling water from a kettle. Stand for 10 minutes for the fennel to soften slightly.

Meanwhile, reserve some fennel fronds for garnishing, then finely chop the rest; you'll want at least 1 tablespoon's worth. Toss into a shallow bowl with the panko crumbs and remaining flaked sea salt. In a separate shallow bowl, combine the flour and pepper. Crack the eggs into a third bowl and lightly beat with a fork.

Heat 7 cm (2¾ inches) of your chosen deep-frying oil in a wide saucepan to 400°F; a panko crumb will turn golden in 10 seconds when the oil is hot enough. Line a baking tray with paper towel, and set a cooling rack over the top.

Drain the softened fennel. Working with one piece at a time, coat it in the flour, then the egg, then dip in the breadcrumb mixture to coat completely. Transfer to the hot oil and cook, in batches, for 3 minutes, or until golden brown. Transfer to the cooling rack to drain as you cook the rest; season with extra salt while it is still hot.

For a quick and easy sweet chili sauce, mix together the sambal and honey until well combined.

Sprinkle the fennel wedges with the reserved fennel fronds. Serve hot, with sour cream and your DIY sweet chili sauce for dipping.

Tips Small or baby fennel bulbs will work particularly well for this recipe. Cut them into quarters for finger-food pieces – or even halves if they're extra-small.

The fennel wedges can be blanched in advance and deep-fried just before it's time to serve – but only batter and crumb them just before deep-frying, so they don't go soggy.

Go gluten-free Rice crumbs or quinoa flakes will fry up nicely under a gluten-free flour.

For vegans Avocado mashed with lemon juice would go down well as a dip alternative. Use the liquid left behind in a can of beans or chickpeas (the 'aquafaba') as a substitute for the eggs in the crumbing stage.

Celeriac

One of the stranger sessions in a film theory class I took at university was analysing David Lynch's *Eraserhead*, an experimental horror film in which the protagonist is plagued by a bulbous baby-like blob (also, some pretty wild hair). Every time I see a celeriac bulb, I'm reminded of that film – bulbous-baby-blob and wild hair combined. At first glance you may be forgiven for assuming that it is the *root* of the 'celery root' (another name for it) you're eating, but it is actually an engorged celery *bulb* – more stem than leaf – and the *actual* roots are the worm-like tendrils tucked up around its base! When cooked, celeriac's mildly earthy flavor and aroma transform to something nutty and herbaceous. It can also be eaten raw, particularly as the grated hero of a remoulade, lending a welcome textural contrast to this classic mayonnaise-based dish that is part-salad, part-condiment.

Celeriac is wonderful in soup, or raw in salad, and in a famous Turkish dish where it is lightly braised in lots of olive oil and orange juice. The citrus gives the dish a lovely, light flavor that complements the fragrant celeriac and helps it keep its color.' – COSKUN UYSAL, TURKEY

BUYING AND STORING

Considering it's still a card-carrying member of the celery clan, you can apply the same principles when shopping for fresh celeriac throughout autumn and winter – the sprightlier the leaves, the fresher the bulb. Don't be too perturbed if all the leaves have been lopped off, as long as the flesh seems firm; it's usually more a case of an overzealous greengrocer than a bad bulb. Roasting the bulb together with its leaves does amplify its flavor, though, so if you can find one with leaves intact, go for that option. Look for celeriac with skin as smooth as possible, for easier peeling and to avoid having to hack too deeply into it later on. Store it unwashed and loosely bagged in the fridge, where it will last for over a week. Celeriac also freezes quite well, so on a slow Sunday afternoon, consider peeling, chopping and freezing it on a tray, then portioning up to use in soups and stews.

Wash 'n' go

When it comes to barriers to celeriac consumption, the biggest is how tricky it is to wash. Those gnarly root tendrils twist and turn into themselves, trapping dirt in the most dastardly of ways, earning itself a reputation as the 'octopus' of vegetables. If you go down the conventional route – root? – of trimming these off, you risk lopping off a third of the bulb along with them. Instead, try soaking the whole thing in a big bowl of water for at least 10 minutes, then cranking on the tap and holding it under running water to encourage any particularly enthusiastic particles to part ways. This also has the added benefit of injecting moisture back into the bulb. If you're in a rush, chop the celeriac into quarters first, as this will help you see how deep and gnarly the root systems are, then use a paring knife to trim as close to the flesh as possible.

WITH COMPLEMENTS

Apple, apple cider vinegar, lemon, mustard (especially dijon, seeded), parsley, potatoes.

SCRAP MEDAL

Although the 'celery' bit of the celeriac will probably be too bitter for dipping into your peanut butter jar, you can pop it into the 'stock-up' bag in your freezer for making veggie stock. It adds a deep earthiness and minerality, without you needing to shell out for an extra bunch of celery.

SALT-BAKED BUTTERFLIED CELERIAC CHEESE

This dish is the epitome of 'ugly delicious': the skin is blackened and shrivelled, yet completely edible, while the flesh inside is herbaceous and bright, and at the same time creamy and unctuous. I can't say enough good things about it. And not because I'm just being nice.

SERVES 4 AS A SIDE DISH

⅓ cup (30 g)
   flaked sea salt
2 celeriac bulbs, 400–500 g
   (14 oz–1 lb 2 oz) each
   (see tips)
50 g (1¾ oz) unsalted
   butter, chopped

½ cup (120 g)
   crème fraîche
100 g (3½ oz) grated
   gruyère or mozzarella
½ bunch of thyme,
   sprigs picked
1 teaspoon celery seeds

Set an oven rack in the middle of the oven and place a foil-lined baking tray underneath. Preheat the oven to 450°F.

Combine the salt and 2 cups (500 ml) of just-boiled water in a large bowl. Stir until the salt has dissolved. Add the celeriac bulbs and carefully roll to coat them in the water; this will help create an easy salt crust, to flavor the celeriac and intensify the heat.

Place the celeriac on the middle oven rack (over the lined baking tray, to catch any cooking juices and keep the oven clean) and bake for 1 hour and 15 minutes, or until a knife easily goes through the fleshiest part, like butter.

Stand for 10 minutes to cool slightly, then use a sharp knife to make an incision along the side of each celeriac so that it can be pried open carefully with your fingertips. (If you find this too difficult, use a butter knife to ease the halves apart.)

Spread the celeriac out onto a baking dish to reveal the flesh, and sprinkle with the butter. Spoon half the crème fraîche over each, then sprinkle with the cheese, thyme sprigs and celery seeds. Season with a pinch of salt and pepper.

Shift the oven rack towards the top of the oven. Preheat the broiler to high and broil the celeriac for 4–5 minutes, or until the cheese is golden. Serve warm, with warmth.

Tips This cheat's béchamel, using crème fraîche or sour cream mixed with cheese and butter, is as easy as layering – no need to stir ... and it works a treat in lasagna, too!

If celeriac is not forthcoming, but kohlrabi is at hand, give this same method a whirl.

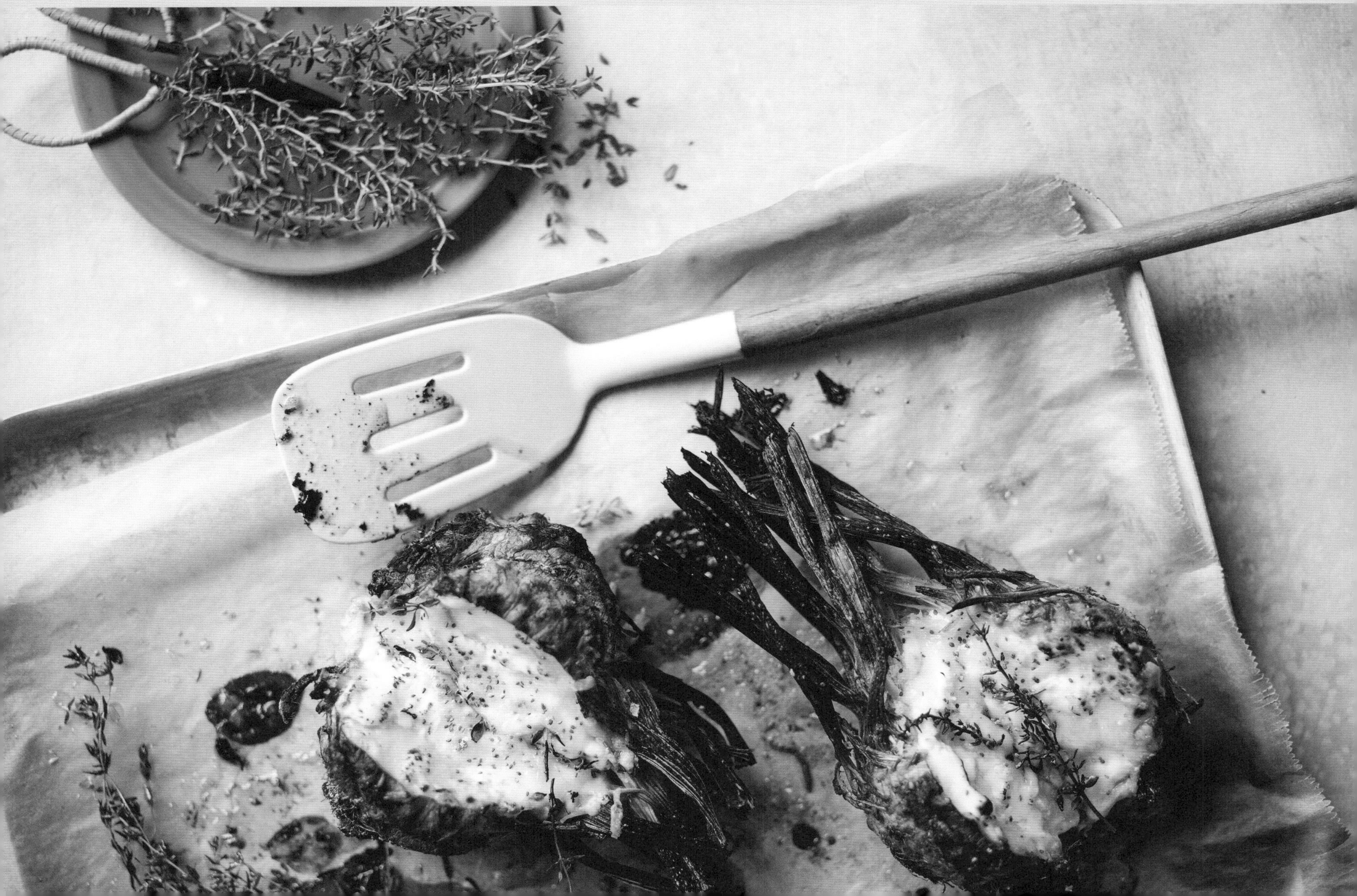

Cauliflower

When it comes to veggie versatility, you can't go past cauliflower. Whether it's whole-roasted, blitzed to a 'cauli couscous' consistency, whizzed up into a soup or pickled into piccalilli, this brilliant Brassica's mild flavor makes it a welcome addition to many meals within many cuisines. You can treat it in the same way as its close relative broccoli, simply steaming or tossing into a stir-fry. It's also proven itself quite the shapeshifter, sliced into thick 'patties' and fried like a steak, or dehydrated into powders and used as an alternative starch for crackers.

'I love cauliflower grilled like a steak and served with a balsamic and olive oil vinaigrette, or puréed as a gratin with sauce mornay in winter, and as a soup, of course.' – PHILIPPE MOUCHEL, FRANCE

BUYING & STORING

Fresh cauliflower's lily-whiteness and delicate flesh make it easy to tell you're picking a winner. Available for most of the year, peaking in autumn, look for a clean canopy (a.k.a. 'curd') and sprightly leaves. For another good indicator, check underneath where the head has been lopped off from the stalk – the more moisture there is at this point, the fresher your florets will be. Any 'ashiness' (in color and texture) of the stalk or discoloration on the curd tell you these heads have seen some things, but it's nothing that the flick of a paring knife or peeler can't solve. Floppy florets are also not the end of the world – use them in a cauliflower soup and people will be none the wiser. It's always more cost effective to buy a whole head, and simply add any leftovers – roasted or steamed – to bulk out whatever dish you're making the next day.

Your cauli can last up to 2 weeks in the crisper if the leaves are sprightly when you buy it. If you insist on going with a cauli half, either stand it in a jar of water on the bottom shelf of your fridge, or wrap it loosely before storing in the crisper to slow the inevitable drying-out process. Incidentally, you can also freeze blanched cauli florets flat on a tray, before packing into portions and popping back into the freezer.

BEYOND CAULIFLOWER: CAULILINI

Also known as 'Cauli Blossom' or Fioretto, these elongated cauliflower stems are punctuated by floret-like blossoms instead of a tightly packed curd. You'll start seeing caulilini on North American fine dining plates sometime in the next few years as the seeds are propagated. Look out for it at farmers' markets and specialty stores, too. My grower sources tell me that a drop on North American shores is imminent! They make fantastic tempura fodder, lightly dipped in fizzy batter and then deep-fried, the fine florets poking out as tender tendrils through the crispness. I like tossing some through stir-fries, too, the stems offering just a little extra crunch, like broccolini. They'll make a gorgeous addition to a serving of Lau's vegetables (see recipe on page 104).

WITH COMPLEMENTS

Anchovies, butter, cheese (especially cheddar, blue, parmesan), chili, cream, curry powder, garlic, lemon (especially zest), pepper.

Rice is nice

Cauliflower 'rice' has become a popular grain-free alternative to its namesake, adding a bonus layer of flavor to any meal. Bypass the pre-pulsed bags and make your own. I simply grate raw cauliflower (or blitz in a food processor if serving more than two), and then ladle my hot curry or casserole over the top to help soften the cauliflower a little. Or, grate it more coarsely and you've just made cauliflower couscous. Genius!

Purple cauli tabouleh

Finely dice ½ green onion and toss in a bowl with 4 diced roma tomatoes and 1–2 crushed garlic cloves, with salt and pepper to taste. Chop 1 purple cauliflower into florets, place in a heatproof bowl, then pour a kettle of boiled water over to cover. Meanwhile, zest and juice 1 lemon, adding the lemon juice to the tomato mixture. Drain the cauli well, then whiz in a food processor with the lemon zest, 1 teaspoon ground sumac and 2 tablespoons olive oil, until finely chopped. Toss through the tomato mixture. Sprinkle 1 cup chopped parsley and ½ cup chopped mint on top, tossing through just before serving. (If no purple cauli is available, look out for other colored caulis – they range from light green through to yellow and orange. Or consider blitzing a cooked baby beet in with white cauliflower to fake the anthocyanin aesthetic!)

SCRAP MEDAL

Cauliflower leaves are surprisingly tasty; roast them as you would kale chips (see page 360) until they're golden and crispy. If you're preparing a recipe that only requires the florets, don't you *dare* throw out the heart – it's my very favorite bit. Slice off the end of the stalk to show you how much woody outer layer needs to be peeled, then use a paring knife or peeler to access the sweet, sweet paler stalk within. Eat this raw as you might a celery stick, and consider sharing with any small people around. It'll hook them on Brassicas for life – and they might even write about it one day. For any left-over cauli, blitz it in a food processor, pour boiling water over, leave for a minute to 'blanch', then drain well. Spread out flat on a tray and freeze, then portion and keep in the freezer to use as needed.

ONE-POT WHOLE-ROASTED CAULIFLOWER

No 21st century vegetable bible would be complete without a version of this dish. That's because when Miznon chef–owner Eyal Shani started dropping whole heads of burnished cauliflower on the dining tables of his restaurants in Tel Aviv, New York and Melbourne, it almost single-handedly (single-headedly?) shifted the way people thought about serving vegetables at home. When we have plant-based diners coming round, this goes on the menu instantly: it's a real people-pleaser. It's also a Nick-pleaser because he does the washing up (as all significant others should). The only thing that might change is the spicing – sometimes I'll go Middle Eastern, rubbing the cauliflower with spices such as cumin and coriander before roasting, finishing with dukkah and pomegranate; other times I'll rub it with some turmeric, make a cucumber raita and serve with plenty of fresh cilantro. Once you understand the principles of steam–roast–garnish, the curd is your oyster. So to speak.

SERVES 4–6

1 head of cauliflower, preferably with some luscious leaves still attached	2 tablespoons olive oil, plus extra for drizzling
	1 teaspoon flaked sea salt, plus extra for sprinkling

Soak the cauliflower in a big bowl of salted water, curd side down, for 5 minutes, then base side down for another 5 minutes, to encourage any 'hop-ons' to hop off into the water. Use your fingertips, and maybe some blasts of running water, to rub the base of any leaves free of residual dirt. Check that the stalk of the cauliflower is flat enough for it to stand upright, trimming if needed.

Dig out an ovenproof casserole dish (I like to use a cast-iron one) that fits the cauli comfortably, with the lid on. Stand the cauliflower in the dish, upright on its stalk. Fill the dish with about two knuckles-worth of cold water. Close the lid and boil/steam over medium–low heat for 15 minutes. The shallow water cooks the thicker base of the cauliflower, while sparing the finer curd, ensuring it won't end up waterlogged or mushy.

Meanwhile, preheat the oven to 500°F.

Remove the lid from the dish, and use a tea towel to carefully lift out the cauli. Drain off the water, then pop the cauliflower back in, curd side up, to let any residual water evaporate for about 5–10 minutes; this will help it crisp up during roasting.

When the cauliflower is cool enough to touch, pull it out onto a chopping board and use your hands to massage the olive oil and salt into every crevice.

Overlap two pieces of parchment paper, to create a wider surface, scrunch into a bowl shape, and place on the base of the casserole dish. Cradle your cauli on top, place in the oven and roast, uncovered, for 25–35 minutes, depending on the size of the cauli, and how much you're willing to let it burn on top without freaking out; I'd usually roast a 1.2 kg (2 lb 10 oz) cauli for 30 minutes.

(Occasionally, I roast the cauliflower with the lid still on to help get even more heat into it – but you can also steam it in a pot, then roast it on a baking tray if you'd prefer to live less dangerously.)

Allow the cauliflower to cool slightly, then lift out gently along with the parchment paper collar, so the cauli doesn't fall apart. Drizzle with a little extra olive oil, sprinkle with a bit more salt flake action and serve.

WHITE & GREEN GIARDINIERA

I love the concept behind this Italian pickle – where you, the 'gardener' are quite literally planting and cultivating your own 'garden' in every jar. Traditionally, the tone is very *tricolore*, with veggies such as white cauliflower, red bell pepper and green celery in the mix, as well as slices of carrot poking out. But I thought I'd make this one all about the green and white of cauliflower varieties. Once you get the hang of this pickle, go right ahead and try it with other veggies too – and fill your pantry, for those rainy days where the only garden you want to pop into is the one in your pantry, waiting to be plonked on your sandwiches and cheeseboards. You will need to begin this recipe 1 day ahead.

MAKES 1 X 6 CUP (1.5 LITER) JAR

½ head of cauliflower
  (about 250 g/9 oz),
  cut into florets
1 small head of Romanesco
  cauliflower/broccoli
  (about 400 g/14 oz),
  cut into florets
3 green onions
  (scallions), sliced 1 cm
  (½ inch) thick
2 small celery stalks,
  cut into 3 cm
  (1¼ inch) lengths
4 garlic cloves, peeled
2 dried bay leaves
2 long green chilis, halved
  lengthwise

¼ cup (35 g)
  flaked sea salt
2 tablespoons
  fennel seeds
2 tablespoons brown
  mustard seeds
300 g (10½ oz) pitted
  green or Sicilian
  olives, halved

Pickling liquid
1½ cups (375 ml) white
  wine vinegar
1½ cups (375 ml) water
  (preferably filtered)
2 teaspoons
  flaked sea salt

Place the cauliflower and Romanesco florets in a large, non-reactive (stainless steel or enamel) bowl, along with the green onion, celery, garlic, bay leaves and chili. Add the salt and toss to coat, then add enough water to just cover the vegetables. Stand to soak overnight.

The next day, wash a 6 cup (1.5 liter) glass preserving or pickling jar in hot soapy water, rinse well and stand it upside down to dry on a rack.

Add 1 tablespoon each of the fennel and mustard seeds to the bottom of the clean, dry jar. Drain the vegetables and combine well with the olives, then cram the mixture into the jar. Top with the remaining fennel and mustard seeds.

In a saucepan, bring the pickling liquid ingredients to the boil over high heat. Use a clean ladle to carefully pour the hot pickling liquid into the jar, leaving a 5 mm (¼ inch) gap at the top. Secure the lid and stand to cool, then store in a cool dark place. You can start to pucker up to your pickle within a couple of days.

The giardiniera will keep in the sealed jar for 2–3 months. Once opened, store in the fridge and use within 1 month, making sure the vegetables are always covered with the pickling liquid.

Tip Garlic can take on a greeny-blue tinge when pickling – but is still perfectly safe to eat. In fact, some cultures prize colored garlic, like 'Laba' garlic, which is auspiciously jade-green for Chinese New Year. If you'd prefer to keep your giardiniera green-garlic free, use filtered water, iodine-free salt and non-reactive cookware for the brine.

KFC: KERALAN FRIED CAULIFLOWER WITH COCONUT CHUTNEY

Puffy popcorn pieces of cauliflower, warmed and wonderful with the spices of South India, complete with a quick and easy coconut chutney. These are already gluten-free and can easily be turned vegan by using coconut yogurt for dipping. Serve as a stunning share-plate, or turn into a killer breakfast by popping a runny fried or scrambled egg or two alongside. If this book isn't smattered with curry-leaf-oily fingerprints within the next hour, I'll be quietly disappointed.

SERVES 4–6 AS A STARTER

½ head of cauliflower
1 cup (150 g) chickpea flour
½ cup (75 g) rice flour
¼ teaspoon baking powder
1 teaspoon flaked sea salt
2 teaspoons
    ground turmeric
2 teaspoons Kashmiri
    chili powder
2 teaspoons mild
    curry powder
1 cup (250 ml) very cold
    sparkling water
1 garlic clove, finely grated
1 teaspoon finely grated
    fresh ginger
rice bran oil, for
    shallow-frying
3 curry leaf branches,
    washed and patted dry
cilantro leaves, to garnish
1–2 limes, cut into wedges
Greek-style yogurt,
    to serve

Coconut chutney
(Makes 1½ cups)
100 g (3½ oz) shredded
    coconut
1½ tablespoons coconut oil
1 teaspoon cumin seeds
1 teaspoon black
    mustard seeds
1 teaspoon chili flakes
20 curry leaves, washed
    and patted dry
1 green chili, chopped
1½ teaspoons
    tamarind purée
1 teaspoon brown sugar,
    or to taste
1 bunch of cilantro,
    chopped

Remove and thinly slice the core from the cauliflower and set aside. Cut or tear the rest of the cauliflower into small florets about 3–4 cm (1¾–1½ inches) in size. Pick the leaves and keep these for frying also.

In a large bowl, combine the chickpea flour, rice flour, baking powder, flaked sea salt and 1 teaspoon each of the turmeric, chili powder and curry powder. Create a well in the middle, add the sparkling water, garlic and ginger, whisking out any lumps. Add the cauliflower florets and mix to coat. Chill for at least 15 minutes, or up to 1 hour.

To make the coconut chutney, place the coconut in a bowl and cover with just boiled water. Stand for 5 minutes to soften. Meanwhile, place the coconut oil, cumin and mustard seeds, chili flakes, curry leaves and reserved cauliflower core slices in a frying pan over medium–high heat and cook for 3–4 minutes, or until the mustard seeds begin to pop and the cauliflower is softened. Transfer to a blender, along with the remaining chutney ingredients and drained coconut. Whiz until smooth and combined, adding 1 tablespoon of water at a time to loosen. Season to taste.

Heat 3 cm (1¼ inches) of rice bran oil in a wok or saucepan over high heat to 400°F; a little batter added to the oil shouldn't take longer than 30 seconds to turn golden brown. Carefully add the well-dried curry leaf branches (they'll make a loud noise!) and cook for 30 seconds, or until crisp. Drain on paper towel.

Working in batches, add the cauliflower florets and leaves to the hot oil after shaking away the excess batter and cook for 3–4 minutes, or until golden. Drain on paper towel.

Strain one-quarter of the cooking oil into a cold saucepan, leaving a 5 mm (¼ inch) shimmer of oil in the pan. Return the pan to the heat with the remaining spices and cook for 1 minute, or until foaming. Add all the fried cauliflower and cook, stirring, for 3 minutes, or until coated and golden. Transfer to a serving platter and sprinkle with the crispy curry leaves and cilantro. Serve with the coconut chutney, lime wedges and yogurt.

DOUBLE DENIM MAC 'N' CHEESE

Remember when Justin and Britney were dating, and went to the MTV Video Music Awards wearing double double denim? Well, between his hair (noodles) and her surname (Spears), I bring you this dish. Often, mac 'n' cheese recipes are let down by too many steps (I'm looking at you, béchamel sauce), so what I love about this one is that the only thing standing between you and a bowl of oozy deliciousness studded with sumptuous asparagus spears is how long it takes to boil the pasta. If you don't have time to fuss around with cooking the veggies, chop the asparagus into fine discs and toss into the colander just before draining the pasta water through it; this will cook the asparagus just enough to take the raw edge off. You can also grate some of the cauliflower through the cooked pasta just before turning off the heat and draining. Pouring plenty of boiling water over a cupful or two of frozen peas in a bowl is another option.

SERVES 4

500 g (1 lb 2 oz) macaroni (or gluten-free pasta)
3–4 bunches of asparagus, about 600 g (1 lb 5 oz) in total
½ head of cauliflower, with leaves
100 g (3½ oz) butter
300 g (10½ oz) Comté (or gruyère or cheddar), grated

250 g (9 oz) parmesan, grated
olive oil, for drizzling

Bonus beurre noisette
80 g (2¾ oz) butter
1 handful of raw or roasted hazelnuts, roughly chopped

Grab your largest pot, fill it three-quarters full of water, add plenty of salt and bring to a vigorous boil. Add the macaroni, setting a timer for 3 minutes before the packet says the pasta will be ready.

Meanwhile, snap the woody ends off the asparagus and reserve them, then slice the spears into bite-sized pieces. Chop the cauliflower into fork-sized florets, and the stalks into bite-sized pieces. Cut the leaves to forkful size and reserve.

Melt the butter in a large non-stick saucepan.

When your timer goes off, pop the cauliflower into the pasta pot, then reset the timer for another 2 minutes. When the timer goes off again, in go the asparagus spears, then reset the timer for 1 minute more. Scoop out and reserve a mugful of pasta water, then carefully pour the asparagus, cauliflower and pasta mixture into a colander to drain.

To make the beurre noisette, pop the reserved asparagus ends and cauliflower leaves in the emptied pasta pot with the butter and hazelnuts. Allow to bubble away and brown over medium heat until the pot smells like you're baking cookies in it. Reserve for garnish.

Meanwhile, sprinkle all the Comté and about 200 g (7 oz) of the parmesan into the other saucepan of melted butter, then add the cooked pasta, veggies and mugful of reserved pasta water. Stir until everything combines into one glorious oozy mess. Season to taste with salt and plenty of cracked black pepper.

Scoop out the brown butter mix across the mac 'n' cheese. Sprinkle each serving bowl with the remaining parmesan, another couple of cracks of black pepper, drizzle with a glug of olive oil and serve.

Double duty **Store your leftovers in an ovenproof dish, so that all you have to do the next day is sprinkle panko or rice crumbs on top, glug with olive oil, finish with some grated parmesan and reheat at 400°F for 10 minutes or so.**

Napa cabbage

With crinkly leaves like a savoy cabbage, and a 'bite-through' akin to a crunchy lettuce, napa cabbage is a brill beginner's Brassica. Grown in warmer, wetter climates, where it's available year round, it is far more flavor-sponging and heat-responsive than its icy cousins, lending itself to fresher hot-weather salads and stir-fries. White or red cabbages often need blanching to soften their woodiness, but raw napa cabbage is already juicy and crisp, making it the perfect addition to a coleslaw. Napa cabbage is also a hero in one of my favorite ferments, kimchi – Korea's spicy answer to sauerkraut. If you don't have kimchi in your fridge, you're missing out. (You may have, as I like to call it, FORKO: Fear Of Regular Kimchi Outage.) Beyond a simple side or snack that's great for gut health, kimchi provides an easy base to dishes that would otherwise take twice or thrice as long to prepare.

'I blanch larger leaves for wrapping dumplings, or shred finely for an Asian slaw, using the leaves and the stem for zero waste and contrasting textures.' – **CHRISTINE MANFIELD, AUSTRALIA**

BUYING & STORING

What the napa cabbage lacks in woodiness, it also loses in robustness, so you'll find it lasts less time in the crisper than your traditional cold-weather cabbages. Often, you'll see napa cabbages sold with their tops lopped off, as the curly leaves start to twist in on themselves and turn a little grey. Similarly, look for that creep of greyscale on napa cabbage halves that have been prematurely sliced – the longer they're left out in the elements, the dryer and crustier the open face will get. That's why napa cabbage is best bought whole and used over a couple of nights. Look for bright, crisp white flesh, and feel for tightly packed leaves. Anything you don't use right away can be wrapped with beeswax wrap or damp paper towel across any exposed bits – but try to use napa cabbage up as quickly as possible because once you've cut in, even the fridge won't save it after 4 days or so. In fact, after big Brassica purchases, my husband, 'The Produce Prophet', says, 'Use the napa cabbage first, or you'll forget about it' – and true to his name, we either feast like napa cabbage wizards, or pull out a magically mangy head at the back of the crisper within a week or so.

COOKING WITH

Aside from the very base of the napa cabbage, which can be washed and popped into the freezer for future vegetable stock, the rest of the cabbage is entirely usable. With a sharp knife, slice from the leafy top into fine ribbons for coleslaw or other salads – its fine flesh is far too agreeable to fuss about with a food processor. Cut into thicker strips for adding to broths or when making kimchi. Keep the leaves whole for wrapping ground meat in – either raw, for san choy bau vibes, or braised for stuffed cabbage leaves, without the need to muck around with blanching. In fact, most recipes that require cabbage can have napa cabbage subbed in; just be sure to reduce the cooking time, or you'll end up with a mushy mess.

WITH COMPLEMENTS

Carrot, cilantro, Kewpie mayonnaise, oyster sauce, sesame (oil, seeds), soy sauce.

SCRAP MEDAL

Save outer leaves from the compost heap by using them in stir-fries, with a good char over high heat – they'll add gorgeous texture and extra freshness, soaking up the sauce just so.

KIMCHI 3-WAYS

Here are three great reasons to either make your own kimchi, or pick up a good jar from the shops with lots of 'active' warnings – that's how you know it's good.

SERVES 3

Kimchi beans

Heat 1 tablespoon olive oil in a frying pan over medium heat. Scoop in ½ cup (75 g) kimchi and allow it to color for 3–5 minutes and become even more fragrant. Stir in 1 cup (180 g) cooked white butterbeans, flatten (with a smaller frying pan) and leave over medium heat for 10 minutes, stirring and flattening now and then, to heat and color the beans and allow the flavors to marry – no need to stand by the stove. Serve on sliced sourdough toast, spread with mashed avocado if desired, and dolloped with Greek-style yogurt.

Kimchi fried rice

Heat a wok or large well-seasoned frying pan until smoking hot. Pour in 1 tablespoon peanut oil and ½ cup (75 g) kimchi. Toss until colored, then scrape out of the pan and reserve. Heat another 2 tablespoons peanut oil and fry 2 cups (370 g) cold cooked white rice over high heat until the rice starts to color, then slide the rice off to the side (or remove if your pan isn't big enough). Crack in 2–3 eggs and fry until a runny sunny-side up. Slip out of the pan and reserve. Pop the rice and kimchi back into the pan, stir through a few times, then splash in 2 tablespoons soy sauce. Taste for seasoning; you may need more soy. Serve topped with the fried eggs, garnished with sliced green onion, and a squirt of sriracha sauce if you're after more kick.

Kimchi aioli

Add 1 tablespoon kimchi juice to a food processor with ⅔ cup (100 g) drained, roughly chopped kimchi. Crack in 1 egg. Combine ¾ cup (185 ml) grapeseed oil and ¼ cup (60 ml) olive oil and then, with the blades running, add the oil combo to the processor in a gentle, steady stream and blitz until an emulsion forms. (If you have an immersion blender with a cup attachment, you can simply put all the ingredients in the cup attachment, pop the immersion blender in so that the blades are at the bottom of the cup, and blitz.) Season to taste. Store in the fridge and serve alongside crispy stuff as a dipper, or as a creamy drizzle. (In the photograph, thin starchy potato strips were fried in sunflower oil until crispy on the outside and soft in the middle.)

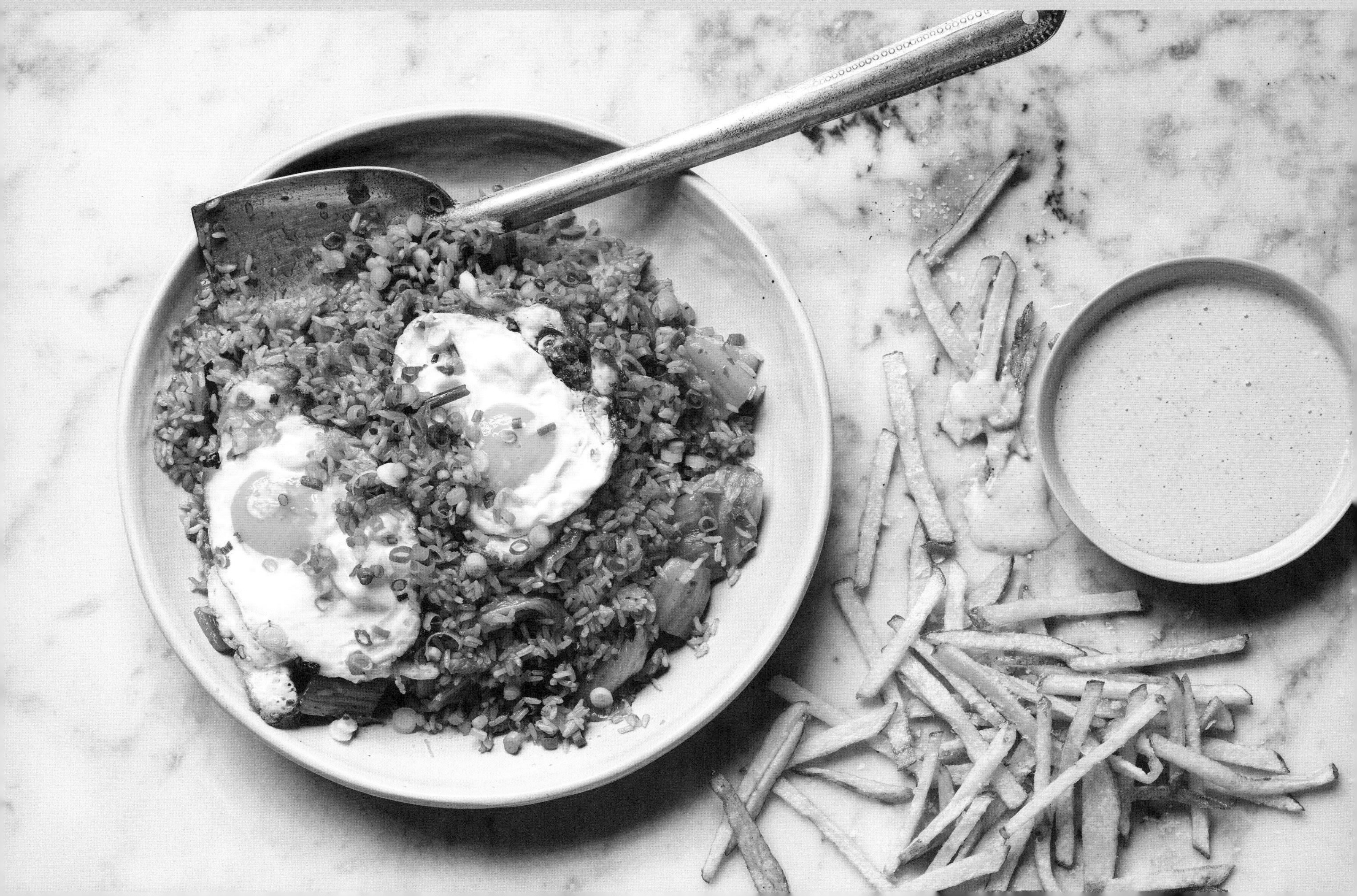

NAPA CABBAGE SLAW
WITH PLUM SAUCE

I'll never forget how grown-up it felt in high school to be moved into our Year 12 common room, complete with an old desk next to a sink that served as our kitchenette, stacked with the few appliances the staff trusted us with – a kettle, a toaster, and a microwave with the buttons well-worn. They didn't have to worry much, as it turned out, because a new wave of culinary innovation was sweeping our cohort: no-cook noodles. That's right – we finally had all the heat sources we needed to actually prepare something worthwhile, and yet instead we were pulling two-minute noodles out of their packets and crunching into them like toast. I'd like to think I've moved some way beyond no-minute noodles, but this slaw, complete with crunchy noodles (the fried kind) and a controversial store-bought honey cashew situation, is just as playful, and properly tasty – even for grown-ups.

SERVES 6–8 AS A SIDE DISH

3 green onions (scallions),
   thinly sliced on an angle
4 radishes, thinly sliced,
   cut into quarters
½ napa cabbage, about
   600 g (1 lb 5 oz),
   finely shredded
100 g (3½ oz) crispy
   fried noodles
⅓ cup (50 g) chopped
   honey cashews

Plum sauce dressing
⅓ cup (80 ml) plum
   sauce (see tips)
¼ cup (60 ml) rice
   wine vinegar
1 tablespoon soy sauce
2 teaspoons sesame oil

Pop the green onion and radish in a bowl, cover with cold water and leave to soak for 5 minutes.

Combine all the dressing ingredients in a bowl and taste for seasoning.

Drain the radish and green onion, then toss in a large bowl with the napa cabbage.

Sprinkle half the noodles and cashews over, and drizzle with half the dressing.

Transfer to a serving dish and top with the remaining cashews and crispy noodles. Serve with the remaining dressing alongside, for last-second drizzling.

Tips **The magic of this salad is in the crunch:dressing ratio, which can get splashed to bits if you dress it too soon. Dish this up on a tray and let your guests dress the salad themselves to maintain the perfect crunch level.**

If you want to use up some left-over *tkemali* (page 368, broccoli steak), sub it in instead of the store-bought plum sauce, for extra zip. Don't @ me.

Longcut **To make your own honey cashews, melt equal parts honey, sugar and butter in a saucepan, then take off the heat and pour in some plain roasted cashews. Scoop out onto a lined baking tray, sprinkle with a pinch of salt and bake at 350°F for 10–15 minutes, until golden.**

Go gluten-free **Use deep-fried vermicelli rice noodles in place of wheat-based ones. Deep-fry in vegetable or canola oil at 400°F until puffy, drain on paper towel and serve. If you'd prefer to keep things simpler, julienne some carrot for crunch instead.**

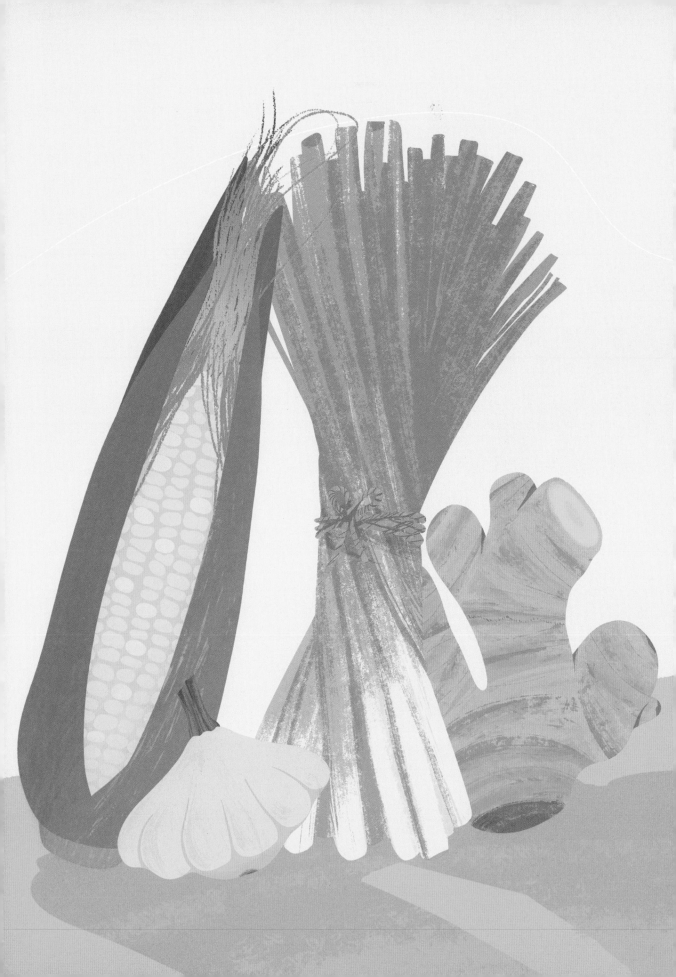

Yellow

* **GINGER**
  + Galangal
  + Turmeric
* **LEMONGRASS**

* **CORN**
* **PATTY PAN SQUASH**

Ginger

I once had a cat called Ginger. We inherited the name when we adopted him from the RSPCA, and I like to think it's because a little Ginger went a long way, and he had more than a little bite to him, especially as he got older. Even though ginger root is closer to blonde, gold or even brown in color, it's the crimson–orange flowers that bloom atop the ginger plant that has given rise to its eponymous etymology. I like to think that it's also because redheads, like this rhizome, and my cat of the same name, tend to be a little on the fiery side (I still have an upper-lip scar to prove it!). So, if you've ever taken a whiff of a cinnamon quill and thought, 'Gee, I wish there was something chewier I could sink my teeth into with this level of warmth and aroma', then get more ginger into your cooking. The root, not the cat, obviously. Even though it's technically a vigorous rhizome rather than a 'vegetable', I'm slipping ginger into the book to encourage you to use it more, because it's one of those sidekick aromatics that makes so many veggies taste infinitely better.

'Ginger is everything in Ghanaian cuisine; it's even in our *mirepoix*. We appreciate its aroma and heat. Sometimes it slaps you in the face, other times it's in the background. At Midunu Chocolates, we make caramelized ginger truffles, called 'Ya', because they're feisty.' – SELASSIE ATADIKA, GHANA

BUYING & STORING

When it's young and fresh, typically in late summer and early autumn, the skin of the ginger root is translucent, sometimes even flushed in parts with the finest of pinks, and you can practically peel it away with the flick of a fingernail. As it ages, however, the skin thickens, going a gorgeous shade of gleaming gold, and the heat intensifies in equal measure. You're probably thinking, 'Oh, so younger is better, right?' Wrong-ish! It really depends on what you're going to do with it. Young ginger is terrific for thinly slicing or julienning into tiny matchsticks for salads, dipping sauces, broths, and any actual ingestion of said root. The flavor is mild, with a very gentle hum at the back of your tongue if you eat enough of it. On the other hand, the heat of older ginger hits you right in the nostrils, and sometimes the tear ducts, filling the air with its warm, subtropical spiciness as soon as you slice in. Don't be deterred by woodiness or fuzziness – the stronger, punchier flavor of older ginger is great for grating into curry pastes, steeping in teas and slicing thickly into stocks and soup bases to be extracted prior to serving. Whether your ginger is young or old, look for firm roots without too many shrivelled bits or signs of mold. If roots with moldy ends are all you can find towards the end of winter, trim these off as soon as you get home so they don't move in on the main body like Samwell Tarly did for Jorah Mormont's Greyscale in *Game of Thrones*.

If you're planning on using your ginger fairly quickly, storing it intact in the fridge door is your best bet. Once you slice into the root and expose its flesh, cover with some beeswax wrap or a paper bag before transferring to the crisper. If you find yourself using a lot of fresh ginger in your general cooking, juices and your morning cuppa, plant a fresh ginger root in a small pot on the windowsill and water generously. Once it shoots, you can shake off the dirt, trim off a knob, then replant the remaining root and regrow. Magic!

COOKING WITH: GROUND VS FRESH

If a recipe calls for ground ginger, you could try substituting fresh, and vice versa, but you'll find that you need much more of the fresh stuff to get the kick you want from ground, and you'll need far less of the ground stuff for the heat that fresh can bring. For best results from dry, add a little at a time, tasting as you go. From fresh, add a pinch of ground cinnamon, too.

FUNCTIONAL FOOD

With a Sanskrit name translating to 'horn body', and the occasional rudely shaped rhizome, ginger's gone and gotten itself quite the reputation. Since making its way to the Western world from South-East Asia, it has been used as both a spicy mood-enhancer and blood-flow accelerator, which is said to increase the sensitivity of erogenous zones. Ginger is also great for staving off the nausea of sea, motion and altitude sickness, as well as the pain-with-gain pangs of morning sickness in early pregnancy. Coincidence? I think not.

WITH COMPLEMENTS

Carrot, Chinese five-spice, chocolate (especially dark), cream, fish, garlic, honey, lemon, lemongrass, lime, pear, pineapple, sesame oil, soy sauce, green onion (scallion), turmeric, vinegar (especially mirin, white wine and cider vinegar).

BEYOND GINGER: GALANGAL

If ginger had a Hulk-like alter-ego, it would be galangal. Sometimes referred to as Thai ginger, its skin is rubier, flesh woodier, and flavor 'punchier', sharper in acid and a little pine-y. When slicing thickly and simmering in broths like *tom kha kai*, don't worry about peeling. For blitzing into Indonesian, Malaysian and Thai curry pastes, hack it into manageable chunks, peel with a paring knife and roughly chop. Galangal can also be stored frozen for up to 3 months without losing any flavor; I'd suggest cutting it into chunks first.

BEYOND GINGER: TURMERIC

The first thing that strikes you about turmeric is its color – vibrant tangerine beneath the finest of skins, staining everything it touches marigold yellow, whether it's used fresh or dry. If you're worried about fingertips, wear disposable gloves, or use the dried and ground variety, sprinkling straight into curries, stews or rice; the general rule for swaps like this is that a 2.5 cm (1 inch) piece is roughly equivalent to 1 teaspoon powder. It is prized for its pungency and bitterness in cooking, as well as its natural antioxidant and anti-inflammatory properties. It is even widely recommended as a daily dosing for joint pain, especially when paired with black pepper to aid absorption.

'There's a kaleidoscopic array of turmeric, in greens, reds, white, rouge, pink and brown. The strangest one I've found was electric blue, in the far north of Thailand.'
– DAVID THOMPSON, AUSTRALIA

MAPLE GINGER-SPICED GRANOLA

One thing that's special about ginger is how differently it can taste, depending on whether it is fresh, crystallized or ground. Ground ginger adds a gentle earthiness and heat to this baked granola, which is toasted until deeply dark, making it the perfect way to start the day – especially with warm milk on blustery winter mornings.

MAKES 9 CUPS (1 KG)

3 cups (270 g) rolled oats

2 cups (200 g) dried
 fruit (I like cranberries,
 blueberries, chopped
 apple)

2 cups (200 g) seeds
 and nuts (such as
 coconut chips, chopped
 pecans, flaked almonds,
 sunflower seeds)

⅔ cup (110 g) crystallized
 ginger, thinly sliced

½ cup (110 g) firmly
 packed brown sugar

1 teaspoon flaked sea salt

¾ cup (185 ml)
 maple syrup

½ cup (125 ml) extra
 virgin olive oil

1 teaspoon vanilla
 bean paste or extract

3 teaspoons ground ginger

1 teaspoon
 ground cinnamon

½ teaspoon
 ground allspice

¼ teaspoon
 ground cardamom

Preheat the oven to 350°F. Line two baking trays with parchment paper.

Place the oats, dried fruit, seeds and nuts, crystallized ginger, sugar and salt in a large bowl. Drizzle with the maple syrup, olive oil and vanilla and mix until well combined.

Spread the granola mixture evenly over the baking trays. Bake for 45 minutes, stirring and swapping the trays every 10–15 minutes, until the granola is toasted and golden. Stir the ground spices through.

Leave to cool slightly, before serving immediately with milk – or allow to cool completely, then store in an airtight container in a cool dark place for up to 1 month.

Tip This 'trail mix' style mix is but a guide, so use the recipe as a base to get through whatever dried fruit and nuts you have in the pantry.

Shortcut Sprinkle a little ground ginger and cinnamon through a store-bought granola, or into your porridge, for a hum of heat and earthiness.

GOLDEN TURMERIC LATTÉ

This golden elixir is a bit like the yoga of hot drinks. It's trendy, it's good for you, you've likely only come to it recently, and now you're obsessed. Yet like yoga, turmeric tonics have long been used remedially in Ayurvedic medicine in India. In its simplest form, it's known as *haldi doodh*, a bedtime beverage with hot milk (or simply water) and a tablespoon of ground turmeric. This version uses fresh turmeric and coconut milk, though you're welcome to sub in whatever milk you have on hand. It's grounding, creamy and soothing, whether you're in activewear-as-day-wear, or your PJs.

MAKES 800 ML (28 FL OZ)

25 g (1 oz) fresh turmeric, about a 2.5 cm (1 inch) knob, peeled (see tip)

10 g (¼ oz) fresh ginger about a 2.5 cm (1 inch) knob, peeled (see tip)

⅛ teaspoon ground black pepper

⅛ teaspoon ground cinnamon

⅛ teaspoon flaked sea salt

⅛ teaspoon cayenne pepper (optional)

400 ml (14 fl oz) coconut milk

1 tablespoon honey, maple syrup or coconut sugar (or to taste)

Using a stainless steel grater, finely mince the turmeric and ginger, popping your grater into a sink with hot soapy water right away. (A bit of elbow grease is needed to scrub the turmeric off your grater, so if yours isn't stainless steel, chop it into thin slices instead.)

Pop the turmeric and ginger into a saucepan with the pepper, cinnamon, salt and cayenne pepper, if using. Add the coconut milk and 350 ml (11 fl oz) water and bring to a simmer, stirring occasionally with a whisk. Give the mix a taste, then add your desired sweetness (or leave it out, if you're 'sweet enough').

If the sediment bothers you, strain the milk through a fine sieve before serving. Otherwise, enjoy chomping on the chunky bits towards the bottom of your cup – they're good for you!

You can store the mixture in a clean glass jar in the fridge for up to 10 days once made. I like to pour my leftovers into a jar and give it a shake to redistribute spices before pouring out a portion.

Tip **If you don't have fresh turmeric and/or ginger, use ground instead. My recommendation would be 1 teaspoon ground turmeric and ¼ teaspoon ground ginger – though prepare for a bit of trial and error, depending on the freshness and intensity of your spices.**

Shortcut **You'll find powdered golden milk blends at most health food shops, but once you work out how to make your own, it's a much more cost-effective way to play. Namaste.**

LAU'S VEGETABLES WITH FRESH GINGER

Whenever people ask me where to go for a 'home-cooked' meal in Melbourne, my answer is Lau's Family Kitchen in St Kilda. Gilbert Lau, founder of the city's iconic Flower Drum restaurant, and his sons Michael and Jason, make you feel like you (and about 50 or so new friends) have literally just come around to theirs for the cleanest, sharpest Cantonese. I've been obsessed with this dish since my first review there many moons ago, and it's still the first thing we order. I asked Gilbert if he wouldn't mind if I borrowed his recipe, and he invited me straight into the kitchen to see how it was made. My husband has requested that we have this dish at least once a week at home, and I'm sure it'll have a similar effect on your loved ones, too.

SERVES 4

500 g (1 lb 2 oz) assorted green vegetables, such as zucchini, snow peas (mangetout), sugar snap peas, baby spinach, bok choy, broccolini, gai lan and napa cabbage, chopped into bite-sized pieces

¼ cup (60 ml) vegetable oil

1 thumb-sized piece of fresh ginger, peeled and roughly chopped

¼ cup (60 ml) chicken or vegetable stock

a pinch of flaked sea salt

a pinch of sugar

Fizzy ginger (optional)

¼ cup (60 ml) vegetable oil

1 thumb-sized piece of fresh ginger, peeled and finely shredded

Blanch any harder vegetables such as gai lan or broccolini in a saucepan of vigorously boiling water – about 2 minutes for the stalks, then add any florets and cook for another minute, before plunging them straight into a bowl of iced water to stop them overcooking. Drain once cooled, then spin to ensure there's no water left on them, as any water will spit when you fry.

Meanwhile, heat a wok or large, wide-based frying pan until smoking hot. (If you're cooking on an induction stovetop, like me, this can take 15–20 minutes.)

For the fizzy ginger, if making, pour the oil into the pan, then add the ginger and cook for 1–2 minutes, or until the bubbles subside and the ginger is crisp. Drain on paper towel.

Heat the oil in the pan. Toss in the ginger, then, working in batches, add the vegetables according to their density – woody/stalky veggies first, then peas of any kind, zucchini or bok choy, finishing with any fine leaves, transferring each batch to a plate as you go.

Return all the veggies to the pan, then pour the stock over and let it absorb a little. Sprinkle in the salt and sugar, give it one final toss, then tip straight out of the pan and serve immediately.

Tip **Baby bok choy is perfect for this dish, but requires a really thorough wash between all the layers. Direct your tap through the heart once you chop the leaves off and quarter, using your fingers to agitate.**

Shortcut **If you've no time for blanching, give any harder veggies a vigorous boil for a minute, before transferring straight into the hot wok. Or just use softer veg for the quickest version.**

SIX-SPICE GINGER COOKIES

If you're a fan of gingerbread, these burnished, chewy-in-the-middle, crunchy-on-the-corners cookies are bang-on. Often, such recipes call for a squillion different separate spices and mean you're shelling out for a whole new spice wardrobe. Instead, I invite you to pop out for a fresh pack of Chinese five-spice – a blend that can vary a little in ratio, but most likely contains a combination of ground star anise, fennel seeds, cassia (or cinnamon), plus peppercorns and cloves. The ground ginger is warming and mouth-filling. Any form of warm beverage with these cookies will unlock even more heady spice; my preference is warm milk or black filter coffee. A few batches of this dough can also be used to bake and build the bougiest gingerbread house your neighborhood has ever seen. Bonus points if you melt hard ginger candies into the window holes for stained-glass windows.

MAKES 50 COOKIES

⅓ cup (115 g)
   molasses; see tips
120 g (4 oz)
   unsalted butter
1 teaspoon baking soda,
   sifted
1 egg, beaten
2⅓ cups (350 g) all-
   purpose flour, plus
   extra for dusting
1½ tablespoons
   ground ginger

1½ teaspoons
   Chinese five-spice
150 g (5½ oz) dark
   brown sugar
¼ cup (55 g) coffee sugar
   crystals (see tips)
¼ cup (70 g) crystallized
   ginger, finely shaved
   with a mandoline,
   coarse grater or very
   sharp knife

In a large saucepan, bring the molasses and butter to the boil over high heat. Add the baking soda and stir well to combine – the mixture will foam and double in size. Set aside to cool slightly, then stir in the egg using a flexible spatula.

In a bowl, mix the flour, spices and brown sugar until evenly distributed, then make a well in the center. Use your flexible spatula to scrape the warm molasses mixture into the flour mixture, stirring just enough for the dry bits to make friends and get rid of lumpy bits.

Transfer to a clean work surface and shape into a ball, then halve and shape into two flat discs. Wrap and chill for at least 1 hour, or even overnight.

Preheat the oven to 400°F. Line three large baking trays with parchment paper.

Lightly dust your rolling pin and work surface with flour, then roll one of the dough discs out 5 mm (¼ inch) thick. Using a 6 cm (2½ inch) cookie cutter (or a scallop-edged saucer from your nanna's china cabinet), cut out your cookies, placing them on the baking trays 1 cm (½ inch) apart. Repeat with the remaining dough.

Sprinkle the cookies with the coffee sugar crystals and crystallized ginger. Bake for 7–8 minutes, or until light golden brown. Leave the baking trays on cooling racks to cool.

These cookies are best stored in an airtight container in the pantry, where they will keep for up to 1 week. They can also be frozen for up to 1 month – so make a double batch, if you're in the mood.

Tips Any dark, treacley sugar syrup will do, such as date, coconut or palm sugar syrup.

Coffee sugar crystals can be purchased from some supermarkets, specialty stores or your best bet: hipster cafes. Demerara sugar is a happy swap, too!

Lemongrass

You may notice that I use the word 'whack' a lot, so you may be forgiven for assuming that when I say lemongrass benefits from a 'good whack', it's a mere figure of speech. But make no mistake, dear reader, fresh lemongrass stems do benefit from a *proper* whack, preferably with the back of a heavy cleaver. What you're aiming to do is release all the pungent, peppery, lemony-ness that lays in wait inside what is essentially the root of a big, dried-out blade of grass. Its bright, zippy aroma and citrusy aftertaste make it a welcome addition to both savory and sweet dishes, be it as the base of a curry paste, infused into chicken or seafood, or in place of lemon in creams and curds. If you're all whacked out, bending and tying a knot in a stem of lemongrass and infusing it into any sort of South-East Asian broth or sauce will help round out the flavor perfectly – like tying a bow on the gift that is your dinner.

'eeled and sliced paper thin, lemongrass lifts a salad dressing to mbrosial levels. I love it in a warm seafood salad with lots of fine erbs, and in soup stocks.' – PALISA ANDERSON, AUSTRALIA

BUYING & STORING

Lemongrass is often sold with part of the leaf blades attached to the pale, slightly bulbous root. The stalky bits dry out quickly soon after harvesting, so don't be too concerned if these look a bit more like something you'd weave with than eat, unless they're especially shrivelled and dried. Pop a bit of your fingernail into the very bottom of the bulbous bit (to minimise any visible damage you may leave behind) and give it a whiff. The swifter the release of aroma, the fresher your stalk. As soon as you get it home, trim off more of the top (as it will leach moisture), then wrap in beeswax or damp towel. It should keep in the fridge for a few weeks.

COOKING WITH

The sweetest, most fragrant part is a few inches from the root, all the way along until the stem starts to darken in hue. Chop off about three knuckles' worth from the root point, chop very finely, or slice into 2 cm (¾ inch) rounds for cooking and remove before serving (or leave in for a rustic effect). Like a teabag, the longer lemongrass is left to steep, the stronger the flavor and aroma it imparts, so add it towards the start of cooking for maximum effect.

FUNCTIONAL FOOD

Lemongrass tea has been found to have healing properties for stomach upsets, with some studies even suggesting that a hunk of freshly sliced (or even dried) lemongrass in your tea on a daily basis can help keep stress in check. Being a cousin of citronella, planting some lemongrass also acts as a natural mosquito shield in your garden.

WITH COMPLEMENTS

Chili, coconut, galangal, garlic, herbs (especially cilantro, mint, Vietnamese mint, Thai basil), fish sauce, makrut lime, palm sugar (jaggery), green onion (scallion), vanilla.

SCRAP MEDAL

Finely chop or blitz the darker tops and woodiest root ends and freeze, then use in marinades and curry pastes straight from the freezer. If you leave a fresh lemongrass root in a glass of water, changing the water every few days, you'll have some fresh shoots within a fortnight.

LEMONGRASS FISH POPS WITH GREEN MANGO SALAD

If a cake pop and a fish cake got together and spawned, you'd have something resembling this dish. Divide by the lowest common denominator and you have yourself a Fish Pop. You could also grill these skewer-free, and sprinkle slices of the lemongrass on top to serve.

MAKES 12

4 lemongrass stems
⅓ bunch of cilantro
500 g (1 lb 2 oz) firm-
    fleshed white fish such
    as monkfish or cod,
    roughly chopped
3 tablespoons good-
    quality Thai green curry
    paste (not too salty)
1 teaspoon palm sugar
    (jaggery)
6 makrut lime leaves,
    finely chopped, plus
    extra to garnish
vegetable or canola oil, for
    brushing

Lemongrass dressing
2 tablespoons fish sauce
2 tablespoons palm
    sugar (jaggery)
    or brown sugar
¼ cup (60 ml) lime juice
    (preferably makrut lime)

1 red chili, bruised
    but kept whole
1 tablespoon peanut oil
a pinch of chili flakes

Green mango salad
1 long green (unripe)
    mango, flesh julienned
1 pomelo, peeled and
    segmented (skin
    and pith peeled),
    then roughly torn
1 banana shallot,
    finely sliced
2 green onions (scallions),
    finely sliced on an angle
⅓ bunch of mint,
    leaves picked
¼ cup (40 g) cashews,
    toasted and chopped
¼ cup (35 g) peanuts,
    toasted and chopped

Cut the lemongrass stems into thirds, reserving the pale white stems for grating into the dressing. Pick the leaves from the cilantro and reserve for the salad; finely chop the cilantro stems and reserve them for the dressing (you need about 1 tablespoon chopped stems).

Put the fish in a food processor. Add the curry paste, sugar and lime leaves and blitz into a rough paste. Have a bowl of water nearby, and line a tray with parchment paper. Using damp hands, squish squash-ball-sized rissoles of the fish mixture onto the 12 lemongrass stems, wetting your palms as needed to stop things sticking. Pop the skewers on the lined tray and chill for 20 minutes to set.

To make the dressing, finely grate the reserved lemongrass stems into a small saucepan (you need about 1 tablespoon grated lemongrass). Add the fish sauce, sugar and 2 tablespoons of the lime juice. Bring to a simmer, let the sugar dissolve, then switch off the heat. Add the bruised chili, peanut oil, chili flakes, the reserved chopped cilantro stems and remaining lime juice, and give it all a stir. Taste for seasoning.

To make the salad, combine the mango, pomelo, shallot, green onion and most of the mint in a bowl. Add most of the reserved cilantro leaves. Sprinkle with the toasted nuts, reserving some for the top. Drizzle with most of the dressing and toss to combine. Top with the remaining nuts and herbs.

Heat a grill pan or barbecue grill plate until smoking hot. Wet a piece of parchment paper until just damp, shake off the excess water and lay the paper on the grill pan (to help stop the fish sticking). Brush the fish pops with oil, then grill for about 4 minutes on each side. Once the surface of the fish pops is firm, pull off the parchment paper and finish them on the naked grill if you'd like decisive char marks.

Serve the skewers alongside the dressed salad, with the left-over dressing in a dipping bowl.

COCONUT TAPIOCA WITH LEMONGRASS CURD & FRESH MANGO

The flavor of lemongrass lends itself to both sweet and savory dishes. This dessert utilizes the zippiness of lemongrass to splice through the richness of coconut cream and accent the bounciness of sago pearls. In much of the world, 'sago' and 'seed tapioca' are sold interchangeably, even though true sago is made using starch from the sago palm, and seed tapioca from cassava. Use whichever one you can find and, since both are technically vegetables, I should probably file this recipe under 'salads' …

SERVES 4

diced mango, or other
    fresh fruit, to serve
julienned lime zest,
    to garnish

Coconut tapioca
150 g (5½ oz) dried
    white tapioca pearls
3 green lemongrass
    stems, bruised
400 ml (14 fl oz) can
    coconut cream
    (Kara is my favorite)
¼ teaspoon salt
1 tablespoon granulated
    sugar (optional,
    particularly if using
    a sweeter cream such
    as Kara)

Lemongrass curd
3 lemongrass stems, white
    part roughly chopped
finely grated zest of
    3 limes (preferably
    makrut, if available)
½ cup (125 ml) lime juice
½ cup (110 g)
    granulated sugar
3 egg yolks, plus
    1 whole egg
80 g (2¾ oz) butter,
    diced

For the tapioca, bring 12 cups (3 liters) water to the boil in a saucepan. Pop in the tapioca pearls and bruised green lemongrass stems and simmer away over medium–low heat for 20–30 minutes, or until soft and only slightly opaque through the center, stirring occasionally.

Drain the tapioca through a fine-mesh sieve, discarding the lemongrass, and rinse with cold water. In a bowl, combine the coconut cream, salt and sugar, if using. Stir in the tapioca. Chill for 1 hour, or until thickened slightly.

For the curd, place the chopped lemongrass in a heavy-based saucepan with the lime zest, lime juice and sugar. Bring to just before the boil, then remove from the heat and stand for 20 minutes to infuse. Strain through a fine sieve and return to the saucepan. Add the egg yolks and whole egg, then whisk until creamy yellow in color. Switch to a flexible spatula and stir continuously for 7–8 minutes as the mixture thickens to a custardy consistency, coating the back of a spoon; if you run a finger through it, the streak should stay put.

Pour the eggy mixture into a blender or food processor and stand to cool for 5 minutes or so. Start the motor, then add the butter cubes, a few at a time, continuing to blend on a low speed until incorporated and smooth.

Strain the curd into a bowl if you plan on using it all, covering directly with a layer of parchment paper to stop it developing a film, and chill for at least 1 hour to cool completely. (Alternatively, strain into sterilized jars and refrigerate until needed; the curd will last unopened for up to 3 months, or 1–2 weeks once you crack in.)

To serve, divide the curd among four glasses. Top with the tapioca, then the mango, and garnish with julienned lime zest.

Tip Instead of granulated sugar, you can use palm sugar (jaggery) or even coconut sugar if you prefer, but for a truly bright-colored curd, stick to the white stuff.

Corn

We've had a while to eke out an excellent ear of corn, given that fossilized corn pollen has been dug up in Mexico from 80,000 years ago. There are hundreds of corn varieties available, including pink, purple and even bi-color cobs with white and yellow kernels. These days, most corn on the market is of the 'super sweet' variety, which retains more of its natural sugars for longer. There are also some novelty styles such as baby corn, which is picked super young and adds great texture to stir-fries and laksa, as well as sun-dried popcorn on the cob, which can be slathered in butter and popped on its cob in a tightly sealed pot on the stove or straight into the microwave.

Corn just grilled with lemon and salt is epic! We also char the
leaves to make powder to flavor cookies, and use the spent cobs
to infuse anglaise for ice cream.' – DARREN ROBERTSON, UK

BUYING & STORING

Believe it or not, corn loses up to 40 per cent of its sweetness within SIX HOURS of being
picked! So, if you want amaize-ing flavor (hey, you know this was always going to get corny!),
look for whole ears, with light green outer husks and dry, bushy 'silks' that haven't started
to get dark or wilty. Corn is at its peak in warmer weather, so summer through early autumn
will give you the sweetest returns. Increasingly, the only kind of corn on offer is de-robed and
imprisoned by plastic wrap on a foam tray. Mind you, this does offer a chance to give the
kernels a keen once-over. Still, I prefer to buy them *au naturel* when I can, both
on principle and for the longer shelf life you'll get from nature's packaging. Give the ends
a whiff: even through plastic, they should smell fresh and sweet, rather than sour or funky.
If the color's a little 'greige' or the kernels have started to dimple, your corn has been
picked too soon or too late, respectively. This will affect the sweetness and juiciness, so
cook it for a little longer to artificially plump it back to its former glory. To check the kernel
quality on a full ear, pull back the husk a little, but be sure to tuck it back in if you're
leaving said corn on the shelf.

Corn's peak freshness is calculated in hours rather than days, so frozen and canned kernels
are a good option if you can't find fresh corn, or can't cook it promptly. Store fresh cobs in
the husk if possible, or remove their plastic prisons as soon as you get home. If the cobs are
starting to smell a little sour at the ends, shave these off and cook the rest right away, then
slice off the kernels and enjoy in all manner of dishes for the next day or so.

COOKING WITH

The less you do to fresh corn, the better. Grab the silky tassel and husks from the top and
pull towards the base to remove, then rub at any remaining silks with your fingers or a veggie
brush. Plop the whole cobs in boiling water for 3–8 minutes until vibrant in color, but don't
salt until after cooking, or you'll harden the kernels. Raw corn can also be sliced off the cob
and served fresh in salads, or in a piping hot broth for sweetness and crunch. The spent cobs
make liquid-gold stock. Freeze them in your 'stock-up' bag, to add extra sweetness to every
veggie stock from now until forever. In summer, barbecued corn goes down a treat, especially
cooked in its husk (nature's foil!). Flaked sea salt is corn's catnip, so sprinkle liberally once
cooked to really make the sweetness sing – like a vegetal salted caramel.

WITH COMPLEMENTS

Butter, cheese (especially parmesan), chili, lemon, olive oil, pepper.

FOOL-PROOF CORN FRITTERS

Once you get the hang of these, you'll be making them all the time, and adding your own go-to combinations beyond these bases. In fact, the more veg you can pack in, the better – think zucchini, frozen peas, shredded red bell pepper and the like. Keeping the corn frozen adds moisture, and saves you having to thaw it in advance. These fritters are not only brilliant for breakfast, steaming hot and crispy, but make for fab lunchbox additions, too.

SERVES 4

2 cups (300 g) frozen corn kernels
½ cup (75 g) self-rising flour (page 23) (I use gluten-free, but you do you)
2 eggs, lightly beaten
⅓ cup (80 ml) milk
½ cup (55 g) grated haloumi
½ teaspoon flaked sea salt
½ teaspoon freshly cracked black pepper
vegetable or canola oil, for shallow-frying

Pop the frozen corn into a bowl with the flour and toss through to coat. Add the eggs, milk, haloumi, flaked sea salt and pepper and mix well to combine. Allow to stand for 15 minutes, or until bubbling a little.

Add in any chosen flavorings (see below; this is where things can get creative).

Heat 1 cm (½ inch) of oil in a large frying pan over medium–high heat. Line a tray with paper towel and set a wire rack on top.

Working in batches, add heaped tablespoons of the batter to the hot oil and cook for 1–2 minutes, or until golden. Turn and cook for a further 1–2 minutes, or until cooked through and golden. Drain on the wire rack and continue with the remaining batter. Serve hot.

Tex-Mex fritters

To the batter, add 1 teaspoon smoked paprika, 1 small grated red onion and ½ bunch of shredded cilantro. Cook as above. Serve with lime wedges, extra cilantro and chili salt, or mayonnaise spiked with chipotle chili or smoked paprika.

Indonesian fritters

To the batter, add 100 g (3½ oz) thinly sliced green or snake beans, 1 teaspoon finely grated ginger and 1 finely chopped seeded red chili. Cook as above. Serve with Vietnamese green or red nuoc cham (page 221).

Indian fritters

Fry the leaves from 2 curry leaf branches, or ½ bunch of cilantro, until crisp, then crumble one-third into the batter. Stir in 1 teaspoon ground turmeric. Cook as above. Serve sprinkled with the remaining leaves, and plain yogurt with a dollop of Cilantro raita (page 280) or mango pickle swirled through.

Tip You can also slice corn kernels off fresh corn and stir these through the batter. However, you'll need to add another tablespoon or so of milk to compensate, until you have the consistency of pancake batter.

CORN SCRAMBLE

This is kinda halfway between a corn fritter and a frittata, and way quicker. Fresh corn cooks faster than you think, and provides a delightful burst of juicy sweetness, while the eggs bind everything just so, like a creamy, textural cloud. I make this often in the weeks following Christmas to get through the left-over ham, but bacon is great too. And if you're meat-free, use goat cheese and/or butter instead to get some extra richness into your scramble.

SERVES 2

1 corn cob
4 streaky bacon slices, or
   2 slices thick-cut ham
40 g (1½ oz) butter
   (optional, if using ham
   instead of bacon, or
   using neither)

6 eggs
2 tablespoons roughly
   chopped dill fronds

Slice the corn off the cob by laying it flat on a chopping board and hacking off a few rows at a time using a sharp knife. Cut the bacon into long thin strips, or the ham into cubes.

Sauté the bacon and corn in a frying pan over medium–high heat for about 4 minutes, until the corn changes color and the bacon starts to get a little crispy on its sides; the bacon will render out its own fat pretty quickly. (If using ham instead of bacon, melt the butter in the pan before frying off with the corn.)

Meanwhile, briskly beat the eggs in a bowl, until a fairly uniform shade of golden yellow.

Pour the beaten egg over the corn mixture, reduce the heat a little, then use a spatula to make figure-eight motions around the pan until everything is incorporated.

Stir the dill through, sprinkle with freshly ground black pepper and turn off the heat just before the eggs stiffen up completely. Serve immediately.

Tip **Feel free to adjust this simple base recipe as per your tastes and your fridge contents. Instead of fresh corn, the scramble could even work with frozen peas or corn, at a pinch.**

Go meat-free **If you're not using bacon or ham, have 40 g (1½ oz) butter and/or goat cheese ready to plonk in. Add the butter once the corn has started coloring up in the pan, and the goat cheese when the beaten egg goes in.**

CORN SOUP

There's a very special place in my heart for corn soup – whether that includes chicken, or not. Corn provides its own broth, locked away in the cob, so anyone who is game – and clever enough to whack it in their stock will be rewarded with plenty of sweet, umami flavor for no added cost. I've included a few more versions with chicken below, but here's a vego version to kick things off.

SERVES 4–6

4 corn cobs
10 green onions (scallions)
8 garlic cloves, thinly sliced
1 teaspoon finely grated fresh ginger
1 teaspoon freshly cracked black pepper
¼ cup crispy fried shallots, plus extra to serve
2 tablespoons soy sauce
1 tablespoon sesame oil

8 cups (2 liters) vegetable stock (or even water)
1 tablespoon apple cider vinegar
2 egg whites, lightly whisked
1 bunch of asparagus, finely sliced (optional)
toasted sesame seeds, to serve

Remove the kernels from the corn, placing both the cobs and kernels in a large saucepan.

Finely slice the green onions, keeping the white and green parts separate.

Add the white green onion bits to the saucepan of corn, along with the garlic, ginger, pepper, crispy fried shallots, soy sauce and sesame oil. Pour in the stock.

Bring to a simmer, then cover with a lid, reduce the heat to low and cook for 45 minutes, or until the corn has softened and the broth is rich with flavor.

Remove from the heat, then use long tongs to remove the corn cobs. Use an immersion blender to briefly whiz the soup until some of the corn has creamed, but you can still see half the kernels.

Pour in the vinegar, add the egg whites and stir with a wooden spoon. Sprinkle in most of the green green onion bits and the sliced asparagus, if using. Let the soup stand for 3–4 minutes, to cook the egg whites in the residual heat.

Divide the soup among serving bowls. Top with the sesame seeds, extra fried shallots and remaining green onion and serve.

Tip When cutting corn, I like to lay the cobs flat on a large wooden board, slicing off a row of kernels before moving to the next. I wouldn't bother with those corn-peeling gadgets out there – they break far too easily.

Extra For chicken and corn soup, use chicken stock instead of vegetable stock. Add 2 whole chicken thighs to the soup during the last 30 minutes of cooking, then pull them out and shred, ready for popping into the bottom of bowls to pour soup over.

Shortcut For a speedy chicken and corn soup, shred a shop-bought barbecue or rotisserie chicken and add this to your bowls before pouring the hot soup over. Bonus marks for buying a discounted chook at the end of the day, when it's had a chance to sweat its juices into the bag. Pour these juices into your soup as your base stock, and use the water you boil the corn in to bulk it out. If you add just enough water for a serve or two, you could be sitting down to a bowlful in under 10 minutes, as soon as the corn has cooked through.

CHEESE-CLOUD CORN COBS WITH APPLE CHIPOTLE BARBECUE SAUCE

If I didn't have you at 'cheese-cloud', then 'apple chipotle' should just about do it. This recipe is pretty much the most 'extra' way to eat a cob of corn, and is so worth it for summer entertaining. The barbecue sauce will find endless uses once you're done with the corn, too. Use it to baste other grill-friendly veggies such as mushrooms, patty pan squash and zucchini, or dip stuff in it instead of straight-up ketchup. Yum.

SERVES 4 AS A SIDE DISH

4 corn cobs, in their husks
olive oil, for brushing
½ cup (125 g) thick
    whole-egg mayonnaise
    (or Garlic aioli, page 37)
25 g (1 oz) pecorino or
    parmesan cheese
finely chopped chives,
    to serve

Apple chipotle barbecue sauce (Makes 2¼ cups)
1 cup (250 ml) apple sauce
½ cup (125 ml) ketchup
½ cup (125 ml)
    barbecue sauce
¼ cup (60 ml) maple syrup
2 chipotle chilis in adobo
    sauce (or use 1 chili if
    you don't like spice),
    finely chopped
1 tablespoon
    worcestershire sauce
1 teaspoon
    smoked paprika

Preheat a grill pan or barbecue on high heat.

Pull back the corn husks, leaving them still attached, and use a vegetable brush (or your fingers) to pull away the corn silks. Submerge the corn in well-salted water for at least 10 minutes, to soften the husks and save them from being incinerated before the corn cooks through.

Shake the excess water off the husks, then massage or brush a little olive oil on them. Pull the husks back over the corn cobs, to protect them from the fierce heat of the grill. Place on the barbecue on the diagonal and cook, turning every 5 minutes, for 15–20 minutes, or until the husks are blackened. Set aside for 10 minutes to cool and steam in their husks slightly.

Meanwhile, combine all the barbecue sauce ingredients and season to taste. (We're making plenty of sauce, but the remainder will keep in a clean airtight container in the fridge for up to 1 month.) Take ¼ cup (60 ml) of the sauce and mix it through the mayonnaise to make a dipping sauce. Pop another ¼ cup (60 ml) of the sauce in a small saucepan and warm slightly.

When the corn is ready, pull back the husks to reveal the corn cobs. Brush with the warmed barbecue sauce and finely grate the cheese over, so that it looks like fluffy cloud cover over the Andes. Sprinkle with chives and serve with the dipping sauce alongside.

Shortcut **Cut or snap the corn cobs in half and boil for 4–5 minutes, until bright yellow. Make the sauce in the meantime. Grate your cheese over, sprinkle with chives and boom, you're done.**

Double duty **Slice the kernels off any left-over corn (even if it's been cheesed) and blitz together with a little cream and/or stock to make creamed corn, or even a smoky chipotle corn soup!**

Patty pan squash

Welcome to gourd's country! Patty pan squash, which also goes by the names baby yellow squash or scalloped squash, really does look like someone packed a bag of glossy yellow zucchini for the road, and then sat on them all the way. Often picked up for the novelty factor alone, many newcomers are most delighted to discover that patty pan squash are both gloriously pretty in the middle of a table, but also really robust to cook with. While conventional zucchini suffer from an internal structure compromised by a considerable slab of soft, seedy real estate, patty pan squash sports a tidier cul-de-sac of seeds, meaning that it'll hold its bite – and brightness – under trying conditions (such as roasting in the oven).

am obsessed with bottlegourd (known as *lauki* in Hindi),
which I find quite versatile. My mother makes a stew out of it with
yogurt, mustard oil, cumin, bay leaf and cardamom. And I love
making savory bottlegourd and yogurt pancakes, which I eat with
a kashmiri chili chutney.' – PRATEEK SADHU, INDIA

BUYING & STORING

Patty pan squash has a delightfully glossy skin – like a sunburst in a squat little package.
You're most likely to see them in the shops at the height of summer. Smaller ones are
sweeter, with larger ones better left for stuffing. Seek out chartreuse stems, as you might
for a zucchini, with no signs of withering, and inspect the squash edges for any bumps and
bruises. Give each one a gentle squeeze and check for too much give, which is indicative of
meddlesome moisture loss. Try to buy them as close to using as possible, as their delicate
flesh and skin mean they'll only last a couple of days in the fridge. For longer-term storage,
dice or roughly chop as you might zucchini and freeze on a tray, then portion out into
containers and stash in the freezer.

COOKING WITH

Treat patty pan squash as you would their more familiar relative, the long yellow zucchini.
Slice horizontally for easy grilling on the barbecue, quarter and toss into curries and
casseroles, grate and batter for fritters, or crumb and fry as you would an actual scallop.
Smaller ones can be braised or roasted whole, while larger ones benefit from 'proportionising'.
If you're going down more of a pumpkin-y route (because they're a relation, too), you can
lop the top off any of your larger golden globes, scoop out their innards with a teaspoon,
chop the innards and stuff them back inside with rice and spice, and/or ground meat and
herbs. Bake in a tomato-based sauce, or simply drizzle with olive oil, wrap in foil
and roast with the 'lids' back on for individual portions of stuffed squashy scrumptiousness.

WITH COMPLEMENTS

Cheese (especially feta, goat's curd, parmesan, ricotta), chili, garlic, herbs (especially basil,
marjoram, oregano, parsley, thyme), red onion.

'TRAFFIC LIGHT' CHIMICHURRI SQUASH

The best part about a dish cooked on a barbecue grill are the char lines – but you don't need to be standing outside swatting away flies to obtain a similar result, thanks to the niftiness of a grill pan. Popping patty pan squash straight onto a grill pan without any oil may seem like a recipe for disaster, but if the pan is sufficiently hot, they'll slip right off, and won't turn into an oily, sloppy mess. If you don't have a grill pan, any heavy-based pan will do – just accept that you'll get char 'splats' rather than grill lines. And whatever you do, keep the oil away from the squash until after it comes off the griddle. Resist!

SERVES 4–6

6–7 patty pan (baby yellow) or other summer squash (or a mix)
250 g (9 oz) cherry tomatoes, quartered
mint leaves, to serve

Red & green chimichurri
1 long green chili, chopped
1 garlic clove, chopped
½ bunch of parsley, leaves and stems chopped
½ bunch of cilantro, leaves and stems chopped
1 small red onion, chopped
1 tablespoon smoked paprika
½ cup (125 ml) olive oil
¼ cup (60 ml) red wine vinegar
1 tablespoon honey
150 g (5½ oz) Roasted bell peppers (page 200), chopped

For the chimichurri, place all the ingredients except the bell pepper in a small food processor and whiz until finely chopped. Season to taste with salt and pepper, then remove about ½ cup of the green chimichurri mixture. Add the bell pepper to the remaining chimichurri mixture in the processor and whiz once more for a red chimichurri. Chill both versions until required.

When you're ready to serve, heat a grill pan for 5 minutes or so, until smoking hot.

Slice each squash in half on the horizontal axis, about 1.5 cm (⅝ inch) thick; if they're on the larger side, you may need to slice them into thirds.

Working in batches if needed, pop the squash halves face side down, in one layer on the hot grill pan and listen for a sizzle and pop: if there isn't one, the pan isn't yet hot enough, so pull them off quickly and wait a little longer. Let the first batch of squash char up for about 3 minutes on each side, then push them to the side of the pan while you cook the rest. (At this thickness, it's nigh on impossible to overcook them – a little bit longer near the heat just means a more tender result.) Brush with most of the green chimichurri.

Toss the cherry tomatoes with the remaining green chimichurri. Spoon the red chimichurri around a platter, then arrange the tomatoes and chargrilled squash over the top. Serve hot, sprinkled with the mint.

Tip **If patty pan squash isn't available, use zucchini instead. Slice into long strips about 1.5 cm (⅝ inch) thick and grill in the same way.**

Shortcut **Slice your squash into thinner rounds and char for about 1 minute on each side, until the flesh softens. And as for the sauce, a sambal, good chili jam or sweet chili sauce will do quite nicely instead of the chimichurri.**

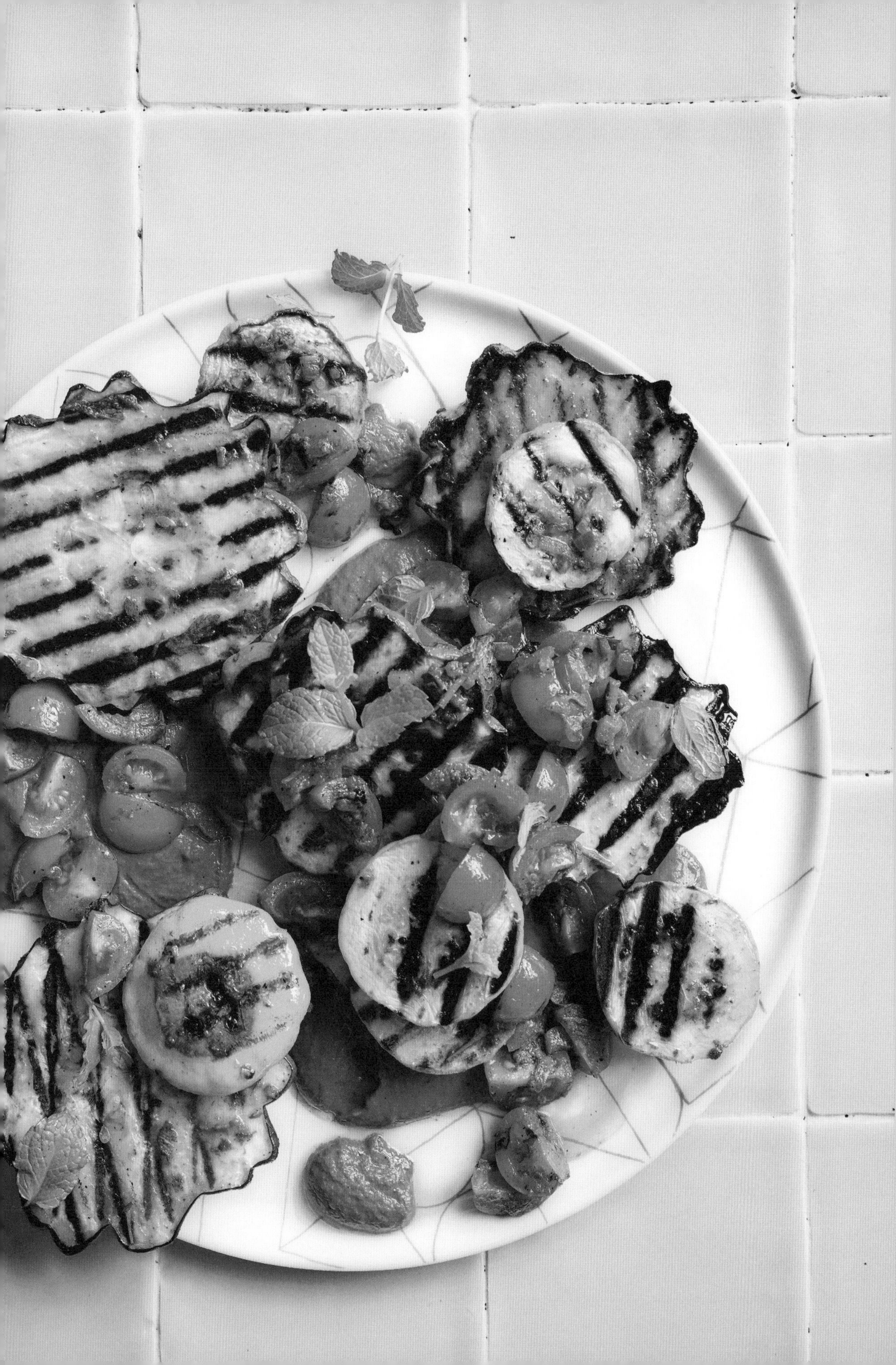

Yellow

Patty pan squash

GOLDEN BUNDT CAKE

When we were photographing this cake, I sent some home with my publisher, whose daughter declared, 'It doesn't taste like a vegetable cake?', which I would agree with – because most of the time, people who put vegetables in a cake do it surreptitiously, trying to 'sneak in a serve'. Here, patty pan squash – or zucchini if you'd prefer – is celebrated with reckless abandon, to the point that you can still see flecks of yellow and green through the moist, velvety sponge. I can't tell you how satisfying it is to eat, and still more satisfying to serve. You'll be fielding questions about it all afternoon. Stay gold, Ponybundt.

SERVES 8

20 g (¾ oz) unsalted
　　butter, melted
2 cups (250 g) coarsely
　　grated patty pan
　　(baby yellow) squash
　　or zucchini
　　(see tip)
½ cup (110 g)
　　superfine sugar
finely grated zest of
　　1 lemon, plus ⅓ cup
　　(80 ml) lemon juice
1 tablespoon finely
　　chopped lemon thyme
　　leaves (or regular thyme
　　leaves, if you must)
¾ cup (180 ml) light extra
　　virgin olive oil, plus
　　extra for greasing

3 eggs
1 cup (250 ml) buttermilk
¾ cup (170 g) brown sugar
½ cup (45 g) desiccated
　　coconut
2½ cups (375 g)
　　self-rising flour
　　(page 23)
½ teaspoon flaked sea salt
1½ cups (175 g) icing
　　(confectioners') sugar

**Dehydrated squash
flowers**

2 patty pan (baby yellow)
　　squash, thinly sliced
　　using a mandoline or
　　sharp knife

Preheat the oven to 350°F. Grease a 25 cm (10 inch) bundt pan with the melted butter, then transfer to the fridge to chill and set.

Place the grated squash, superfine sugar, lemon zest and lemon thyme leaves in a bowl and mix to combine. Stand for 10 minutes to macerate.

Add the oil, eggs, buttermilk and brown sugar to the bowl, mixing well. Add the coconut, then sift in the flour and salt. Use a wooden spoon to combine, without overmixing.

Transfer to your cake pan and bake on the middle rack of the oven for 1 hour, or until a skewer inserted in the cake comes out clean. Leave to cool in the cake pan on top of a wire rack for 10 minutes, then invert the cake onto the wire rack to cool completely.

If making the dehydrated squash flowers, flick the oven on to 250°F. Place the squash slices on a wire rack so that the slices will droop over. Pop into the oven for 20 minutes, or until dried into frilly 'flowers'.

Meanwhile, get the icing going. Place the icing sugar in a bowl, add ¼ cup (60 ml) of the lemon juice and mix to combine. Add more lemon juice, a teaspoon at a time, to achieve a smooth, spoonable icing consistency.

Spoon the icing over the cooled cake, then garnish with the squash flowers. This cake keeps extremely well, covered loosely with beeswax wrap or foil and stored on the bottom shelf of your fridge. Not that you'll have much left, mind you.

Tip **If you're using zucchini but still want to keep the paler sponge, just peel off the skin, or leave it on for maximum veg cake realness.**

Shortcut **The icing is optional, as are the dehydrated 'flowers'. Try dusting the cake with icing sugar instead, decorating with fresh lemon thyme leaves, and/or serving with a dollop of plain yogurt.**

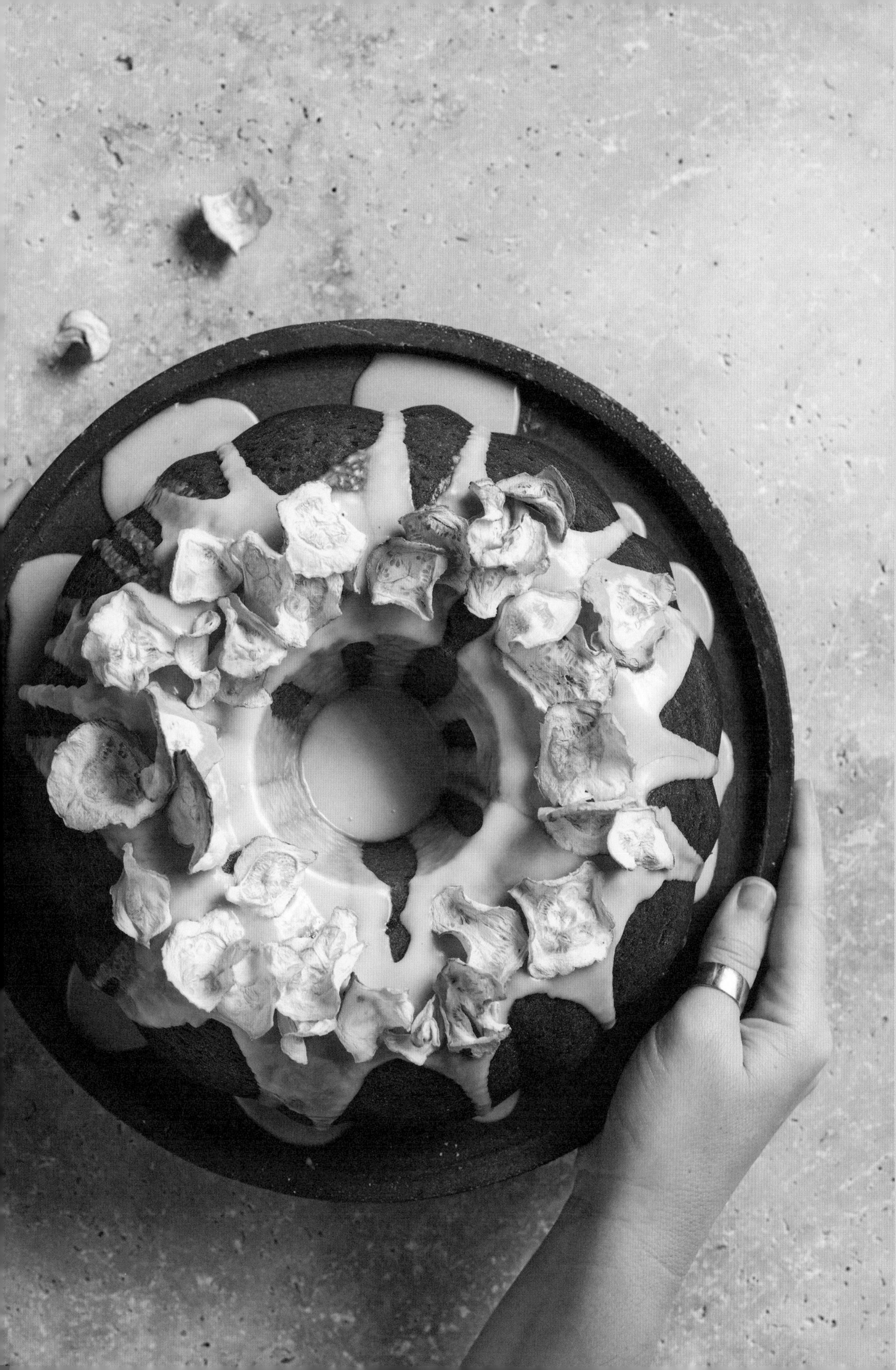

Orange

* **CARROT**
* **SWEET POTATO**
* **BUTTERNUT SQUASH**
  + Spaghetti squash
* **PUMPKIN**

Carrot

If you've ever tried to grow your own carrots, you'll likely have been disappointed to discover that achieving the goal of long, straight and even uniformly *orange* specimen is quite the feat. That's because carrots weren't originally orange at all. They were probably purple, white or even yellow – all the colors we now associate with fancy heirloom varieties. It wasn't until the 16th century that orange carrots began to be cultivated by the Dutch, to show support for the powerful Orange–Nassau family, who were like the Hiltons of their day. As their hold on power in the Netherlands waxed and waned, the possession or sale of orange carrots was occasionally seen as tantamount to treason. Nowadays, the family are the nation's constitutional monarchs, and the whole country – particularly its sports fans – are still orange mad. And as for those once treasonable carrots? They're the second-most popular vegetable in the world, after potatoes.

'I'm all about carrots. I roast them, juice them, spiralize them, slice them and serve them raw. I purée, dehydrate, bake and fry them. Everyone thinks of carrots as simply sweet, but if you roast them long enough they develop some bitterness to match. They have a brightness that brings out the best in other vegetables, too.' – AMANDA COHEN, CANADA

BUYING & STORING

We're fortunate enough to have treason-free carrots – orange and otherwise – available all year round, but they're most exciting during the cooler months when you see those heirloom varieties crop up more often. The heirloom ones are best for braising, stewing and roasting whole, or perhaps even pickling, as their flavor is deeper, the densely packed fibers holding their shape better under heat. Purple carrots can stain dishes with their anthocyanin pigment just like beets and red cabbage. For chomping into raw and grating into salads, you can't go past the fragrant fluoro-orange ones, which have a syrupy aroma and a sweet crunch. If you spot some carrots still with their leafy accoutrements attached, look for bushy tops with bright green foliage – as you would for herbs (carrots are related to dill and parsley, after all). If buying topless carrots, give them a whiff. They should smell sweet, the skin should be shiny and not turning ashen, and the root should be robust rather than bendy. The longer you plan to cook them for in dishes, the thicker the carrot should be, so for braises and so on that are simmered low and slow, select dense, stumpy carrots. Growing underground, carrots love the cold, so storing them in the crisper is best.

Cut the tops off when you get your bunch home, and store these as you would herbs. The leaves can be used in place of parsley in a recipe, but you'll have to bump up the salt and fat content, as they can be quite bitter. If you're chopping carrots into sticks and ferreting away for afternoon snacks, or to pop into lunchboxes at the last minute, store them in a sealed container with iced water.

FUNCTIONAL FOOD

Before you skip this bit, assuming I'm about to roll out the same old trope about carrots helping you see in the dark, read on. Because guess what ... it's fake news! Quite literally, in fact. During World War II, or so the story goes, the British Air Force needed to hide the fact that they were using advanced radar technology to detect and shoot down enemy planes. So, the government put together a disinformation campaign, complete with propaganda posters, making out that the secret to the sudden spike in night vision was due to pilots popping carrots like Popeye popped spinach (which is a whole other story, actually). The growers of Great Britain benefited from a sudden spike in the sales of carrots – something that would've been advantageous at a time when fancy food was scarce, but root

veggies were abundant. Strategically speaking, whether the ruse worked depends on who you ask, but there are accounts, apocryphal as they may be, of German fighter planes loaded up with bunches of carrots, just in case. I should probably mention, though, that carrots are rich in vitamin A, which is great for eye health in general – just don't expect to stop needing the flashlight on your smartphone any time soon.

WITH COMPLEMENTS

Cheese (especially feta, goat, gruyère, parmesan), cream, ginger, olive oil, orange (especially zest), sage, spices (especially cinnamon, cloves, nutmeg).

133

ZESTY GLUTEN-FREE CARROT CAKE

This is just about the moistest carrot cake you'll ever bake. The cream cheese icing, with a hit of freshly grated orange zest on top, is like buttering bread to its corners, and the spices and nuts make every mouthful exciting. Back when my mother-in-law started baking *sans* gluten, it was nigh-on impossible to find good alternative flours, but these days, gluten-free mixes are readily available. If you'd prefer to stick to regular all-purpose flour , go right ahead, but I like to try and factor in dietaries when I bake, considering the delighted look on people's faces when they find out they *can* finally have their cake and eat it, too!

SERVES 6-8

2 carrots (320 g/11½ oz), peeled
1 thumb-sized piece of fresh ginger, peeled
150 g (5½ oz) walnuts, roughly chopped
200 g (7 oz) dark brown sugar
½ cup (125 ml) olive oil
4 eggs
1 teaspoon natural vanilla extract
1 teaspoon ground cumin
½ teaspoon ground cinnamon
2 cups (300 g) all-purpose gluten-free flour

pinch of salt
1½ tablespoons baking powder
1 teaspoon baking soda

Cream cheese icing
500 g (1 lb 2 oz) cream cheese, softened
120 g (4 oz) unsalted butter, softened
1¼ cups (155 g) pure icing (confectioners') sugar, sifted
grated zest of 1 orange, plus extra to garnish

Preheat the oven to 400°F. Line the base and sides of a 13 cm x 24 cm (5 inch x 9½ inch) loaf pan with parchment paper.

Coarsely grate the carrots, ginger and walnuts using a food processor or box grater (a rough chop for the nuts with this option, thanks). Set aside.

In a bowl, mix together the sugar and olive oil until you have a thick, brown paste.

Whisk in the eggs, one at a time, making sure each is incorporated before adding another. Add the carrot mixture, vanilla, cumin and cinnamon and stir to combine using a spatula.

Sift in the flour, salt, baking powder and baking soda and stir until there are no lumpy bits. Pour into the loaf pan and bake for 45–50 minutes, or until a skewer inserted in the middle comes out clean.

Place the loaf pan on a wire cooling rack and let the cake cool in the pan.

For the icing, beat the cream cheese, butter, icing sugar and orange zest in a food processor or using an electric stand mixer until very smooth.

Lash the icing thickly over the top of the cooled cake. Grate over some extra orange zest before serving.

Tip This carrot cake has no eat-by date; keep it icing-free, then slice and freeze, and even toast as you would banana bread. It's best stored in an airtight container in the fridge, and is the kind of cake you can bake the night before, refrigerate and slather with icing just before serving, in as theatrical a manner as you dare.

Shortcut Ditch the cream cheese icing and instead simply sieve or sift some icing (confectioners') sugar over the cake, and maybe extend yourself to grating some orange zest over the top.

CARROT TOP RIGATONI

When you're lucky enough to score a bunch of carrots with the green tops still on, treat them like you might any leafy herb and blitz them into a zesty pesto. Using pepitas instead of pine nuts means this one is nut-free, which means pesto-lovers who don't love nuts can dig in with zesto. Praise be!

SERVES 4

2 bunches of Nantes carrots, leafy tops detached and washed with extra vigilance (see tips)
½ cup (75 g) pepitas (pumpkin seeds), plus extra to serve
50 g (1¾ oz) pecorino, chopped, plus extra grated to serve

zest and juice of 1 lemon
2 garlic cloves, peeled
1 teaspoon flaked sea salt
½ teaspoon freshly ground black pepper
½ cup (125 ml) extra virgin olive oil
400 g (14 oz) rigatoni pasta
50 g (1¾ oz) arugula leaves

Bring a large saucepan of well-salted water to the boil.

Reserving a few for serving, plunge the carrot tops into the boiling water for 20 seconds, or until wilted. Remove using long tongs, reserving the pan of water, and place in a sieve under cold running water until cooled.

Squeeze the water from the leaves and place them in a food processor, along with the pepitas, pecorino, lemon zest and juice, garlic, salt, pepper and olive oil. Whiz until a fine paste forms. Taste for seasoning, then set aside.

Peel the carrots, then use the veggie peeler to cut the flesh thinly, on an angle, into skinny rounds.

Bring the saucepan of water back to the boil. Add the pasta and cook according to the packet instructions, adding the carrot rounds in the last minute.

Reserve 1 cup (250 ml) of the pasta cooking water, then drain. Return the pasta and carrot to the saucepan, along with the pesto and half the reserved cooking water, and stir to coat, adding more cooking water as needed. Fold the arugula through.

Transfer to a serving platter or individual bowls. Serve sprinkled with the reserved carrot tops, extra pecorino and pepitas.

Tips Carrot tops are notoriously gritty, particularly after heavy rain. To keep the texture of this pesto chunky for all the right reasons, soak them in a bowl of cold water for 10 minutes to let the grit release.

If you can't find pecorino, parmesan is fine. Choose one with a bit of age; 12 months or more would be grand.

Pepitas and carrot tops can occasionally be a bit on the bitter side, so be sure to taste and correct before serving. A little extra salt and olive oil should do it.

Substitutions If you can't find carrot tops, use basil or parsley to make your pesto.

To turn this fully plant-based, omit the pecorino and add more pepitas, olive oil and salt to counteract any potential bitterness.

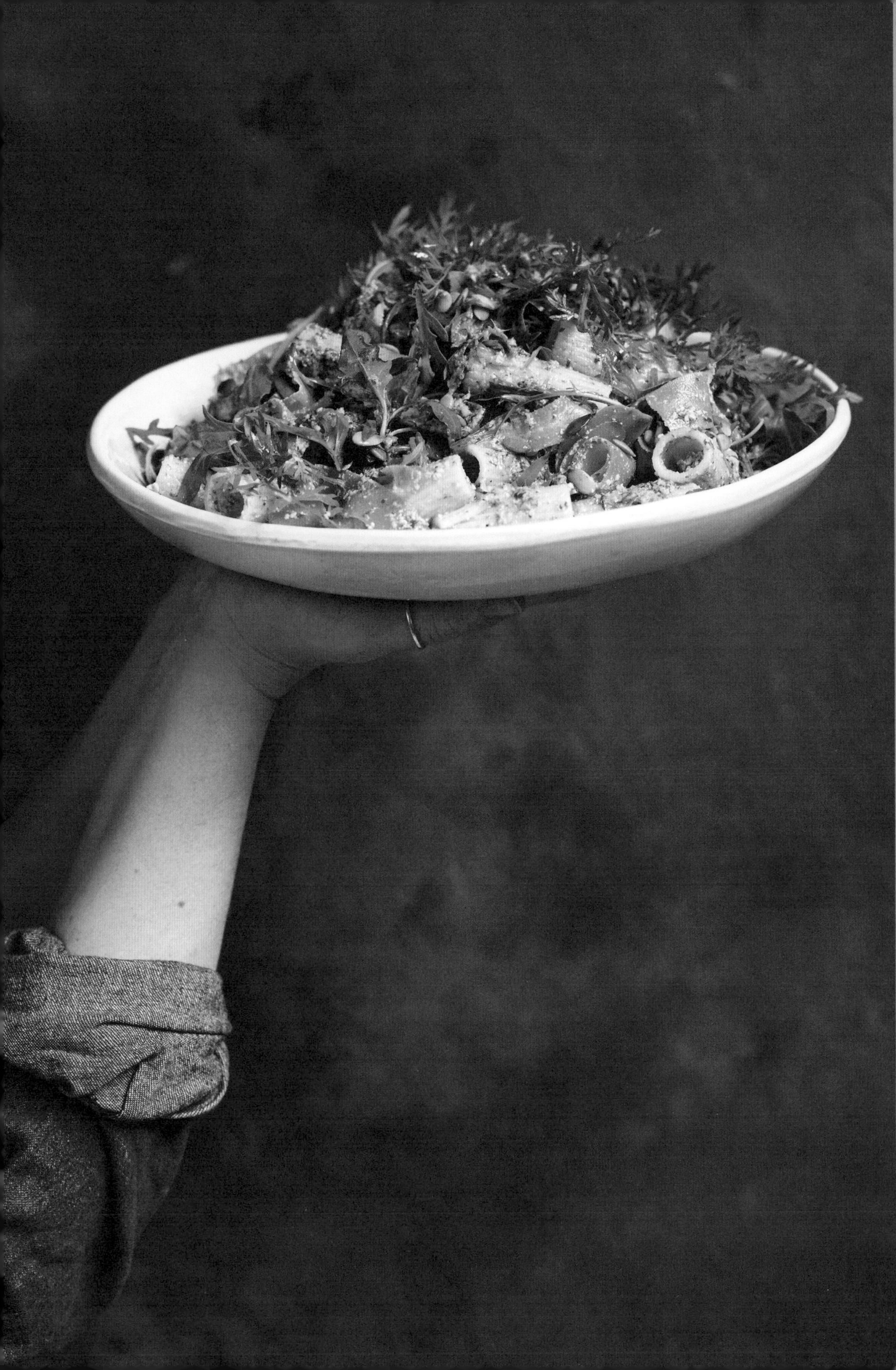

CARROT SOUFFLÉS WITH CRISPY CARROT TOPS & SALSA VERDE

If you're the kind of person who takes one look at a soufflé recipe and thinks, 'Nah!', I don't blame you. They can be pretty intimidating – especially the cheffy ones. That's why I asked my mate Phil Wood for his famous carrot soufflé recipe at Pt. Leo Estate winery in Victoria's Mornington Peninsula, which is an absolute revelation – then worked out an easier version for home. Cheffy deep-fried carrot tops, entirely optional.

SERVES 8

100 g (3½ oz) butter,
   plus extra for greasing
650 g (1 lb 7 oz) small
   carrots, peeled and cut
   1 cm (½ inch) thick
1 teaspoon caraway
   seeds, lightly toasted
1 tablespoon honey (one
   with a slightly stronger
   flavor works well here)
1 teaspoon flaked sea salt
50 g (1¾ oz) parmesan,
   finely grated, plus
   extra to serve
⅓ cup (50 g) all-purpose
   flour

1½ cups (375 ml) milk
3 eggs, separated
crushed pistachio nuts,
   to garnish

Salsa verde
½ cup basil leaves
   (or leafy green carrot
   tops if you have them)
½ cup parsley leaves
2 tablespoons capers
¼ cup (60 ml) lemon juice
   (about 1 lemon)
¼ cup (60 ml) extra virgin
   olive oil

Preheat the oven to 400°F. Butter eight ¾ cup (180 ml) soufflé molds or ramekins, in upward strokes.

Whiz the salsa verde ingredients in a small food processor until finely chopped. Set aside.

Add the carrot to a saucepan, along with the caraway seeds, honey, salt and 2 cups (500 ml) water. Bring to a gentle simmer, then cover with a cartouche (for instructions, see the butter carrot recipe tips on the next page). Cook over low heat for 15–20 minutes, or until the carrot is fork-tender.

Transfer 400 g (14 oz) of the carrot to a blender. Sprinkle parmesan into the bottom of each mold, then swirl around so it sticks up the walls. Distribute the remaining carrot among the molds.

Return the pan to the heat. Melt half the butter, then stir in the flour with a wooden spoon. Cook, stirring constantly, for 2 minutes, or until the butter–flour mix (a.k.a. 'roux') is golden brown and smelling distinctly of cookies. Swap over to a balloon whisk and slowly add the milk, whisking until it's at a simmer. Cook over low heat, stirring frequently with a wooden spoon, for 5–6 minutes, or until the sauce is the thickness of mashed potato.

Spoon the sauce into the blender and whiz with the carrot until smooth and puréed. Whiz in the remaining 50 g (1¾ oz) butter. Leave to cool for 10 minutes, then blitz in the egg yolks.

Meanwhile, beat the egg whites to soft peaks using an electric stand mixer.

Scoop a spoonful of egg white into the carrot mix, then use a flexible spatula to gently fold the rest of the whites into the cooled carrot mixture in figure-eight motions. Fill the molds three-quarters full, using your thumb to clean up the edges.

Place the molds on a baking tray and into the oven for 15–18 minutes, or until the soufflés are risen and golden. Serve immediately, sprinkled with extra parmesan and crushed pistachios, and topped with a spoonful of salsa verde.

GAJAR MAKHANI – INDIAN-STYLE BUTTER CARROT

Curries are always better the next day, or even a few days afterwards. Most veggie curries, though, start to get mushy after a day or two – except this one. Carrots are the ideal density to last as long as you need them to, and soften just enough with heat to be perfectly *al dente*. Make your carrot chunks bite-sized, serve with steamed rice and naan bread and leave the cutlery in the drawer – this is hand food! Any left-over gravy is good enough to mop up with naan or roti bread. Or try mixing in some picked charcoal-roasted chicken meat for a quick and easy butter chicken, before or after the carrot is all gone.

SERVES 4–8

50 g (1¾ oz) butter
2 tablespoons vegetable oil
1 cup (150 g) raw cashews
2 garlic cloves, finely chopped
1 tablespoon finely grated fresh ginger
1 tablespoon brown mustard seeds
4 curry leaf branches, leaves picked (about 35–40 leaves)
1 bunch of cilantro, leaves picked, stems and roots washed well and finely chopped
3 teaspoons garam masala
1 teaspoon ground turmeric
1 teaspoon ground cardamom

1 teaspoon mild chili powder
1½ cups (375 g) Greek-style yogurt
800 g (1 lb 12 oz) carrots, peeled and cut into 3 cm (1¼ inch) pieces on the diagonal
1 tablespoon brown sugar
700 g (1 lb 9 oz) tomato passata (strained tomatoes)
1 cup (250 ml) coconut cream, plus extra to serve
steamed basmati rice, to serve
naan or roti bread, to serve

Heat the butter and oil in a wide saucepan over medium–high heat. Add the cashews and toss for 3 minutes, or until toasted and golden.

Add the garlic, ginger, mustard seeds and curry leaves and cook, stirring, for 2 minutes, or until aromatic. Set aside half the cashew mixture for serving.

Add the cilantro stems and spices to the pan and cook, stirring constantly, for 1 minute, or until fragrant.

Stir in the yogurt until combined, then add the carrot and stir to coat. Stir in the sugar, passata, coconut cream and 1 cup (250 ml) water and bring to a simmer.

Cover the surface of the curry with a cartouche (see tips) to stop the sauce cooking down too quickly – or you could partially cover the pan with a lid. Simmer over low heat for 45 minutes, or until the thickest piece of carrot you can find is fork-tender, and the gravy has thickened and reduced slightly.

Serve drizzled with extra coconut cream and sprinkled with the reserved cashew mixture and cilantro leaves, with rice and naan or roti bread.

Tips Creating a 'cartouche' out of parchment paper encourages even, gentle cooking, without sweating. It's handy for gentle poaching, and low-and-slow broth-making. Make a cartouche by folding a square-ish piece of parchment paper into quarters, then cutting a rounded edge with scissors, to fit the diameter of your pot. Cut a little bit of the middle out, too, to make a little blow-hole for air to escape.

Fantastic naan and roti bread are readily available at Indian supermarkets. Look for ones with a short shelf life and not too many ingredients. Try popping them over some heat to take on an almost-authentic tandoor char, or into the toaster to crisp up a little.

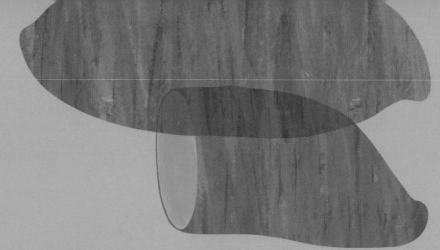

Sweet potato

Known to our Kiwi cousins as kumara, sweet potato is one of those 'Tough Mudder' tubers that stands the test of time, so you can almost always find the most common type – the orange one – in amongst the other 'stuff to be roasted' corner at your chosen potato purveyor. What *will* change throughout the year, however, is the *size* of the sweet potato on offer, from bulbously built, like the forearm of a biker, down to thumb-sized, with the best stock during the warmer months. Colors will also vary – from gold, to purple, and back again. If you're wondering whether color makes a difference to flavor, in the case of sweet potato, the answer is yes! Purple sweet potatoes are higher in starch and tend to make for sweeter fries when you're roasting, while also keeping their shape well. The small red sweet potatoes are absolutely delicious roasted whole, with the skin on, turning into a surprise mash on the inside.

'Sweet potato takes me back to my childhood in New Zealand, where kumara is a favorite. I love roasting it in its skin until soft and caramelized.' – MONICA GALETTI, SAMOA

BUYING & STORING

As with any root veg, you're seeking strong tubers that are in no way bendy – which would indicate they've been sitting around for longer than you care to know. And a bit of dirt never goes astray, as it acts as a natural barrier to extend shelf life. Select sweet potatoes of a similar size, to simplify preparation, particularly if you are planning on roasting them whole, so they all cook through at around the same time. Even though these are closer in relation to water spinach than actual potatoes, their storage method remains the same. Store them in a cool, dark place, away from any direct sunlight, and they should keep for about a month. Unlike potatoes, however, you can store these near onions without causing any damage to either.

COOKING WITH

I don't bother peeling sweet potatoes, because the skin is full of nutrients, and helps them hold their shape. Their knobbly shape can make it a bit tricky to cut into uniform pieces for roasting, but try to keep the pieces a similar size, to ensure even cooking. I love having left-over roasted sweet potato for adding flavor and texture to soups, wraps, sandwiches and anything involving egg. Thanks to their low glycemic index, they're a fantastic option for an energy-boosting breakfast (hello, sweet potato fritters and hash browns). Ghanaian chef Selassie Atadika tells of a Liberian recipe for braised sweet potato greens: 'I do a rosti with sweet potatoes and add some curry powder to the batter, serving with coconut chutney. I've been playing around with braising the greens in coconut milk. Eat them as is or puréed, and as a dip for sweet potato chips.'

WITH COMPLEMENTS

Avocado, bacon, butter, cheese (especially goat, feta, parmesan), cinnamon, cloves, cilantro, cumin, honey, maple syrup, nutmeg, olive oil, sour cream.

SCRAP MEDAL

Sweet potato peelings can be deep-fried and tossed with cayenne pepper for a crunchy snack, one that is made even more satisfying by the fact that you're basically a waste warrior. If you chance upon sweet potato in the wild, you'll be delighted to know that its leaves are also edible – sautéed, or blanched and popped through salad, as you would spinach.

CAYENNE SWEET POTATO FRIES

Some people think sweet potato fries are some kind of 'less than' version of potato fries, but I'm not one of them. In fact, I believe they're a completely different proposition and deserve to be treated as such – particularly because you don't need to faff about with parboiling and roasting and frying as you might for the regular potato version. Just take advantage of food science by adding a sprinkling of starch to the outside to help encourage even more crisp-factor.

SERVES 4

4–6 sweet potatoes, about 600 g (1 lb 5 oz), washed and scrubbed (no need to peel)

2 tablespoons gluten-free flour or cornstarch

2 tablespoons vegetable or canola oil

1½ teaspoons smoked paprika

1 teaspoon cayenne pepper

1 teaspoon garlic powder

2 teaspoons flaked sea salt

Cut the sweet potatoes in half, then stand them on the flat side and cut lengthwise into fries just over 5 mm (¼ inch) thick (the more similar in size the better).

Meanwhile, preheat the oven to 450°F. Line two baking trays with foil.

Pop the fries into a bowl that's big enough to toss them around in. Sprinkle with the flour and toss about to coat. Drizzle with the oil and use your fingers to lightly swirl the fries in the bowl, rubbing in any visible powdery spots with your fingertips.

Arrange the fries across the baking trays, making sure not to overcrowd them – each fry should have enough room to extend its arms (if it had any). Roast for 30–35 minutes, or until the fries are completely soft through the middle.

Wipe out the big bowl you tossed the fries in, then toss in the paprika, cayenne pepper, garlic powder and flaked sea salt. As soon as the fries come out of the oven, add them to the bowl and toss to coat in the seasonings. Enjoy hot.

Tip Ovens can be notoriously temperamental, and you'll know yours best. You may need to swap the trays around halfway through the bake so all the fries get their fair share of heat action, or turn the trays in the oven to keep any hot spots from staying on the one area for too long.

Shortcut Slice the sweet potato into thin rounds with a mandoline, then toss with the oil and bake in a single layer on the foil-lined trays in a preheated 375°F oven for 15–20 minutes, or until crispy, turning them over halfway. Toss with the spices and serve.

PURPLE LOADED SWEET POTATO

ow of course you know the first thing I'll tell
ou is that if you can't find purple sweet potato
which certainly tends to be more seasonal than
e orange – use regular ones instead. However,
you can get your hands on purple ones, this is
e perfect recipe to showcase them. Some
arieties are purple both inside and out, which
oks super dramatic, while others are purple
skin only and white in flesh. That's why I love
at this recipe keeps the jackets on the sweet
otatoes, so that you get some color regardless.
eeping the skin on is also a good way of ensuring
at the whole thing doesn't collapse under the
eight of the loaded filling … go big, or go home.

ERVES 4

tablespoons extra
 virgin olive oil
teaspoon
 smoked paprika
x 250 g (9 oz) purple
 sweet potatoes, washed
 and scrubbed
cup (35 g)
 flaked sea salt

125 g (4½ oz) sour cream
125 g (4½ oz) fresh
 or canned corn
 kernels, drained
1 cup (100 g) coarsely
 grated cheddar
cilantro leaves, to serve
chopped chives, to serve

Preheat the oven to 425°F. Line a baking tray with
parchment paper.

Combine the olive oil and paprika in a small bowl
and set aside to infuse.

Cut a 4 cm (1½ inch) slit into the top of each sweet
potato (find the natural balance point where it will stand
level, or slice a small bit off the base so that it doesn't
roll about).

Combine the flaked sea salt and 2 cups (500 ml)
just-boiled water in a heatproof bowl and stir until
dissolved. Add the sweet potatoes and roll in the salted
water to coat.

Pop the sweet potatoes on the baking tray and bake
for 40–50 minutes, until you can poke a paring knife all
the way through.

Remove from the oven and leave for 5 minutes to
cool slightly. Then, use the slit in each sweet potato
to push out and open up the sweet potatoes, to make
room for some toppings.

Divide the sour cream among the sweet potatoes
and sprinkle with the corn and cheddar. Drizzle with the
paprika oil, season with salt and pepper and finish with
the cilantro and chives. Serve warm.

Double duty **Try this combo with smaller sweet
potatoes, or even the sweet potato fries opposite,
loading them up with all the fillings over a platter.**

Shortcut **Place the sweet potatoes in a microwave-safe
dish. Make a small slit across the top (where the sweet
potato will be opened up) and lightly brush the skin
with paprika oil. Microwave on high for 8–10 minutes,
or until cooked through. If still firm, continue cooking
at 1-minute intervals until just cooked.**

DARL'S DAL

This is my good mate Jane 'Grylltown' Grylls' dal recipe, and she has one of the best palates in the biz, as you'll taste when you make this. Add extra veg for more color and texture, too; anything in the bottom of the crisper will get a new lease on life bathed in this rich, coconut-y soup. In the colder months, Jane likes to cook the dal at 375°F for an hour or two in the oven to keep her house in country Victoria warm, while eliminating the need for stirring. 'Double bonus!' is what she calls it.

SERVES 4-6

1 tablespoon olive oil
50 g (1¾ oz) butter
1 yellow onion, diced
2 large garlic
    cloves, grated
1.5 cm (⅝ inch) piece
    of fresh ginger, grated
1 bunch cilantro stems,
    rinsed well, then finely
    chopped (reserve the
    leaves for serving)
300 g (10½ oz) squash,
    cubed
200 g (7 oz) sweet potato,
    chopped into 1 cm
    (½ inch) discs or chunks
1 tablespoon ground or
    fresh turmeric, or to taste
1 tablespoon
    garam masala
1 tablespoon curry powder
a pinch of chili powder

2 curry leaf branches
    (about 20 curry leaves)
1 cinnamon stick
2 bay leaves
400 ml (14 fl oz) can
    coconut milk
400 g (14 oz) can
    tomatoes (optional)
1 cup (200 g) split red
    lentils, rinsed
2 cups (500 ml)
    vegetable stock
50 g (1¾ oz) palm sugar
    (jaggery), grated
juice of ½ lemon
100 g (3½ oz) baby
    spinach leaves
1 cup (150 g) frozen
    or fresh peas
plain yogurt, to serve
sliced red chilis, to serve
lemon wedges, to serve

Heat the olive oil and butter in a large ovenproof casserole dish. Add the onion and sauté over medium-low heat with the lid on for about 8–10 minutes, until the onion turns translucent, then add the garlic, ginger and cilantro stems and give it all a good stir.

Add the squash, sweet potato, spices, curry leaves, cinnamon and bay leaves. Stir for another few minutes.

Deglaze the pan with the coconut milk (and tomatoes if using), thoroughly scraping the bottom of the pan. Stir in the lentils, stock, palm sugar and 1 cup (250 ml) water.

Bring to the boil, giving everything a considered stir every now and then, and simmer for 20–25 minutes, until the lentils have broken down and become creamy rather than chalky, and the sweet potato is fork-tender.

Remove the cinnamon stick and bay leaves. Stir in the lemon juice, then check the flavor balance, adding salt and freshly ground black pepper to taste.

Just before serving, add the spinach and peas and cook for a final 2 minutes, until the peas are just cooked and the spinach has wilted.

Serve topped with a dollop of yogurt, sliced chili and the reserved cilantro leaves, with lemon wedges. This dal also freezes really well, so portion any leftovers into packs for the freezer.

Shortcut Simmer the lentils separately in 4 cups (1 liter) filtered water or stock for 25 minutes. Meanwhile, sweat the onion in another saucepan. Grate the squash and sweet potato and add the onion with the spices and other dal ingredients, then combine together once the lentils have cooked.

Go vegan Use coconut oil and coconut yogurt instead of butter and yogurt.

Double duty Use an immersion blender to blitz the dal into a spiced lentil and veg soup.

SWEET POTATO SHEPHERD'S PIE

One thing I love about sweet potato is the way that it steams, collapses and turns into mash inside its skin when baked long enough. Here, this method is put to full use to create a mash for the top of a classic shepherd's pie, skin and all, for bonus crunch. We've used pork and beef to bulk out and flavor the mixture inside the pie, but you could just as easily go to town on mushrooms cooked down in a pan, or use Mushroom tempeh ground (page 428), or even beans and lentils. The next time a shepherd comes calling – whether he eats plants or sheep – make this pie.

SERVES 4–6

1 kg (2 lb 4 oz) small
   sweet potatoes, washed
3–4 good rasps of
   fresh nutmeg
50 g (1¾ oz) unsalted
   butter, melted
¼ cup (60 ml) extra
   virgin olive oil, plus
   extra for brushing
60 g (2 oz) pancetta,
   finely diced
300 g (10½ oz) free-range
   ground pork
400 g (14 oz) grass-fed
   ground lamb or beef
1 onion, finely chopped
1 carrot, finely chopped
1 celery stalk,
   finely chopped

2 tablespoons
   worcestershire sauce
1 garlic clove,
   finely chopped
2 tablespoons
   tomato paste
1 cup (250 ml) beef stock
2 tablespoons half
   and half cream
   (or whole milk)
1 cup (140 g) frozen peas,
   thawed slightly
finely chopped parsley,
   to serve
crispy fried shallots,
   to serve

Preheat the oven to 425°F. Poke the sweet potatoes all over with a fork. Arrange in a baking dish and bake for 45 minutes, or until softened through; some may even leak out a sweet potato 'caramel', like tree sap.

Remove from the oven and leave to cool slightly, the roughly chop the sweet potatoes (no need to peel) and toss in a bowl with the nutmeg, butter and 1 tablespoon of the olive oil. Set aside.

Grease a 10-cup (2.5 liter) casserole dish with oil.

Meanwhile, fry off the pancetta in a dry deep-sided frying pan over medium–high heat until golden. Remove the pancetta to a bowl. Squish the ground meat in a bow to combine, splash another tablespoon of oil into the pan, then add the ground mixture, pressing it down as one big patty. Leave to brown for 4 minutes on one side, then break up and stir for another 3 minutes on high heat. Pop into the bowl with the pancetta.

Pour the remaining oil into the pan. Add the onion, carrot, celery and worcestershire sauce and cook, stirring frequently, for 8 minutes, or until the veggies are fully softened. Add the garlic and cook for a further minute, c until aromatic. Return the ground and pancetta to the pan, stir in the tomato paste, stock and cream and simmer for 3–5 minutes, or until slightly reduced.

Stir in the peas, then transfer the ground mixture to the casserole dish. Top with the sweet potato mixture, sprinkle with flaked sea salt and bake for 30 minutes, or until golden and bubbling. Serve sprinkled with parsley and fried shallots, with a salad on the side.

Tip The better the quality of the ingredients, the better the flavor will be. I'd much rather you bought less ground meat, but of the highest quality, and bulked it out with cooked-down mushrooms or beans and lentils, please.

Sweet & savory
sweet potato galettes
(pages 152–153)

SWEET & SAVORY SWEET POTATO GALETTES

Although its name would indicate that 'sweet potato' is a 'sweet' ingredient, it is most often used in savory applications. Here, its natural sweetness is balanced beautifully with salty feta in a savory free-form pie, while its dessertiness is put to full effect in a sweet galette with maple and cinnamon – plus a very Americana touch of toasted marshmallows. Woah! You might even like to halve the filling recipes and make one of each for your next party. But be warned: the crowds will swarm!

GALETTE CRUST

MAKES 2 GALETTES

3 cups (450 g) whole-wheat flour, plus extra for dusting
1 teaspoon flaked sea salt
250 g (9 oz) cultured butter, chopped
1 tablespoon apple cider vinegar
200 ml (7 fl oz) chilled water

Place the flour and flaked sea salt in a bowl. Rub in the butter with your fingertips until the mixture resembles coarse breadcrumbs. Add the vinegar and chilled water, bringing the mixture together with your hands to form a crumbly dough. Divide into two equal portions, then shape each into a disc. Enclose in beeswax wrap or plastic wrap and chill in the fridge for 30 minutes until firm.

Line two baking trays with parchment paper, leaving some overhang.

On a lightly floured surface, roll out each pastry disc to form a 40 cm (16 inch) circle. Use a rolling pin to hang the pastry over and transfer to the baking trays. Chill in the fridge until needed, or even overnight.

SAVORY SWEET POTATO, LEEK & THYME

SERVES 8

300 g (10½ oz) sweet potato, thinly sliced crossways
200 g (7 oz) marinated feta
2 tablespoons extra virgin olive oil (or use the oil from the marinated feta), plus extra to serve
1 small leek, pale part only, thinly sliced
2 garlic cloves, thinly sliced
½ bunch of thyme, leaves picked, plus extra to garnish
⅓ cup (100 g) caramelized onion jam
1 egg, lightly beaten
2 teaspoons caraway seeds
flaked sea salt, for sprinkling

Preheat the oven to 425°F.

Toss the sweet potato, feta, olive oil, leek, garlic and half the thyme leaves in a bowl. Spread the caramelized onion jam over the pastry discs, leaving a 5 cm (2 inch) edge. Top with the sweet potato mixture.

Brush the pastry edges with the beaten egg. Sprinkle the caraway seeds and flaked sea salt over the top, then pour any remaining egg over the sweet potato center. Sprinkle with the remaining thyme leaves.

Place in the oven and reduce the oven temperature to 350°F. Bake for 1 hour, or until the pastry bases move easily on the tray, checking halfway through and covering the galettes with foil if they darken too much. Drizzle with a little extra olive oil and sprinkle with extra thyme. Cut into wedges and serve.

SWEET POTATO & MAPLE

SERVES 8

300 g (10½ oz) sweet
  potato, scrubbed, thinly
  sliced lengthwise
½ cup (125 ml)
  maple syrup
1 teaspoon ground
  cinnamon
¼ teaspoon ground
  nutmeg
1½ cups (150 g)
  almond meal

¼ cup (55 g) raw sugar,
  plus extra for sprinkling
1 egg, separated
1 teaspoon vanilla bean
  paste or extract
¼ cup (25 g) natural
  flaked almonds
2 cups (180 g)
  marshmallows, cut
  in half with scissors

Preheat the oven to 425°F.

Place the sweet potato slices in a bowl, add the maple syrup, cinnamon and nutmeg and toss well to combine and coat.

In another bowl, combine the almond meal, sugar, egg white and vanilla. Spread the almond paste over the pastry discs, leaving a 5 cm (2 inch) edge.

Remove the sweet potato pieces from the maple syrup mixture, reserving the remaining syrup in the bowl, and lay them over the almond base. Add the egg yolk to the remaining maple syrup, mix to combine, then brush over the pastry, pouring any remaining over the sweet potato center. Sprinkle with the almonds, and sprinkle with extra sugar.

Place in the oven and reduce the temperature to 350°F. Bake for 1 hour, or until the pastry bases move easily on the tray, checking halfway through and covering the galettes with foil if they darken too much.

Remove from the oven and arrange the marshmallow halves over the top. Turn the oven up to 450°F and bake for a final 5 minutes or so.

Cut into wedges and serve.

Tip If you're only making one galette at once, you can freeze one of the uncooked pastry discs for up to 4 weeks; just remember to first wrap it well. You'll only need half the quantity of your chosen topping.

Shortcut If you've made a batch of galette pastry and stashed a disc in the freezer, thaw it on the counter and add any left-over roasted veg plus feta on top. Bake until the pastry is golden.

Butternut squash

So here you are, with a pumpkin in one hand and a butternut squash in the other, and a question mark above your head. The first thing you might be thinking is: are they different? And the answer is: yes and no. Yes, in that the flesh of butternut squash – also known as butternut pumpkin! – is drier than that of pumpkin and tends to be more fibrous, which means it also holds together better than pumpkin might under heat. And also no, in that you could substitute butternut squash for pumpkin and vice versa in most recipes. If you're in a rush, butternut is a better choice, because it's easier to cut, and has a smaller hollow for seeds and pulp in its heavier bottom. If you're looking to roast something whole and serve it with theatrical aplomb to a tableful of plant-eaters, look no further than butternut squash. Split it lengthwise with a sharp sturdy knife, scoop out any seeds, slather with some form of marinade, then roast flesh side down at 190°C (375°F) for about 45 minutes, or until tender when poked with a fork.

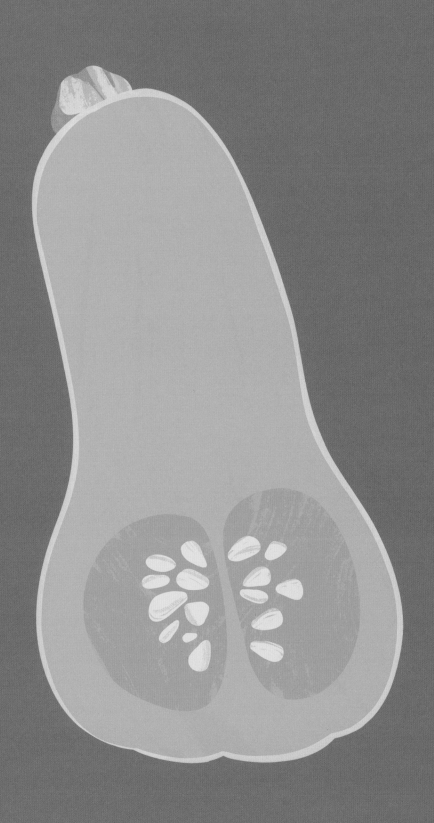

t a glance, they are the same matte color as my austere
tate-school walls, but inside the boring ends and the nutty
egins. Peeling is an offence in my kitchen, and steaming is
crime! Treat them ROUGH: generous chunks, hot roasting
nd fierce sautéing will reward you.' – SIMON BRYANT, UK

BUYING & STORING

Butternuts are bound to receive a few knocks and blows before they even hit the shopping basket, but any sporting deep cuts or soft spots are best avoided. A thicker skin shows it has had a chance to ripen well on the vine, as these cooler weather gourds like to take their time getting ready. Feel for one that's heavy for its size, as this shows that it is fresh and hasn't started drying from inside out. You can also test this by tipping the butternut on its side and seeing how it balances in your palm – if it tips too far towards the top, this means the bottom is probably more hollow than flesh. Store butternuts in a cool, dark place, away from moisture, and they should keep for at least a month. If you're only using half, chop it in half horizontally to minimise the exposed surface area, and store it covered in the fridge. Once roasted or steamed, you can pop any leftovers in the fridge for slipping into sandwiches, wraps and salads, or smushing into mash. Incidentally, you can also freeze the mash for later use – it makes a great thickener for soups, and a simple sauce for pasta and risotto, topped with a sprinkling of toasted pepitas or pine nuts. I prefer to snap-freeze fresh chunks on a tray, then pop them into a container so that they're easy to portion out as needed. You can do this with pumpkin, too, but freezing works particularly well with butternut's firm, drier flesh.

WITH COMPLEMENTS

Cayenne pepper, chives, cumin, garlic, herbs (especially oregano, cilantro, mint), nutmeg, olive oil, paprika.

BEYOND SQUASH: SPAGHETTI SQUASH

If you're a fan of zucchini 'noodles', you can put down your spiralizer, because Mother Nature has done all the heavy lifting for you. Spaghetti squash is an especially fibrous member of the squash family, which, once cooked, yields strands of golden gourd-geousness at the flick of a fork. The flavor is, admittedly, on the mild-verging-on-bland side, but this makes it even more perfect as a neutral stand-in for actual spaghetti. Many traditional recipes recommend boiling, but I think spaghetti squash is waterlogged enough to justify roasting instead. Halve it lengthwise, scoop out any seeds, flip the halves over and poke some holes in the skin with your fork, then roast flesh side down at 400°F for 30–40 minutes. Once softened, use a fork to scoop at the flesh, which will thread up faster than you can say, 'Gee, I can't wait to fill this with parmesan, garlic and olive oil and serve it in its skin like a bowl'!

BUTTERED BUTTERNUT SQUASH

You know what I love more than a play on words? Burnt butter – or *beurre noisette*, if you're fancy. As the butter's milk solids cook in the pan, your whole kitchen will fill with the most delicious nutty aromas – and you'll know it's ready when that scent gives off baked-cookie vibes. Although sage is a classic herb to splice through *beurre noisette*, this recipe is more about the balance of sweet/crunch/herb/salty to get too precious about how you get there. Feel free to get creative: if you have other nuts, go for it; try another soft herb if sage doesn't float your boat, and even anchovies instead of olives would be a great addition. It wouldn't even bother me if you subbed the butter out for olive oil and turned the recipe fully plant-based – just don't go trying to make 'burnt oil' sauce ... instead, follow the 'double duty' instructions below and roast your squashed bits alongside the squash.

SERVES 4

1 butternut squash
1 teaspoon brown sugar (muscovado is my fave here)
1 teaspoon flaked sea salt
⅓ cup (80 ml) olive oil, plus an extra 1 teaspoon
100 g (3½ oz) macadamia nuts

80 g (2¾ oz) butter
50 g (1¾ oz) kalamata olives, unpitted
1 handful of fresh sage leaves, plus extra to garnish

Preheat the oven to 400°F, with a baking tray inside.

To slice the squash in half, insert a sharp knife through the middle along one side, spin the squash over without removing the knife, then slice through the other side. Scoop the seeds out. Use a squash hollow as a bowl to make a paste with the sugar, salt and 2 tablespoons of the olive oil, then rub into the squash halves.

Pull the hot baking tray out and carefully line the base with a sheet of parchment paper. Drizzle another 2 tablespoons of olive oil across the middle of the baking tray and lay the squash halves, face side down, across the oily bits. Transfer to the oven and roast for 40–50 minutes until a fork can be poked through the top of the skin.

With 15 minutes to go, wrap the macadamia nuts in a clean tea towel. Use a rolling pin, pestle or the bottom of a bottle to crush the nuts up a bit.

Tip the crushed nuts into a cold frying pan. Add the butter and remaining 1 teaspoon olive oil and place over medium heat. Squash the olives between your thumb and forefinger to split them in half and pop out the pits. Toss the pitted olives and the sage into the butter mixture and gently sizzle for about 2–3 minutes, until the butter has turned as nut-brown as the nuts.

When the squash is ready, pile the nut mixture into the squash hollows, drizzling any left-over buttery sauce around the squash. Garnish with extra sage, season and serve.

Shortcut **Roast the squash a day ahead and reheat in a 400°F oven while the nuts cook. You'll have a dramatic vego roast on the table in about 10 minutes flat.**

Double duty **For an easy appetizer, toss the olives and macadamias in a small ovenproof dish with a glug of olive oil and roast for 8–10 minutes at 425°F.**

SEVEN-SPICE BUTTERNUT TAGINE

Few dishes can boast being both moreish – in that you just cannot ever have enough – and Moorish, as in pertaining to north African cuisine. Tagine is one of them. You'll end up with more spice mix than you need, but the leftovers will stay fragrant in a jar for up to 2 months, and are a fabulous addition to dishes like the pea pilaf on page 447. Although 'tagine' actually refers to the specialty dish the ingredients are cooked in, there's no need to shell out for more kitchenware: any cast-iron or shallow ovenproof casserole dish with a lid will do.

SERVES 6

1 medium butternut
squash
⅓ cup (80 ml) extra
virgin olive oil
1 yellow onion,
finely chopped
1 bunch of parsley,
leaves picked and
finely chopped,
stems finely sliced
2 garlic cloves, finely sliced
¼ cup (50 g) sultanas or
chopped dried apricots
2 tablespoons dried
barberries (optional)
400 g (14 oz) can
chickpeas, drained
and rinsed
2 x 400 g (14 oz) cans
whole peeled tomatoes
2 tablespoons
pomegranate molasses,
plus extra to serve
2 red bell peppers, cut
into wedges

a good pinch of
flaked sea salt
½ cup (80 g) walnuts,
lightly crushed
mint leaves, to garnish
lemon zest, to garnish
flatbreads or couscous,
to serve

Seven-spice
(Makes ½ cup)
2 tablespoons ground
black pepper
2 tablespoons ground
cumin
1 tablespoon ground
coriander
1 tablespoon ground cloves
2 teaspoons ground
nutmeg
2 teaspoons ground
cinnamon
1 teaspoon ground
cardamom

Combine all the seven-spice ingredients in an airtight jar, giving it a shake to evenly distribute the spices.

Preheat the oven to 400°F and line a baking tray with parchment paper.

Using a sharp knife, chop your squash in half lengthwise. Scoop out the seeds, then cut into quarters. Coarsely grate 1 cup (150 g) of the squash and set aside, then chop the rest into 3 cm (1¼ inch) cubes.

Heat ¼ cup (60 ml) of the olive oil in an ovenproof casserole or cast-iron dish over medium heat. Add the onion and parsley stems. Cover and cook, stirring occasionally, for 8–10 minutes, or until the onion has softened and become translucent. Sprinkle in 1 tablespoon of the spice mix, scrape in the grated squash, garlic, sultanas and barberries, if using. Cook for 2 minutes, or until glossy and incorporated.

Stir in the chickpeas, tomatoes, pomegranate molasses, and an extra 400 ml (14 fl oz) can full of water. Bring to a gentle simmer, cover, then transfer to the oven and cook for 1 hour, or until the sauce has thickened.

Meanwhile, toss the diced squash in a bowl with the bell pepper and remaining olive oil, then spread across the baking tray. Sprinkle with flaked sea salt and roast for 25 minutes, or until the squash is cooked through and slightly golden.

Fold the roasted squash and bell pepper through the tagine. Sprinkle with the walnuts, chopped parsley leaves, mint leaves and lemon zest. Drizzle with extra olive oil and pomegranate molasses, then serve immediately with flatbreads or couscous.

Shortcut **Instead of roasting the squash and bell pepper from scratch, use left-over roast veggies.**

Double duty **Heat the leftovers in an ovenproof dish, crack an egg or two in, and serve with toasted left-over flatbreads. Or, scoop any left-over couscous on top and reheat in the oven for a tagine 'gratin'.**

Pumpkin

When the fairy godmother chose a pumpkin for Cinderella's carriage, she wasn't just waving her wand willy-nilly. These versatile members of the gourd family are hardy, hold their shape well when baked, make for terrific transportation to balls (just kidding!), keep for months in a cool, dry spot and can be eaten so many ways – grated raw through salads, mashed through rice pudding in unctuous steamed forkfuls, or roasted (my favorite), with leftovers blitzed into soup. In North America, where pumpkin is also seen as an ingredient for sweet dishes, its popularity peaks seasonally – and by 'seasonally', I mean as Jack-o-Lanterns at Halloween (an actual variety with a thick skin and fairly tasteless flesh), and as pumpkin pie at Thanksgiving (often out of a can). Of course, people all around the world enjoy pumpkin in curries, tagines and casseroles, adored for its sweetness, texture and creaminess.

'My mother is an incredible gardener and we always had pumpkin in abundance. Fast forward 35 years to the Attica kitchen – pumpkin was spectacularly unfashionable, but we devised a new way of cooking it, which involved steaming it for 12 hours with no seasoning. I felt pumpkin deserved its time in the sun. So did our guests, who frequently named it their favorite dish on our menu.'
– BEN SHEWRY, NEW ZEALAND

BUYING & STORING

The best time for pumpkin is autumn through to early winter. Depending on the variety, the color will vary, but you're looking for a firm, dry stem on top, with no signs of mold, which is a indicator of potential rain damage and dramatically docks its shelf life. Also, the longer the stem is, the longer the pumpkin is likely to last. A hollow-sounding pumpkin is a ripe one, so give it a good tap, and listen for the sound of something resembling a basketball. If you're no feeling confident, buy one that has already been cut in half, so you can check on the firmnes of its flesh, as well as vibrancy of color and any tell-tale slime – but use it quickly, because th exposed flesh will turn, as though at the stroke of midnight. Warts and discoloration of the skin (patchy bits that look like they've been bleached by the sun) are actually an indicator of ripeness, too, so don't be deterred. There are plenty of interesting types nowadays, but my favorite is the Japanese pumpkin, or kabocha squash. It has a lovely, sweet flavor, a finer skir that can be roasted and eaten, and holds its shape nicely during roasting.

When left whole and stored properly, pumpkins can last several months in a cool, dry place, elevated off the ground. I like to turn mine every couple of weeks to avoid pressure and liquid pooling underneath. Remember to periodically check for soft spots, which should be dealt with immediately, lest you lose the whole thing. Once cut, keep the exposed surface away from oxygen by covering with beeswax wrap and storing in the fridge. If you've cut the pumpkin open for just the one dish and you won't use the rest for ages, cut it into cubes and freeze, ready for roasting, steaming or stewing when you're up for another hit.

WITH COMPLEMENTS

Brown sugar, butter, cheese (especially goat, feta, gruyère, parmesan), cinnamon, cloves, cream, ginger, maple syrup, nutmeg, orange (especially zest), sage.

SCRAP MEDAL

If you do feel inclined to peel your pumpkin, don't throw the peel away – instead, it can be tossed with olive oil and salt and roasted at 350°F until crispy. Pumpkin seeds, or pepitas as they're usually referred to when hulled, are one of the most prized bits of 'offal' in the vegetable world. If you have a whole pumpkin that's rich in seeds, you can take those riches straight to the bank! Or at least the oven. You'll have to wash the seeds thoroughly first, making sure to shed as much of the stringy pumpkin innards as possible (which can be added to vegetable stock, so don't throw them out either). Once that's done, roast them in a 170°C (325°F) oven until they're golden and dried out, listening for the tell-tale 'pop', and checking after 20 minutes. The same can be done with butternut squash seeds. I often like to garnish pumpkin dishes with pepitas, or simply toss them with honey and soy sauce and roast them, for grazing on. As a matter of fact, I'm reaching for one now ...

Brace yourself

Pumpkin is the most injurious of all vegetables. Between its awkward angles, hard flesh and glossy (read 'slippery') skin, cutting into it can be an accident waiting to happen. The risks can be mitigated by using a heavy blade to break the pumpkin down into manageable pieces (a good cleaver is helpful here), with a towel folded across the top as a guard for when you pull it out again, and then using a knife with a finer blade for peeling and slicing. In fact, unless you're planning on whizzing flesh into a fancy soup or are really keen to preserve its orange color, I wouldn't bother peeling the pumpkin at all. Seek out unwaxed, thinner-skinned pumpkins (check for any handy halved ones if you're unsure), and you'll never have to break a sweat (or a nail) again.

Pumpkin soup

Preheat the oven to 400°F. Take half a medium-sized pumpkin, leave the skin on and chop into 2 cm (¾ inch) chunks. Toss them into your biggest mixing bowl, with some bruised garlic cloves (keep the skins on), halved top-n-tailed shallots (skins on, of course), thyme sprigs, a few roma tomatoes, a good pinch of flaked sea salt and a glug of olive oil, mixing to coat. Pour into a baking dish. If you're feeling decadent, pour about 2 tablespoons heavy cream over the top. Roast for 20–25 minutes, until the pumpkin is completely soft. Pop the garlic cloves and shallots out of their skins, and into a blender. Remove the pumpkin skins with the flick of a paring knife or sharp spoon if you'd like the soup to be vibrant orange (otherwise don't bother), then add the pumpkin and remaining pan ingredients to the blender with 4 cups (1 liter) stock and blitz to combine.

Classic zesty
pumpkin risotto
(page 168) and
Arancini (page 170)

Honey
pumpkin risogalo
(page 169)

GRATE PUMPKIN RISOTTO & RISOGALO

I like to think of this recipe as a three-fer ... or a four-fer if you're feeling particularly creative. For one thing, learning to cook risotto is a great skill to acquire all on its own, considering all of the different veg–spice flavor combos you can play with. Take the same amount of butter, rice and grated pumpkin and you could find yourself on the road to risogalo, the gorgeous Greek rice pudding that is like a hug in a mug. Cool down the risotto mix and you're cruising to canapé city, with the ultimate finger food: arancini – savory, stuffed with cheese, or even sweet, using the risogalo leftovers, drizzled with syrup.

CLASSIC ZESTY PUMPKIN RISOTTO

SERVES 4

80 g (2¾ oz) unsalted butter

3 French shallots, finely chopped

2 garlic cloves, finely chopped

2 cups (250 g) coarsely grated pumpkin

1½ cups (330 g) arborio rice

1 tablespoon extra virgin olive oil

2 cups (500 ml) just-boiled water

3 cups (750 ml) chicken or vegetable stock

finely grated zest and juice of 1 lemon

50 g (1¾ oz) parmesan, finely grated, plus extra shavings to serve

Persian feta, to serve

1 bunch of parsley, leaves picked and finely chopped, stems finely chopped

1 tablespoon finely chopped chives, to serve

Melt 60 g (2 oz) of the butter in a large, wide heavy-based frying pan or saucepan over medium heat. Add the shallot and cook for 2 minutes or so, until it starts sizzling, then pop on a lid for 5 minutes and reduce the heat. Lift the lid and stir for a minute or so, until softened and translucent.

Add the garlic and pumpkin and cook for 2 minutes, or until softened but not colored. Stir in the rice and olive oil and cook for 3 minutes to toast and coat each grain in butter.

Remove from the heat, pour in the hot water and stir to combine. Return to a low heat and cook, gently stirring occasionally, until most of the liquid has been absorbed.

Pour in ½ cup (125 ml) of the stock and continue the process, adding the remaining stock ½ cup (125 ml) at a time until the rice is cooked through and has absorbed most of the liquid. This usually takes around 18 minutes.

Remove from the heat and stir in the lemon zest and juice, the remaining 20 g (¾ oz) butter and the parmesan. Close the lid and let everything relax for a minute or so.

Season with salt and pepper to taste. Spoon the feta over and serve sprinkled with the parsley, chives and extra parmesan.

HONEY PUMPKIN RISOGALO

SERVES 4

0 g (2¾ oz)
  unsalted butter
½ cups (330 g)
  arborio rice
⅓ cup (85 g) sultanas
  (golden raisins)
  cinnamon stick, or
  1 teaspoon ground
  cinnamon
  est and juice of ½ orange
  est of 1 lemon
  cups (250 g) coarsely
  grated pumpkin
  ½ vanilla bean,
  seeds scraped (or 1
  teaspoon vanilla bean
  paste or extract)
  ¼ cup (60 ml) honey, plus
  extra to serve

2 cups (500 ml)
  just-boiled water
2½ cups (625 ml) milk
½ cup (125 g) crème
  fraîche, plus extra
  to serve
chopped honey cashews
  (or other nuts), to serve

**Quick candied
orange zest**
zest of 1½ oranges,
  thinly shredded
  into long strands
1 cup (220 g)
  granulated sugar

Melt the butter in a large, wide heavy-based frying pan or saucepan over medium heat. Add the rice, sultanas, cinnamon and orange and lemon zest. Cook, stirring, for 3 minutes to toast and coat each grain of rice in butter.

Add the pumpkin and vanilla and stir to coat. Cook for a further 2 minutes to soften the pumpkin slightly. Remove from the heat and stir in the honey and hot water. Cook over low heat, gently stirring occasionally, until most of the liquid has been absorbed.

Add ½ cup (125 ml) of the milk and continue the process, adding the remaining milk ½ cup (125 ml) at a time until the rice is just cooked through and has absorbed most of the liquid. Usually this takes about 18 minutes.

Meanwhile, for the candied orange zest, put the orange zest in a heatproof bowl, cover with boiling water, then strain. Place the sugar and ½ cup (125 ml) water in a wide pan over high heat and stir for 4 minutes, or until the sugar has dissolved. Reduce the heat, add the zest and simmer for 5–10 minutes, or until candied and sticky. Remove with a slotted spoon, reserving the syrup (try adding to poached fruits, or the Rhubarb on page 207).

Remove the rice from the heat and stir in the crème fraîche. Cover and stand for 5 minutes to thicken slightly.

Serve with an extra dollop of crème fraîche, an extra drizzle of syrup and a sprinkling of candied orange zest.

ARANCINI

MAKES 24 CANAPÉ-SIZE ARANCINI

1 quantity cooked risotto
(page 168) for savory
arancini, or 1 quantity
cooked risogalo (page
169) for sweet arancini,
cooled completely
2 eggs
1 cup (150 g) all-purpose
flour
3 cups (180 g) panko
breadcrumbs
rice bran oil, for
deep-frying

Savory
100 g (3½ oz) mozzarella,
chopped into 1 cm
(½ inch) pieces
1 bunch of basil,
leaves picked
Garlic aioli (page 37),
to serve

Sweet
½ cup (125 ml) honey
100 g (3½ oz)
dark chocolate,
finely chopped
strawberries, to serve
icing (confectioners')
sugar, to serve

Chill the rice mixture in a 24-hole ice cube tray (with each hole being about 1 tablespoon capacity).

Lightly beat the eggs in a bowl. Place the flour in a separate bowl, and the breadcrumbs into a third bowl.

Shape the chilled rice into balls, rolling the mixture between your palms, with a bowl of water nearby to keep your hands sticky-free.

At this point, if making savory arancini, create an indent in each and add the mozzarella. Roll once more between your hands to coat the cheese in the rice.

Roll the balls in the flour, then the egg, and finally the breadcrumbs. Chill for 20 minutes to firm up slightly, or up to a day ahead.

When ready to cook, fill a large saucepan three-quarters full with oil and place over medium–high heat until the oil reaches 400°F – you'll know it's at the right temperature when a cube of bread dropped into the oil turns golden brown in 15 seconds. Cook the balls in five batches for 2–3 minutes, or until nicely golden, briefly draining each batch on paper towel.

To serve the savory arancini Carefully add the basil leaves to the hot oil, standing back as the oil will spit. Cook for 1 minute, or until the bubbles subside. Remove with a slotted spoon and drain. Sprinkle the warm arancini with salt and crush the crispy basil over. Serve with aioli alongside for dipping, or on a bed of the cheat's sugo from the gnocchi on page 300.

To serve the sweet arancini Drizzle the warm arancini with honey and sprinkle the chocolate over so that it begins to melt. Sprinkle with strawberries, dust with icing sugar and serve warm.

Tips If you'd prefer to bake rather than fry, preheat the oven to 400°F, pop the arancini on a lined baking tray and bake for 20–25 minutes, until golden and crispy.

You can fry, cool and freeze your arancini in smaller portions for serving up later, too! They'll last for up to 3 months in the freezer; reheat in the oven at 400°F until warmed through.

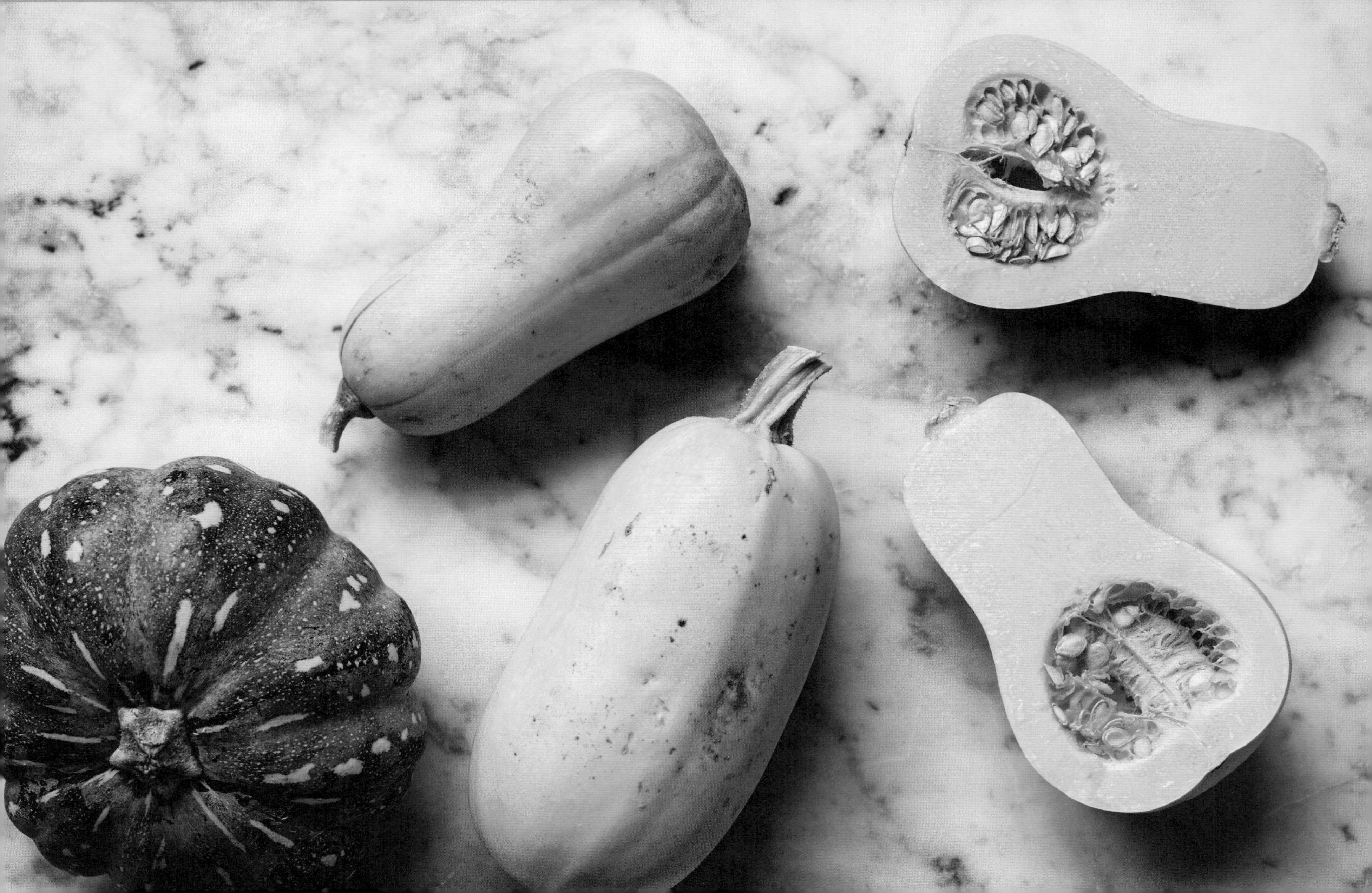

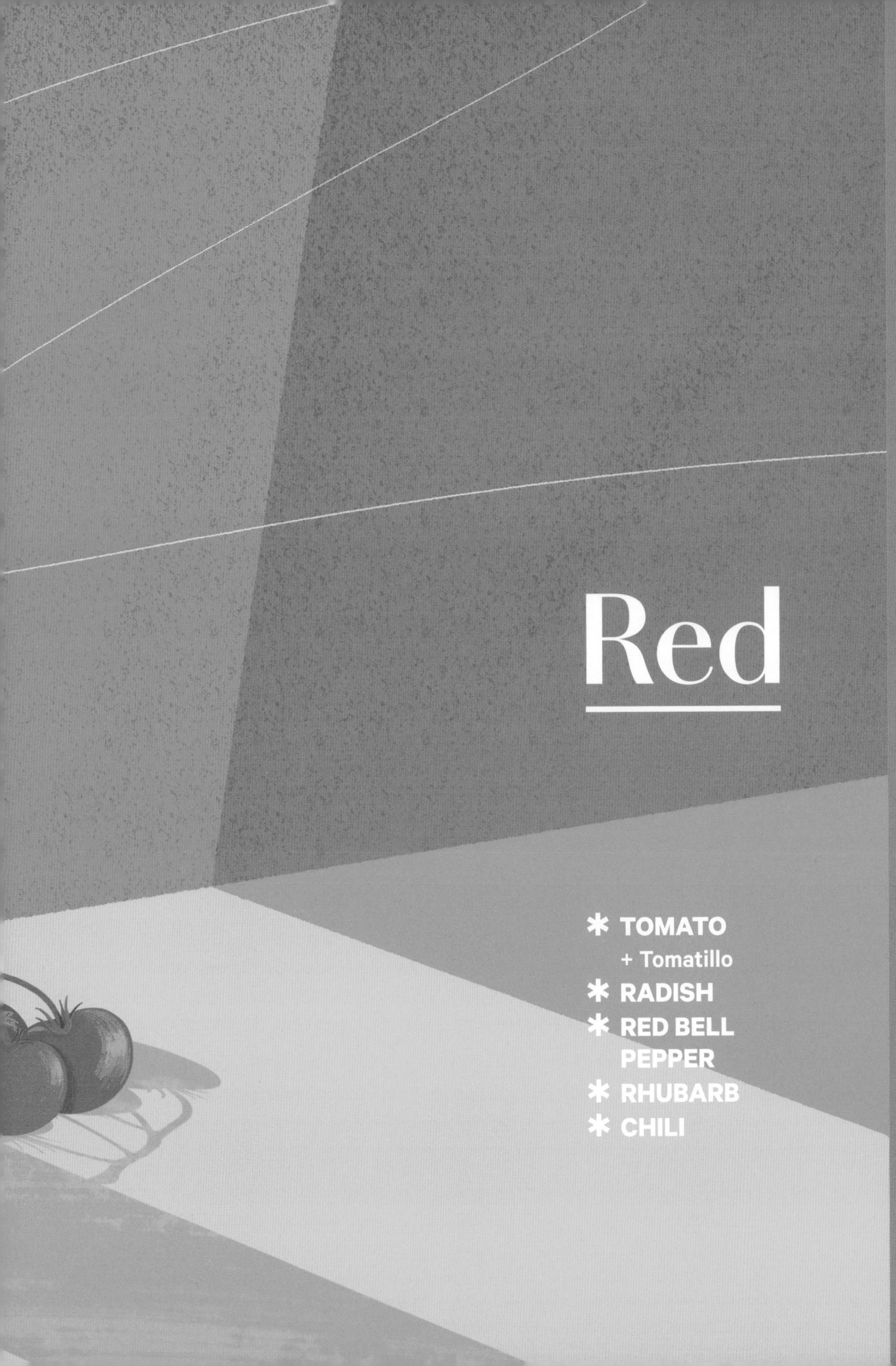

Red

* **TOMATO**
  + Tomatillo
* **RADISH**
* **RED BELL PEPPER**
* **RHUBARB**
* **CHILI**

Tomato

Tomatoes are a high-summer delight. I know you can find them year round, but don't be fooled: those hard orange spheres you come across in winter are not worth your pennies! If you're a tomato fiend (like me), opt for canned tomatoes or bottled passata (strained tomatoes) in the colder months. If you're lucky enough to have some growing, or have a neighbor with a vigorous tomato vine and a low fence, look no further – home-grown tomatoes are always the sweetest, because they haven't had to endure the indignity of refrigeration. Farmers' markets and farm gates are your next best bet, as many offer heirloom varieties in a multitude of summery hues. Knobbly, pleated varieties such as Ox Heart, or those with unusual colors such as Green Zebra or Black Russian, are extra special, so don't be put off by uneven shapes or textures – just try to pick those that are more flesh than fold. Thin-skinned tomatoes are best for serving fresh in salads, but if you're looking for tomatoes to pickle, slow-roast or ferment, make a bee-line for the greatest preserver of them all: the oblong roma tomatoes, also known as plum tomatoes.

Tomatoes are so important to our family and our cooking. Tomato Day was something I didn't really appreciate until I got much older, when I could see its part in teaching future generations the value of preserving the abundance of a seasonal product as well as the cultural traditions that come with it. Now I think it's the most special day in the Italian calendar.'
GUY GROSSI, AUSTRALIA

BUYING & STORING

For sweet, sun-ripened tomatoes, your best shopping tool is your nose. When tomatoes are ready for picking, they give off a particularly pungent aroma that can best be sniffed out at the stem – or truss, as it's called. If they're especially good, you'll be able to smell them from quite a distance, so keep your nose alert. Tomatoes should feel heavy and yield slightly to a squeeze – like a cheek, not a sponge. Trussed tomatoes, and those with a bit of vine or stem still attached, will keep best. Cherry tomatoes are often sold in a plastic punnet of some description, but some independent grocers will swap the plastic punnets for a paper bag (or your BYO cloth one) at the counter, and then return the punnets back to the grower, or at least recycle them. If your grocer hasn't cottoned on yet, encourage them to get on board.

Tomatoes belong in your fruit bowl, not the fridge! This was a revelation to me, too. Their delicate skin and watery flesh makes them highly susceptible to absorbing fridge odors, ruining their sweet aroma and flavor. Plus, being warm-weather lovers, the coldness of a fridge really dampens their exuberance. If you're buying tomatoes in advance, go for firmer ones, whereas last-minute purchasing means you can afford to go squishier – which often means cheaper and more flavorsome. When it comes to canned tomatoes, schools of thought differ, between 'buying local' or grabbing a can from the 'old country'. Whichever way you swing, try to find cans that are labelled 'BPA free' and contain no ingredients besides tomatoes.

FUNCTIONAL FOOD

Ever hear the expression "grow together, go together"? Tomato and basil are a classic example of two plants that punch well above their weight when coupled up. Not only do they taste sublime together in cooking, but any avid gardener will tell you they also help each other grow. Besides sharing soil nutrients, basil helps to enhance the natural sweetness of tomatoes, and protects them from bugs by wafting its basil-y aroma all over the place. That's why you'll often see them planted together in thriving kitchen-garden patches. And for those seeking to mend a broken heart, tomatoes, which yield their own little heart-shaped chambers once split down the middle, are packed full of antioxidants, vitamins A and C, folic acid, beta-carotene and, most pertinently, lycopene – a carotene that has been found to help with wound healing, lowering blood pressure and reducing inflammation, amongst other benefits. Incidentally, the natural benefits of lycopene are more readily accessed when some form of lipid (a.k.a. 'fat') molecule is involved ... includir its classic Mediterranean partner, olive oil! Liberally season your tomatoes with salt and pepper before adding the oil, to help the flavors absorb (fat acts like a barrier to the wate wedges of tomatoes), then splash on the oil and toss to combine. Hold off on adding any fresh herbs until just before you're ready to serve, though – the weight of the oil molecule will make the leaves wilt like a sad face emoji.

WITH COMPLEMENTS

Basil, bell pepper, cheese (especially mozzarella, parmesan), eggplant, garlic, olive oil, onion, shellfish, zucchini.

SCRAP MEDAL

Whenever you blanch tomatoes, try dehydrating the skins to turn into tomato powder! It's so simple: you can microwave the skins on high for 4–5 minutes until dried out, or leave in the oven on its lowest temperature overnight, with the door slightly ajar. Once done, blitz them up with a little salt and maybe some cayenne pepper, to rim your Bloody Mary glasses, or sprinkle on poached eggs. You can also deep-fry the skins as a garnish, or freeze in a 'stock-up' bag for vegetable stocks, soups and stews.

BEYOND TOMATO: TOMATILLO

Tomatillos, or 'little tomatoes', look quite like green (or occasionally purple) tomatoes, wrapped in a filigreed husk known as a 'calyx', like cape gooseberries. That's because all three are nightshades; the only difference being that while tomatoes, with their mild, sweet flavor, really took off around the world, gooseberries and tomatillos – with their slightly stick highly herbaceous and astringent tang – remain more specialty in their production. If you're of the mind to make an authentic Mexican salsa verde, or want to make the ultimate fried green tomatoes, then you need to track some down quick-smart. Look for firm fruit, with heavy husk coverage, and don't peel this back until you're ready to cook.

Layering up

Often, when a recipe calls for tomatoes, varying the ways in which you dish them up means extra depth of flavor, without much more fussing about. Cooking down fresh tomatoes creates a thick, rich sauce, whereas adding them towards the end offers pops of acidity. The juiciness of passata (strained tomatoes) is enriched with a teaspoon or two of syrupy tomato paste, while a can of chopped or even whole tomatoes adds texture and body, as the don't tend to break down the way fresh ones do. Sometimes, a pinch of sugar can enhance

'A very ripe tomato with salt and olive oil can be as refreshing as a glass of water on a hot summer's day.' – ANA ROŠ, SLOVENIA

their naturally sweet flavor, too. And if all else fails and you feel like your dish still needs some 'oomph', a dash of tomato ketchup never goes astray – either towards the end of cooking, or squirted on the side of the plate.

To blanch or not to blanch?

That is the question. And the answer really depends on what you plan on doing with your tomatoes. If your intention is to whack them into a chunky tomato soup or pasta sauce, it's entirely feasible to give blanching the flick. I only blanch when it's necessary, for instance when I don't want the silky flavor of cooked tomato to be interrupted by skin on the tooth. Bring your biggest pot of water to the boil, and use a serrated paring knife to slash an 'X' into the bottom of each tomato. Also, prepare a big bowl of iced water. Working in batches of five or so, drop your tomatoes into the boiling water for 20–30 seconds, transfer to the iced water using a slotted spoon, then peel as soon as the tomatoes are cool enough to touch.

Tomato passata

I tried to find out the etymology of 'passata', and came up with variations of 'paste', 'passed' and 'past' – which, when combined, tells the story of this crimson tide in its entirety. It's a runny paste, made by passing tomatoes through a sieve, making full use of excess produce into the years ahead, sustaining Italian families – and lovers of tomato-rich cuisines – through the seasons when sunshine is only available passed across the table in bottle form.

Wash 2 kg (4 lb 8 oz) very ripe tomatoes well – the riper, the better. Quarter them, then spread out on a baking tray lined with parchment paper. Drizzle with 1 tablespoon olive oil, sprinkle with 1 teaspoon salt, then bake in a preheated 400°F oven for 45 minutes, until they blister and soften enough to squash upon impact. (Alternatively, simmer in a large pot for 45 minutes, or until the tomatoes have collapsed, stirring now and then; some people like to add herbs such as basil or thyme, or aromatics such as onion and garlic as well.) Pass through a mouli (potato mill) or a sieve, or blitz in a blender, skin and all, until puréed to your liking. Pour into hot sterilized jars and seal right away. Check your jar lids: if they pop to concave by the next morning, you'll have a whole year to use it. If any don't pop, put them in the fridge and use in 2 weeks. Refrigerate after opening, regardless.

CONFIT CHILI TOMATOES

My friends Sandra and John inspired this recipe by serving up a sensational tomato sugo for lunch at theirs. The key, it turned out, was in low- and slow-ing the toms. I've mangled their method a little, to make it even easier to recreate, but the essence is there. They couldn't agree on whose recipe it was, and now I think we can all agree that it's, well, everyone's. Whack these on top of the bruschetta overleaf for peak Italianality.

MAKES 1 X 3 CUP (750 ML) JAR

1 kg (2 lb 4 oz) cherry
   tomatoes on the vine
½ cup (125 ml) extra
   virgin olive oil
1 teaspoon granulated
   sugar

flaked sea salt, to taste
5–6 large garlic
   cloves, halved
chili flakes, to taste

Preheat the oven to 250°F.

Pop the cherry tomatoes onto a baking tray, still attached to their trusses (green vines). Drizzle the olive oil evenly over the tomatoes, sprinkle with the sugar and salt, then sprinkle the garlic and chili flakes over the top, making sure the garlic is submerged in the oil.

Roast for 1½–2 hours, until the tomatoes are very tender, but still keep their shape. Remove from the oven and leave to cool a little. Ease off the garlic skins.

Use immediately, or transfer the tomatoes and their lovely herby oil to a clean 3 cup (750 ml) container with a tight-fitting lid. They will keep well in the fridge for up to 2 weeks; just return them to room temperature or warm them gently before serving.

Longcut If you'd prefer a more delicate mouthfeel, consider peeling the skins off your tomatoes. The easiest way is to slice off the tops and use this point to peel, after momentarily dunking into boiling water, then popping straight into a bowl. No need to fiddle with iced water here – the residual heat is enough to nudge the skins, and you won't have to worry about losing flavor into the water. Dehydrate the skins and blitz with salt for rimming your Bloody Mary cocktails

TOMATOES ON TOAST 3 WAYS

Toms on toast: need I say more? That's all this spread has room for, anyway …

EACH VERSION MAKES 4 PIECES

Bagel shop tomatoes

Melt 50 g (1¾ oz) butter in a frying pan. Add 2 halved bagels, cut side down, and toast them in the butter until golden. Meanwhile, thickly slice 3 heirloom tomatoes and dress them with fancy vinegar (such as malt or sherry), or some liquid from the pickled onions on page 282. Spread ½ cup (125 g) cottage cheese over the toasted bagel halves. Top with the tomato slices and some sliced pickled onion or fresh red onion. Garnish with basil and plenty of freshly cracked black pepper and serve.

P&T on brioche

Spread 4 toasted brioche slices with ⅔ cup (180 g) crunchy peanut butter. Cut 250 g (9 oz) cherry tomatoes in half, season with ⅛ teaspoon cracked black pepper, then pile on top of the brioche. Drizzle with 1 tablespoon honey. Serve topped with 3 tablespoons chopped toasted peanuts, if desired, and any mild baby herbs with smaller leaves, such as parsley or basil.

Blistered balsamic toasts

In a hot grill pan, toast 4 slices of sourdough bread, then remove from the pan. In the same hot pan, cook 250 g (9 oz) cherry tomatoes (a medley of colors is great) and ½ cup (75 g) pitted black olives for 4–5 minutes, until the tomato skins start to burst. Scrape the mixture into a bowl and toss with ⅓ cup (80 ml) olive oil, 2 tablespoons balsamic vinegar and some freshly cracked black pepper, squishing the tomatoes slightly. Halve 1–2 garlic cloves and rub the cut surface over the toasts. Top with the tomato mixture and sprinkle with parmesan shavings and thyme leaves.

FATTOUSH PLATTER

Most tomato-heavy cuisines have some form of tomato/bread/oil combination salad that takes full advantage of their sauciness as a way of softening stale bread, and said bread's sponginess for soaking up said sauciness. The etymology of the salad known as fattoush sits somewhere around 'crushing', from its Arabic origins, referring to the crushed flatbread within. Here I've kept things extra large, so that you can do all of the 'crushing' yourself. Let guests pick and choose their favorite bits, like a salad smorgasbord, and just remember to go heavy on the crispy pita, because it's pretty addictive …

SERVES 4

½ cup (125 ml) olive oil
¼ cup (60 ml) lemon
   juice, plus lemon
   wedges to serve
3 garlic cloves, crushed
6–8 tomatoes of various
   shapes and sizes,
   sliced into rounds
3–4 smallish Lebanese
   cucumbers, roughly
   chopped
   (or finely mandolined
   if you're feeling fancy)
1 red bell pepper, sliced

½ red onion, finely sliced
⅛ teaspoon ground sumac
1 tablespoon finely
   chopped parsley
1 tablespoon finely
   chopped mint
lemon wedges, to serve

Crispy pita
4 small pita pockets or
   2 large pita breads,
   cut into triangular
   bite-sized pieces
2 tablespoons olive oil

Preheat the oven to 450°F.

Combine the olive oil, lemon juice and garlic in a bowl, to make a dressing. Season with salt and pepper.

Combine as much (or as little) of the tomato and cucumber on the platter along with the bell pepper and onion. Sprinkle with the sumac, and drizzle with ¼ cup (60 ml) of the dressing and let everything get friendly.

Meanwhile, for the crispy pita, toss the pita triangles in the olive oil, spread on a baking tray and bake for 10 minutes, or until golden and crispy.

Arrange the pita triangles on the platter. Sprinkle with the herbs and serve straight away, with lemon wedges and the dressing alongside.

Tip Pita bread is often discounted as it approaches its use-by date. Snap it up and freeze for using in this recipe, or simply bake as directed above and serve with whatever creamy stuff you have in the fridge.

Shortcut Toast the whole pita breads in the toaster, then 'crush' into smaller bits to serve.

Radish

Whether it's rotund like a reddish Christmas bauble, popping with watermelon pink from inside out, or elongated with a dusky dip-dye, the radish is a ravishing thing to behold. I love tossing thinly sliced radish through salads for a punch of color and crunch, and serving breakfast radishes whole (with tops still on!) alongside whipped butter as part of a brunchy buffet. Raw radish flavor ranges from a mellow mustardiness towards the tonsils to straight-up pungent and peppery – which you can accentuate with a seeded mustard dressing, or mitigate with something creamier. They keep their color and shape quite well under heat, and any especially burnished bits will just add to the rustic appeal. Radish tops can be used as you might peppery arugula leaves – finely sliced through salads or simmered into soups and stews.

'We make a radish carpaccio, sliced with a mandoline and soaked
n icy water to accentuate its crispness. Use it in a salad, or simply
erve with butter and sea salt, or to accompany seafood such as
quid, cuttlefish or trout.' – MAURO COLAGRECO, ARGENTINA

BUYING & STORING

Peaking in spring, radishes are almost always sold in bunches with the green tops attached. The color of these can vary between a brighter or deeper green – both are fine, as long as the leaves are stiff to touch, with no visible slime. Bugs love radish tops, so don't be deterred if there are a few hungry holes through a leaf or two – it's a good indicator they're tasty enough for anyone to eat. Colors can range from reddish pink to white, through to magenta, purple and even black. Radishes lose their color and density as they age, so seek out the brightest-looking bunch, with a plump shape that's heavy for its size, and no give when squeezed. The skin should be cool to touch, and the flesh underneath as white as possible; any discoloration means too long on the shelf (or the fridges out the back). The less green there is near the start of the stalk, the better, as more green means they've had sun exposure and won't last as long.

If your bunch has the greens still attached, detach them as soon as you get them home. If you're not using the radishes for a few days, trim off the stems, too, as they'll leach moisture (unless, of course, you want to keep the cute tapered shape for roasting or serving whole – in which case, keep them attached but monitored). Wash your radishes right away and, without drying, pop them into a container with a damp cloth or paper towel, and into the fridge. This will offer the radishes a damp, cold environment, akin to the soil from whence they came.

COOKING WITH

Wash radishes especially well, since they're prone to catching grit, particularly around their stalks. Greens need a vigilant soak in a bowl and at least three wash-n-spins in the salad spinner to ensure they don't leave your soup disappointingly gritty. Soak the radishes themselves in cold water for at least an hour before slicing, or even overnight when serving whole, to ensure they're extra clean and gleaming, and to replenish any lost moisture and accentuate their crunch-factor. Being naturally bitter and hot, radishes quite like fat and they love salt, so a glob of good butter and flaked sea salt is all they need to really shine.

WITH COMPLEMENTS

Butter, cheese (especially cottage, blue, feta), cucumber, herbs (especially chervil, chives, dill, mint, parsley), green onion (scallion), vinegar (especially apple cider, chardonnay vinegar).

BREAKFAST RADISH QUICKLE WITH WASABI MAYONNAISE

A 'quickle' is exactly as it sounds – a quick pickle. The more porous the fruit or vegetable, the quicker it pickles – which means radish, with its spongy interior plumped up by sheer water content, is a perfect candidate. Serve this radish quickle for breakfast with wasabi mayo as the French enjoy theirs with butter, or alongside a main meal for a pop of acidity and crunch.

SERVES 4–6 AS A SNACK

1 bunch of breakfast
    radishes, with the
    leafy tops, washed and
    scrubbed of any grit
1 cup (250 ml) white
    wine vinegar
1 tablespoon pink
    peppercorns, plus extra
    crushed peppercorns
    to serve
2 teaspoons
    flaked sea salt

2 teaspoons honey
1 garlic clove, bruised
1 long red chili,
    halved lengthwise
½ cup (125 ml)
    Kewpie mayonnaise
2 teaspoons wasabi paste
togarashi or Daikon leaf
    furikake (page 52),
    to serve

Trim the outer radish stems, keeping the smaller leaves intact. Halve the bigger radishes and keep the smaller ones whole. Divide the radishes among two 1½ cup (375 ml) heatproof dishes or mugs.

In a saucepan, bring the vinegar, peppercorns, salt, honey, garlic, chili and 1 cup (250 ml) water to the boil. Pour the mixture over the radishes, doing your best to avoid the leaves so they don't wilt. Stand for 15 minutes to pickle.

Mix the mayonnaise and wasabi in a small bowl until suitably pale green. In another small bowl, combine some crushed pink peppercorns with togarashi or furikake.

Once the radishes are pickled to your liking, eat them straight from the dish, using the leaves and stem as a handle to dip in the wasabi mayonnaise and the togarashi sprinkle.

Alternatively, the radishes can be pickled in an airtight container in the fridge for up to 1 week.

Tip Radishes gather a lot of grit in the crevices between the leaves and roots. Try fully submerging them in cold water for 10–15 minutes after scrubbing and inspecting, to ensure any residual grit is left behind

Double duty Left-over pickled radishes can be tossed into salads or slotted into burgers. The wasabi mayo makes a great spread on sandwiches and wraps, or drizzle it over seafood and other vegetables.

HERB-BUTTER GLAZED RADISHES

Like clockwork, after a weekend's fresh produce purchases, there's a bowl of radishes somewhere on my parents' kitchen counter. By midweek, the bowl's still there, and the radishes are wondering what their purpose is in life. Sometimes I'll stop by and pop them in iced water overnight to refresh. Other times, they end up in the oven – where they turn out looking something like this. In the spirit of abundance, I'm taking this opportunity to also show you how to make compound herb butter – something that will come in handy for way more purposes than you think. It's great through any veggies you're roasting, on a steak, or for making a quick garlic bread (see the Garlic bread shortcut on page 38).

SERVES 4

1 kg (2 lb 4 oz) radishes (2 bunches), soaked
1 tablespoon olive oil

Compound herb butter
2 garlic cloves, roughly chopped
½ teaspoon flaked sea salt
¼ cup picked tarragon leaves, plus extra to garnish
¼ cup picked parsley leaves, plus extra to garnish
185 g (6½ oz) salted butter, softened

Preheat the oven to 400°F.

Cut the larger radishes in half, leaving the root end and a little of the green stem attached for decorative effect. Cut any very large radishes into quarters.

Toss with the olive oil, spread on a baking tray and pop into the oven for 20 minutes.

Meanwhile, make the herb butter. Blitz the garlic, flaked sea salt and herbs together in a food processor until a rough paste forms, then add the butter and pulse to combine. Place the herb butter on a sheet of plastic wrap, parchment paper or beeswax wrap and roll up into a log, using the pressure of your fingers.

Slice off a quarter of your butter log, and chop into small pieces. Add it to the baking tray and mix it through the radishes to glaze them. Wrap the remaining butter log tightly and stash it in the freezer for later use.

Roast the radishes for a further 5 minutes.

Serve warm, sprinkled with extra herbs and a sprinkling of flaked sea salt, and topped with another blob of herb butter if desired.

Tip **This dish will also work with baby turnips or Nantes carrots, at a pinch.**

Shortcut **Instead of making the herb butter, mix some crushed garlic and a knob of butter through the roasted radishes when they're just softened, then bake for another couple of minutes.**

Red bell pepper

Native to the Americas, bell pepper belongs to the nightshade family and is variously known as a sweet pepper in the United Kingdom. Although you can buy red, green, yellow, orange, pink and even purple bell peppers, you'll no doubt be astonished to discover that many of these grow on the same vine, but are simply picked at varying stages of ripeness! Green bell peppers are picked before they're ripe, so tend to have more bitterness, while red ones are picked at peak ripeness, after their natural sugars have had a chance to develop. They're available for much of the year, but are at their most affordable (and sweetest) during the summer months.

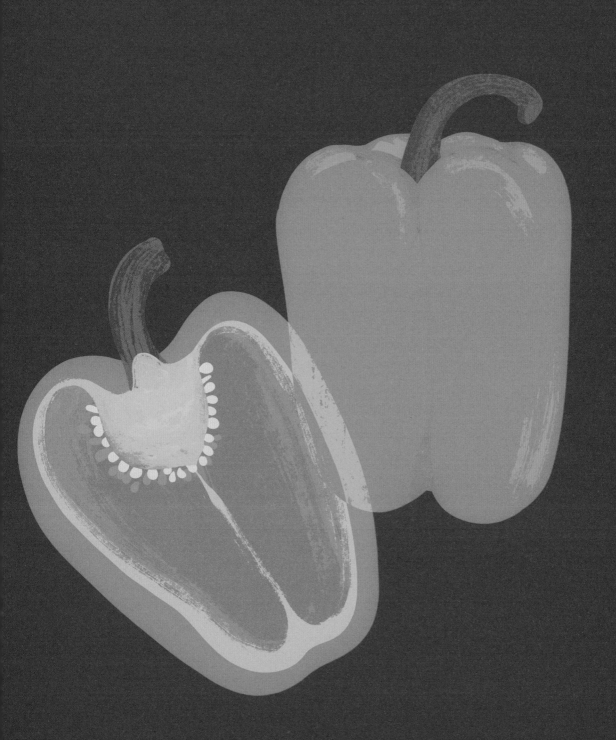

'One should listen to one's veg a little more; they certainly know how they like to be treated. Bell peppers are powerful things, objects of intensity, and shouldn't be trifled with when cooking. They command a certain reverence if they are to play nice, like that guest at a dinner you always have to deliberate where to seat. Do that well and they are the life of any party.' – IVAN BREHM, BRAZIL

BUYING & STORING

Bell pepper's skin is quite fine – almost like the flesh is growing slightly quicker than the skin itself, and is trying to stretch to accommodate. I like to use the 'balloon' analogy when shopping for these, because it gives you a good sense of what to look for, regardless of the color. You're after glossy firm skin, with no wrinkles or deflated spots. Try to avoid any with darkening around the bell pepper's folds, as these could be indicative of internal mold. Some bell peppers have three lobes, and others have four; I like to pick out three-lobed ones for slicing into salads (less curves to fuss around with), while four-lobers have a stronger base of gravity, so they're better for stuffing or baking without tipping over and spilling out their innards. A common gardening theory is that the number of lobes relates to the gender (and even *sweetness*) of the pepper, but seeing as it's the flower and not the fruit that has the sexual orientation, this one's a myth. Your best bet for picking a sweet pepper is, as always, to give it a good whiff – it should smell a bit like paprika or chutney.

If you're planning on using them within a few days, bell peppers actually cooperate well outside of the fridge – it helps them keep their crunch. Any longer, though, and it's best to store them loosely bagged in the crisper section. Their delicate skin and juicy flesh needs room to move, so try not to pack them in tightly with too many other things in there. And remember not to pile other heavy veggies on top, as bruising is a sure road to spoil-town for these guys. They're also very sensitive to smells and gases in general, so don't leave them too close to apples, pears and especially bananas. If you're the kind of person who likes to wash all of your produce as soon as you get it home, take care to thoroughly dry your bell peppers afterwards, as any moisture makes for mangy, moldy bits.

COOKING WITH

I like to keep the fancier-colored varieties for tossing fresh into salads, for novelty value and juicy crunch. Green ones are great for any heavy-duty cooking, such as stuffing and/or bakin for prolonged periods. Red bell peppers are superb for sautéing, the hot oil encouraging them to become glazed and glossy, eking out even more caramel-y notes as they soften. Bell pepper is the most inclusive member of the capsaicin family. While chili is fiery and fierce on the front palate, the bell pepper is happy to just hang back and be the sweet, unassuming one (until you get a wayward squirt in the eye). If you like the flavor of roasted bell pepper (page 200) but don't have an open flame, try quartering, seeding and roasting in a hot oven for 20 minutes or so, until blistered. Speaking of seeding, I find the easiest way is to take the seeds out along with the stem, by cutting the flesh as close to the join between the green stem and the bell pepper from the top, then twisting it all out in one fell swoop. Another method is to slice horizontally across the top fifth of the bell pepper, then pull out the exposed membrane and seeds.

WITH COMPLEMENTS

Cheese (especially goat, mozzarella, parmesan), eggplant, garlic, herbs (especially basil, cilantro, parsley), olive oil, paprika, potatoes, red onion, vinegar (especially balsamic, red wine, sherry), tomatoes.

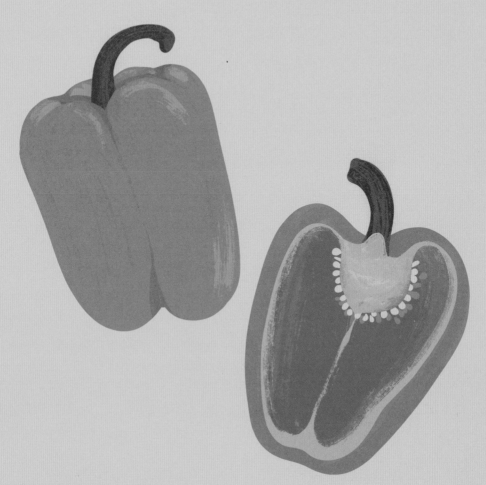

One-pan
romesco soup
(page 198)

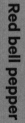

ONE-PAN ROMESCO SOUP

Hailing from Catalonia, romesco is traditionally a vivid red sauce served alongside fish. Considering the hero ingredients, tomatoes and bell peppers, were both introduced to the region by merchants and sailors returning from the Americas, this would once have been quite a decadent dish. It can be as much of a soup as a sauce, with the simple addition of some extra stock, a little crispy crouton action and an entirely incongruous but delicious ball of burrata – a fresh Italian mozzarella-style cheese that should have no place here, but totally works.

SERVES 4–6

4 red bell peppers, quartered, seeds removed
1 garlic clove, bruised
250 g (9 oz) cherry tomatoes, on the vine
400 g (14 oz) canned whole peeled tomatoes
1 teaspoon smoked paprika, plus extra to serve
½ teaspoon cayenne pepper
2 cups (500 ml) vegetable stock (see tip)
½ cup (125 ml) extra virgin olive oil, plus extra to serve
2 tablespoons sherry vinegar
½ cup (65 g) slivered almonds
4 small balls of burrata (optional)

Garlicky croutons
350 g (12 oz) sourdough bread, cut into croutons
2 garlic cloves, finely grated
2 tablespoons olive oil
50 g (1¾ oz) unsalted butter, melted

Preheat the oven to 400°F.

In a large casserole dish or roasting pan, combine the bell pepper, garlic and all the tomatoes. Sprinkle with the paprika and cayenne pepper. Pour in the stock, olive oil and vinegar, sprinkle with the almonds and give it all a stir.

Cover with a lid or foil and bake for 45 minutes, or until all the ingredients are softened.

Remove the lid or foil, and increase the oven temperature to 450°F. Bake for a further 15–20 minutes, or until the almonds are slightly toasted.

Meanwhile, for the garlicky croutons, pop all the ingredients in a bowl and mix to coat evenly. Transfer to a baking tray and roast near the top of the oven for the last 15 minutes of baking. Remove from the oven and stand until required.

In quarter batches, transfer the contents of your roasting vessel to a blender and whiz until smooth, transferring each batch to a soup pot. (Alternatively, transfer the whole lot to a soup pot and purée with an immersion blender.)

Bring the soup to a simmer and season to taste. Ladle into bowls and drizzle with olive oil. Sprinkle with a pinch of paprika and sprinkle the croutons over. If using the burrata, add one ball to each bowl and use a knife to pierce the skin to let the cheesy goodness escape into the soup. Serve immediately.

Tip If you have any 'pepper tears' handy from the roasted bell peppers on page 200, use them as part of the stock for this soup, for added smoky bell pepper flavor.

Double duty This soup also makes for a killer chicken parmigiana sauce – it's pretty thick already, so there's no need to reduce it down, either.

ROASTED BELL PEPPERS

My Babushka Zina was always hunting for fresh produce in the bargain section, one step away from the bin (before food-rescue organizations came on the scene, of course), eking out the good bits from the bad with the deft flick of a paring knife, and turning them into delicious after-school snacks and inexpensive, Soviet Bloc dinners. I'm still constantly drawn towards this min-shelf-life/max-flavor section, picking out the soft fruits for freezing or baking, juicy veg for, well, juicing – and, if I'm lucky, bright red bell peppers with the odd squishy bit (easily fixed with a paring knife) for turning into strips of slippery roasted piquancy with a capsi-can-do attitude! Pop them into salads, sandwiches and wraps, and onto antipasti platters. Use the left-over oil for dressing and saucing.

MAKES 1 X 3 CUP (750 ML) JAR

1 kg (2 lb 4 oz) red bell peppers
¼ cup (60 ml) red wine vinegar
½ cup (125 ml) extra virgin olive oil, plus extra for covering
1 teaspoon freshly cracked black pepper
1 teaspoon sweet paprika (optional)
2 garlic cloves, finely sliced
6 bay leaves
2 teaspoons flaked sea salt

If you plan on storing these for longer than 1 week, wash the jar you are using in hot soapy water, rinse thoroughly and stand it upside down on a rack to dry.

Preheat a grill plate on a barbecue to high. Add the whole bell peppers and cook for 25 minutes, or until the skins are blackened, turning every 5–10 minutes. Alternatively, preheat the broiler to high and cook the bell peppers directly on the oven rack closest to the broiler, with a baking tray underneath. Or, if you have a gas cooktop, rest the bell peppers over the exposed flame, using ovenproof tongs to hold and turn them now and then until fully blackened all over. (Warning: this method will leave your gas cooktop with some clean-up!)

Transfer the bell peppers to a heatproof bowl and cover tightly with foil. Stand for 5–10 minutes to steam.

Use the foil to peel off the bell pepper skins (this is great for friction AND helps protect your fingertips from burning). Pull off the stems (which will help with getting rid of most of the seeds), and remove any remaining seeds. Strain and reserve the liquid in the bottom of the bowl (see tip), then rinse and slice the bell peppers.

In a large bowl, combine the remaining ingredients. Add the bell pepper slices and mix to coat.

Serve immediately, or pop the bell pepper slices in a jar, adding more oil to ensure they are covered completely, and seal the lid. The bell pepper will keep in the fridge, submerged in oil, for up to 3 months.

Tip **The sweat and juice that comes off the grilled bell pepper is like liquid gold. Chef Jeremy Fox anointed it with the perfect name: 'pepper tears'. Use it in any place you'd usually use a stock – soups, sauces, gravies, dressings and the like.**

Shortcut **Buy some roasted bell pepper from a deli, then marinate it in the same mixture, after gently heating the oil, vinegar and aromatics first.**

PIPÉRADE

Hailing from the Basque region, this cross between salsa roja and a ratatouille is fantastically versatile, served alongside meat or fish for a piquant side dish, or as the main event with crusty bread. What I particularly love about this version is that it's much quicker and cleaner than the usual rigmarole of charring bell peppers over an open flame for extra burnished flavor (though if that's more your speed, check the recipe opposite). It's the ultimate multi-tasking methodology – the bell peppers bubble and burn away under the broiler while you build up the sauce.

SERVES 4-6

tablespoon olive oil,
  plus extra for drizzling
yellow onion, finely sliced
garlic cloves,
  roughly chopped
tablespoon tomato paste
teaspoon brown sugar
teaspoon salt

1 teaspoon *piment
  d'espelette* or
  hot paprika
400 g (14 oz) can whole
  peeled tomatoes
2 green bell peppers,
  sliced into long thin
  strips

Preheat the oven or broiler to 500°F, or as high as it will go.

Warm the olive oil in a large ovenproof saucepan over medium–low heat and sweat the onion with the lid on for 5–7 minutes, until translucent.

Stir in the garlic, tomato paste, sugar, salt and chili powder. Pour the tomatoes between your fingers and give them a squash as they tip into the pan, stirring to combine. Let the mixture bubble away with the lid on.

Meanwhile, coat the bell pepper with a drizzle of olive oil and spread on a baking tray in an even layer. Whack into the oven or under the broiler for about 15 minutes, or until the bell pepper edges char up and the flesh softens.

Add the bell pepper to the pan, pop the lid back on and let the flavors come together over medium heat for another 5 minutes before serving.

Tips **If you feel like taking this dish to the next level, do take the time to roast the bell pepper over an open flame, peeling off the burnt bits and slicing it into thin strips before adding to the sauce.**

Green bell peppers have a strong, bitter flavor that can be quite intense for some – so feel free to use a combination of yellow, red and green ones. It looks extremely pretty this way, too!

Shortcut **If you've already made yourself a batch of roasted peppers, turn them into pipérade by popping them into the pan in the final step.**

Double duty **You *know* this is gonna make an epic base for baked eggs. Just bring the mixture to a simmer in an ovenproof pan, then make some holes, crack an egg into each and pop under the broiler until they just start to set. Top with a little more paprika and let the residual heat cook the eggs through – and hey presto, you have shakshuka!**

SAMOSA-MIX STUFFED PEPPERS

A bell pepper's natural cup shape lends itself to stuffing with no great effort – you could say it's a 'capsicup', even. I love the notion of popping a heavily spiced mix in there, whether it's something like the filling from a subcontinental samosa, or something of your own design. Any shaped bell pepper will work – from the conventional bell pepper to the rarer bullhorn, if you can find it. Just remember to par-bake them first, to soften them up a little, then stuff to your heart's content.

SERVES 6

6 red and/or yellow
   bell peppers, halved
   lengthwise,
   but left intact
⅓ cup (95 g) Greek-style
   yogurt
3 garlic cloves, crushed
crushed papadams,
   to serve (optional)
cilantro leaves, to serve

Samosa mix
500 g (1 lb 2 oz) medium-
   sized floury potatoes,
   such as desiree,
   peeled and cut into
   2 cm (¾ inch) pieces
¼ cup (60 ml) mustard oil
   or vegetable oil
2 teaspoons yellow
   mustard seeds

1 tablespoon
   ground turmeric
1 teaspoon curry powder
1 teaspoon garam masala
1 teaspoon freshly cracked
   black pepper
2 garlic cloves,
   finely chopped
2 thin green chilis,
   thinly sliced
1–2 curry leaf branches,
   leaves picked and
   chopped, plus extra
   to garnish
400 g (14 oz) ground beef
1 cup (140 g) frozen
   peas, thawed
1 tablespoon brown sugar
1 tablespoon white vinegar

Preheat the oven to 425°F.

Start by making the samosa mix. Pop the potatoes in a saucepan and cover with cold well-salted water. Bring to the boil over high heat, then reduce the heat to medium and cook for 15 minutes, or until cooked through. Strain and stand until required.

Meanwhile, heat the mustard oil in a frying pan over medium–high heat. Once you can feel the heat emanating from the pan with your palm hovering 10 cm (4 inches) away, add the mustard seeds and stir – they'll begin to pop almost instantly. Scoop out half the seeds and reserve. Now add the turmeric, curry powder, garam masala, pepper, garlic, chili and curry leaves and cook, stirring occasionally, for 1 minute, or until fragrant.

Add the beef to the pan. Using a potato masher to break up the bits, cook and stir for 5 minutes, or until browned and golden. Stir the potatoes, peas, sugar and vinegar through. Season with salt and pepper.

Pop the bell peppers on a baking tray, cut side down, and roast for 10 minutes, or until they are beginning to sweat and are warmed through.

Remove the seeds and membranes from the bell peppers, then fill the cavities with the samosa mix. Return to the oven on the highest rack and roast for 5–10 minutes, until charred and crisp.

Meanwhile, combine the yogurt, reserved mustard seeds and garlic. If using the papadams and extra curry leaves, quickly fry them up.

Spoon the yogurt over the bell peppers, garnish with cilantro and serve immediately, with the papadams and fried curry leaves if desired.

Shortcut **Bake some frozen samosas while the bell peppers bake, then stuff the whole samosas inside the capsicups. It may take a little squashing, but that's all part of the fun, yes? Or, dice the bell pepper and add to the samosa mix, wrap in filo or puff pastry, then bake.**

Rhubarb

Rhubarb was once so venerated that it fetched a higher price than cinnamon and saffron, and even the Pope was sent a gold case with rhubarb seeds for planting in the Vatican. That's because it had to be lugged over from the rugged mountains across China and Mongolia, whence it originated, and because its trade and cultivation was tightly controlled by the Russian monarchy. By the 17th century, the Romanovs had established a rhubarb monopoly via the Baltic, helping finance Catherine the Great's extensive military expansions, and driving the rest of Europe NUTS. A 'rhubarb race' ensued, which finally ended when some seeds were smuggled out of Russia by a former physician to the Tsars, and these seeds thrived across the United Kingdom. Rhubarb also made its way to America care of industrious Russian sailors, who used it to treat scurvy, and by the late 19th century it had begun to earn a new nickname there: 'Pie Plant'.

love rhubarb, in a sweet or savory application. Its marriage
artner is lemon thyme – either picked and on top, or blended
to cold vegetable oil and drizzled over stewed rhubarb.'

JO BARRETT, AUSTRALIA

BUYING & STORING

More often than not, rhubarb is sold with its giant elephant-ear leaves lopped off. Sure, the leaves are high in oxalic acid and other compounds that are poisonous if eaten, but they're also a very clear indicator of how long that rhubarb has been sitting on the shelf. If the leaves are still present, you know what to do – find the stalks with the sprightliest-looking Dumbo ears. If the leaves are already gone, look towards the root instead. When rhubarb is picked at the right time, it pulls right out of the ground, taking the thicker root end with it. When picked early, the root stays put, and your rhubarb is a uniform thickness along the whole stalk. This isn't the end of the world, mind you, but it *will* mean you'll have to use more sugar to counteract the astringency of under-ripe stalks. Late winter into early springtime is when rhubarb is at its best, but you'll still find decent bunches of it all the way into summer, too. If using within a few days, store the stalks like cut flowers in a jar of water, loosely bagged to protect them from ethylene-producing fruit and veg. For longer storage, wrap stalks as you would celery – in the crisper, loosely wrapped in beeswax or foil, allowing some air to escape without letting the stalks dry out. Rhubarb also freezes quite well, so wash, dry, chop into chunks, freeze on a tray, then transfer into labelled, portioned containers for up to a year.

FUNCTIONAL FOOD

While we think of rhubarb as a pleasantly pink punctuation to pudding, it was first cultivated for a far more functional task: easing constipation! In traditional Chinese medicine, it belongs to the class of herbs used for 'purgative, downward draining', drawing out heat from the body, and accelerating movement in the stomach and intestines – an effect that makes it popular in herbal preparations to this day. It's the fiber in rhubarb, along with compounds known as anthraquinones, that can help keep you regular, so a few stewed or poached batons of rhubarb can be a useful (and delicious) addition to your breakfast spread.

WITH COMPLEMENTS

Apple, cardamom, cheese (especially blue, haloumi), cinnamon, cream (clotted, pure, ice cream, crème fraîche, mascarpone), ginger, lemon, orange, strawberries, vanilla.

RHUBARB ROAST-UP – TWO WAYS

Rhubarb is one of the vegetable world's wiliest shapeshifters – morphing firstly from 'vegetable' to 'frui' in our culinary consciousness, and transforming with gentle cooking from crimson-colored celery-like stalks into silken salmon-hued strands. I love stewing rhubarb with apple and having it at the ready for wintertime crumbles, or simply serving it with a heaping of yogurt or clotted cream. And while rhubark has earned itself a sweet reputation, it has plenty of savory appeal, too. Make yours work double duty by using half a bunch for a savory sweet-n-sour brunch combo with shallots and cherry tomatoes on grilled haloumi, and the rest for a sweet breakfast featuring classic flavor friends: strawberries and vanilla. You might even like to pull both versions out at once for indecisive friends who've stayed the night

ROASTED RHUBARB
ON GRILLED HALOUMI

SERVES 4

4 rhubarb stalks,
    about 250 g (9 oz)
2 French shallots,
    thinly sliced
¼ cup (60 g) brown sugar
2 tablespoons red
    wine vinegar
1 teaspoon cracked
    black pepper
1 teaspoon flaked sea salt

100 g (3½ oz) cherry
    tomatoes, halved
200 g (7 oz)
    haloumi, sliced
    1 cm (½ inch) thick
2 tablespoons olive oil
purple basil leaves,
    to serve (optional)

Preheat the oven to 400°F. Line a baking dish with parchment paper.

Cut the rhubarb into 4 cm (1½ inch) lengths, then cut the thicker pieces in half, so all the slices are about 1 cm (½ inch) thick, for even cooking.

Place the rhubarb, shallot, sugar, vinegar, pepper and salt in the baking dish. Cover tightly with foil and bake for 10–15 minutes, or until the rhubarb has softened but still holds its shape.

Place the tomatoes in a heatproof bowl. Using the parchment paper, lift the rhubarb from the dish and pour the whole mixture over the cherry tomatoes in the bowl. Stand for 5 minutes, to slightly cook the tomatoes in the residual heat.

Meanwhile, heat a non-stick frying pan for at least 5 minutes. Coat the haloumi slices in the oil and fry for 2–3 minutes on each side, or until golden.

To serve, arrange the rhubarb, tomato and onion over the haloumi, then spoon the cooking juices over and sprinkle with purple basil, if using.

OASTED RHUBARB WITH
TRAWBERRIES & VANILLA

ERVES 4

rhubarb stalks,
 about 250 g (9 oz)
cup (60 g) brown sugar
hely grated zest and
 juice of 1 orange
00 g (3½ oz)
 strawberries,
 thinly sliced
 cups (375 g) Greek-
 style yogurt

½ teaspoon vanilla bean
 paste or extract
1 tablespoon honey
1 teaspoon rosewater
 (optional)
Maple ginger-spiced
 granola (page 102), or
 shortbread biscuits,
 crumbled

Preheat the oven to 400°F. Line a baking dish with parchment paper.

Cut the rhubarb into 4 cm (1½ inch) lengths, then cut the thicker pieces in half, so all the slices are about 1 cm (½ inch) thick, for even cooking.

Place the rhubarb, sugar, orange zest and juice in the baking dish. Cover tightly with foil and bake for 10–15 minutes, or until the rhubarb has softened, but still holds its shape.

Place the strawberries in a heatproof bowl. Using the parchment paper, lift the rhubarb from the dish and pour the mixture over the strawberries. Stand for about 5 minutes to let the strawberries relax in the residual heat.

Meanwhile, combine the yogurt, vanilla, honey and rosewater, if using, in a bowl or cup.

Serve the sweet rhubarb mixture sprinkled with granola or crumbled biscuits, with the yogurt alongside.

Roasted rhubarb
on grilled haloumi
(page 206)

Roasted rhubarb with
strawberries & vanilla
(page 207)

GLUTEN-FREE RHUBARB & APPLE CRUMBLE

This is my mother-in-law Jackie's crumble, and it's one of my favorite ways to make use of left-over winter fruit. It's gluten-free, making it perfect for when you're not sure what kind of dietaries are about to walk through the door, and is also very simple to prepare ahead. The fruit can be stewed days before, with the crumble rubbed together and sprinkled over just before guests arrive – or skip the crumble and serve the blushing bowls of stewed fruit with a side of natural yogurt or cream. Speaking of cream, I hope Jackie doesn't mind my addition of a crème anglaise, which is just a fancy name for a runny custard. You don't have to make it, but you'll be glad you did.

SERVES 6–8

1.2 kg (2 lb 10 oz) granny smith apples, peeled and chopped into 3 cm (1¼ inches) pieces

500 g (1 lb 2 oz) bunch of rhubarb, cut into 2 cm (¾ inch) batons

2 tablespoons brown sugar

1 cinnamon stick

2 star anise

Crumble

120 g (4 oz) cold butter, cubed

100 g (3½ oz) gluten-free all-purpose flour

½ cup (100 g) brown sugar

⅓ cup (70 g) rolled oats

¼ cup (30 g) roughly blitzed hazelnuts, toasted

¼ cup (40 g) roughly blitzed almonds, toasted

¼ cup (25 g) almond meal

1 teaspoon baking powder

¼ teaspoon ground allspice

Crème anglaise

4 egg yolks

⅓ cup (75 g) granulated sugar

1½ cups (375 ml) half and half cream

2 teaspoons vanilla bean paste or extract

Pop the apple, rhubarb, sugar, cinnamon stick and star anise in a large heavy-based saucepan. Pour in ¼ cup (60 ml) water, cover and simmer for 30–40 minutes, stirring occasionally, until the apple softens to a purée; some mild chunks are fine for texture. Leave to cool slightly, then transfer to a 6 cup (1.5 liter) baking dish.

Preheat the oven to 425°F.

To make the crumble, lightly rub together the butter and flour in a bowl with your fingertips, then stir in the rest of the ingredients with a wooden spoon. Sprinkle it over the stewed fruit, heaping it into each nook and cranny. Bake for 15–20 minutes, or until the top is golden.

Meanwhile, make the crème anglaise. Whisk the egg yolks and half the sugar in a bowl until pale. Bring the cream, vanilla and remaining sugar to a simmer in a heavy based saucepan, stirring until the sugar dissolves. While whisking, slowly pour the hot cream over the egg yolk mixture to combine. Pour into a clean saucepan (you can wash and dry the one you used) over medium–low heat. Cook, stirring constantly, for 6–8 minutes, or until the mixture coats the back of a wooden spoon, and you can put a finger through it and the streak stays put. Strain through a fine sieve and keep warm for serving.

Serve the crumble warm, with the crème anglaise.

The stewed fruit will keep for up to 1 week in the fridge.

Tips Chinese five-spice contains all the spices you need for this dish (and a few more, so use sparingly).

For extra texture, reserve two handfuls of the chopped apple, squirting a little lemon juice over to stop it browning. Once the fruit has stewed, mix the raw chopped apple through, then bake as normal.

Shortcut Poke holes in an apple using a fork, dice up some rhubarb, then microwave them with a little water on high for 6–8 minutes, until soft. Top with granola and serve with yogurt, sprinkled with ground cinnamon.

Chili

It's fascinating to explore the drift of the chili pepper from New World to Old. And by 'drift', I mean as fast as the sails of the 16th-century ships could take them. Spanish and Portuguese conquistadors were particularly enamored of the piquancy chilis added to food, reminiscent of the black peppercorns that were popular and expensive back home. Industrious sailors started popping dried chilis (packed with vitamin C) in their pockets as a way of staving off scurvy, which is how chilis ended up in the cuisines of Africa, India, South-East Asia and the Middle East. A sprinkle of ground cayenne pepper – another moderately hot variety of chili – gently warms the cockles of any stew; chopped fresh red or green chilis transform a bland salad into a taste sensation; chili sauce makes the tastebuds pop; dumplings are nothing without a hit of chili oil; and stuffed jalapeño poppers are just plain revelatory. As a general rule, the smaller the chili, the hotter it will be – consider a small red bird's eye, versus a larger fatter jalapeño, carefully.

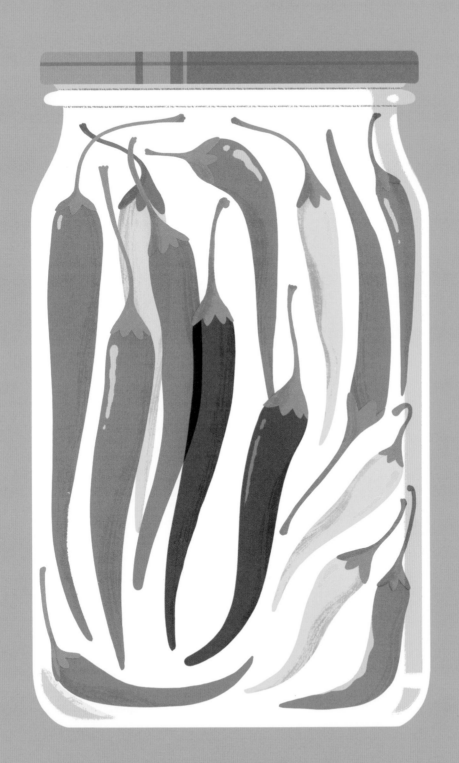

'Jalapeño and habanero are my favorite chilis to work with. I like to dry chilis and then blend them with salt, or infuse them into oils. I also like to blend soaked chilis with chocolate for my chicken mole.' – ROSIO SANCHEZ, MEXICO

BUYING & STORING

Fresh chili has a glossy smooth skin like a bell pepper ... unless you're in scorching territory, with the likes of Ghosts or Reapers (their name should give the game away), where the skin looks pock-marked, as if by searing hot oil. When buying chilis, try to grab them by the stalk, which should be bright green, with no signs of mold or sliminess. Store your chilis in your fridge's side compartment. Pull the stem off gently, wrap in cloth or paper towel, and they should last a week or two. If you're only using a little at a time, chop and freeze fresh chilis in portions for popping into soups, stews and sauces as needed; this works best with green chilis, as red ones lose their color when frozen. You can dehydrate your own red chilis, by slicing them in half lengthwise, removing the seeds, and then drying, either using a dehydrator, or in the oven on its lowest temperature overnight, with the door chocked open. They can also be roughly chopped, tossed with coarse salt and air-dried to make a cheap and cheerful 'chili salt' for sprinkling and gifting. Create your own whole fresh chili oil by scoring surplus chilis, popping them into sterilized, wide-mouthed bottles or jars, then covering with heated olive oil. The oil will intensify with time, and can be used to fire up dressings, marinades and glazes, storing in the fridge for up to 2 months. Chilis are also one of the easier edibles to grow, particularly in warmer climates, so for heat-heads with a mildly green thumb and a windowsill, that might be an option too.

COOKING WITH

For fresh chilis, if you're unsure of your guests' heat-tolerance, scoop out the membranes and seeds with the edge of a teaspoon, and reserve half the allotment to be added at the table. Infuse a long red chili into hot chocolate for a decadent, devilish drink. If you're just after a hum, your three amigos are ground paprika, cayenne pepper and chili flakes. Paprika is the mildest of the three; smoked for darker sauces, and sweet for lighter ones. Cayenne pepper is HOT – an eighth of a teaspoon is roughly equivalent to a whole bird's eye chili. Flakes are the great in-betweener – hotter than paprika, fruitier than cayenne. I love them in a chili oil for dumplings. To make your own, heat 1 cup (250 ml) of neutral-flavored oil over medium–low heat with 3–4 tablespoons chili flakes and a few pinches of salt for 5 minutes, then allow to cool and pour into a clean jar, flakes and all. Store in the fridge, and it'll keep at its best for around 6 months. Whole dried chilis are complex, smoky and versatile. With fruity acidity and vibrant color, brighter red or orange dried chilis such as chipotle are best for chicken, fish and vegetables, while darker dried chilis such as ancho – with plum hues through to brown and black – work well with dark, gamey meats and mushrooms, or when making sauces such as mole for deeper, prunier flavor. Dried chilis like these need to be rehydrated before grinding or blitzing. Cut the stem off with some scissors, split the skin and tap or scrape the seeds out before soaking, as these can be bitter or musty. For a bolder, more intense flavor, chili aficionados will, before soaking, fry dried chilis in a little oil until they pop and glisten, or dry-toast them until colored. Keep the chili-soaking water to loosen the mixture in the blender, using in place of an equivalent amount of liquid in your recipe.

FUNCTIONAL FOOD

Peppercorns and chili peppers aren't even remotely related, with the heat in the former due to the natural compound piperine, and the latter capsaicin. In the wild, these are a plant's defense mechanism against being eaten; in humans, they trick the brain into thinking your mouth is on fire, releasing endorphins and dopamine in response – which is why some people get hooked on heat. A chili's capsaicin content is measured on the Scoville scale: the more capsaicin, the hotter the burn. If you do get caught out with a chili that's blowing your head off, reach for milk rather than water. Unlike water, which slides right off any capsaicin that has attached itself onto your tongue, the casein in milk will cut right through it, like detergent through grease, and the burning should subside with a few big gulps.

WITH COMPLEMENTS

Avocado, beans (green and/or canned), coconut (water, milk, cream – anything coconut-y), cilantro, corn, curry leaves, fish sauce, garlic, ginger, lime.

Heat seeker: the Scoville scale

Cold	Spicy	Hot	Hot Hot	Fiery Hot	Scary Hot
0 Scovilles	2K–50K Scovilles	50K–100K Scovilles	100K–500K Scovilles	500K–1.5M Scovilles	1.5M+ Scovilles
Bell pepper	Jalapeño chili	Bird's eye chili	Habanero chili	Ghost pepper	Carolina reaper
Gypsy hybrid	Serrano chili	Cayenne pepper	Red savina	7 Pot pepper	7 Pot douglah
		Tabasco chili	Scotch bonnet	Brain strain	Trinidad scorpion
		Chile de arbol			

JALAPEÑO BUSINESS

I hope you don't think I'm trying to get all up in yo' business when I tell you that these poppers must be on your 'to make' list. Because they are, quite frankly, The Business – creamy, smoky, with a gentle heat that's easy to serve up, and please just about everyone, too. Use this recipe as a base, and add your own spin to the filling – be it extra herbs and spices, or in doubling down on cheese.

MAKES 12 POPPERS

12 jalapeño chilis
   (see tips)
200 g (7 oz) cream cheese
½ teaspoon smoked
   paprika (plus extra
   for sprinkling)
½ teaspoon garlic powder

1 tablespoon cilantro
   stems, finely chopped
   (you can use the
   leaves for garnishing,
   if you like)
¼ teaspoon salt, plus extra
   for sprinkling
100 g (3½ oz) cheddar,
   grated

Preheat the oven to 425°F. Line a baking tray with parchment paper.

Hold your chilis by the stems and use a small serrated knife to make a slit in the top, like a suspicious squinty eye. Using the knife or a teaspoon, scoop out the membrane and seeds. Give the chilis a tap and a rinse to get rid of any sneaky seeds.

Put the cream cheese, paprika, garlic powder, cilantro stems and salt in a bowl and mix together with a fork, smushing to combine.

Use a teaspoon to press the mixture into each popper, leaving an indent for the cheddar.

Fill the indent with cheddar (you knew this one was coming). Pop the poppers (ha!) onto the baking tray and bake for 13–15 minutes, or until the cheese is bubbly. If you'd like a little extra burnish, give them a quick blast under the broiler.

Sprinkle with a smattering of paprika and serve.

Tips This recipe works with both red and green jalapeños, as they're actually the same chili, although the green ones do hold their shape slightly better as they are firmer, being less ripe.

Keeping the cheddar separate from the cream cheese helps save the filling from bubbling over, but you can mix it all together if you're pressed for popper-prepping time.

SMOKY BAKED BEANS

Is there anything more satisfying than having some flavor-packed baked beans to look forward to for breakfast? These fully loaded baked beans take advantage of paprika-laden chorizo sausage, as well as the piquancy of tomatoes, to offer a warming bowl of beans that are much grander than the sum of their parts (which, let's face it, simply involves opening a few cans and stirring). If you'd prefer to go chorizo-free, that's totally cool – just up the olive oil, paprika and cumin factor and we'll call it square.

SERVES 4

1 smoked chorizo
   sausage, skin removed,
   finely diced
1 tablespoon olive oil
1 onion, finely diced
2 garlic cloves,
   roughly chopped
½ teaspoon ground cumin
½ teaspoon sweet paprika
1 dried ancho chili, finely
   sliced (optional)
2 x 400 g (14 oz) cans
   whole peeled tomatoes

2 teaspoons tomato paste
1 teaspoon brown sugar
1 teaspoon flaked sea salt
2 x 400 g (14 oz) cans
   cannellini beans,
   drained and rinsed
4 eggs
finely chopped parsley,
   to serve
warm toast, to serve

Fry the chorizo in an ovenproof pan until it starts to release some bright orange oil. Pour in the olive oil, add the onion and stir well to combine, then pop a lid on and sweat for at least 10 minutes, or until translucent.

Stir in the garlic, cumin, paprika and chili, if using. Add the tomatoes, tomato paste, sugar and salt, breaking the tomatoes into chunks using a wooden spoon. Bring to a simmer.

Meanwhile, preheat the oven to 400°F.

Stir the beans into your tomato mixture and allow the flavors to meld as the oven heats up.

Pop the pan into the oven and bake, uncovered, for 10 minutes.

Remove from the oven and use a wooden spoon to make 4 holes in the mixture. Crack in the eggs, then bake for a further 5–6 minutes, or until the egg whites are white and the yolk is par-cooked (it will finish cooking in the residual heat).

Sprinkle with parsley and serve hot, with toast.

Tip Most white beans will work in this recipe, but if you can get your hands on some Spanish *pochas* beans, give them a whirl – their flavor is just unbeatable in this dish.

Shortcut A can of baked beans can be spruced up with herbs, spices and chili in this same way. Look for ones that aren't too high in added sodium and sugars.

CHILI SAUCES

If there's one thing I've learnt about chili, it's that being a hot-head seems to be universal. Pretty much every cuisine has some variation on a chili theme, adding their own flourishes using locally available ingredients to add sweetness, sourness and the occasional creaminess factor to balance out the spice.

SUDANESE DAKWA (CHILI & PEANUT SAUCE)

MAKES ABOUT 3 CUPS (750 ML)

1 white onion,
　coarsely grated
juice of 1 lemon
1 cup (250 ml)
　vegetable stock
2 long red chilis, seeded
　and finely chopped
1–2 garlic cloves,
　finely chopped
1 cup (240 g) crunchy
　peanut butter

2 teaspoons
　flaked sea salt
1½ teaspoons baharat
　(make sure your spice
　mix has rose petals
　in it, otherwise add
　½ teaspoon rosewater
　or rose petal powder)
2 large tomatoes,
　coarsely grated
cilantro leaves, to serve
　(optional)

Place the onion and lemon juice in a bowl and stand for 10 minutes to pickle slightly.

Pour the stock into a large frying pan and bring to the boil. Add the pickled onion mixture and chili and cook for 1–2 minutes to soften slightly. Incorporate the garlic, peanut butter, salt and baharat, bring to the boil, then simmer until the mixture reduces by one-third. Stir in the grated tomato and season to taste.

If serving straight away, stir in the cilantro, if using.

Alternatively, wash a 3 cup (750 ml) jar or sauce bottle with hot soapy water, rinse well and leave to dry. Pour the hot sauce in, seal and store in the fridge for up to 1 month. To serve, warm over low heat, then stir in the cilantro.

Serve as a dipping sauce, or drizzle over vegetable, chicken or lamb skewers.

INDONESIAN SAMBAL WITH PINEAPPLE

MAKES ABOUT 2 CUPS (500 ML)

200 g (7 oz) long red
　chilis, chopped
1 red bell pepper, chopped
　(optional, to tone down
　the kick)
2 garlic cloves, peeled
3 cm (1¼ inch) piece of
　fresh ginger, peeled
　and chopped

225 g (8 oz) canned
　pineapple in juice
1 tablespoon
　flaked sea salt
1 cup (250 ml)
　white vinegar
¼ cup (55 g)
　granulated sugar

Wash a 2 cup (500 ml) jar with hot soapy water, rinse well and stand to dry.

Place the chili, bell pepper (if using), garlic, ginger, pineapple (and juice) and salt in a food processor. Whiz until finely chopped.

Transfer to a saucepan with the remaining ingredients. Bring the mixture to the boil, stirring, then cook for a further 10–15 minutes, or until most of the liquid has been absorbed.

Transfer the hot sauce to the jar and seal the lid. The sambal will keep sealed in a cool dark place for up to 6 months. Once opened, it will keep in the fridge for up to 1 month.

Serve as a condiment alongside anything that needs a spicy kick – from rice, to veggies, to soups and curries.

HONKIGNESE (VEGO) XO

MAKES 3 X 14 OZ (400 ML) JARS

0 g (1¾ oz) dried
  shiitake mushrooms
 cups (1 liter)
  vegetable stock
 cup (150 g) fermented
  black beans, rinsed
50 g (9 oz) canned
  bamboo shoots, drained
 cup (50 g) raw peanuts
 French shallots, chopped
2 garlic cloves, chopped
0 g (1 oz) fresh ginger,
  peeled and finely
  chopped (about
  2½ tablespoons)
 long red chilis,
  seeded and chopped

1 cup (250 ml) peanut oil
2 tablespoons sesame oil
⅓ cup (90 g) tomato paste
¼ cup (30 g) Korean chili
  flakes (from Asian
  shops, used for kimchi)
2 tablespoons chili flakes
1 teaspoon sichuan
  peppercorns
½ cup (125 ml) shaoxing
  rice wine
2 tablespoons soy sauce
2 tablespoons Chinese
  black vinegar
4 star anise

Place the dried mushrooms in a bowl and cover with the
stock. Place the beans in a separate bowl and cover with
cold water. Soak both overnight at room temperature.

The next day, drain the beans, then rinse and drain
once more. Transfer to a large tray lined with paper towel
to dry. Drain and reserve the liquid from the mushrooms,
then transfer the mushrooms to a food processor and
whiz until coarsely chopped. Transfer to the tray lined
with paper towel to dry out.

Add the bamboo shoots and peanuts to the food
processor and whiz until finely chopped, then transfer
to the same tray. Finally, whiz the shallot, garlic, ginger
and fresh chilis in the food processor until finely
chopped but not puréed.

Heat the peanut and sesame oil in a large
heavy-based saucepan over medium–high heat.
Add the mushroom, bean and bamboo shoot mixture
and cook for 10 minutes, or until beginning to crisp.

Add the shallot mixture and cook for a further
0 minutes, or until it starts sticking to the bottom

of the pan. Stir in the tomato paste, all the chili flakes
and the sichuan peppercorns, then cook for 1–2 minutes,
or until darkened.

Deglaze the pan with the rice wine, stirring well,
and bring to a simmer. Add the soy sauce, vinegar,
star anise and reserved mushroom soaking liquid.
Bring to a gentle simmer and cook for 20–25 minutes,
or until the mixture has reduced and most of the liquid
has been absorbed.

Meanwhile, wash three 400 ml (14 fl oz) jars with
hot soapy water, rinse well and stand to dry.

Transfer the hot mixture to the clean jars and seal
the lids. The XO will keep in sealed jars in a cool dark
place for up to 6 months. Once opened, keep in the
fridge and use within 1–2 months.

Serve as a condiment to enhance anything from
tofu to rice to stir-fried veggie dishes.

VIETNAMESE GREEN OR RED NUOC CHAM

MAKES ABOUT ¾ CUP (185 ML)

¼ cup (60 ml) fish sauce
juice of 1 lime
1 garlic clove, finely grated
1 small cucumber,
  finely chopped
1 long green or red chili,
  thinly sliced

2 tablespoons rice wine
  or white vinegar
1 tablespoon
  granulated sugar

Combine all the ingredients in a clean ¾ cup (185 ml)
jar or airtight container. Store in the fridge and use
within 2 weeks.

Serve as a dipping sauce with Vietnamese dishes
such as rice paper rolls, spring rolls or skewers, use as
a salad dressing or seafood marinade, or pour over rice
or noodles.

Purple

* **TURNIP**
  + Rutabaga
* **BEET**
  + Golden beet
* **RADICCHIO**
  + Endive
* **ARTICHOKE**
* **EGGPLANT**

Turnip

Traditionally, the pretty purple-tinged turnip has copped a rough rap for being the 'Beggar's Brassica', which can best be attributed to its capacity for growing well under trying conditions, and being under-appreciated by careless cook through no fault of its own. It is true that turnips, when overcooked, lose their purple hue and become pallid in both taste and color, and – as all brassicas are wont to do – waft a sulfurous stench throughout the house, soaking into all soft furnishings and probably walls. However, if we simply stopped boiling and started browning them instead, turnips become sweet, gem-like globs, fork-tender, with a hint of mustardy heat. Turnips also respond extremely well to being pickled, retaining their solid constitution and providing a crunchy 'kerpow!' in kebabs and shawarma dishes. I'm particularly fond of plopping a small peeled beet inside the jar, as its color quickly seeps into the turnip chunks, painting them a spectacular shade of fuschia – especially handy for brightening dishes that are dangerously teetering on fifty shades of brown.

'For me, cooking vegetables is so much more complex than a piece of beef or lamb. One favorite, which we've been doing for several years, is the tagliatelle of turnip. Cooked in an emulsion of parmesan rind, butter, dashi and nutmeg, we serve it with greenhouse pesto or a game ragout, depending on the season.' – S AT B A I N S , U K

BUYING & STORING

Whether it's particles of dirt attached to root ends, or bruises and discoloration from transport, all are easy to spot on a pearlescent turnip. Luckily, unless you're planning on slicing finely and quick pickling, or peeling and serving as crudités, any brown bits will soon be peeled off or roasted away. Smaller and mid-sized turnips are sweetest, with the flavor becoming spicier and the texture woodier as they age; save the bigger ones for pickling. You'll likely find the smaller ones in summer, while autumn and winter stocks are bigger and more robust. Those with their tops still attached are always preferable – firstly because it's a marker of freshness when they're still bright green and billowy, but also because they're extra bang-for-buck. Slice the tops off as soon as you get them home, and wrap and store as you would herbs. Just soak and spin them well before cooking, as these kinds of greens are notoriously gritty.

BEYOND TURNIP: RUTABAGA

Though the turnip as we know it – white and maybe a little purple – was probably cultivated in Eurasia, by the 16th century in Scandinavia (hence its alternative name, Swede) the rutabaga was gaining a fine reputation for its robustness, both in growing and in flavor. Thought to be a hybrid of turnip and cabbage, the rutabaga can be subbed in for turnip, with a few marked differences. The most noticeable is color: rutabaga are ombré shades of yellow-orange-brown, with the occasional pop of purple. They're also larger, and unlike turnips, keep their sweetness even when bigger. Some even say rutabaga have a superior flavor to turnips, so if you're a stickler for authenticity, dishes such as Scottish 'neeps and tatties', Cornish pasties and Southern glazed rutabaga are ones for which they should be sought. Unless you're roasting and serving whole, or keeping them fresh for crudités (where baby turnip works best), it's worth giving a rutabaga a try. A final note: pay attention to the outer skin of rutabaga, which is often coated with a thin layer of paraffin wax before selling to stop it drying out. This is why most recipes call for the skin to be peeled before cooking, but you can also clean the wax off with a rough vegetable brush and hot water.

WITH COMPLEMENTS

Allspice, bacon, butter, caraway seeds, cream, herbs (parsley, thyme), juniper berries, lemon.

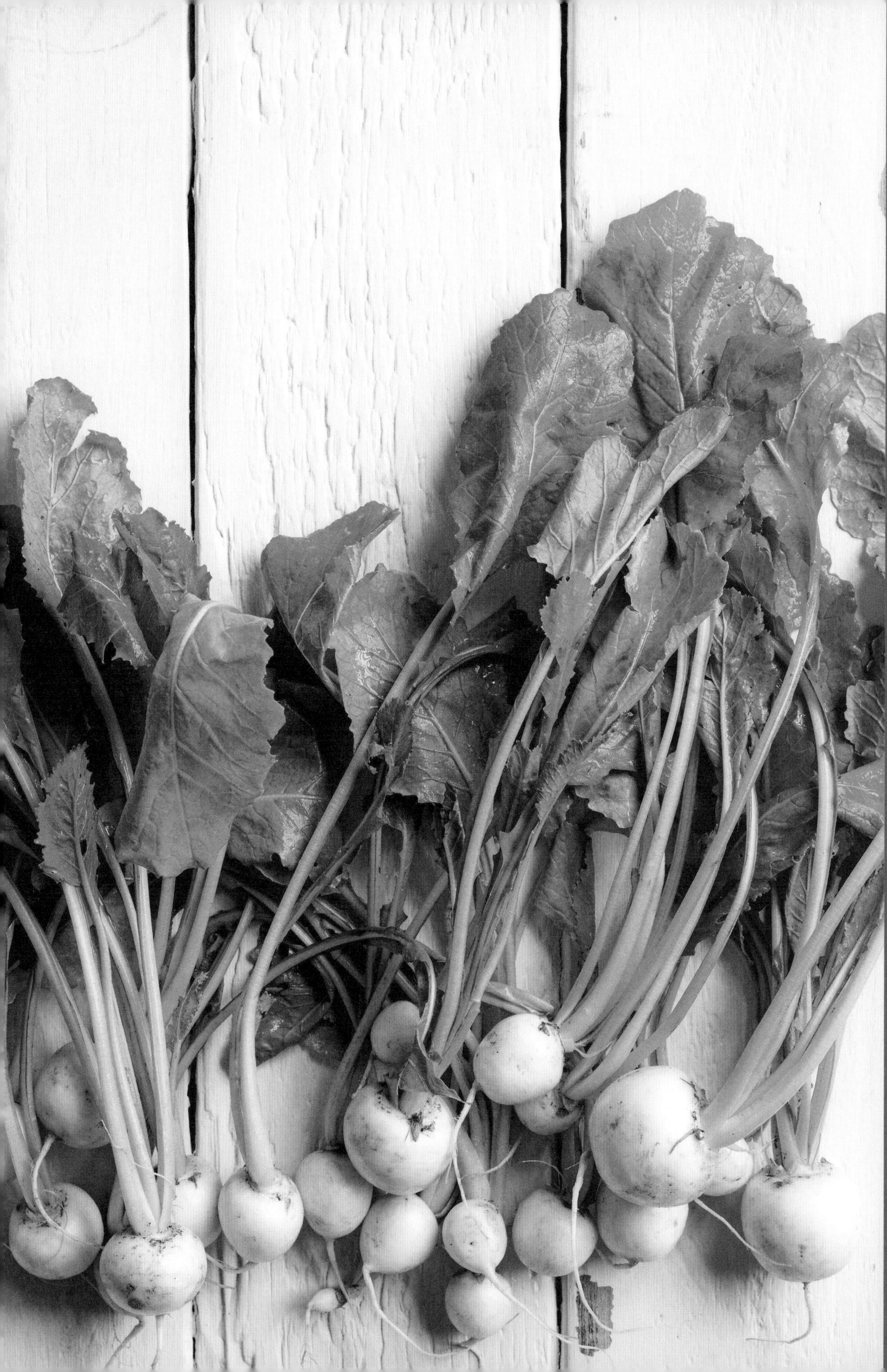

CIDER-BRAISED TURNIPS WITH SOURDOUGH CRUMB

Turnips are a surprisingly versatile ingredient – in fact, I like to think of them as albino beets. Like beets, turnips love being baked, especially when they're given a flavorful broth to soak up, like in a braise. Here, that broth is cider-spiked, and the funky, floral, fruity flavors, alongside the softened baby turnips which are naturally a little sweet, plus crunchy sourdough crumbs on top, make this a little like a savory crumble.

SERVES 4

800 g (1 lb 12 oz) baby turnips

100 g (3½ oz) unsalted butter, chopped

2 French shallots, thinly sliced

1 celery stalk, or the stalks of 1 fennel bulb, finely chopped

1 tablespoon dried juniper berries, bruised

1 teaspoon coriander seeds, crushed

2 cups (500 ml) apple cider

1 cup (250 ml) chicken stock

1 teaspoon brown sugar

1 cup (110 g) sourdough breadcrumbs

30 g (1 oz) parmesan, finely grated

finely grated zest of 1 lemon

dill sprigs, to serve

Clean and trim the turnips, leaving a 2 cm (¾ inch) stem. Halve the bigger ones.

Heat half the butter in a heavy-based saucepan. Add the shallot, celery and spices and cook, stirring frequently, for 3 minutes, or until softened. Add the turnips, cider, stock and sugar and season with salt and pepper. Bring to the boil, then cover with a cartouche of parchment paper (see tip) and cook for 15 minutes, or until the turnips are tender.

Remove the parchment paper and continue to cook for a further 8 minutes, or until the sauce has reduced and the turnips are tender. Transfer to a heatproof serving dish.

Preheat the broiler to high.

In a bowl, combine the breadcrumbs, parmesan, lemon zest and remaining butter, then sprinkle the mixture over the turnips.

Place the dish under the broiler for 3–5 minutes, or until the topping is golden. Sprinkle with dill, freshly cracked black pepper and flaked sea salt and serve.

Tip Make a cartouche by folding a piece of parchment paper in half, then in half again. Cut a hole in the center fold, and then cut the outside in a semicircle to fit your pan. Open the paper out, check that it fits the pan, then pop it on top to help slow the evaporation of the liquid without reincorporating any steam.

Double duty Toss some arugula through any left-over baby turnips and crumbs, together with some sort of soft cheese like goat or feta, for a quick and easy salad for lunch.

PICKLE ME PINK TURNIPS

Aside from being incredibly striking, these magenta marvels are full of salt-n-vinegar sass that is fantastic fodder for a falafel (or any enrobed meat-veg-wrap combo) and late-night fork-in-jar cravings. Turnips suck up the beet color along with any aromatics quickly, yielding yummy half-moons within a day. The flavor will intensify the longer they are submerged in the liquid, but the texture peaks at about a week.

MAKES ABOUT 800 G (1 LB 12 OZ)

⅓ cup (25 g) flaked sea salt

⅓ cup (75 g) granulated sugar

100 g (3½ oz) beets, chopped into 1 cm (½ inch) cubes

2 garlic cloves, peeled and bruised

zest of 1 lemon

1 teaspoon black peppercorns

4 bay leaves

800 g (1 lb 12 oz) turnips, peeled and cut into 2 cm (¾ inch) half-moons

1 cup (250 ml) white vinegar

Pop the salt, sugar, beets, garlic, lemon zest, peppercorns, bay leaves and 2 cups (500 ml) water in a saucepan over high heat and bring to the boil. Remove from the heat, add the turnips and leave to cool completely, then stir in the vinegar. Strain the turnips into a jug, reserving the spices and liquid.

Wash a 1.6 liter (55 fl oz) jar with hot soapy water and leave to dry. Add the turnips and spices. Pour in the liquid, all the way to the top, to cover the turnips. Seal the lid, then leave in a cool dark place for 5 days to pickle.

The lid should properly seal in this time, due to the pressure from the pickling; it should pop to concave. If it doesn't, store the jar in the fridge and use within 1 month. Otherwise, you can store in a cool dark place for up to 3 months.

Tip Baby turnips can be pickled halved, while larger turnips are best as wedges or batons.

Double duty Who am I kidding ... these never make it into a dish! I just eat them straight out of the jar.

RUTABAGA SPIRAL TIAN WITH BALSAMIC GLAZE

This is such a visually arresting dish, and frankly, such a fabulous way of making use of a veg that is so often seen as a bit drab. You can also get creative with what else you layer up into a tian – from ratatouille combos of zucchini, eggplant, tomato and summer squash, to borschy tian with beet, carrot and turnip. A mandoline will come in handy, but some of the fancier food processors will do the job, too.

SERVES 4–6

1.2 kg (2 lb 10 oz) rutabagas or turnips, thinly sliced with a mandoline

¾ cup (185 ml) olive oil

1½ teaspoons flaked sea salt

1½ tablespoons granulated sugar

1 teaspoon freshly cracked black pepper

100 ml (3½ fl oz) vegetable stock

Caramelized balsamic (page 340), to serve

Preheat the oven to 400°F.

Put the rutabaga slices in a bowl. Drizzle with a few tablespoons of the olive oil, then sprinkle with the salt, sugar and pepper and toss until well coated.

Arrange the rutabaga slices in a round baking dish in a spiral pattern, starting from the outside and working your way in.

Drizzle with a little more olive oil, then pour the stock into the bottom of the pan. Cover with foil and bake for 45 minutes, or until the rutabaga is knife-tender.

Remove the foil from the dish. Glaze the rutabaga slices with the remaining olive oil and bake for another 30–35 minutes, or until burnished on top.

Drizzle with the caramelized balsamic and serve to gasps at the table.

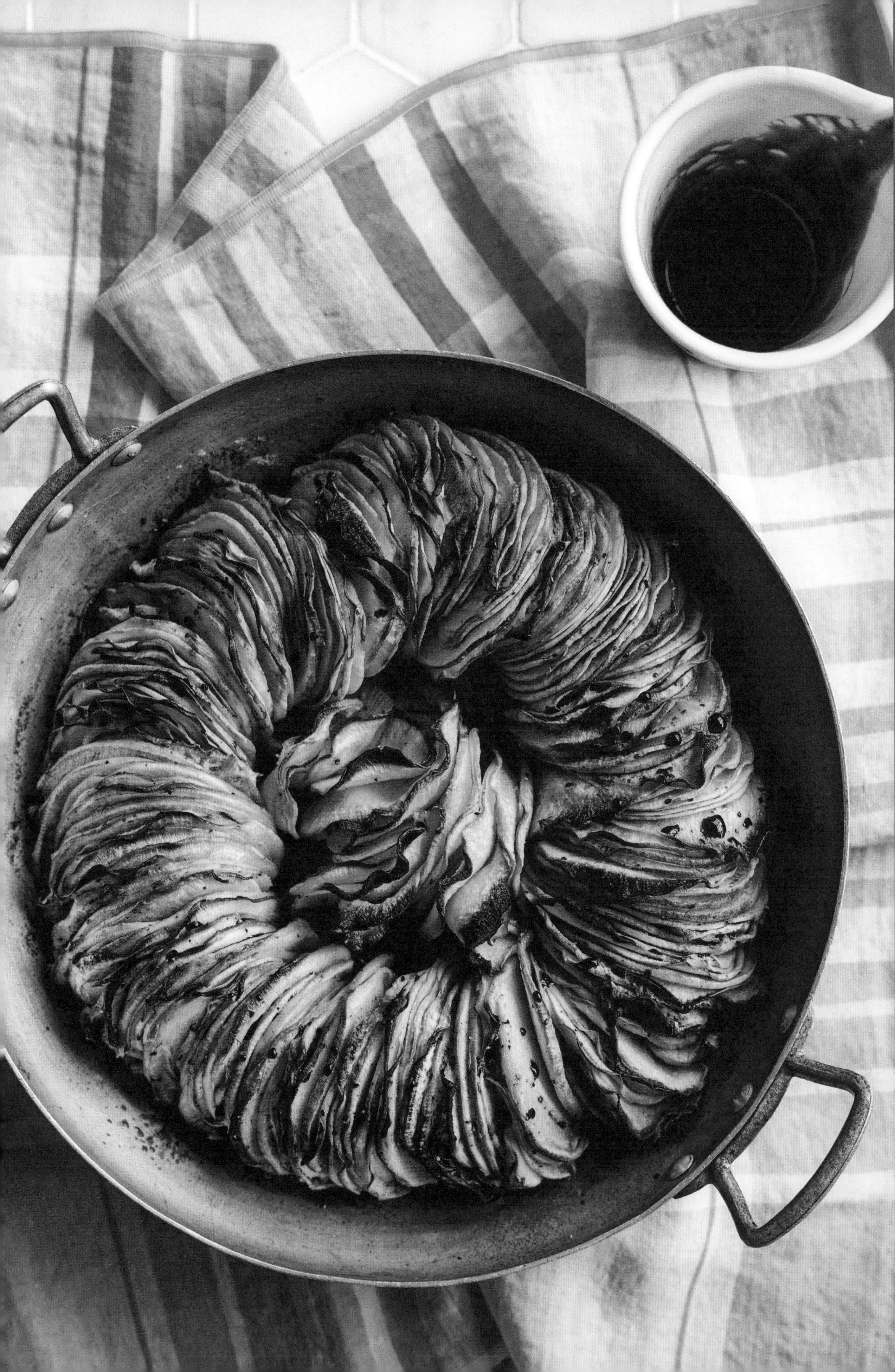

Beet

Forget 'blue blood' – my veins run *purple* with the juice of a billion beets! If, however, you didn't grow up with after-school borsch, allow me to introduce you to the Dark Prince of the vegetable world. With its bold, earthy flavor and unmistakable magenta hue, this root veg is sure to leave an indelible mark ... on clothes, tablecloths, dishes and hands. Raw, steamed, boiled or roasted, beet enhances any dish you add it to with both color and taste – though, in true royal fashion, it's always better as the star of the show, so think about keeping the other elements simple and letting the beet set the beat. Beet greens are also incredibly tasty, being card-carrying members of the same family that gives us spinach and chard ('chard-carrying members', then?). Blanch and blitz these greens into dips or sauté as you would spinach, but save the smaller leaves for tossing into your next beet salad, for the ultimate root-to-stem conversation starter. And remember to soak both leaves and bulb well – this is not the kind of 'earthiness' we are going for.

> 'Beet is one vegetable whose texture really benefits from low-temperature cooking. We even extract the liquid that comes off during cooking and turn this intensely red juice into a vinaigrette or sauce.' – JOAN ROCA, SPAIN

BUYING & STORING

Greengrocers often offer bunches of fresher or smaller beets with their greens still on, particularly in winter when beets are at their loudest, as well as older or bigger beets loose much of the year through. If attached, the leaves should stand to attention, with glossy, wavy edges and no signs of slackening or slime; the odd bent or broken bit is fine, as this is usually indicative of an overzealous shop-packer rather than a defective product. Mid-sized, roundish red and purple beets are the most commonly available, but don't go past the oblong Cylindra variety whenever you come across it, as it's great for uniform slicing. Beyond the familiar reds and purples, beets can be white, golden, or multi-hued – such as the Bulls-eye or Chioggia beets, which are fuschia on the outside, and striped white and pink within. No matter the color, beets will start to lose the luster in their skin the longer they're out of the ground, turning decidedly muted, like someone has turned the brightness down on your screen. As long as the beet itself is still firm to touch and the root end hasn't started to wrinkle and wither, the color will come good again once you give them a good wash and scrub before cooking.

Separate roots from leaves as soon as you get beets home. Store the tops as you would any leafy greens, wrapped in damp paper towel or cloth. When bought fresh, beets can live in your crisper for up to a fortnight, as long as you keep the dirt on and give them a squeeze to check for moisture loss every now and then. Freezing works best if you boil the beets first, chop into chunks and lay them out to flash freeze on a tray, then portion out into labelled containers for the freezer, where they'll keep for a good year or so. You can also pickle your own beets by boiling until fork-tender (30–45 minutes, depending on size), slipping the skins off once cooked, then popping into clean jars and covering with a spiced pickling liquid, made with equal quantities of water and vinegar and one part sugar.

COOKING WITH

If you're looking to serve them whole or grate raw into a salad, go for beets the size of squash balls, as these will give you a pretty presentation, and yield the added benefit of leaves for picking into the salad, too. For soups or giant jacket beets, go big or go home. Unlike their fellow root veggies, beets don't tend to become woodier as they age and grow, so there's no harm in using bigger ones – just bear in mind that you'll need to set aside ample time to ensure they're cooked through. If you're serving baked or boiled purple beets as part of a broader dish, keep them isolated until the last moment, as they're likely to bleed into everything. Even yellow beets have this potential, though not as diabolically as red ones.

It would be remiss of me not to mention that beets also have a reputation as the gift that keeps on giving, causing the odd lavatory conniption while trying to recall whether you'd grated some beets into that risotto last night.

BEYOND BEET: GOLDEN BEET

The golden child of the beet family, these are sweeter and milder than purple beets, and don't make a mess of everything they touch. Texturally speaking, they are also less fibrous, with thinner skins, giving more scope for keeping them raw and shredding into salads, or slicing thinly and serving with soft cheeses. Golden beets also make for quicker pickling, and look especially dramatic glowing in a jar bobbing with dill and spices. They have a much higher starch content than purple beets, and their lighter color makes them susceptible to dark spots. If you've ever tried roasting them using the same hot 'n' heavy principles as for the purple ones, you may have been confronted by an unbecoming 'fade to black' effect through the center, or you might pull them out of the fridge the next morning to find darkness creeping in around any edges. This can be mitigated by roasting them low and slow at around 300°F until they're fork-tender, or boiling them rather than roasting. If storing them overnight before using, try tossing in equal parts oil and an acidic agent such as white wine vinegar or lemon juice.

WITH COMPLEMENTS

Caraway, cheese (especially cream cheese, blue, goat), citrus (especially lemon, orange, blood orange), herbs (especially chervil, chives, dill, parsley, tarragon), honey, horseradish, garlic, vinegar (especially balsamic), walnuts.

Can do!

If you have a beet hankering but are in a hurry, pre-cooked beets – either canned or vacuum-packed – are worth considering. Check the label for extra ingredients such as sugar or acetic acid, which can affect the flavor – though, if you've ever had a 'proper' burger in Australia, you'd know that canned beet slices are ideal for slipping in for some extra pickle-factor. Vacuum-packed beets, increasingly found alongside fresh beets, are peeled and cooked, with nothing added, and ready to serve straight out of the pack. As well as making mid-week beet dishes a cinch, they're also great for packing to take along on trips off-the-beaten-track, when you're not sure how much fresh produce is around – just add a packet of mixed salad leaves and a sprinkling of trail mix and there'll be smiles all round.

GRATE BORSCH

Borsch was served almost every day when I was growing up. The ingredients were cheap, and it was easy for mum to make big batches of. All my big brother Stan and I had to do when we came home from school was to pour what we needed into a small pot and heat it up – or whack it in the microwave if we were in a rush to get back to *Widget the World Watcher* on telly.

These days, I still insist on having a batch of borsch in the fridge whenever possible. It's a convenient and delicious way of getting eight or so different veggies in one whack, so that even if we're on the run, or out for a fancy (read: rich!) meal, we still feel satisfied and nourished at the end of the day. In summer, turn this into a gazpacho-style cold soup by whizzing it up to a purée with an immersion blender once cool, and serving cold with slices of cucumber, radish, grated garlic, dill and sour cream.

SERVES 6–8 (WITH LEFTOVERS)

1 onion, roughly chopped
2 garlic cloves, roughly chopped
2 tablespoons olive oil
700 g (1 lb 9 oz) cauliflower (½ large one, or 1 small), or 2 heads of broccoli
½ small cabbage (or ¼ of a larger one), shredded
2 carrots, shredded
2 celery stalks, thinly sliced, tops reserved for garnishing
2 beets (400 g/14 oz), shredded

12 cups (3 liters) vegetable or chicken stock
juice of ½ lemon
⅓ cup (80 ml) sauerkraut or pickle brine (optional)

To serve
dill sprigs
sour cream or crème fraîche
grated garlic
croutons or thinly sliced baguette

Whack the onion and garlic into a big saucepan with the olive oil. Let them start to sizzle over medium heat, then pop the lid on and allow the onion to sweat away in its own juices for 5–10 minutes until translucent, stirring occasionally.

Meanwhile, turn the cauliflower upside down and cut into the core at an angle, so that the florets all come off with a pull. Now pull them apart until they're bite-sized. Set aside.

Once the onion has sweated down and is fragrant, add the cabbage, carrot, celery and beets. Pour in the stock, then supplement with extra water (preferably filtered) until your pan of choice is three-quarters full. Squeeze in the lemon juice (to keep the brightness of the beets) and add a good pinch of salt.

Bring to the boil, then reduce the heat and simmer for another 10 minutes. Add the cauliflower florets and cook until the shredded beets are easily bitten through, but not mushy and the cauliflower softens slightly; keeping some 'bite' here is the key for both flavor and texture.

Season to taste with the brine, if using, as well as salt and freshly ground black pepper. Garnish with dill and the reserved celery leaves, and serve with sour cream, grated garlic and croutons – or what you will!

Extra **This is one dish where *schmaltz* (chicken fat, duck fat) enriches the flavor in a most delightful way. You could also add a little butter when sweating the onions, or a spoonful of jam or honey for sweetness.**

PARCEL-ROASTED BEETS WITH JEWELLED COUSCOUS

There's a lot of drama to this dish, which takes a pretty jewelled couscous and makes it even more beautiful with the addition of a rainbow of beets.

SERVES 6

finely grated zest and juice of 1 orange

2 tablespoons pomegranate molasses, plus extra to serve

1 teaspoon flaked sea salt

1 teaspoon freshly cracked black pepper

⅓ cup (80 ml) extra virgin olive oil

2 bunches (350 g/12 oz) of baby golden, bulls-eye or mixed beets, trimmed, leaving 4 cm (1½ inch) of stem attached, any smaller leaves picked and reserved for salad

1 red onion, finely chopped

1 bunch of parsley, leaves picked and chopped, stems finely chopped

⅓ cup (60 g) dried apricots, chopped

½ teaspoon ras el hanout

1 cup (200 g) instant couscous

1½ cups (375 ml) chicken or vegetable stock

seeds from ½ pomegranate

½ cup (65 g) chopped pistachios

mint leaves, to serve

Preheat the oven to 425°F.

In a bowl, combine the orange zest and juice, pomegranate molasses, salt, pepper and 2 tablespoons of the olive oil.

Cut out two 40 cm (16 inch) rounds of parchment paper. Place one round over a medium-sized bowl, then add half the beets and half the orange juice mixture. Bring all the sides of the parchment paper in like you would an Australian Christmas pudding, then bind tightly with kitchen string. Place on a baking tray and repeat to make another parcel.

Bake the parcels for 30 minutes, or until the beets are tender when pierced with a knife. Remove from the oven and leave to cool slightly. Remove the string from one of the parcels and carefully tip the beets and juices into a large bowl, then repeat with the other parcel. Halve or quarter the beets and return to the bowl, tossing to coat in the juices.

Meanwhile, heat the remaining 2 tablespoons olive oil in a saucepan over high heat. Add the onion, parsley stems, apricot and ras el hanout and cook for 3 minutes, or until the onion has softened.

Add the couscous and stir to coat and heat through. Pour in the stock and bring to the boil, then cover and remove from the heat. Stand for 10 minutes to steam the couscous.

Use a fork to break up the couscous, then transfer to a bowl with the parsley leaves. Gently toss to mix.

Pile the couscous onto a serving platter. Spoon the beets and juices over, then sprinkle with the pomegranate seeds, pistachios, mint and beet leaves (if using) to serve.

Tip If you're using mixed baby beets, you might like to separate the darker-colored ones from the light to stop the colors bleeding into each other. The color will also bleed into the couscous, so keep the darker beets separate until just ready to serve. You could also try the muffin pan method on page 242, if you're feeling experimental.

Shortcut Many grocery stores now stock ready-boiled beets, which could easily slip into this dish if you're in a hurry.

Go gluten free Use blitzed cauliflower couscous (page 83) to speed this salad up even further, and add a bonus bit of veg, too.

BEET & HONEY ROASTED WALNUT SALAD

Roasted beets belong in salad, and they absolutely adore nuts. Here, the nuts are roasted with honey, which adds another note of sweetness to play off the soil sweeties that beets are. Make the elements the night before a soirée, keep the ingredients separate from each other, then assemble on the spot in seconds. That's what my friend Celia, who tested this recipe out on her co-workers, did. And they all asked for the recipe. Here it is.

SERVES 4

12 small beets; baby ones that are on the larger side would be perfect	¼ cup (60 ml) extra virgin olive oil
1 cup (115 g) walnuts	60 g (2 oz) baby arugula leaves
2 tablespoons honey	150 g (5½ oz) creamy blue cheese, thinly sliced or crumbled
¼ cup (60 ml) sherry vinegar	

Preheat the oven to 425°F. Grease and line a baking tray with parchment paper.

Trim the beets, leaving a 3 cm (1¼ inch) stem attached. Wash the trimmed leaves, if you have any, and chill in iced water until required.

Take a 12-hole muffin pan and place a beet in each hole. Fill the holes three-quarters full with cold water. Cover the pan with foil, then bake for 40–45 minutes, or until the beets are cooked through and tender when pierced with a knife. Remove from the oven, pull the foil off and leave to cool for 15 minutes.

Meanwhile, pop the walnuts on the lined baking tray. Drizzle with the honey, sprinkle with flaked sea salt and bake for 6 minutes, or until the walnuts are toasted and the honey is bubbling. Remove from the oven and leave to cool and crisp, then roughly chop and set aside.

Remove the beets from the muffin holes with tongs, then use your fingertips to remove the skins. Cut into wedges, transfer to a bowl with the vinegar and olive oil, then toss to coat. (You can leave the beets to steep overnight, either covered on the counter if it's a cool evening, or in the fridge and brought back to room temperature for serving. If so, store the toasted walnuts in an airtight container to keep them crisp.)

To serve, sprinkle a platter with the arugula leaves. Pour over the beets and juices from the bowl, then sprinkle with the walnuts and cheese.

Tips Roasting each beet in a water bath in a muffin tin means each one is individually taken care of. This method also means you can use different colored beets – such as Bulls-eye and golden beets – and the colors won't bleed into each other, so feel free to get creative.

If you're *sans* muffin pan, try roasting the beets in a parchment paper parcel, as you would for the jewelled couscous salad on page 240.

CHEATROOT RELISH

Relishes can be a lot of work, which we often don't got time for. That's why this one uses precooked beets and store-bought cocktail onions as the base, so all you have to do is whiz. Wheeee! This is such a quick 'whatever' recipe, that it really doesn't deserve investment in special jars. Just hold onto any glass jars from store-bought ferments, jams or nut butters, and transfer whatever you won't eat right away into them for later. Be sure to keep plenty of this relish aside for serving alongside frittata, inside sandwiches, or with bangers and mash for dinner.

MAKES 650 G (1 LB 7 OZ)

500 g (1 lb 2 oz)
    precooked beets,
    coarsely grated
225 g (8 oz) jar pickled
    cocktail onions (or
    120 g/4 oz pickled red
    onions from page 282),
    plus ½ cup (125 ml) of
    the pickling liquid

1 granny smith apple,
    cored and chopped
¼ cup (60 g) firmly
    packed brown sugar
5 cloves
½ teaspoon
    ground allspice

Wash 850 ml (29 fl oz) worth of jars in hot soapy water and stand to dry on a rack.

Place the beets, pickled onions and the onion pickling liquid in a food processor. Add the apple and sugar and whiz until finely chopped.

Transfer to a wide saucepan or deep-sided frying pan and add the cloves, allspice and 2 cups (500 ml) water. Bring to the boil, reduce the heat to medium and simmer for 20 minutes, or until most of the liquid has been absorbed.

Transfer the hot relish to the clean jars and seal the lids. You can also pop some in the fridge in a lidded glass container if you're planning to eat it straight away, or within 2–3 weeks.

Alternatively, transfer the jars to a medium–large saucepan, then pour in enough water to cover. Bring the water to the boil, then turn the heat off and stand for 15 minutes. Remove the jars from the water and allow to cool. Check that the seal on the lids has popped to concave. If not, return the jars to the water, bring back to the boil and repeat the process.

The sealed jars will keep in the pantry for up to 4 months. Once opened, store in the fridge, and use within 1 month.

Tip You'll find precooked baby beets vacuum-sealed in the fresh fruit and vegetable section at most supermarkets.

Shortcut You can try making this with canned beets, too. Just sweat down some onion and apple, then add the spices, sugar, garlic and chopped beets and simmer away for 15 minutes until concentrated.

Rainbow
labneh balls
(page 246)

No-bake
beet salad
(page 246)

NO-BAKE BEET SALAD WITH RAINBOW LABNEH BALLS

I probably shouldn't bring attention to this, but there are way too many beet salads in this book. I'm actually a bit addicted to them. I love the way beets can change texture, from soft and syrupy in a bake, to firm and al dente when served like this – and the color alone gives enough drama that guests are sure to comment. Some beets lend themselves better to this kind of application than others. If you can manage it, find some Bulls-eye or golden beets, which have a finer composition, or at least seek out baby purple beets, which are less fibrous too.

SERVES 4–6

Rainbow labneh

250 g (9 oz) Greek-style
    yogurt
2 tablespoons
    ground sumac
2 tablespoons pink
    peppercorns, finely
    chopped or crushed
3 tablespoons dukkah
    (preferably with
    pistachio nuts)
2 tablespoons
    poppy seeds
2 tablespoons freshly
    cracked black pepper
3 tablespoons finely
    chopped dill fronds

Pomegranate dressing

2 tablespoons
    pomegranate molasses
1 teaspoon dijon mustard
1 garlic clove, peeled
    and bruised
1 teaspoon honey
¼ cup (60 ml) olive oil
¼ cup (60 ml) blood
    orange juice

Salad

6 baby bulls-eye beets,
    washed and scrubbed
6 baby golden beets,
    washed and scrubbed
3 cups (150 g) baby kale
    leaves or arugula
1 blood orange, halved
    (optional)

Start on the rainbow labneh the night before. Line a sieve or colander with cheesecloth or a clean tea towel. Pop the yogurt in, then hang the sieve over a bowl and leave in the fridge for the liquid to drain. By morning, the yogurt will have become much firmer. (Reserve the whey – the liquid left in the bowl – for making pancakes, or your own yogurt.)

Combine all the dressing ingredients in a jar and shake to emulsify. Alternatively, use a whisk – this dressing should be thick and glossy. Taste for sweetness. If the blood orange is quite bitter, add an extra teaspoon of honey. Leave in the bruised garlic until just before serving, to let the flavor infuse as much as possible.

To roll the labneh, set up a small fingerbowl of water for keeping your palms moist. Set up four saucers or plates: one with the sumac and pink peppercorns; one with dukkah; one with the poppy seeds and cracked pepper; one with dill. Set up a lined baking tray.

Use a teaspoon measure to shape balls of labneh, gently rolling them between your palms, then tossing in one of the saucers and applying a little pressure to help the crust of spices or herbs stick. Lay the rolled rainbow balls on the baking tray. Once all of them are done, pop them in the fridge for 20 minutes to firm up.

Meanwhile, prepare the salad. Thinly slice all the beets using a mandoline and place in a serving bowl. Drizzle the dressing through the beets, tossing to coat. Pop the kale leaves on top, ready to be tossed through just before serving (this will keep the kale from wilting on too much contact with the oil).

Once the salad has been tossed, arrange the blood orange halves on the sides, if using, then the rainbow labneh balls on top. Encourage guests to scoop at the labneh balls in the bowl, and then fork them into theatrical creamy dressing on their plates, with a bonus squeeze of blood orange if they're so inclined.

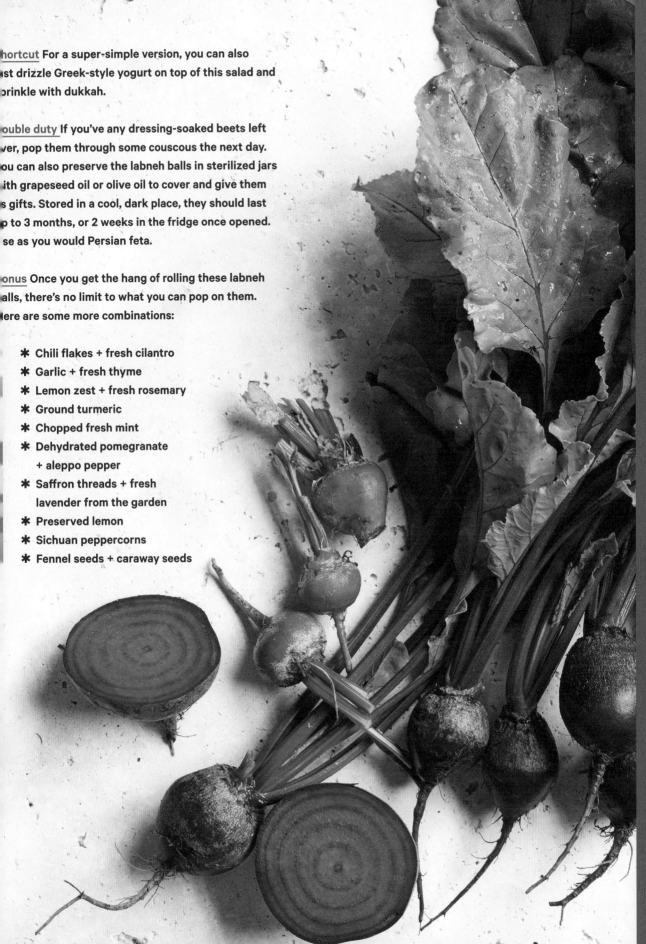

Shortcut For a super-simple version, you can also just drizzle Greek-style yogurt on top of this salad and sprinkle with dukkah.

Double duty If you've any dressing-soaked beets left over, pop them through some couscous the next day. You can also preserve the labneh balls in sterilized jars with grapeseed oil or olive oil to cover and give them as gifts. Stored in a cool, dark place, they should last up to 3 months, or 2 weeks in the fridge once opened. Use as you would Persian feta.

Bonus Once you get the hang of rolling these labneh balls, there's no limit to what you can pop on them. Here are some more combinations:

* Chili flakes + fresh cilantro
* Garlic + fresh thyme
* Lemon zest + fresh rosemary
* Ground turmeric
* Chopped fresh mint
* Dehydrated pomegranate
  + aleppo pepper
* Saffron threads + fresh
  lavender from the garden
* Preserved lemon
* Sichuan peppercorns
* Fennel seeds + caraway seeds

BLENDER BEET BROWNIE (BBB)

This oozy, gluten-free skillet sweetie takes inspiration from Claudia Roden's world-famous orange-almond cake, where oranges are boiled until completely soft, then used to give both flavor and moisture to an almond meal base. Except I've brownie-fied this with the addition of dark chocolate and whizzed it into a wintry wonderland with beets. I'm especially enamored with the color – a kind of deep burgundy that could almost be red-velvet – and the flavor of chocolate cakes. I like to keep this brownie quite gooey in the middle (like a lava cake), but if you'd prefer to slice and be more sensible, bake it for a little longer.

SERVES 6-8

1 orange (preferably organic)

1 beet of a similar size to the orange, plus 1 small finely sliced beet

200 g (7 oz) butter, melted

200 g (7 oz) dark chocolate, melted, plus 50 g (1¾ oz) extra, chopped for the top

3 eggs

1 cup (220 g) granulated sugar

1 teaspoon natural vanilla extract or paste

2 cups (200 g) almond meal

½ cup (75 g) all-purpose gluten-free flour

½ cup (55 g) unsweetened cocoa powder

½ cup (70 g) walnuts

1 teaspoon baking powder

¼ teaspoon flaked sea salt

yogurt, to serve

Boil the whole orange and beet together in a saucepan, topping up with boiling water regularly to keep them covered. Cook for about 1 hour, until both are soft, and you can put a skewer through them.

Line a 20 cm x 30 cm (8 inch x 12 inch) brownie pan or skillet with parchment paper. (I line all the way up the sides if I'm using a brownie pan and plan to turn the whole thing out, but for the skillet version, simply lining the base of the pan will do.)

When the beet is cool enough to handle (but still warm), use some paper towel or a teaspoon to create some friction and help slip the skin off.

Preheat the oven to 400°F.

Pop the warm beet in a blender or food processor, along with the orange, butter and the 200 g (7 oz) chocolate. Blitz to combine, keeping the machine whirring until a smooth purée forms. Add the eggs, sugar and vanilla and blitz until incorporated.

In a bowl, mix together the almond meal, flour, cocoa, walnuts and baking powder, then add these to your blitz-machine and give it a few pulses, until the lumps of flour have mostly incorporated – but not too much, lest you bake a brick!

Pour the batter into the brownie pan or skillet, then dot with the extra chocolate and beet slices and sprinkle with flaked sea salt. Bake for 40–45 minutes, until the brownie is fudgey and still moist. Don't bother doing the skewer test ... it'll lead you astray.

Allow to cool slightly before digging in. Serve warm with yogurt as a decadent pudding, or cut into small slices for lunchboxes and mid-afternoon snacking. Store in an airtight container in the fridge, where it'll happily keep for at least 1 week (but who are we kidding here?).

Tip I use a mandoline to thinly slice the beets for garnishing, but you can also peel it into strips using a vegetable peeler.

Shortcut Before baking, scoop out ⅓ cup (80 ml) of the batter for zapping in a microwave-proof mug to make a mug cake. It's not as oozy, but if you're desperate and can't wait, the option is there for you.

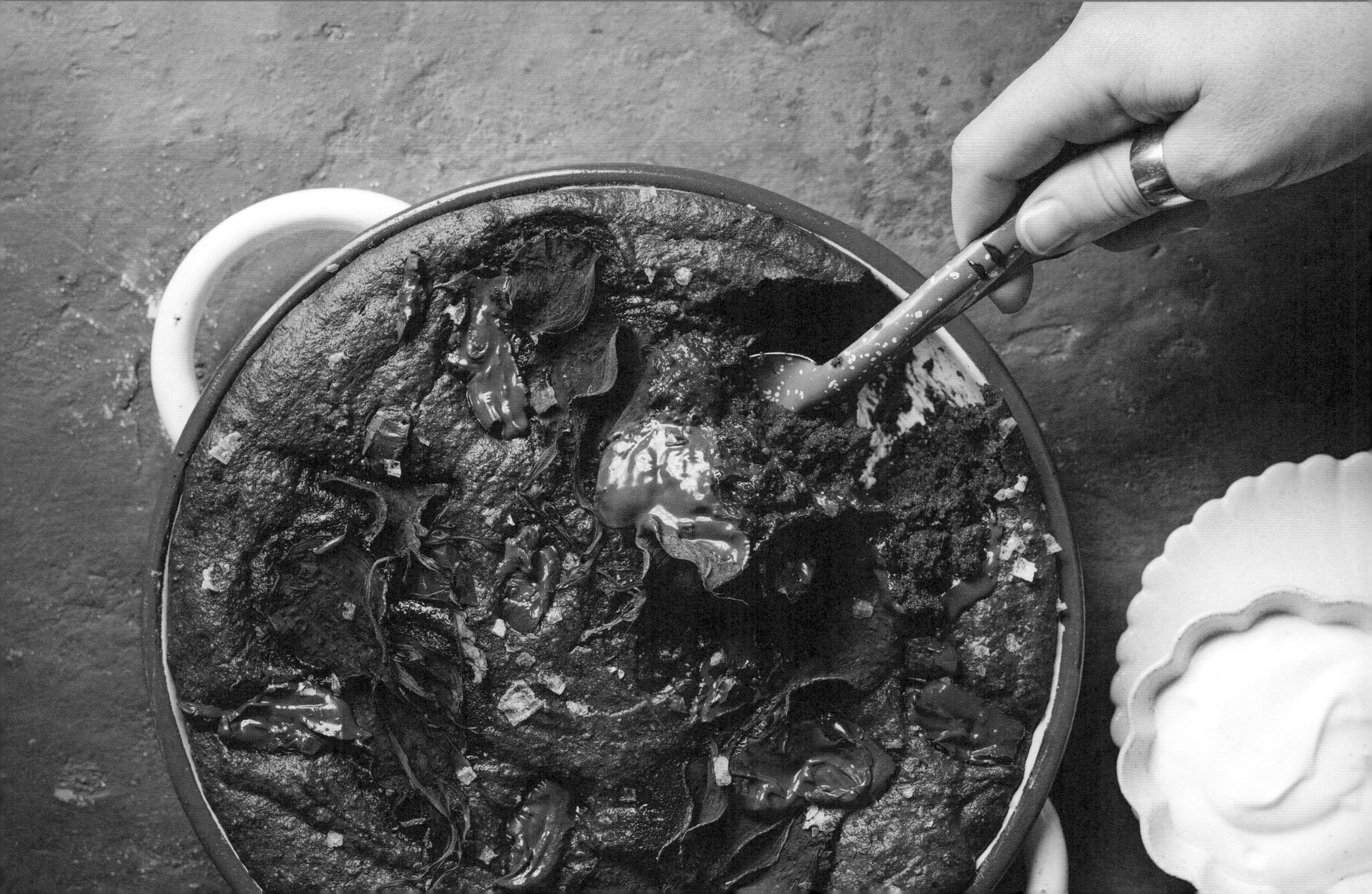

Radicchio

If you're partial to a negroni, or Campari on ice, check out this dark Italian chicory. People either love radicchio, or are yet to learn to. Its bitterness *can* be confronting, particularly in heirloom varieties that haven't been mellowed through breeding to make them more lettuce-y. But if you can get past the initial blast of bitterness across the front palate, and mitigate it with a good pinch of salt, olive oil, and an acidic element such as citrus or balsamic vinegar, you'll be amply rewarded. If you're new to radicchio, try some raw in a salad with more conventional leaves such as lettuce, arugula and red-veined sorrel, or some other variation of pre-mixed small young mesclun leaves. Taste a radicchio leaf, then either tear it or finely slice – the stronger the bite, the smaller the bits.

Radicchio is good raw and cooked, roasted and fried. It's sweet
nd bitter at the same time, making it very versatile. I like every
ype of radicchio, from Chioggia to Treviso. A pairing I recommend
s radicchio splashed with Sicilian red wine vinegar, enjoyed with
bottle of Nero d'Avola wine.' – CICCIO SULTANO, ITALY

BUYING & STORING

You can buy whole heads of radicchio, leathery leaves tightly tucked, or torn leaves sold loose, peaking in mid-winter through spring. Typically, the paler the leaves and veins, the milder the flavor. Named after their Italian regions of origin, some varieties are sweeter and softer than others, such as Castelfranco, with magenta-speckled yellow leaves; at the other end of the spectrum, Chioggia, which is round and taut like a red cabbage, but with clearer cream veins and finer leaves, weaves the back of your tongue with its astringency. Smack bang in the middle is Treviso, with its elongated, oblong shape and shrunken base stem. If the head has been shrink-wrapped, or the radicchio is being sold as torn leaves, check the bottom of the base or the edges of the leaves – the closer to creamy in color, the fresher your pick.

Radicchio is extremely susceptible to drying out or wilting in the arid landscape of the crisper. Wrap with damp paper towel or cloth, bag up and store towards the top of the pile, so you don't forget to use it. If you want to pick as you go, tear off only as many leaves as you need at a time, and try not to expose too much of its surface to the air by slicing into it. Like any delicate leaf, radicchio begins to wilt as soon as you even mention the word 'oil', so only dress when you're ready to serve. If you're planning on taking some for lunch the next day, pop some fresh torn leaves in a clean jar and add these to the dressed leftovers for extra crunch and freshness.

BEYOND RADICCHIO: ENDIVE

If you think the bitterness of radicchio is just 'rad', meet endive – the genus of leafies that prides itself on its bite. I love using frisée, otherwise known as 'curly endive', as part of my salad mix, both for its texture and the astringency it offers as a counterpoint to creamy dressings. Individual leaves of witlof – particularly the pale yellow variety – also make wonderfully dainty edible canapé serving spoons.

WITH COMPLEMENTS

Butter, capers, cheese (blue, feta, parmesan), chili, chorizo, eggs, fennel, garlic, herbs (chives, parsley, rosemary, thyme), lemon (juice, zest), mustard, nuts (hazelnuts, pine nuts, walnuts), olive oil, orange (juice, zest, blood orange), prosciutto, vinegar (balsamic, sherry).

BRONZED RADICCHIO WITH CAPER & SOUR CHERRY DRESSING

Radicchio is one of those bitter leafies that really comes alive when it's blasted with heat to burnish it, and then teamed with salty, sweet and tart flavors. I love the way that the bright orange zest and emerald-green chives play against the deep purple leaves of the radicchio – and dried sour cherry is such a sharp, syrupy addition to the red wine vinaigrette.

SERVES 6–8 AS A SIDE DISH

2 heads of radicchio
finely grated zest and
  juice of 1 orange
⅓ cup (80 ml) red
  wine vinegar
¼ cup (40 g) dried
  sour cherries
200 g (7 oz) haloumi,
  crumbled

¼ cup (45 g) capers
  (see tip)
⅓ cup (80 ml) extra virgin
  olive oil, approximately
½ bunch of chives,
  finely chopped

Preheat the oven to 450°F. Line a baking tray with parchment paper.

Stand each radicchio on its base, then slash a medium-sized cross into the top of the leaves, deep enough to penetrate through the layers, but not so deep that they start to fall apart.

In a small saucepan, heat the orange juice and vinegar until just simmering, then add the dried cherries, mixing well, and stand for 5 minutes to soften.

Meanwhile, spread the haloumi and capers on a baking tray and drizzle with some of the olive oil. Transfer to a lower shelf of the oven. Pop the slashed radicchio on a rack above the haloumi, then roast for 12–14 minutes, or until the leaves are very dark and almost burnt, and the haloumi is golden.

Remove the radicchio from the oven and pull at the slashes to separate the leaves a little further. Transfer to a plate or bowl.

Pour the cherry vinaigrette over and sprinkle with the haloumi crumb mixture, chives and orange zest. Give it all another glug of olive oil and serve.

Tip If your capers are in brine, drain them well before baking. If using capers in salt, pop them in a colander and give them a quick spray with cold water to remove the salt, then shake off the excess water and drain these well, too.

Shortcut You can also use a milder radicchio (such as the broader Chioggia) and tear the leaves into more of a salad, drizzling with olive oil, orange juice and red wine vinaigrette.

RADICCHIO & SAUSAGE PASTA

This one is all in the timing: if you multi-task properly, you'll have the whole dish done faster than a pizza delivery. I've made this recipe so often that my hands are now practically on autopilot from step to step. And trust me – once you try it, you'll add it to your rotation quick smart. If I'm in the mood for extra green stuff, I'll add half-n-half spiralized zucchini to the pasta (*à la* the bolognese on page 380), so I've included the instruction for that as an optional extra.

SERVES 4

500 g (1 lb 2 oz) spaghetti
¼ cup (60 ml) olive oil
500 g (1 lb 2 oz) Italian sausages (see tips), removed from their casings
1–2 garlic cloves, finely chopped or crushed
1 small fennel bulb, finely sliced, fronds reserved for garnishing

2 tablespoons sake (optional)
1 head of radicchio (see tips), shredded
2 zucchini, spiralized (optional)
100 g (3½ oz) Parmigiano Reggiano, grated

Bring a big pot of well-salted water to the boil. Add the pasta and cook according to the packet instructions.

Meanwhile, heat a large, deep-sided frying pan over medium heat. When the heat emanates from the pan with your palm hovering above, pour in a tablespoon of the olive oil, then add the sausage meat and hack at it with a wooden spoon to break it up into crumbly bits. Once the meat has browned, add the garlic and fennel and cook for 3 minutes, or until softened slightly, then deglaze the pan with the sake, if using, or a splash of water or vinegar.

Transfer the meat mixture to a bowl. Toss the radicchio into the pan, splash in another tablespoon of oil, crank up the heat and let it wilt and color.

When the pasta is cooked, reserve a mugful of the pasta cooking water. If using the zucchini, pop it in a colander, then drain your pasta through it so the hot pasta water softens it slightly.

Return the meat to the pan, along with the drained pasta, and zucchini if using. Sprinkle in about half the parmesan and pour in the reserved pasta water. Stir everything about until the sauce reduces and thickens.

Portion into bowls. Top with the remaining parmesan and olive oil, the fennel fronds and plenty of freshly cracked black pepper and serve.

Tips With so few ingredients, make them count. The quality of the sausages is particularly critical, seeing as they form the basis of the dish, so make this your moment to try a fancy sausage. A little definitely goes a long way! You're looking for free-range pork, natural casings, and no 'fillers' such as breadcrumbs, etc.

A more bitter variety of radicchio would really suit this recipe – but chicory, frisée or witlof would work well, too.

Artichoke

Whoever looked at an artichoke and thought, 'Gee, I wonder if this thistle would taste any good steamed, with lemon and olive oil?' is to be commended, both for their culinary commitment and their courage. I can just imagine them, thinking they were in the clear once they'd hacked through the spiky outer armor, only to be met with a mouthful of 'choke' – both noun and verb – in the center ... as though they'd grabbed a dandelion flower-head and *sucked in* rather than blowing out. What possessed them to persevere must surely be what appeals to any true artichoke lover today: nuts. Cooked artichoke tastes of hazelnuts, with the aroma of spruce, while the texture of its heart, once cleaned, is like butter. You need to be in the mood to properly fuss around with artichokes, because they *are* fiddly to clean, which is why people often set aside a weekend to jar their own. However, you can circumvent all of that by choosing immature artichokes that haven't yet sprouted the fuzz, or by steaming it whole, then avoiding the choke and using the tips of the leaves as handles while you dip the softened base of each into something rich and lemony – like a hollandaise – and rasping with your teeth. I'm nuts for it.

'For a great starter, finely slice artichokes on a mandoline, toss them into an emulsion of lemon juice and extra virgin olive oil, salt, pepper and finely chopped parsley, and spread over thinly sliced raw beef. Finish with Parmigiano Reggiano and crispy red Asian shallots. The raw nuttiness of the artichoke is superb with the beef and the parmesan.' – KAREN MARTINI, AUSTRALIA

BUYING & STORING

Buying fresh produce is always a multi-sensory undertaking – I've lost count of how many times I've told you to take a whiff of something to check if it's ripe. But with artichoke, it's another sense that comes into play for picking a winner: your hearing. In springtime, when artichokes are rife, squeeze the leaves of an artichoke and the meaty ones that are ready for action will *squeak* back at you, while the ones that have started to lose their pep will remain quite silent. Any long stems on larger artichokes are also indicative of freshness, as it is the stem that starts to deteriorate first. Artichokes are extremely susceptible to oxidizing and will turn black at any hint of air, so black spots on the stem are nothing to be afraid of – as long as the rest of the thistle is looking (and sounding!) crisp. This susceptibility to oxygen is also to be taken into account when storing – artichokes don't love being left exposed in the fridge, so be sure to bag or wrap them before storing them there. Incidentally, as long as your kitchen is cool enough, the best place to store artichokes is in a vase on the countertop, their stems trimmed on the diagonal, as you would cut flowers, where they'll thrive for over a week, with a water change every couple of days.

PREPARING

You can never be too prepared when prepping artichokes. As soon as an artichoke's cell structure is damaged – through tearing or slicing – it'll start to discolor. You can stop this enzymatic reaction in its tracks by counteracting with acid in the form of lemon juice or vinegar. Before you even touch an artichoke, grab yourself a lemon and slice it in half, then pop one lemon half next to your chopping board. If you plan on boiling the artichokes pretty quickly, squeeze the other lemon half into your cooking water before adding the small batch of trimmed artichokes to simmer away. Or, if your plan is to prepare a bunch of them – which can be a slow and arduous process, to be honest – instead squeeze that lemon half into a big bowl of cold water for the artichokes to bob around in as soon as you finish preparing each one, using the other lemon half next to your chopping board like an immunity shield, rubbing the juicy face across any exposed surfaces as you go.

WITH COMPLEMENTS

Breadcrumbs, broad beans, butter, cheese (especially emmental, goat, parmesan), garlic, herbs (especially bay leaves, mint, parsley), lemon, nuts (especially hazelnuts, walnuts), potato.

Jartichokes

When you have a hankering for artichoke, but they're not in season or you don't have time for all the preparation rigmarole, pick up a jar of artichokes from your local deli. Although oil-preserved artichoke hearts are an antipasto mainstay, the jury's out over whether the ones in oil or in brine are better for cooking with. I prefer the ones in oil, as it helps to further soften any stowaway tough leaves, while others, like the great Jane Grigson, think this softening makes them too slimy. If you like a firmer heart, briny artichokes are generally the way to go, but check the ingredients list – the higher vinegar or acetic acid is on the list, the sourer the mix. And whatever you do, avoid canned artichokes, unless you like the distinct tang of metal in your mouth. For the truest artichoke flavor, though, seek out frozen artichoke hearts. When thawed, these behave as they would if you'd boiled fresh ones, spread them on a tray and frozen them yourself – which you may like to do if you have a couple of spare hours when artichokes are in peak season, along with marinating your own artichoke hearts.

Steamed artichokes with lemon & olive oil

To avoid the fiddle-factor of trimming artichokes, simply add some water to a pot, whack a bamboo or collapsible steamer on top and bring the water to the boil. Meanwhile, wash your artichokes well under running water, then trim the stems and tops to help the artichokes fit in the steamer, standing upright if possible. (The stems can be steamed independently, grilled, or even hacked of their woody outer bits to the lighter-colored core and served raw in a salad.) Steam baby artichokes for about 10 minutes, medium to large ones for 25–30 minutes, and big mammas for 30–40 minutes (these can lay on their side in the steamer, too). Check the water every now and then to ensure there's still some water steaming away. Squirt with plenty of fresh lemon juice, drizzle with olive oil and season with salt and pepper. Serve like a finger food, where people can pull at the leaves and then eat the tender bases by rasping them between their teeth, dipping into Garlic aioli (page 37) or a little bowl of bonus lemon juice, olive oil and crushed garlic.

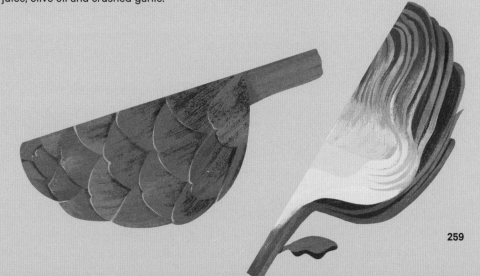

SAFFRON ORZO WITH CHARRED DELI ARTICHOKES

Some dishes are family heirlooms, others happy accidents, while some are simply divine inspiration. This one is the latter. And when I say 'divine', I truly mean it. Saffron and artichoke are two of Greece's (many!) gastronomic gifts to the world.
If you're to believe Greek mythology, it's Zeus himself we have to thank for the artichoke, after he transformed a homesick goddess into a thistle. Here, through time and heat, the thistle is returned to her golden glory, resting on a bed of unctuous orzo – or *kritharaki* as it is known in Greece – dappled with the sunshine glow of saffron. Aptly, Zeus was said to have slept on a bed of saffron, so you could say that this dish is a reunion of sorts for the king of Olympus and his ex. Awkward.

SERVES 4

⅓ cup (80 ml) olive oil
6 cooked artichokes
    with stems (see tip),
    halved lengthwise
2 French shallots,
    finely chopped
1 bunch of parsley, stems
    finely chopped, leaves
    picked and chopped
1½ cups (330 g) orzo
    (or risoni)

3 cups (750 ml)
    vegetable stock
a good pinch of
    saffron threads
2 teaspoons finely
    chopped preserved
    lemon
½ cup (60 g) hazelnuts,
    lightly toasted, then
    roughly chopped

Heat 2 tablespoons of the olive oil in a large frying pan over high heat. Add the artichokes cut side down and cook, without touching, for 4 minutes, or until charred and golden. Remove and drain on paper towel.

Add the remaining oil to the pan over medium–low heat. Add the shallot and parsley stems and cook for 4 minutes, or until softened. Add the orzo and cook, stirring, for 2 minutes, or until glossy and slightly toasted. Pour in the stock and bring to the boil, then reduce the heat to low. Add the saffron, then cover and cook for 12–15 minutes, or until the orzo is cooked through. Stir in the preserved lemon.

Place the artichokes on top of the orzo, face side up. Cover and cook for 3 minutes to warm through.

Transfer to a serving dish and sprinkle with the chopped parsley and hazelnuts. Serve warm or cold.

Tip Most continental delis sell two types of marinated artichokes – one preserved in oil, which tends to be just the heart, the other most likely kept in brine, with more of the leaf intact. Whichever you choose is up to you. Jarred artichokes are more than a suitable replacement if these fancy ones are not forthcoming.

Shortcut Instead of orzo, use instant couscous, frying up the artichokes while the kettle (or vegetable stock) comes to the boil. Stir saffron into the couscous just before pouring the hot liquid over it.

Double duty This dish is one step away from being a pasta salad. Chop or tear the marinated artichokes into chunks, crumble some feta on top and serve cold – it's a fantastic 'bring a plate' or desk-lunch option.

Eggplant

Eggplant is moody and mysterious, its taut skin as dark and glossy as the fender of a Rolls-Royce Phantom. Its Italian name *melanzane* ('crazy apple'), is testament to the reputation its nightshade cousin Belladonna garnered in ancient Rome – first as a medicine, then a potent poison. People believed the new arrival, introduced by Arab traders in the Middle Ages, could cause all manner of ails, such as madness and melancholy. How it came to be called 'egg' plant has a far more literal explanation. These first arrivals (some varieties of which are still popular in India, China and Thailand) were far smaller, more oval in shape, and often off-white in hue – like an egg. However, breeding for color and sweetness turned the 'egg' decidedly deep purple. Its other common name, *aubergine*, goes back to the Sanskrit *vatin-ganah*, as it was said to aid in 'holding the wind' (which means exactly what you think it means). Creamy, salty fillings and condiments, from mayo to miso, complement its sharpness and nuttiness, inviting you back in for another bite. Speaking of 'bite', if an eggplant dish catches on the sides of your tongue, it may not have been cooked for long enough. More is more when it comes to cooking eggplant! It might keep the 'wind' at bay, but heartburn is just an *al dente* slice away.

'I love eggplant. I like to slice it in half and bake it, so the middle colors up. If we cook it over a gas flame, or better yet on the grill, it takes on a smoky flavor, which is great for baba ghanoush. If we fry them, we first brine them in milk and salt, drain thoroughly, then rub them in thick flour so they take in as little oil as possible. I usually serve them with intense sauces such as white miso with ginger, romesco sauce, or with molasses if fried.' – ALBERT ADRIÀ, SPAIN

BUYING & STORING

The luster and squeak of a ripe, fresh eggplant is unmistakable, whatever the variety, particularly when they're busting out in late summer into autumn. Look for ones that are hard, heavy for their size, with unbroken skin and a glossy, vibrant color – whether deep aubergine Italian ones (for sautéeing and roasting), rounder plump purple Indian ones (for stuffing), long slender dark or paler purple Japanese and Chinese eggplants (for pickling and grilling), the striped cream and purple Sicilian ones (great as fries!), or the small round green or white Thai eggplants (for popping whole into curries). Give the stem a squeeze: it should feel rough-textured and firm (careful of the occasional prickle). The points at the bottom of the stem cap should still sit flush against the skin – if they've started to lift, you're looking at some shrinkage. Dark spots on the stem are mostly okay, as long as they're still dry and firm; these are usually caused by tight packing and transport. If older, spongier specimens are all that are available, seek out ones that are uniformly softening, with no discernible brown soft spots that you could almost poke a finger through. These eggplants would benefit from peeling, salting and slow-braising. While our first instinct might be to store eggplants in the fridge, they are actually better stored in a cool, dark place such as the pantry, in a bag of some description. Avoid storing potatoes and onions nearby, as these will accelerate decomposition.

COOKING WITH

Beneath its glossy exterior, the flesh of an eggplant is spongy to the touch and creamy in color, turning a golden shade of greeny-brown when cooked, and absorbing any fat and flavors it is teamed with. This porousness also lends itself particularly well to taking on the smoky flavors from grilling or roasting at high temperatures, as best showcased by the dip that rivals hummus for world domination: baba ghanoush. If you're making baba ghanoush at home and have access to an open flame, leave your eggplant whole and uncovered over medium heat, rotating it occasionally, until dry and blackened on the outside, and completely soft in the middle (30–45 minutes). Poke a slit in the side and hang your eggplant over a bowl or sink to drain of excess moisture. Scoop the flesh off the skin with a tablespoon if you like, or keep the skin on for the 'rustic' route. Add tahini, garlic, paprika, ground coriander (and fresh too, if so inclined), a squeeze of lemon juice, olive oil and salt to taste, then fork together for a chunky baba ghanoush, or blitz in a food processor for a smooth result. Even if you're not making baba ghanoush, eggplants generally taste best when they're charred and smoky, or baked long enough to become silky and slippery. Grill your eggplants dry, then wait until they're golden brown on both sides before brushing them with oil and aromatics such as garlic and spices, so your eggplanty sponge doesn't soak up all the oil and turn greasy. Alternatively, bake them whole at 400°F with a glug of olive oil and a sprinkling of flaked sea salt until soft (about 40 minutes), or slice and roast until golden using the same method (15–20 minutes). I like to leave the stem on for presentation, halve the eggplants from end to end, score them in a lattice pattern, char the cut side face-down in a dry, hot, well-seasoned pan, and then bake until soft – that way I get the best of both worlds and the flavor is phenomenal. Its ability to transform from firm to pliable through heat is put to full advantage in dishes where eggplant becomes the wrapping for rice and ground meat for braising, or for one of my favorite Georgian dishes: walnut-stuffed eggplant rolls (page 266).

WITH COMPLEMENTS

Breadcrumbs, bell pepper, cheese (feta, goat, parmesan, ricotta), chili, cilantro, garlic, ginger, honey, lemon, mayonnaise, miso, nuts (cashews, pine nuts, walnuts), olive oil, parsley, pomegranate, sesame oil, soy sauce, tahini, tomato, yogurt.

To salt or not to salt?

Salting is often listed as a step in eggplant recipes (especially in older cookbooks), although it's hardly ever necessary. Initially it was recommended to 'draw out the bitterness', but the current thinking is that salting is more likely to just trick the tongue into experiencing eggplant's natural bitterness as 'creaminess'. Salting does, however, break down eggplant's spongy cell structure, pulling out moisture and making it easier for oil to penetrate. You don't need to salt fresh, firm eggplants, or if you're popping smaller ones into curries (where their slight bitterness is a desired depth-enhancer), or if you plan on cooking any eggplant for an extended period. It's when you choose to fry eggplant that salting really comes in handy – giving you that creamy-in-the-middle, crispy-on-the-outside gold. Cut your eggplants as per the dish instructions, then season liberally with flaked sea salt and allow to stand for at least 30 minutes (an hour is even better). You'll see the eggplant start to sweat pretty quickly, and will be flabbergasted by how much moisture you can extract. Be sure to pat dry with paper towel or a clean cloth before using, and keep in mind that there's probably no need to salt the dish until tasting at the very end, given how well seasoned the eggplant is already.

BADRIJANI: WALNUT EGGPLANT ROLLS

Whenever I'm asked to sum up Georgian food, I always fire back 'walnuts, garlic, coriander'– it may as well be our holy trinity. Whether these are blitzed in, stirred through, or sprinkled on top, many vegetable dishes in the cuisine benefit from this combination, from spinach to beets to eggplant. I particularly love this version, where the trinity is whizzed into a paste, along with some classically Caucus spices. It's then wrapped in golden-roasted eggplant, its bitterness and bite sweetened and mellowed through some quality time in the oven.

SERVES 4–6 AS A STARTER

5–6 small–medium
  eggplants, 1.5 kg (3 lb 5
  oz) in total
olive oil spray
1 cup (120 g)
  shelled walnuts
1 garlic clove, peeled
1 teaspoon white
  wine vinegar
½ teaspoon
  ground coriander
½ teaspoon curry powder

pomegranate seeds,
  to serve
cilantro leaves, to serve

Pomegranate sauce
⅓ cup (80 ml)
  pomegranate molasses
⅓ cup (80 ml) tahini
⅓ cup (80 ml) extra
  virgin olive oil

Preheat the oven to 400°F. Line three baking trays with parchment paper and spray with olive oil spray.

Cut the eggplants vertically into slices 8 mm (⅜ inch) thick. Try to keep the 'butts' on each side to a minimum, as these don't fold too well. Arrange on the lined baking trays in a single layer, then spray with olive oil spray. Bake for 50–60 minutes, turning over halfway, until golden on both sides, softened and cooked through.

Meanwhile, blitz the walnuts, garlic, vinegar, spices and ¼ cup (60 ml) just-boiled water in a blender until a smooth paste forms. Season with salt and pepper.

Combine all the sauce ingredients and set aside.

When the eggplant is completely pliable, remove from the oven and leave until cool enough to handle. Scoop a teaspoon of the walnut paste onto one of the short edges of each slice, then roll, pressing the end over and resting it on this side to keep it secure.

Arrange the eggplant rolls on a platter. Drizzle with some of the dipping sauce and sprinkle with pomegranate seeds and cilantro. Serve with remaining sauce.

Tip Walnuts are up there with pine nuts in being highly susceptible to rancidity once cracked. Beware of sealed packets with a long shelf life, particularly if the nuts look powdery. Either take the time to crack your own, or buy them from a bulk store where you can audaciously ask to taste before you buy. Store any left-over nuts in an airtight container in the fridge.

Shortcut You can circumvent the walnut shelling by subbing in crunchy peanut butter (or any nut butter) instead. To speed up the eggplant side, salt the slices, pat them dry and grill instead of baking – they'll turn out slipperier, but they'll cook more quickly. Drizzle with molasses instead of the pomegranate sauce.

Double duty Any left-over nut paste can be loosened off with mayonnaise and tossed through your next salad as a creamy, aromatic dressing. It's also a fab addition to the Georgian lobio on page 354.

CAPONATA IN A JAR

Whether it's Greek *briam*, Georgian *ajapsandali*, French ratatouille or Italian caponata, you'll find a version of this vegetable stew in most cuisines. What I like about this one is that it's part preserve, part dip, part meal in a jar. Zippy red wine vinegar and lemon, tempered by syrupy raisins (or other dried fruit) give caponata its distinctive *agrodolce* (sour–sweetness) flavor. The ingredients can also be thinly sliced, fried off, dressed, then packed down layer by layer to form a pretty pattern for gifting. Caponata is great with grilled bread, or warmed through and served as a side. Or for a substantial vego main, serve it on a bed of polenta, grating plenty of parmesan on top. If you're getting to the end of a jar, this caponata can also be whizzed into a piquant eggplant dip, too.

MAKES ABOUT 5 CUPS (1.25 LITERS)

¼ cup (45 g) raisins

¼ cup (60 ml) red
   wine vinegar

1 kg (2 lb 4 oz) eggplant,
   cut into 2 cm (¾ inch)
   cubes

1 tablespoon flaked
   sea salt

2 tablespoons extra
   virgin olive oil

2 small red onions, cut into
   1 cm (½ inch) cubes

2 celery stalks, cut into
   2 cm (¾ inch) cubes

1 bunch of parsley,
   leaves finely chopped,
   stems finely sliced

2 garlic cloves,
   finely chopped

100 g (3½ oz) caper berries,
   stalks removed, sliced

400 g (14 oz) canned
   cherry tomatoes

zest of 1 lemon

vegetable or canola oil,
   for shallow-frying

Wash 4 x 300 ml (10½ fl oz) jars in hot soapy water and stand to dry.

Place the raisins, vinegar and 1 cup (250 ml) just-boiled water in a heatproof bowl. Leave for 5 minutes.

Toss the eggplant and flaked sea salt in a colander and place over a bowl to drain, giving the eggplant the oc squeeze to massage the salt in and draw the liquid out.

Heat the olive oil in a saucepan over medium–high heat. Cook the onion, celery and parsley stems for 4 minutes, or until softened. Add the garlic and caper berries and cook for 1 minute, until aromatic. Stir in the tomatoes, lemon zest and soaked raisin mixture. Simme for 15 minutes, or until the liquid has reduced by half.

Meanwhile, heat 5 cm (2 inches) of oil in a wide saucepan over high heat. Squeeze the eggplant to remove any remaining liquid. Working in batches, deep-fry for 3–4 minutes, or until golden. Drain with a slotted spoon and add directly to the bubbling sauce. Continue with the remaining eggplant.

Stir the chopped parsley through and taste for seasoning. Spoon into the prepared jars while hot and seal the lids. Place the jars in the fridge if you're plannin to eat the caponata straight away, or within 2–3 weeks.

Alternatively, transfer the jars to a saucepan and pour in enough water to cover the jars. Bring the water to the boil, then turn the heat off and stand for 10 minutes. Remove the jars from the water and allow to cool. Check that the seals have popped to concave. If not, return the jars to the water, bring back to the boil and repeat the process. The sealed jars will keep in the pantry for 3–4 months. Once opened, store in the fridge and use within 1 month.

Shortcut Instead of deep-frying, roast the eggplant on baking trays drizzled with olive oil for 20 minutes at 425°F. You'll lose some of the cube drama of the eggplant, but it lets you get on with other things.

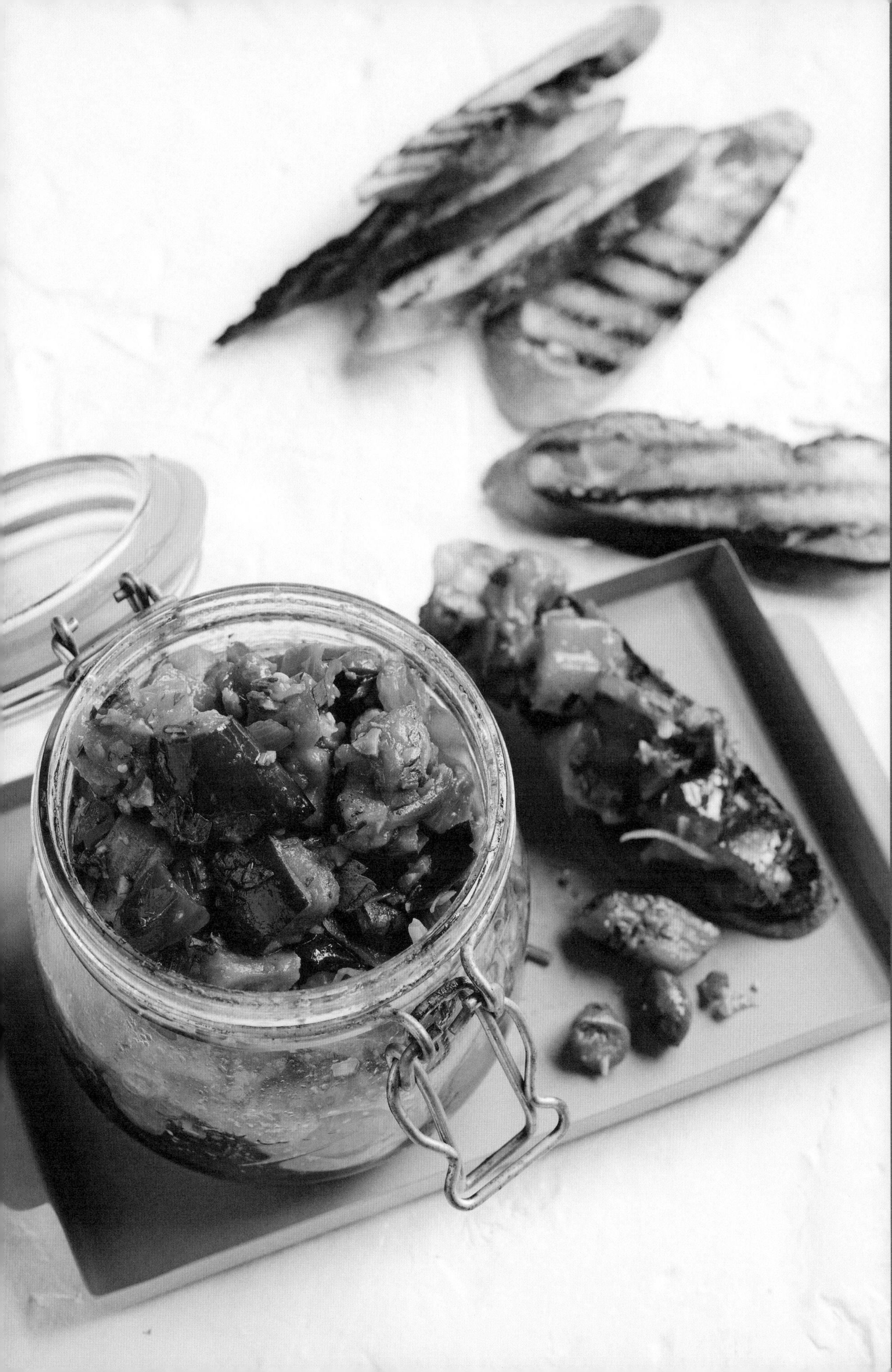

SICHUAN STICKY EGGPLANT

Sichuan cuisine is punctuated by punchy, vibrantly red sauces and searingly hot dishes. Among them all, though, is this sticky eggplant dish – otherwise known as 'fish-flavored eggplant', even though the only fish in it is a few tablespoons of fish sauce. For me, this is a dish that not only tastes absolutely stupendous, but also brings back many bittersweet memories of a day spent taking the late legendary restaurant critic Jonathan Gold around some of Melbourne's many foodie haunts, including to the famous Dainty Sichuan restaurant. He gave me one heck of a good piece of advice about food writing that I think about often. J-Gold said, 'A food writer can be three things, but never all together – they can be well liked, they can write well, or they can stick to a deadline.' I'll let you guess which category I find most challenging.

SERVES 4–6

1 kg (2 lb 4 oz) eggplant, sliced into 1 cm (½ inch) thick batons

2 teaspoons flaked sea salt

⅓ cup (80 ml) honey

¼ cup (60 ml) Chinese black vinegar

¼ cup (90 g) soybean chili paste (see tip)

¼ cup (60 g) crispy chili oil with peanuts (see tip)

2 tablespoons fish sauce

juice of 1 lemon

¾ cup (110 g) cornstarch

rice bran oil, for frying

2 small red chilis, thinly sliced

3 garlic cloves, thinly sliced

2 tablespoons toasted white sesame seeds

sliced green onion (scallion), to serve

steamed rice, to serve

Place the eggplant in a colander and toss with the flaked sea salt. Place over a bowl to drain for 1 hour, or until softened.

Meanwhile, make the sauce. Combine the honey, vinegar, chili paste, chili oil and fish sauce in a wok over medium heat. Bring to the boil and cook, stirring frequently, for 4 minutes to reduce the liquid slightly. St in the lemon juice, then set aside.

When ready to cook, push down on the eggplant to release the excess water. Transfer to a bowl and toss with the cornstarch.

Heat 5 cm (2 inches) of oil in a large saucepan over medium–high heat to 400°F, or until a cube of bread dropped into the oil turns golden in 15 seconds. Add the chili and garlic slices and fry for 1 minute, or until crisp. Remove with a slotted spoon and drain on paper towel.

Working in batches, shaking off any excess cornstarch as you go, deep-fry the eggplant for 4 minutes, or until light golden and crisp, yet soft in the middle. Remove with a slotted spoon and drain on a cooling rack set over paper towel. Continue with the remaining eggplant.

Bring the sauce in the wok back to the boil. Add the eggplant and stir to coat in the sauce.

Transfer to a serving dish and sprinkle with the crispy chili and garlic, sesame seeds and green onion. Serve with steamed rice.

Tip You'll find Chinese black vinegar, soybean chili paste and crispy chili oil at all good Asian grocers. If you don't have one nearby, try checking online.

Double duty This salty caramel (more 'salt' than 'caramel', but only just) is absolutely delicious on any vegetable you have handy. Try it with last night's roas veg, tossed through as a salad dressing loosened off with peanut oil – or even just drizzled over a simple bowl of rice and green onion.

Brown

* **ONION**
  + Red onion
  + Shallot
* **POTATO**

* **JERUSALEM ARTICHOKE**
* **YAMS & TUBERS**
* **MUSHROOMS**
  + Truffles

Onion

The very etymology of 'onion' gives a clear indication of its high regard since ancient times – the word stemming from the Latin for 'one' or 'unity'. And there's no doubt onions unify a dish. They are the *one* ingredient no cook should be without, and they are a non-negotiable in my cooking. The smell of these sulfurous bulbs sweating in a pan mean something scrumptious this way comes. No matter the cuisine – or whether it's a stew, a curry, a pasta or a soup – all roads lead to our pantry door, where onions of varying sizes and colors lay in wait to offer oomph to practically every savory dish. Even when I'm simply whacking fresh ingredients into a salad or between slices of bread, onion i what 'makes' it – the crisp sweetness and tang elevating th delicious savoriness of everything within. Dicing onions is great option when you want heaps of flavor fast, and for the onion to dissolve into a sauce. If you want texture, slice your onions finely and sauté slowly, or chop them roughly if you plan on blitzing, and keep them chunky for roasting. Just make sure you have plenty in storage at all times, because 'one' onion is never enough.

Packed full of flavor, onions are so versatile: slowly roasted with thyme, turned into onion tarts or served with Lyonnaise sauce, then there's onion soup, onion salads, onion pickles and onion jams … I could go on, but I think onions are right up there as one of the best and most cost-effective of all vegetables.'
CLARE SMYTH, NORTHERN IRELAND, UK

BUYING & STORING

Onion layers tend to dry out from the outside in, so look for firm bulbs, where the skin is still quite tight. Knicks and bruises will diminish their shelf life, but if such specimens are all you have access to, particularly deep into late winter right before the next harvest, just be sure to use the most banged-up ones first. Your run-of-the-mill yellow onion (white fleshed, brown skinned) is terrific for everyday cooking, and you'll find yourself sweating and caramelizing it on a daily basis across practically every cuisine. Cipollini onions are flat and round, and have a mild, sweet flavor that's fabulous for roasting and baking – I love to use these in tarts when I can find them. White onions are worth a look-in if you want something that is milder than a red onion (see page 278) and still sweet raw; they also love being barbecued.

    Seeing as they're a bulb, onions do have a tendency to shoot if not stored correctly. Keep them away from any direct sunlight, moisture and potatoes (specific but necessary – the two have a diabolical effect on each other), in a well-ventilated place, and they'll keep for around a month. Once you've sliced off an onion half, cover with wrap of some kind, and store in the fridge, where it'll dry out within the week; keep it in the fridge door so you don't forget! When it does look a little shrivelled, slice off the most exposed area, and the rest will be right as rain. If you're that way inclined, sweat or caramelize a double-batch of onions when you're cooking with time to spare, and store the extra half in the fridge, or freeze it in smaller portions, ready to be popped out and thawed in the pan for quick sauces or soup bases.

COOKING WITH

Sweat diced onions in your fat of choice (butter or ghee, olive or peanut oil, or even coconut oil) and cover with a lid to keep the liquid from evaporating and burning the delicate dice – this means you don't have to stand over the oven, stirring and stirring. I like to lift the lid every now and again and give them a stir to help with contact-heat, leaving the lid off for the last 2 minutes or so; otherwise, I can get on with the rest of my food prepping. 'Sweating' means you want the onion to end up translucent, so keep the heat medium–low and be patient – the process should take around 10–15 minutes, depending on how much onion you've packed into the pan. Caramelized onions glow up to a gorgeous golden-brown color, because you've taken the lid off maybe 5 minutes into the sweating process, and increased the heat to medium; if they look to be caramelizing too fast, add a dash of water, vinegar or wine and keep stirring. Some cooks will add a sprinkle of brown sugar to accelerate the caramelization process and enhance the onion's natural sweetness; others like to flick in a star anise or two for the same reason. Onion is also the basis of any good mirepoix, sofrito or *refogado* – the base aromatics for stocks, broths and sautés. The general ratio is two parts onion to one part celery and carrot, though occasionally, fennel, leek and even mushroom makes an appearance. Some versions suggest you sweat the onion first; others don't even require you to peel the onion – the skin is full of flavor after all – and simply ask you to pull it out whole once the dish is cooked.

BEYOND ONION: RED ONION

Red onion is great for eating raw in salads, or slicing finely over smoked salmon or herring. It's also terrific spiked through kebab skewers for the barbecue, but I would avoid trying to use it in place of yellow onions for slow sweating or caramelizing. Its extra sweetness – put to full advantage as a raw ingredient – is due to a highly volatile sugar content that can easily burn, so think twice before popping it in the pan, and if you must do so, be extra vigilant about heat control. The 'red' in the onion comes from anthocyanin, the same pigment contained in other red- and purple-tinged fruit and vegetables, and it is great to capitalize on this attractive coloring by pickling red onion, where the pickling liquid turns an appealing pink, too. If you're keeping your salads onion-free because you find raw onion too astringent, try soaking sliced red onion in water for 5 minutes or so, to remove some of its 'bite', then draining before tossing through a salad.

BEYOND ONION: SHALLOT

Here we're talking the purple-tinged, multi-bulbed variety of allium – not the long, thin green green onions or scallions that are mistakenly called shallots in some regions. Shallots, also known as eschalots, look like a miniature onion, so you may be wondering, 'Why should I bother fiddling around peeling something so teeny when there are bigger onions to fry?' But it's actually their teeny-ness that makes shallots worth fiddling with! These pocket rockets are little flavor pouches that are a milder, sweeter punch of trademark allium pungency which, when roasted whole, yield into silky sheets of savory, toffee-like sweetness, especially at their edges. They're also prized fresh as an addition to dressings and dipping sauces – think oyster mignonette or delicate tartare sauce. There are three primary varieties you should be aware of: 'French shallots', which have golden brown skin and are squat like a miniature onion, 'red Asian shallots', which are equally stout and look like a shrunken red onion, and the elongated 'banana shallots' that look more like tiny torpedoes. Recipes usually tell you which to seek out, but generally speaking, banana shallots are handy when you're required to do any kind of fine slicing and dicing, due to their uniform shape, whereas curries – especially Thai ones – ask for red Asian shallots, while the others are better for roughly chopping into organic shallot-y shapes for roasting and braising. Shallots also love being pickled with an acid such as chardonnay vinegar. Finely sliced and doused in a mixture comprising a pinch of sugar, salt and the same amount of vinegar to shallot, they'll keep in the fridge for several days as a simple but classy addition to leafy salads, or you can finely dice the shallots and use the same pickle mix as a perfectly piquant topping for fresh oysters.

WITH COMPLEMENTS

Butter, cheese (especially cheddar or anything alpine), garlic, nutmeg, thyme, tomatoes, vinegar.

No more tears

Every rose has its thorns, and every onion threatens to sting your tear ducts with volatile compounds. But both are worth the pain. And it's these sulfuric compounds that are responsible for the pungent, savory, surprisingly meaty qualities that we so appreciate in cooked onions. So, be prepared. Let your onions bob around in a bowl of water in the fridge for 30–60 minutes to help slow down the volatile chemicals that act as 'lacrimators' (a.k.a. tear inducers), while simultaneously softening the onion's papery, brittle skin into easy-to-peel sheets. Choose a well-ventilated place to slice your onion – open a window and turn on the kitchen range-hood if need be. Use your sharpest knife, to minimise bruising, lessening the potential for sulfur molecules bursting forth unnecessarily. Finally, by slicing the onion lengthwise and using the root-point as a handle, you'll be keeping the most volatile compounds flat against the board, and making it easier to slice it as a complete unit, without bits flying everywhere.

ONION & PEA BHAJI BITES

I cook with a lot of onion, but it's usually a softened, sweated hum rather than a snappy shout. Here, onion's sweet–savory unctuousness is well and truly the hero, with its spiced bhaji bark as loud as its crispy crunchy bite.

SERVES 4 / MAKES 18

1½ cups (215 g) frozen peas, thawed and drained

2 yellow onions, thinly sliced

1 teaspoon flaked sea salt

½ cup (75 g) chickpea flour (besan)

½ cup (75 g) all-purpose flour

2 teaspoons mild curry powder

1 teaspoon ground turmeric

½ teaspoon baking powder

vegetable or canola oil, for shallow-frying

Cilantro raita

1 cup (20 g) firmly packed cilantro

¼ cup (5 g) firmly packed mint leaves

½ cup (125 g) Greek-style yogurt

1 garlic clove, peeled

1 long green chili, seeded and chopped, plus extra slices to serve

finely grated zest and juice of 1 lemon

To serve

torn iceberg lettuce leaves

sliced green chili

mint leaves

thinly sliced red onion

lemon wedges

Place the peas, onion and salt in a bowl and use your hands to squeeze and acquaint the mix with itself. Stand until required.

Blitz all the cilantro raita ingredients in a small blender, or use an immersion blender to purée and blitz until green. Season to taste, then chill until required.

In a bowl, mix together the flours, spices and baking powder. Add 200 ml (7 fl oz) water and whisk until smooth. Fold the onion mixture through until coated.

Pour 3 cm (1¼ inches) oil into a wide saucepan and heat to 400°F; a cube of bread or blob of batter dropped into the oil will turn golden in 15 seconds when the oil is hot enough.

Working in batches, gently add 1 tablespoon of the bhaji mixture to the hot oil and cook, turning halfway, for 3 minutes, until golden and crisp. Drain briefly on paper towel.

Serve the bhaji hot, on lettuce leaves, sprinkled with chili, mint and onion, with lemon wedges and the cilantro raita alongside.

Tips To thaw the peas, place in a sieve under cold water for 1 minute, then drain.

For the most dramatic designs, use a spider or wide-based skimmer to fry the bhaji, encouraging the onion to spread out and tangle up by gently swirling the batter in the skimmer around in the oil.

Dietaries Go dairy-free by using coconut yogurt in the sauce, and add a splash of lemon juice to make up the acidity.

Using gluten-free flour instead of all-purpose flour will also work quite well.

DOB: DOUBLE ONION BURGER

There's something about loading up a burger with extra bits and bobs that makes it even more satisfying. Doubling down on onion cuts through the richness and adds sweetness and crunch in the form of crispy onion rings. Fattier ground beef makes for a better patty; look for anything around the 15–20 per cent fat mark. And don't worry – much of it will render out in the pan, and will just help to keep everything nice and juicy. Lush!

SERVES 4

500 g (1 lb 2 oz) grass-fed
    ground beef
1 egg, lightly beaten
1 garlic clove, finely grated
2 tablespoons smoky
    barbecue sauce, plus
    extra to serve
1 teaspoon flaked sea salt
2 tablespoons
    vegetable oil
4 slices cheddar

Pickled red onions
3 small red onions,
    thinly sliced
2 thyme sprigs
1 teaspoon black
    peppercorns
2 garlic cloves, peeled
    and bruised
1 cup (250 ml) white
    wine vinegar

Onion rings
1 cup (250 ml)
    buttermilk (or kefir)
½ teaspoon mild
    chili powder (or
    smoked paprika)
1 teaspoon salt
1 teaspoon freshly
    ground black pepper
2 yellow onions, thickly
    sliced, into rings about
    1.5 cm (⅝ inch) thick
1 cup (150 g) all-purpose
    flour
vegetable oil, for
    shallow-frying

To serve
halved burger buns
shredded lettuce
sliced tomato
sliced beets (optional)
sliced cornichons
extra sauces, to taste

If you like, you could begin this recipe 1 day ahead.

For the pickled onions, place the onion, thyme sprigs, peppercorns and garlic in a sieve. Pour some just-boiled water over to soften slightly. Transfer the mixture to a sterilized jar, pour the vinegar over and push down to cover. Seal the lid and leave for at least 2 hours, or until bright red in color, then transfer to the fridge. The pickled onions will keep in the fridge for up to 1 month.

For the onion rings, combine the buttermilk, chili powder, salt and pepper in a shallow dish. Add the onion, then cover and chill for 1 hour or, even better, overnight.

To make the patties, place the beef, egg, garlic, barbecue sauce and flaked sea salt in a bowl. Squish together with your hands for 5 minutes, or until well combined and stiffened. Divide into four balls, then press into 12 cm (4½ inch) wide patties. Pop an indent into each to help it cook and expand without doming. Chill for 10 minutes (or up to 24 hours) to firm up.

When ready to cook, heat the oil in a large frying pan over medium–high heat. Add the patties and cook, turning halfway, for 6 minutes, or until just cooked through. Transfer to a plate and keep warm.

Meanwhile, to finish the onion rings, place the flour in a bowl. Heat 2 cm (¾ inch) of oil in a wide saucepan over medium–high heat to 400°F, or until a cube of bread dropped into the oil turns golden in 15 seconds. Drain the rings of excess liquid and toss in the flour. Fry in batches for 3–4 minutes, or until golden and crisp. Drain on paper towel, sprinkling with salt and pepper.

Assemble each burger bun with the salad, cornichons, sauces, a patty topped with a cheese slice, the pickled onion and some onion rings. Finish with the bun tops and serve the remaining onion rings alongside.

Go meat free **Instead of a patty, use a dry-grilled portobello mushroom, cooked on its gill-side first to help draw out moisture and concentrate the flavor.**

The 'any kind of onion'
tarte tatin
(page 286)

THE 'ANY KIND OF ONION' TARTE TATIN

If you've ever had a tarte tatin starring apples or pears, you might find yourself wondering what onions, leeks and shallots are doing in a dessert. And it's certainly true that this dish, which originated at the Hotel Tatin in France over 120 years ago, was likely never intended as a savory. But if you think of it as an open-faced pasty or upside-down vegetable tart, it starts to make a lot more sense. I love the way the puff pastry shatters into buttery flakes on your lips, while the onions, caramelized to an indecent level, are silky and slippery. At the end I've also included some other veggie options for the tarte, because once you get the hang of it, this might just never leave your entertaining rotation.

SERVES 6–8

350 g (12 oz) onions of
  your choice (such as
  leeks, red onions or
  French shallots), peeled
  and cut into 1 cm
  (½ inch) thick slices
all-purpose flour, for
  dusting
2 frozen all-butter puff
  pastry sheets, thawed
½ cup (110 g)
  granulated sugar
2 tablespoons fortified
  wine (such as sherry)
1 tablespoon white
  wine vinegar

50 g (1¾ oz) butter
½ teaspoon ground
  white pepper
2 anchovies in oil, finely
  chopped (optional)
1 handful of thyme sprigs
  and/or fresh bay leaves,
  plus extra to serve
crumbled marinated
  feta or goat cheese,
  to serve
purple basil leaves,
  to serve

Preheat the oven to 425°F.

Place the onions in a heatproof bowl and cover with just-boiled water. Leave for 10 minutes to soften slightly, then drain well and stand on a tray lined with paper towel to dry.

On a lightly floured work surface, stack both pastry sheets on top of each other. Using a rolling pin, roll the pastry out to a rough 26 cm (10½ inch) square. Transfer to a tray and chill until required.

Place the sugar and ¼ cup (60 ml) water in a 23 cm (9 inch) ovenproof frying pan or skillet over medium heat. Cook, swirling constantly, until the sugar dissolves. Increase the heat to high and leave to cook without disturbing for 5 minutes, or until you blink and it's suddenly turned into a golden caramel.

Remove from the heat. Carefully – the mixture will sizzle! – add the wine, vinegar, butter, pepper, anchovies and herbs of choice. Return to the boil and swirl to combine.

Carefully arrange the onions over the hot caramel so that they are tightly packed, then place the pastry over the top, tucking the edges in to give you a cool rustic edge on the flip-side.

Bake for 30 minutes, then remove from the oven and cover with foil to prevent burning. Return to the oven and bake for a further 30 minutes, or until the pastry is cooked through and the caramel is bubbling.

Remove from the oven and leave to stand for 10 minutes.

To serve, place a flat plate over the pan, then carefully invert the tart. Sprinkle with flaked sea salt and cracked black pepper, some crumbled cheese and fresh herbs.

Bonus Experiment with these other vegetable options
for a savory tarte tatin:

* Pumpkin + sage
* Ratatouille – zucchini
    + red onion + red bell pepper
    + eggplant
* Parsnip + carrot + caraway seeds
* Beet + goat cheese
* Pine mushroom + thyme
* Potato + rosemary
* Artichoke + lemon zest
* Asparagus + parmesan
* Tomato + mozzarella + basil

Tip If you don't have an ovenproof frying pan or skillet,
you can use any frying pan to make the caramel. After
stirring in the vinegar mixture, transfer the caramel
to a (roughly) 20 cm baking dish or shallow tray (we
used a shallow tray for the French shallot tarte tatin
in the photo on page 284). Add the onions to this and
continue with the recipe.

Shortcut You could make individual little tartlets
too, by using a pastry cutter slightly bigger than the
onion or shallot you've chosen. Slice the discs of onion
to soften and burnish in the pan with the caramel as
per the recipe, then fish them out and pop puff pastry
on top of each, baking for 20–25 minutes, until the
pastry is golden.

NO-TEARS ONION SOUP

Onion soup was once thought of as food befitting only peasants, and so isn't it the ultimate irony that these days it is often more likely to be associated with the fanciest of French restaurants? This silky, slippery broth is so much easier to make than the original, because it involves no peeling, let alone slicing! A luxury indeed.

SERVES 4

1 tablespoon extra virgin olive oil

25 g (1 oz) unsalted butter

1 kg (2 lb 4 oz) yellow onions, skin left on, halved lengthwise, ends removed

2 garlic bulbs, skin left on, halved horizontally

6 dried bay leaves

½ bunch of thyme, leaves picked, plus extra to serve

½ teaspoon ground allspice

1 teaspoon freshly cracked black pepper

1 teaspoon flaked sea salt

½ cup (125 ml) dry white wine

1 tablespoon all-purpose flour

4 cups (1 liter) beef, chicken or vegetable stock

1 tablespoon sherry vinegar or white wine vinegar

1 baguette, torn into big chunks, or 4 chunky bits of stale bread

150 g (5½ oz) grated gruyère (or cheddar)

finely chopped chives, to serve

Preheat the oven to 350°F.

Heat the olive oil and butter in a large ovenproof casserole dish over medium–high heat. Add the onions, garlic, bay leaves, thyme, allspice, pepper and flaked sea salt and cook for 2 minutes, or until fragrant. Stir in the wine, then cover and bake for 1 hour, or until the onion and garlic have softened.

Set the garlic bulbs aside until cool enough to handle. Slip the skins off the onions using tongs.

Place the dish back over medium–high heat and sprinkle the softened onion flesh with the flour. Cook, stirring with a wooden spoon, for 5 minutes, until golden.

Squeeze the garlic flesh from the bulbs into the dish. Pour in the stock, vinegar and 2 cups (500 ml) boiling water. Bring the mixture to the boil and simmer for 5–10 minutes, or until the liquid has reduced slightly.

Preheat the broiler to high. Arrange the bread on top of the soup and sprinkle with the cheese and extra thyme. Broil for 8–10 minutes, or until the cheese is golden and melted.

Serve immediately, sprinkled with chives.

Shortcut Thinly slice the onion and garlic (the smaller you cut them, the quicker they'll cook). Sweat them in a pan with the oil and butter until translucent, then let them caramelize while you warm some stock with the bay leaves, thyme and allspice (or even a *herbes de Provence* blend). Broil the bread with a slice of cheese on top for 5 minutes, or until the cheese melts. Remove the aromatics from the stock, then ladle into bowls with the caramelized mixture. Taste for seasoning, then dip your cheesy breads in. No sweat!

Double duty If you have oniony broth left over, pour it into some hollowed-out stale bread rolls, sprinkle with gruyère or cheddar and broil until oozy. YUM!

BURNT SHALLOT & CRISPY BROCC ORECCHIETTE

This is an exciting recipe to me because it uses broccoli in two different ways, keeping it textural and interesting. And it's also low maintenance in terms of chopping and peeling – particularly when it comes to the shallots. Simply slice them in half, top-n-tail and char their faces, and the skins will slip right off, revealing silky sweet purple flesh that is creamy and mouth-coating. I like to spike this with fresh crushed garlic just before serving for some extra kick, but you're welcome to leave this out if you'd prefer to keep things mellower.

SERVES 4

300 g (10½ oz) orecchiette

1 head of broccoli, florets roughly grated, stalk finely chopped

6 French shallots, skin on, halved lengthwise, roots and tops trimmed

1 tablespoon olive oil

2 cups (200 g) finely grated parmesan, plus extra to serve

zest and juice of 2 lemons

chili flakes, to taste

2 garlic cloves, crushed (optional)

Bring a large saucepan of well-salted water to the boil. Add the pasta and cook according to the packet instructions, adding the broccoli stalks in the last minut of cooking. Reserve 1 cup (250 ml) of the pasta water and drain the rest.

Meanwhile, pop the shallots, cut side down, in a larg saucepan over medium–high heat and leave to darken and soften as the pan heats up – this will take about 8–10 minutes. Pick the shallots out with tongs, squeezir the flesh free of their skins.

Add the olive oil to the pan, then sprinkle in the grated broccoli to let it crisp up. Once crisp, remove half the grated broccoli and reserve for garnishing.

Return the shallots to the pan with the remaining grated broccoli. Pour in about ⅔ cup (170 ml) of the reserved pasta water to deglaze the pan and infuse the flavors further. Sprinkle in the parmesan and bring to th boil, allowing the water to reduce and thicken to a sauc Add the pasta, along with the lemon zest, lemon juice, chili flakes, plenty of freshly cracked black pepper, and the crushed garlic, if using. Stir to combine.

Divide among serving bowls, sprinkle with the reserved broccoli and extra parmesan and serve immediately.

Tip If you have any broccoli leaves, crisp these up in the pan with the shallots, then pull them out and drair ready for fancy garnishing.

Extra This recipe is made EXTRA delicious with the addition of some pan juices from a roast chicken. Add them once the shallots are burnt and let them melt and ooze into the sauce.

Potato

When you consider the climatic and seismic volatility of the region from whence they came – the Andes, with volcanic eruptions, huge temperature fluctuations and ice-covered peaks stretching along the longest mountain range in the world – it seems an unlikely origin story for one of the world's most prolific crops (fifth, after sugarcane, corn, rice and wheat). But that's exactly what has given the potato its staying power. No mud, no lotus. No volcano, no potato, so to speak. And although any good cook can tell a roasting potato from a boiling potato from a mashing potato, this barely scratches the surface of varieties logged and preserved at the International Potato Center's Peruvian headquarters: 5000 and counting. Potato recipes now abound in most parts of the world, and you will no doubt have a family favorite that reminds you of home. For me, boiled potatoes loaded with butter and red onion, served with oily fish such as herring, mackerel or sardines, remains a Sunday brunch tradition. Christmas Day wouldn't seem right without a big bowl of classic potato salad. And who could say no to dunking their hand into a bag of chips, hoping to pull out a 'wish chip' or two (they're the ones that are folded over – don't forget to make a wish!).

'A potato is not just a potato – it's every kind of thing. And there are so many different dishes you can cook with it. Plus, they have enough minerals and vitamins to live off, which unfortunately my Irish forebears learnt the hard way.' – PHIL WOOD, NEW ZEALAND

BUYING & STORING

Though you'll be able to find potatoes all year round in shops, they definitely taste best when they're properly in season during the cooler months – and lend themselves well to cold weather cooking, too. I like to buy bigger potatoes dirty, because they store better, but new potatoes and baby potatoes are almost always dirt-free, which is fine as long as you use them quickly. Any green bits will need to be cut out before cooking (the toxin solanine is responsibl here and not to be messed with), as will any potato eyes or purple shoots – but I don't mind buying slightly sprouted potatoes, because this tells me they're still vibrating with life. If you're trying to decide between spending a bit more on organic, potatoes are one crop where it would make a big difference, as they suck up everything that's been put into the soil. New potatoes, with their paper-thin skins, are a delightful find in summer and make for fantastic potato salads. Along this same vein (but not quite as special) are baby potatoes, the little potatoes you'll find most of the year, which are smaller versions of the same potato varieties – they're just cuter, and take less time to cook. When buying for specific dishes, I'm always thinking about starch content: high starch means dry-fluffy; low starch means waxy-creamy. Waxy potatoes hold their shape well for boiling, but become a gluey mess if you try to mash them, while starchy potatoes are fantastic for roasting, but fall apart easily – which makes them perfect for fluffy fries, not stews. The general rule I go by is to keep pink potatoes for stewing, roast the yellow potatoes, and boil the new potatoes and baby potatoes. These days, there's often some pretty handy labelling going on, so keep an eye out for any instructions, or ask your friendly greengrocer for their recommendations – it'll make a big difference to your end result. Unlike waxy potatoes, which only become gluey when mashed, starchy potatoes are naturally sticky – in fact some people even make glue out of it. If you've hedged your bets

Which spud for which dish?

Low starch	Mid starch	High starch
Loosely packed starch cells	**Moderate starch levels**	**Densely packed starch cells**
> Bond together when cooked	> All-purpose: when in doubt, here's where you live	> Dry, fluffy when cooked
> Salads, casseroles		> Roast potatoes, wedges, chips, fries, mash

and bought two varieties, to see which best fits your purpose, slice the potatoes in two and check which one leaves the stickier white residue – or won't even slide off the knife.

Spuds prefer a cool, dry, dark place. Any exposure to sunlight is a no-no, because they'll start to sprout faster than you can say, 'Chips and fries aren't the same!' The closer you can keep the environment to subterranean, the longer they'll last. And whatever you do, don't store them anywhere near onions! Although the two of them prefer the same cool and dry storage conditions, they're a terrible influence on each other, releasing moisture that causes sprouting and shooting, respectively. If you have only a small storage area that is cool, dry and dark, prioritise your potatoes, as they are especially sensitive to light. When bought fresh and stored properly, potatoes can last for months, especially when you add a surprising element to your spud bag – an apple! – which will stop them from sprouting. Don't let your spuds wallow in the fridge, unless you're in the tropics. While a little fridge time isn't a bad thing for promoting the metabolising of starch into sugar – great for sweeter roast potatoes – if you leave them in there for more than a day or two, the taste of your potatoes will suffer.

PREPARING

I like to leave the peel on my potatoes as often as possible – a good scrub with a vegetable brush in a bowl with plenty of water is usually all they need, popping out any eyes, sprouts, bruises or green bits with a paring knife and/or the sharp point of a peeler. If you *are* peeling potatoes, let them bob around in some cold water while you do the rest – this will keep them from turning greige. It's also much easier to peel potatoes once they've boiled and cooled a little.

COOKING WITH

How can you cook with potatoes? More like, how *can't* you! As a neutrally flavored, starchy tuber, potatoes are the ultimate carrier of richness in purées, mashes and in fondant form, build body and structure in chowders and soups, go from crispy to creamy when roasted, baked, and even fried (have you ever let a chip melt in your mouth?), and create bases for salads and casseroles when boiled or braised.

Speaking of boiling, make sure you bring potatoes up to the boil in cold water rather than adding them to hot water – this helps them to cook through properly, rather than pulverising the outside before the inside softens. Many recipes that don't call for it will benefit from parboiling – or, more accurately, par-simmering, where potatoes bubble away until only just fork-tender, then get finished with a second (often higher-temperature) cooking method. Nowhere is this more pronounced than with the Triple-Cooked Fry, made famous by Heston Blumenthal. Though the original method requires arduous effort and time – parboiling, cooling, low-temperature frying, then high-temperature frying to finish – it's easy to apply a double-cook approach to fries, wedges and roast potatoes. Parboiling them first helps break down some of the potato's starches at a lower temperature, so that when you finish off with a high-temperature roast or a fry, the inside becomes especially fluffy, while the outside gains a bona fide crispy golden crunch.

> **'Every young person should learn to cook mashed potatoes with lots of butter.'** – J P McMAHON, IRELAND

Potatoes also love fat – oil, butter, cream, milk, cheese – and we love this combo right back ... I'm yet to meet someone who isn't partial to a little (or a lottle) Paris mash. Though it may seem counterintuitive, it's the starchier potatoes that produce the perfect purée. The key is to make the starch work for you, creating loose, fluffy potato particles that quickly bind with your chosen fat. Waxy potatoes take more effort and time to mash, thereby activating too *much* starch, and yielding a – gulp! – lumpy result. Trying to avoid overworking the spuds is also why it is always recommended to use a ricer, masher or drum sieve to process your cooked potatoes, rather than a food processor. The other thing you're trying to avoid are waterlogged potatoes, because this makes it harder for the mash to come together. This is why experts recommend baking potatoes on a layer of coarse salt to draw out moisture, but if you *must* boil (it is quicker, especially if you chop the potato into chunks first), simmer your spuds in salted water until fork-tender, drain the water, and leave the cooked potatoes in the pot to allow the residual heat to encourage more liquid to evaporate. Finally, it's important to be mindful of the temperature of your milk and butter – warm milk, cold butter. Warm milk will prevent the potatoes from seizing and turning a bit blue; cold butter will help distribute the butterfat and milk solids consistently around the mix, while yielding an emulsified purée.

Spuds – step by step

Roasted/fries	**Mashed**	**For salads**
Parboil > plenty of fat > high heat	Bake on salt OR boil and let the steam escape > THEN mash with warm milk, cold butter	Boil OR steam until fork tender > THEN peel OR leave skin on

WITH COMPLEMENTS

Butter, cheese (especially cheddar, gruyère), chives, curry powder, garlic, pepper, rosemary, sour cream, thyme.

MASH, CRACKLE & POP

Whenever I make mashed potatoes (which is not as often as I'd like, frankly), I'm always tempted to keep the skins on – because, flavor! But this makes for a mottled mash, and the mouthfeel is all wrong. Enter: potato skin crackle. Once the boiled potatoes are pushed through the sieve, the skins get fried up until they turn into crispy, crackling CRACK, for want of a better word. Even if you're making this just for two, commit to the full batch and you'll have plenty of ways to repurpose and reinvent in the days to come – see over the page, and the mushroom zrazy on page 320, for instance …

SERVES 4–6 AS A SIDE DISH

1 kg (2 lb 4 oz) medium-
   sized floury/roasting
   potatoes, such as Yukon
   gold, scrubbed
2½ tablespoons
   flaked sea salt
1 cup (250 ml) half and
   half cream
120 g (4 oz) unsalted
   butter, cubed
½ teaspoon ground
   white pepper

2 tablespoons extra
   virgin olive oil
finely grated zest
   of 1 lemon
1 garlic clove, finely grated
parsley leaves and
   chili flakes (optional), to
   serve

Pop the potatoes and 2 tablespoons of the flaked sea salt in a large non-stick saucepan and cover completely with cold water. Bring to the boil over high heat, then simmer fo 25–30 minutes, or until fork-tender, ensuring the potatoes are always submerged, adding more hot water if needed.

Drain the potatoes in a colander and give them a good shake to loosen the skins. When the potatoes are cool enough to handle, remove and reserve the skins.

Return the pan to medium heat with the potato innards, cream, butter, pepper and remaining flaked sea salt, using a butter knife or wooden spatula to slightly chop up the potatoes some more. Bring to a simmer, then cover and cook for 5 minutes, or until the potatoes have collapsed and submitted to the cream.

Nestle a fine sieve over a large bowl and pour the potato mixture through, pushing with a spatula. Once all the mixture has been pushed through, stir gently with a flexible spatula and season. Transfer to a warmed serving dish and cover with a lid or tea towel to keep warm.

Return the pan to the heat and add the olive oil. When the oil is hot, add the reserved potato skins and cook for 4–5 minutes, or until crispy and golden. Turn off the heat, and stir the lemon zest and grated garlic through.

Spoon the crispy potato skin mixture over the warm potato mash and serve hot, with a sprinkling of parsley and chili flakes if desired.

Tips You could use a sharp-tipped knife to create crosses on the skin of the potatoes before cooking; this will loosen the skin and help with peeling later.

   Letting the boiled potatoes steam out in the pan before sieving means less of a waterlogged result. A drum sieve works best, but a fine-mesh sieve will do.

Shortcut Halve or quarter the potatoes to reduce the cooking time. This will also speed up peeling, because you don't want to miss out on the crackly skin!

   If you're keen on a crispy crackle, but not up for a mash, once the potatoes have steamed out a little, pop them on a baking tray, glug with plenty of olive oil squash with a masher and then roast in a hot oven for 5–10 minutes, until golden crusty bits form.

MASH-UP GNOCCHI WITH CHEAT'S SUGO

The words gnocchi and cheat's aren't often seen together in a recipe title, yet between the left-over mash bulked out with powdered mashed potato, and the one-pan tomato sugo that takes all of 10 minutes to make, you'll have a restaurant-quality bowl of gnocchi before you can ask, 'Order in?' Did I mention it was gluten free?

SERVES 4

Cheat's sugo
⅓ cup (80 ml) olive oil
4 garlic cloves,
    thinly sliced
400 g (14 oz) can whole
    peeled tomatoes
100 g (3½ oz) baby
    spinach leaves
grated parmesan, to serve

Mash-up gnocchi
2 cups (460 g) mashed
    potatoes (page 298)
2 cups (100 g) dehydrated
    potato flakes (used to
    make mashed potato,
    found in a packet in the
    canned vegetable aisle)
2 eggs, lightly beaten
½ teaspoon ground nutmeg
⅓ cup (50 g) gluten-free
    flour, plus extra for
    dusting

Shortcuts The sugo works a treat with shop-bought gnocchi. Or, make these gnocchi and splash in some ready-made pasta sauce – or, better yet, some burnt sage butter sauce from page 158, or melted compound butter from the roasted radishes on page 190. You can also fry these gnocchi in a pan without boiling them first – just heat some olive oil and brown on all sides.

For the sugo, warm the olive oil in a large frying pan and cook the garlic over medium–low heat for 2–3 minutes, or until just turning golden. Add the tomatoes and mash them up a bit, then cook for 5–7 minutes, until the sauce has thickened. Remove from the heat and set aside.

Meanwhile, for the gnocchi, combine the mashed and dehydrated potato in a large bowl using a wooden spoon or flexible spatula. Add the eggs, nutmeg and a pinch of salt and black pepper and stir well to combine. Sprinkle the flour on top and incorporate it into the mixture using your hands, until a soft dough forms. It will feel extremely loose, but worry not – it does come together as it cooks. And because we're using gluten-free flour, you don't have to stress about overworking the dough and activating too much gluten.

Line a large tray with parchment paper, overhanging the edges. Divide the dough into four pieces, then roll each into a 2 cm (¾ inch) thick sausage on a clean work surface, using light hands and fingers. Transfer the 'sausages' to the lined tray, spacing them evenly. Using a pastry cutter or similar, cut the dough into 2 cm (¾ inch) pieces. Sprinkle with extra flour and roll about gently to coat. Set in the fridge for 15 minutes or so.

Bring a large saucepan of salted water to the boil. Use the parchment paper to lift the gnocchi off the tray, then gently plop a quarter of the gnocchi at a time into the boiling water to cook for 1–2 minutes, or until they all float up to the surface.

Remove with a slotted spoon and add straight into the pan of sugo, reserving the pasta water. Cook the sauce and gnocchi over high heat for 1 minute, or until warmed through.

Meanwhile, use the slotted spoon to dunk the baby spinach leaves into the pasta water, give the spoon a tap to remove excess water, then drop the blanched leaves straight into the sugo.

Spoon into serving bowls and serve with parmesan.

ALL-SEASONS POTATO SALAD

Potatoes are a fantastic flavor carrier, and a fantastic 'flavor to carry' to parties – in a bowl, as a salad. Here are four seasonal ways to pimp up your parboiled spuds.

Autumn

Place 800 g (1 lb 12 oz) cooked new and purple potatoes (chopped into bite-sized pieces) in a large bowl. Add the leaves of 1 small romaine lettuce, a handful of chopped chives and dill and 1 sliced avocado. Dress with 100 g (3½ oz) sour cream, seasoned with salt and pepper.

Spring

In a large bowl, lightly toss 800 g (1 lb 12 oz) cooked fingerling potatoes, 100 g (3½ oz) flaked hot-smoked trout, 1 finely sliced red onion, 250 g (9 oz) chopped Lebanese cucumber, 3 sliced celery stalks and a handful of dill. Dress with ¼ cup (60 ml) olive oil and the juice of ½ lemon, then season with salt and pepper.

Winter

Lightly fry 3 tablespoons drained capers in olive oil until crisp. Stack a handful of mint leaves on a chopping board, roll them up and finely slice. Halve or quarter 100 g (3½ oz) drained jarred artichokes. Toss everything in a large bowl with 800 g (1 lb 12 oz) cooked new potatoes, the zest of 1 lemon and 100 g (3½ oz) crumbled feta. Combine ¼ cup (60 ml) olive oil, 2 tablespoons lemon juice, a splash of feta brine (if you have it) and 1 crushed garlic clove, season with salt and pepper and use to dress the salad.

Summer

Dice 3 bacon slices and fry in a dry pan until crisp. Place in a large bowl with 800 g (1 lb 12 oz) cooked new potatoes (or boiled waxy potatoes, chopped into bite-sized pieces). Add ¼ cup (30 g) black olives, ½ cup (60 g) sliced cornichons, 2 finely chopped green onions (scallions) and a handful of chopped chives. Combine ⅓ cup (80 g) mayonnaise, 1 tablespoon olive oil and 1 tablespoon dijon mustard, season with salt and pepper, drizzle over the salad and gently toss together.

Jerusalem artichoke

Jerusalem artichokes, or sunchokes as they are also known, have a pretty short season, making them one of those 'blink and you'll miss it' marvels of wintertime. They're also in season right around when people are reaching for ginger and lemon tea to stave off the common cold, so my first piece of advice is to look for the sign that says 'Jerusalem artichoke', lest you confuse it with ginger! Indeed, there's a lot of confusion as far as these knubby tubers are concerned. Firstly, they *don't* come from Jerusalem, but rather derived their name from the French for sunflower – *girasol* – which somehow became 'Jerusalem' over time. Secondly, they're not even artichokes, just similar in taste to the heart of an artichoke, without all the cleaning … well, maybe a little cleaning.

love to play a poor-man/rich-man game with these. You take this
gly little vegetable, roast until the skin's really dark and the inside
soft, then put something really decadent on it, like crème fraîche
nd caviar, or trout roe.' – ALLA WOLF-TASKER, RUSSIA

BUYING & STORING

For once, I won't be telling you to seek out the freshest tubers, because fresh Jerusalem artichokes are high in inulin (see below), which will give your guts a workout. Instead, look for cleanish, knobbly tubers, with fairly light exposed flesh – and even if they're a little soft, proceed with my blessing. Try to find uniform shapes so that they cook for the same amount of time, otherwise you'll need to halve the larger ones to suit. Shapes with less bulbous growths will mean less cleaning, too. These are a root veggie, so benefit most from being stored in a cool, dry place, away from direct light. You can extend their shelf life by storing them in the crisper, wrapped in paper towel or a cloth bag to help absorb excess moisture.

COOKING WITH

With their sweet, nutty flavor, Jerusalem artichokes are like a souped-up potato, and do in fact make a sublime soup (see page 307)! Roasted, they are a great addition to a Sunday roast, and fun in a potato salad. Peel strips and deep-fry for chips, to create drama and texture in fancier dishes – especially great when teamed with a purée. However you choose to cook them, if you decide to peel them, have a bowl of water on hand to let them bob around in, as they'll start to discolor as soon as their flesh is exposed. If you're leaving the skin on, scrub with a vegetable brush and scrape out any blackened bits with a paring knife.

WITH COMPLEMENTS

Butter, cream, herbs (bay leaves, chervil, chives, cilantro, parsley, rosemary), fennel, garlic, lemon, mayonnaise, spices (fennel seeds, nutmeg, pepper, star anise).

Fartichokes!

Yes, Jerusalem artichokes really are a 'farty animal', but for very good reason. They're rich in inulin, a soluble fiber that is a great prebiotic, helping cultivate healthy gut bacteria. It does mean, though, that as the good bacteria get their munch on, they produce gas, and so do you. You can help mitigate this natural side effect by adding a form of acid (lemon juice, tomato, vinegar) to your recipe, or pickling or fermenting the chokes. Or, soak them overnight for roasting, sautéing, frying or boiling the next day, to help break down the starchy carbs within.

CRISPY SMASHED JERUSALEM ARTICHOKES WITH CAPER GREMOLATA

Jerusalem artichokes are a bit like potatoes – except sweeter and nuttier when heated, which is why they lend themselves so well to a method that I love applying to spuds, too – a flatten-fry. The most marked difference is that these knobbly tubers are much less likely to all be one uniform shape, which makes it far more difficult to ensure that each one is consistently cooked through with a parboil. That's why I prefer to steam Jerusalem artichokes instead, and check them as I go. It always gives me plenty of time to blitz up a caper gremolata, which is a perfect briny counterpoint.

SERVES 4

800 g (1 lb 12 oz) Jerusalem artichokes, washed and scrubbed
finely grated zest and juice of 1 lemon
¼ cup (60 ml) olive oil, plus a splash extra for the dressing
1 teaspoon flaked sea salt
1 teaspoon sherry vinegar

3 tablespoons baby capers (see tips), drained and roughly chopped
3 tablespoons finely chopped parsley
2 garlic cloves, finely chopped
1 red chili, finely chopped (optional)

Soak the artichokes in a big bowl of iced water with the lemon juice for at least 45 minutes to help counteract some of the inulin, and give you a crispier result, too.

Steam the artichokes in a steamer basket or bamboo steamer, set above a saucepan of rapidly bubbling water for 15–20 minutes, or until fork-tender, giving them the odd poke to see if they'll yield; having a kettle nearby to replenish the hot water is always a good idea. Grab the smaller ones out onto a tray once they're soft, waiting for the larger ones until they're good and ready. More is more here, so feel free to err on the side of over-steaming if you're not quite sure if they're ready.

Preheat the oven to 450°F.

Pop the artichokes in a roasting pan. Drizzle the olive oil over them, then toss to coat. Spread them out, with a little distance between each one. Use a potato masher to press down and break the skins, but still retain some shape. Turn them over so that the flat, oilier sides are facing up. Roast for 10–15 minutes, or until crispy.

Combine the remaining ingredients in a little bowl. Loosen the gremolata with a little extra olive oil, until it resembles a marinade rather than a dressing. Season to taste, spoon over the artichokes and serve.

Tips I like to roast these in some *schmaltz* if I have any left over from roasting a chicken. It gives an added layer of flavor that is irresistible.

You'll find capers in salt or in brine, and both are perfectly acceptable here. If using the ones in salt, give them a quick rinse and drain, just to keep the rest of the seasoning in check. However, if you're frying capers as a garnish, the ones in salt are perfect just as they are.

Extra These are fab with a dab of the herby compound butter from the roasted radishes (page 190) or a drizzle of the balsamic glaze from the rutabaga tian (page 232).

Shortcut Mandoline the Jerusalem artichokes into thin strips, then toss in oil, spread on a baking tray and bake at 400°F for 15–20 minutes, until crispy. The gremolata is optional but delicious, or you could sprinkle liberally with flaked sea salt and sweet paprika.

ROASTED JERUSALEM ARTICHOKE & TOMATO SOUP

When I was interviewing one of my favorite Australian chefs, Alla Wolf-Tasker, for this book, I was so glad she named Jerusalem artichokes as her favorite ingredient. 'In the depths of winter when there's not much around, Jerusalem artichokes are fantastic,' she told me. 'You've got to give them a good scrub, though. Everyone worries about farting, but I learnt years ago from a French chef that if you make a soup with them and add some tomato (such as tomato passata), it takes that side effect away.' *Dushenka!*

SERVES 4 / MAKES 8 CUPS (2 LITERS)

- 0 g (1¾ oz) unsalted butter, melted
- kg (2 lb 4 oz) Jerusalem artichokes, washed and scrubbed
- 00 g (1 lb 2 oz) cherry tomatoes on the vine, chopped, truss reserved
- garlic cloves, bruised
- red onion, quartered
- 1 bunch of sage, leaves picked
- 1 teaspoon freshly cracked black pepper
- 1 teaspoon flaked sea salt
- 8 cups (2 liters) chicken or vegetable stock
- ¼ cup (60 ml) extra virgin olive oil
- cream, to serve

Preheat the oven to 400°F.

In a large roasting pan, toss the butter, artichokes, tomatoes, garlic, onion, half the sage and all the pepper and flaked sea salt. Bake for 20 minutes, or until the artichokes are golden.

Pour in the stock and add the truss from the tomatoes. Cover with foil. Return to the oven and cook for 45 minutes, or until the vegetables are softened. Discard the truss.

Purée the mixture until smooth and combined, either using a heatproof immersion blender in the pan (being careful of splatters), or in a blender.

Heat the olive oil in a small frying pan over medium–high heat. Add the remaining sage leaves and fry for 1–2 minutes, or until crispy. Remove and reserve both the oil and leaves.

Ladle the soup into bowls and finish with the crisp sage leaves, a drizzle of the sage oil and a swirl of cream to finish. Serve immediately.

Tip When Jerusalem artichokes aren't in season, go double or nothing on truss tomatoes for a silky tomato soup.

Shortcut Pop a can of whole peeled tomatoes in with last night's roasted Jerusalem artichokes, warm your stock with a few roughly chopped garlic cloves, then blitz it all up in a blender.

Yams & tubers

If you live in a temperate or tropical part of the world, chances are there'll be several kinds of colorful yams and edible tubers to call your own. In North America, yams and sweet potatoes are often used interchangeably, though seeing two side-by-side, a yam is much more fibrous. So why the confusion? It stems from the fact that these starchy tubers – the underground energy source for distinctly different plants – look similar enough in their bulbousness to have earned themselves confusingly interchangeable names, depending on where you are in the world, and which became more common there first. The good news is, once you've figured out how to cook one yam or tuber, it's fairly easy to understand how to cook the others.

'Salsify is an extraordinary vegetable that is underappreciated. It carries a flavor of oysters, cucumber and brine that, when caramelized in a hot pan, transforms into notes of toasted hazelnuts. Be careful though when preparing salsify, as the sap may stain your fingers black, and without acidulated water, your salsify will suffer the same fate. Raw, sautéed, roasted or cooked in a white sauce, salsify is versatile, and above all delicious!'

– JOSH NILAND, AUSTRALIA

BUYING & STORING

You'll most likely come across local yams in cooler weather at farmers' markets, farm gates and specialty greengrocers. Treat smaller ones as you would young potatoes, choosing evenly sized shapes so they cook at the same rate, and avoiding any that are sprouting. Larger roots such as jicama or cassava should be free of big dents and soft spots, but some darkening and fissures are acceptable, as long as they're shallow enough to be peeled out. Ask the grower how they usually cook them – they may have a whole new method for you to try. Stored in a paper bag in a cool, dark place, your yams should be good for at least a few weeks.

COOKING WITH

Soak them in a big bowl of water for at least 20 minutes, then scrub with a rough vegetable brush. This gets rid of plenty of the gritty bits, and anything remaining is really just roughage. Many yams, especially when young, can be peeled, then grated or finely sliced and eaten raw in salads – such as jicama, which gives a crisp, apple–radish taste and texture to a slaw. When roasted, yams often turn a paler shade of yellow or beige, with a nutty flavor, texture reminiscent of floury potato, and the odd hint of lemony zest (especially with roasted oca). Their starch content also lends itself to being deep-fried, particularly lotus root chips – just wash some lotus roots well, slice finely on a mandoline and deep-fry until golden brown. Other tubers, such as water chestnuts and tiger nuts, are best used as a base for desserts and drinks – such as in the traditional yum cha favorite, water chestnut cake, or the Spanish *horchata de chufa*, made from soaked, blitzed and fermented tiger nuts.

WITH COMPLEMENTS

Chili, ginger, honey, lime, olive oil.

SALT-BAKED YAM TACOS (YACOS!)

Presented for your consideration, the best plant-based taco, possibly ever? Roasting yams – oca, jicama, youlk or whatever you can find – on salt draws water out and intensifies the texture and flavor, so what you're left with is the chew of chicken, with the lightness of fish. If you're not in the mood to taco 'bout it, turn this dish into a salad by omitting the tortillas and mozzarella and tossing everything together in a bowl instead.

SERVES 4–6

500 g (1 lb 2 oz) rock salt
800 g (1 lb 12 oz) jicama
    or yam of choice
1 bunch of cilantro,
    stems and leaves
    finely chopped
4 green onions (scallions),
    finely chopped
3 long green chilis, seeded
    and finely chopped
2 garlic cloves,
    finely chopped
juice of 1 lemon
juice of 1 lime, plus extra
    wedges to serve
18 small tortillas

200 g (7 oz) vegan or
    mozzarella cheese,
    thinly sliced
1 teaspoon
    smoked paprika
¼ cup (60 ml) extra
    virgin olive oil
½ teaspoon
    ground coriander
shaved red cabbage,
    to serve
watercress sprigs,
    to serve

Preheat the oven to 425°F. Place the salt in a roasting pan, in a thick layer. Add the yams, pressing them into the salt. Bake for 1 hour, or until fork-tender.

Meanwhile, combine the cilantro, green onion, chili, garlic and lemon and lime juice in a bowl. Season with salt and pepper.

When the yams are cooked, remove from the oven and leave until cool enough to handle, then peel and chop into small bite-sized pieces.

When ready to serve, place the tortillas on three baking trays and arrange the cheese slices on top. Sprinkle with the paprika and bake for 3 minutes, or until the cheese is just melting. Smear the cheese with the back of a spoon.

Heat the olive oil in a frying pan over high heat. Add the ground coriander and cook briefly, until aromatic. Add the yams and toss to warm through. Stir through the fresh cilantro and chili mixture, then use to top the tortillas.

Sprinkle with cabbage and watercress and serve immediately, with lime wedges.

Tip Yams are a fantastic source of the prebiotic fiber inulin, feeding the good bacteria in your gut. (If you're thinking 'that sounds familiar', you've probably been reading the Jerusalem artichoke entry ...) Inulin is great for our guts in the long term, but can wreak gaseous havoc in the short term, especially if the yams are particularly fresh. If you're the sort of person whose bowels move with ease, it might be worth delaying the gratification on this dish and soaking your chosen yam overnight.

Mushrooms

It would seem a big omission for a reference book such as this to be missing a mushroom entry ... yet mushrooms are not actually a vegetable at all. They belong to the world of fungi – 'The Third Kingdom' – and we're still discovering their magic, medicinally, psychedelically and gastronomically. Mushrooms are prized for their earthy savoriness and *umami*, along with their texture – springy and light when raw, silky and slippery when cooked. With their sponge-like internal structure, they have the ability to soak up sauces while retaining their shape, making them a tasty meat substitute in casseroles and on the barbecue. It's these properties that also render them the most *disliked* 'vegetable' on the roster, especially by kids. This can usually be linked back to one bad soggy 'shroom experience, often many years earlier. If you (or someone you love) is in this camp, I hope you've come to this entry because there's some inclination, deep down, to give them another chance

'One of my favorite ways to cook mushrooms is simply hot pan, butter, garlic, mushrooms, parsley/marjoram and a good amount of seasoning. Since jumping on the vegan bandwagon, I also enjoy making a good mushroom wellington – and then there's always the mushroom carpaccio I learnt to make while working in Northern Italy.' – TOBIE PUTTOCK, AUSTRALIA

BUYING & STORING

Use your nose to find the freshest fungi. They should smell earthy, but not eggy, and should feel springy, but not spongy – and definitely not slimy (unless you're looking at slippery jacks). Most commercially grown mushrooms – such as buttons, cups and portobello – are cultivated in big, temperature-controlled sheds, which makes them readily available all year round. However, you can access the rarer, more robustly flavored varieties in autumn through winter, when the rains start to make conditions optimal for wild-picking. I'm always partial to a tight little button, but fresh shiitake have also captured my heart. I love how they add bucket-loads of umami* character to any dish you slice them through – from broths and stir-fries to Italian bolognese (as heretical as this may seem). If you can't find fresh, locally grown shiitake, Asian grocers stock dried shiitake waiting to be reinvigorated in some water – and don't forget to add that murky water back in to your cooking liquid of choice as a mushroomy stock. Other exotic varieties such as enoki, oyster and king brown mushrooms make for super stir-fry additions. I loved stumbling upon slippery jacks and pine mushrooms on family foraging expeditions as a child, and am still mad for them – a likely story for many a migrant child. You'll be able to track down these wild-foraged varieties at markets and specialty greengrocers, or head out on your own adventures in local pine forests – just be sure to bring along a knowledgeable guide. The general rule with mushrooming is that if you've any doubt, leave it out. Or, as my dad likes to say: 'Any mushroom is edible ... once.'

Mushrooms are highly porous, and prone to mushiness, so they're best stored in a cool, dry place. Keeping them in the fridge with all those other fridge smells is fraught with future funk and will also dry them out, so if you're leaving them in there, consider storing them in an open paper bag inside the fridge door – that way you'll be reminded that they exist, and will use them up before they spoil. Never store them in a plastic bag, as they'll sweat and turn into soup (and not in a good way). Stocking up on dried mushrooms such as shiitake or porcini is a smart way of having bonus flavor on hand without worrying about shelf life. You can dry your own fresh mushrooms, too – in a low oven overnight, or on trays outside in the sun for a few days if the sun is strong enough and flies aren't rampant. Mushrooms can also be frozen, but I'd steam them first for 3–5 minutes, then cool and freeze in portions.

COOKING WITH

There are two schools of thought when it comes to cooking mushrooms. You're likely familiar with the conventional wisdom that encourages you to keep them dry, start with a dry pan, batch-cook, and generally treat them with kid-gloves. But the new-school thinking from fungi enthusiasts flips this on its head. Enter 'wet-frying'.

Mushrooms are 90 per cent water, with a sponge-like cell structure that can handle plenty of heat without breaking down. Dry-frying might yield plenty of caramelization, but it comes at the price of tenderness as the natural moisture evaporates entirely or, for larger mushrooms, the outside chars before the inside gets the chance. With wet-frying, you're welcome to wash or soak mushrooms as much as you need, which is a double bonus if they're foraged. Start them in a hot pan with just enough water or stock to cover. Leave on a high heat, bubbling away until the water evaporates and the mushrooms start to sizzle. For larger or more fibrous ones (like pine mushrooms), you may want to add extra liquid and repeat the process. Now you can add fat like oil, butter or *schmaltz*, and aromatics like garlic or shallots.

Bigger mushrooms – like portobello or field – are great for stuffing with cheese, herbs and the like. If you're going to stuff and bake, consider first roasting them dry and unstuffed, stem side up, for around 15 minutes to dry them out (consider this a blind-bake of sorts), and then pop the stuffing in for as long as that takes to cook. When using rarer or more delicate mushrooms such as lion's mane, fresh shiitake or morels, less is more. All you really need to do is drop them into an already warmed broth for a couple of minutes to heat through and infuse, or into a hot, wet pan to warm and color a little, let the water evaporate, then chuck in a knob of butter and season to finish.

BEYOND MUSHROOMS: TRUFFLES

Another fungus that's well worth a look is the truffle – both Périgord (black) and Magnatum (white). Though they might look like fossilized poop, truffles are one of the most expensive fresh ingredients by weight. If you want to get the most bang for your buck, buy a small truffle that's as uniform as possible, and so earthily fragrant you'll feel like you've been teleported into a gloomy cave as soon as the purveyor pops the lid on a stash. Truffle aroma has been likened to everything from smelly socks to the tousled bedsheets of a brothel, and it's that sexy, inimitable funk that you're after; something that's been synthesised in products like truffle oil. However, before you bounce out for a bottle, please do me a favor and desist. While true truffles contain over 50 aromatic compounds, the fake version pulls out just one. Spare your pennies and pick up a fresh truffle in season – early winter for Périgords is a safe bet, while white truffles are rarer and might require ordering from a specialty grocer. Most importantly, hold off on shaving either (with a truffle slicer or fine grater) until just before you're ready to serve – the aroma is extremely volatile, and dissipates under too much heat. Use just enough heat to help open up the flavors and bind them to your chosen plain, fatty, carby dish – I'm talkin' eggs, potatoes and pasta. Any offcuts are best left in a jar of salt, which will draw the flavor into itself, or blitzed and folded through softened butter, then frozen for the most decadent compound butter of them all.

'Wild mushrooms are my go-to. At the end of summer, forests become abundant with flora and fauna such as deer. For me there's no greater joy than heading into the forest in autumn and picking under the pine needles and discovering the mushrooms underneath. It's pretty magical.' – MICHAEL HUNTER, CANADA

WITH COMPLEMENTS

Butter, cheese (feta, goat, gruyère, parmesan), cream, garlic, nutmeg, onion, sage, star anise.

*Umami – ummmm, say what?

It's a term that comes up in reviews, recipes and food writing in general, and modern chefs and cooks are *obsessed* with it, but what is it? Umami, otherwise known as 'the fifth taste', was 'discovered' by a scientist at the turn of the 20th century, and translates loosely to 'savory' or 'delicious'. Its discovery by Kikunae Ikeda in Japan should come as no surprise, since Japanese cuisine is *full* of umami. From shiitake to seaweed, miso to dashi, and of course the Japanese mayonnaise, Kewpie, which contains more synthesised umami than it does actual egg. That 'synthesised umami' I'm referring to is monosodium glutamate, more commonly known as MSG – a controversial ingredient, much maligned for apparently wreaking havoc with people's systems, which seems to be more psychosomatic than physiological, based on most recent studies. Whether you actively avoid it, or partake in the odd two-minute-noodle dabble, glutamates in general are addictive … and readily available in some of the world's most-loved foods. Cheese, beer and wine, dark chocolate, aged meats and funky ferments are all chock-a-block with naturally occurring glutamates – which is probably what makes them all so addictive. Nutritionally speaking, umami also goes some way towards promoting a sense of satiety, so foods that contain glutamates make us feel more satisfied. Mushrooms, tomatoes, spinach, cabbage, corn and sweet potato are among the most umami-rich vegetables. Fascinatingly, breastmilk has also been found to contain plenty of glutamates – about the same amount as artificial MSG, in fact. This goes some way towards explaining why we're so attached to it in the first place: 'Oooh, Mommy!'

Shiitake have a depth that is unparalleled in the mushroom world. They have a unique ability to blend into the background when minced, and come to the fore when served in large pieces. They absorb flavors, and add texture and unctuousness. I love that they can easily be substituted for meat, or add a caramelized note when sautéed with soy sauce.' – NIKI NAKAYAMA, US

Mushroom varieties

Pine Bright orange, tart, with a firm texture that lends itself to being finely sliced or even braised. Peel any pine needles off with a deft fingernail or a blast of water – they're waxy enough to handle it.

Chanterelles Golden in color and trumpet-shaped, these are finer in texture than pines but more robust than morels. Sauté in butter, add to pasta or other carby dishes (a la the fry-up on page 322) or pickle, Russian style!

Morels As rare as hen's teeth and just as curious looking, these benefit from a good tap to dislodge grit in their stem and divets, and need nothing more than frying in a bit of butter.

Shiitake I love popping fresh baby shiitakes, whole (or torn if large), through pasta dishes, such as the shallot pasta on page 290. Also available dried.

Lion's mane Growing in popularity due to their ability to support nerve repair, the texture of these mushrooms is reminiscent of crabmeat, especially when poached in a light broth. Pan-frying this as a steak is fab too!

Enoki Resembling bean sprouts with tiny little mushroom caps, enoki collapse into silky ribbons in stir-fries, and are just as comfortable being deep-fried and served as a crunchy golden garnish.

Porcini These are available powdered for instant umami in sauces, dried and, very occasionally, fresh. All are perfect through scrambled eggs. Grill fresh ones as you might a steak, or sauté slices in butter.

NOT MUSHROOM FOR ERROR PIE WITH DUCK FAT PASTRY

Mushrooms are perfect in pies because they keep their shape and take on all the other flavors. I love the depth you get here from frying them down – so meaty, textural and savory – and the bonus flavor from using duck (or goose) fat in the pastry, or even just the fat (*schmaltz*) left behind after roasting a chook. You can of course simply use extra butter in the pastry, or use a quality frozen shortcrust pastry and mix some duck or chicken fat through the mushroom mixture to enhance the flavors. If you can't find porcini powder, blitz some dried porcini mushrooms in a blender, or rehydrate them, squeeze out the excess water (and use it in the pastry) and toss through the mushroom mixture.

SERVES 6

750 g (1 lb 10 oz) mixed
  mushrooms, thinly
  sliced (we used button
  and portobello)
40 g (1½ oz) butter
1 leek, pale part only,
  finely sliced
1 yellow onion, finely sliced
2 tablespoons dried
  porcini powder
1 teaspoon dried tarragon
½ teaspoon
  ground nutmeg
1 tablespoon flaked
  sea salt
¼ cup (35 g) all-purpose
  flour
2 tablespoons
  sherry vinegar

1 egg yolk, lightly beaten
good-quality ketchup,
  to serve

Duck fat pastry

3 cups (450 g) all-purpose
  flour, plus extra for
  dusting
1 teaspoon freshly
  cracked black pepper
1 teaspoon salt
100 g (3½ oz) duck fat
  or rendered chicken fat
100 g (3½ oz) salted
  butter, chopped
2 tablespoons sour cream
2 tablespoons apple
  cider vinegar

For the pastry, combine the flour, pepper and salt in a bowl. Toss the duck fat and butter through. Using just your fingertips, gently rub them into the flour until the mix resembles coarse crumbs. Make a well in the center. Pour in the combined sour cream, vinegar and ¼ cup (60 ml) cold water then, using a small knife, cut together to form a dough, taking care not to overwork it. Transfer to a lightly floured work surface and knead into a ball, then divide into three evenly sized balls. Flatten into discs, then wrap and chill in the fridge for 1 hour.

Meanwhile, make the filling. Pop the mushrooms in a large frying pan over high heat with enough water to cover. Allow the liquid to boil and evaporate completely, listening for the sizzle. Add half the butter to the pan and toss the mushrooms until golden, then set aside. In the same pan, sweat the leek and onion in the remaining butter until softened. Add the mushrooms back, sprinkle in the porcini powder, tarragon, nutmeg and salt, stir in the flour, splash in the vinegar and cook, stirring, for about 3 minutes, or until your eyes stop stinging.

Grease a deep 27 cm (10¾ inch) pie dish. On a lightly floured work surface, roll out one piece of pastry to a 3 mm (⅛ inch) thick round, then use the rolling pin to lift it over the dish and press it in with your fingers. Roll the remaining pastry into long rectangles about 3 mm (⅛ inch) thick, cut into 2–3 cm (¾–1¼ inch) wide strips and transfer to a lined tray. Chill all the pastry in the fridge again for 15 minutes. Use this time to shape any excess into decorative pastry mushrooms.

Meanwhile, preheat the oven to 425°F.

Fill the pie base with the mushroom mixture. Arrange the pastry strips in a lattice pattern over the filling, pressing the sides and strips together to seal.

Place the pie dish on a baking tray and brush the pastry with the beaten egg yolk. Arrange any decorative pastry mushrooms on top and brush again. Bake for about 45 minutes, or until the pastry is golden.

Cool slightly, then serve warm, with ketchup.

MUSHROOM-STUFFED POTATO ZRAZY WITH SATSIBELI

Pronounced ZRAH-zii, these are a bit like all-in-one rissoles. A genius combination of everything you'd pop on your plate for lunch or dinner, stuffed into a pan-fried, oblong-shaped parcel: crisp-crusted mashed potatoes, filled with sautéed cabbage, ground meat or, in this case, mushroom *duxelles* (an intensely flavored mushroom and onion mix). *Satsibeli* is Georgia's answer to tomato salsa, made the traditional way before the advent of food processors – using a box grater – with the very untraditional addition of harissa.

MAKES 10

2 cups (500 g) cold
    mashed potato
    (see page 298)
1 egg yolk, beaten
⅔ cup (100 g) all-purpose
    gluten-free flour
½ teaspoon ground
    white pepper
2 tablespoons olive oil

Mushroom *duxelles*
100 g (3½ oz)
    unsalted butter
400 g (14 oz) mixed
    mushrooms (preferably
    fresh shiitake and
    buttons), finely chopped
2 yellow onions,
    finely chopped
1 teaspoon flaked sea salt

Satsibeli
2 medium-sized tomatoes
½ white onion, peeled
2 garlic cloves, peeled
¼ cup finely chopped
    cilantro stems
    and leaves
2 teaspoons
    sherry vinegar
2 teaspoons harissa paste
½ teaspoon flaked sea salt
½ teaspoon
    granulated sugar
1 teaspoon ground
    fenugreek (optional)

For the *duxelles*, melt the butter in a wide-based frying pan. Add the mushrooms and onion, sprinkle with the salt and cook them down in the butter over low heat for 1 hour, stirring occasionally, until the mixture is dark brown, dry and fragrant. Leave to cool, preferably overnight in the fridge.

When you're ready to cook, combine the mashed potato with the egg yolk, flour and pepper in a bowl, then form into 10 equal-sized balls. Flatten into palm-sized discs, stuff with 2 teaspoons or so of the *duxelles* mixture, then fold the mash over to cover and shape int rissoles. Have a small bowl of water nearby to keep you palms damp and stop the mixture sticking to your hand

Heat the olive oil in a frying pan. Working in batches fry 3–4 *zrazy* at a time over medium heat for about 4 minutes on each side, until golden and crispy all over. Allow to rest for a minute or so before serving.

For the *satsibeli*, grate the tomatoes, onion and garl on the fine teeth of a box grater, then combine with the rest of the ingredients. Taste the mixture and adjust to your liking; it should be garlicky, sweet–sour and punch you a little bit in the nose.

The *zrazy* can be stored in the fridge for up to 4 day and served at room temperature with the *satsibeli*, or refried for a few minutes on each side over medium hea to warm through, if you'd prefer.

Tips **Using mashed potato from the fridge is best, so that the butter stays cold and firm, making it easie to work the mixture. If your hands heat it up too muc pop it back in the fridge to reset a little while you make the *satsibeli*.**

The mushroom *duxelles* is great as a filling for cheese toasties, inside pastry or dumplings, as a past sauce base or most classically in beef wellington.

FOREST FLOOR FRY-UP

One of my strongest memories of autumn is going mushroom picking with my parents in Victoria's High Country, then spending the afternoon pinching pine needles off slippery jacks and saffron milk caps (a.k.a. pine mushrooms) with great anticipation for dinner, where any 'shrooms that didn't end up in pickle jars would be fried up with potato and *smetana* (sour cream) to look something like this. Well, the 1990s new-migrant kitchen version, at least – less fancy cast iron, more 40-year-old enamel – spiked with sour pickles or gherkins to cut through the richness of it all. It's a great way to use up left-over parboiled potatoes. In fact, I like to boil up some extra spuds whenever I'm cooking them, just to use them in a dish like this.

SERVES 4

600 g (1 lb 5 oz)
   fingerling potatoes
4 French shallots,
   finely chopped
150 g (5½ oz) butter
500 g (1 lb 2 oz) mixed
   exotic and/or wild
   mushrooms, such as
   shiitake, oyster, enoki,
   king brown, slippery
   jacks, pine (see tips)

2 tablespoons olive oil
½ bunch of dill,
   roughly chopped
1 teaspoon salt
½ teaspoon cracked
   black pepper
⅓ cup (80 g) sour cream
roughly chopped sour
   pickles (see tips),
   to serve

Pop the potatoes into a saucepan, with just enough cold well-salted water to cover. Bring to the boil, then reduce the heat and simmer for 20–25 minutes, until fork-tender.

Meanwhile, in a large frying pan, sweat the shallot in 100 g (3½ oz) of the butter over medium–low heat for 5 minutes, or until golden. Set aside in a large bowl.

Leaving the residual butter gloss in the pan, crowd in your mushrooms, splash in ½ cup (125 ml) water, then let this liquid evaporate over medium–high heat until you hear the sizzle. Now splash in the olive oil to encourage caramelization. Add to the bowl of shallot.

Drain the potatoes, chop into bite-sized pieces and fry in the remaining 50 g (1¾ oz) butter for about 4 minutes, until starting to get crispy. Toss the shallot and mushrooms through, then stir in the dill (reserve a few fronds for garnishing), salt and cracked pepper.

Dollop with the sour cream, sprinkle with pickles and reserved dill and serve.

Tips **When in season, slippery jacks and pine mushrooms are scrumptious here, but any edible mushrooms of different shapes and textures will work**

   Sour pickles cut through the richness and add color to the dish. Look for brands where vinegar is low on the list; 'dill pickles' are always good.

Double duty **Reheat any leftovers in a non-stick frying pan with olive oil or butter until they start getting crispy bits again, then pour 2 beaten eggs per person over the top. Pop under a hot broiler and you'll have yourself the world's quickest potato tortilla (if you don't count Ferran Adrià's version using potato chips).**

Dark
Green

* **SPINACH**
  + Swiss chard
  + Chicory
* **ARUGULA**
  + Nettle
* **HERBS**
* **KALE**

* **BROCCOLI**
  + Gai lan
  + Broccolini
* **ZUCCHINI**
  + Zucchini flowers
* **CUCUMBER**
* **BEANS**
  + Bean sprouts
* **OKRA**

Spinach

When I think of spinach, I think of David Copperfield (the magician, not the Dickensian character). Put it in a pan, close the lid, and *poof* it's gone. That's because spinach is more than 90 per cent water, and cooking reduces its volume by three-quarters. Its flavor is as mild as its color is vibrant – which is why, well before the statues and the sailor men, spinach dishes made themselves endemic in every cuisine since the Persians. Where would India be without palak paneer, or China without stir-fried ginger spinach, or Greece without spanakopita? It was introduced to France by the Italian queen responsible for bringing an Italian influence to French cooking – Catherine De Medici, who requested spinach so often that anything containing the leafy green was referred to as 'Florentine', like the eggs. Its color is a little bit magic, too. Blanch and blitz and you'll have a vivid green chlorophyll-heavy paste that can add color to pasta, sauce and homemade playdough.

'I find greens really inspiring – raw, roasted, sautéed, blanched, etc.
I'll blanch Swiss chard stems and leaves separately, then mix with
flour, butter and milk, top with cheese and bake for an excellent
gratin. Spinach and nettles get stirred into soups at the end, and make
their way into pasta dough or filling.' – DANIELLE ALVAREZ, US

BUYING & STORING

You'll most likely find fresh spinach in bunches, with roots and stems still attached, or as baby leaves, either loose or bagged. It's available year round, but late autumn into early winter is when it's at its springiest. If bagged up, look out for sweaty bits and softened tips on any of the leaves. Loose spinach should feel bouncy to the touch, and squeak when you start bagging it up – handle with care, as the leaves are quite delicate, and any bruised bits will turn the whole batch. I keep some in the freezer for an extra bit of green, but if you've got the option, fresh is always better. Spinach powder is readily available, and worth considering beyond a scoop into smoothies – a teaspoon of powder is equivalent to about half a bag of baby spinach (I told you it disappears!), so try it out if you're greening up a pasta dough or soup.

The key with keeping spinach fresh is to keep it dry. Pick out any mangy leaves prior to storing, then wash and spin in a salad spinner until they're as dry as possible (salad spinners are a life-saver in a salad-scoffing household). Use the spinner or another container lined with paper towel or cloth to store the spinach in, and check it every couple of days. If the spinach is starting to look a little limp, or if you have a surplus, make your own frozen spinach portions by immersing the spinach in boiling water for 30 seconds, then squeezing out all the excess liquid, squirting on some lemon juice to help keep the color, freezing in fistfuls on a tray, and finally transferring to a container for later use.

COOKING WITH

Spinach has a deep dark-green color that can hide a lot of grit – which will be in particular abundance if there's been any rain about. Even if a package of baby spinach says 'washed', it will still benefit from a couple of whirls around the salad spinner. When sautéing spinach in a pan, there's no need to add water – just use a lidded pan with high sides, keep the heat on medium–low to keep the bottom leaves from catching, and as soon as you close the lid, the spinach will begin to release its own juices. Once this happens, take the lid off and give it the odd stir, to ensure that the entire bunch gets cooked through evenly, and as much of the liquid is released as possible. If the pan is looking particularly soupy, drain off any excess liquid before melting in a knob of butter (and crushed garlic, if you're that way inclined), stirring until the spinach becomes glossy. If you're using the leaves as part of a recipe – such as in a tart or curry – consider sautéing them first, but stop at the butter. Squeeze out the excess moisture before layering it over pastry or through an egg mix; this will help your fat of choice to bind with the spinach and stop the dish becoming soggy.

FUNCTIONAL FOOD

It turns out that Popeye may indeed have been onto something – or 'on something'. In recent trials carried out by researchers in Berlin, a chemical extract from spinach was found to have steroid-like effects on strength-training, with the world anti-doping agency backing the study to investigate whether to put *spinach* on its list of banned substances! The findings will be a relief to spinach-loving athletes the world over, because although it was discovered to be pumping with ecdysterone, a person would have to eat up to 16 kilos of spinach over 10 weeks to get any sort of marked improvement.

WITH COMPLEMENTS

Bacon, butter, cheese (especially Comté, feta, parmesan, ricotta), cream, eggs, garlic, ginger, lemon juice, nutmeg, pepper, sesame seeds, soy sauce.

BEYOND SPINACH: SWISS CHARD

While beets are cultivated for their roots, other family members are prized for their leafy foliage alone. Swiss chard can be white-stalked with deep green leaves, red-veined, or in the case of rainbow chard, an ombré-hued combo of red-pink-orange-yellow stalks with waxy plumage. Treat all the chards as you might kale or mature spinach, either pulling the leaves off the stalks against the grain, or using scissors to trim as close to the woody stalks as possible. The stalks can be braised separately, as you would celery or other watery vegetables. The flavor of chard is very mild – slightly earthy and a little bitter, though the bitterness fades with cooking.

BEYOND SPINACH: CHICORY

Though closer in relation to endive, the way you cook chicory is all about the low and slow, more akin to Swiss chard and spinach. As with all bitter greens, this one is fantastic for digestion, and behaves best when teamed with something creamy (like olive oil, butter, and/or cheese) or lifted with plenty of acid from fancy vinegar or citrus. Horta (vrasta), a classic Greek take on boiled greens, takes full advantage of both of these, braising the chicory with sweated onion and garlic, and finishing with a crumble of feta and plenty of freshly squeezed lemon juice.

GREEN EGGS FLORENTINE

Spinach is almost always an after-thought when it comes to a cooked breakfast – a compensatory bit of green stuff for all the other fried fodder. 'Oh, a bit of spinach on the side,' you say, or squint to find some poking out from under egg on egg. Here, perfectly poached eggs – Nigella Lawson-style – are sandwiched between spinach for a bit of bougie brunch-time indulgence. The vinegar reduction is great with just about everything, but is especially good here in the hollandaise sauce.

SERVES 4

120 g (4 oz)
   unsalted butter
2 egg yolks
120 g (4 oz) baby
   spinach leaves, plus
   extra to serve
⅓ cup (80 ml) vinegar
   (see tip)
8 eggs
4 English muffins,
   halved and toasted
¼ teaspoon paprika
lemon wedges, to serve

**Vinegar reduction
for everything
(Makes 1 cup/250 ml)**
2 cups (500 ml) white
   wine vinegar
stalks from 1 bunch of dill
   (reserve the leaves for
   another use)
2 bay leaves
6 cloves
1 teaspoon black
   peppercorns
1 teaspoon fennel seeds

Tip Adding acid to the poaching water helps the egg whites coagulate. Don't waste your fancy vinegar on this – use any light-colored one, like white or apple cider vinegar, or lemon juice.

Shortcuts Instead of the vinegar reduction, use white wine vinegar in the hollandaise and egg-poaching water. And instead of wilting fresh spinach, blitz some spirulina powder through your finished hollandaise for a hit of green.

To make the vinegar reduction, place all the ingredients in a saucepan over medium–high heat for 10 minutes to reduce by half. Remove the dill stalks, and reserve 2 tablespoons of the liquid. Pour the remaining hot liquid into a clean jar, seal and store in a cool, dark place. It will keep unopened for 6 months, or refrigerate and use within 1–2 months.

Melt the butter in a frying pan. Meanwhile, whiz the egg yolks and 1½ tablespoons of the reserved vinegar reduction in a blender until pale. With the motor running, add the hot melted butter in a steady stream, slowly incorporating until the sauce is thicker and pale. The butter should be hot the whole time, to cook the egg yolks. (Alternatively, put all the ingredients in a small heavy-based pan on the lowest heat, and whisk relentlessly until the sauce thickens.)

Once all the butter has been incorporated, wilt the spinach leaves in the same pan for a minute or so, then pop into the blender with the hollandaise and stand until required; the hot spinach will keep the hollandaise warm.

To poach the eggs, half-fill a wide saucepan with water and bring to the boil. Reduce the heat to low. Add 2 tablespoons of the vinegar to the simmering water. Working quickly, stir the water with a wooden spoon to create a whirlpool. Crack 2 eggs at a time into a small bowl and splash with another 2 teaspoons of the vinegar. Gently pour into the center of the water, and repeat with another 2 eggs and another 2 teaspoons vinegar. Cook for 3 minutes, or until the whites are opaque. Remove with a slotted spoon and set aside to drain. Poach the remaining eggs in the same way.

Meanwhile, whiz the spinach into the hollandaise until green and thick. Pile an egg on each muffin half and spoon the hollandaise over. Sprinkle with paprika and salt, top with extra spinach and serve with lemon wedges.

Double duty For a great accompaniment to *steak frites*, turn the hollandaise into a spinach béarnaise by adding some tarragon, chervil and finely diced shallot.

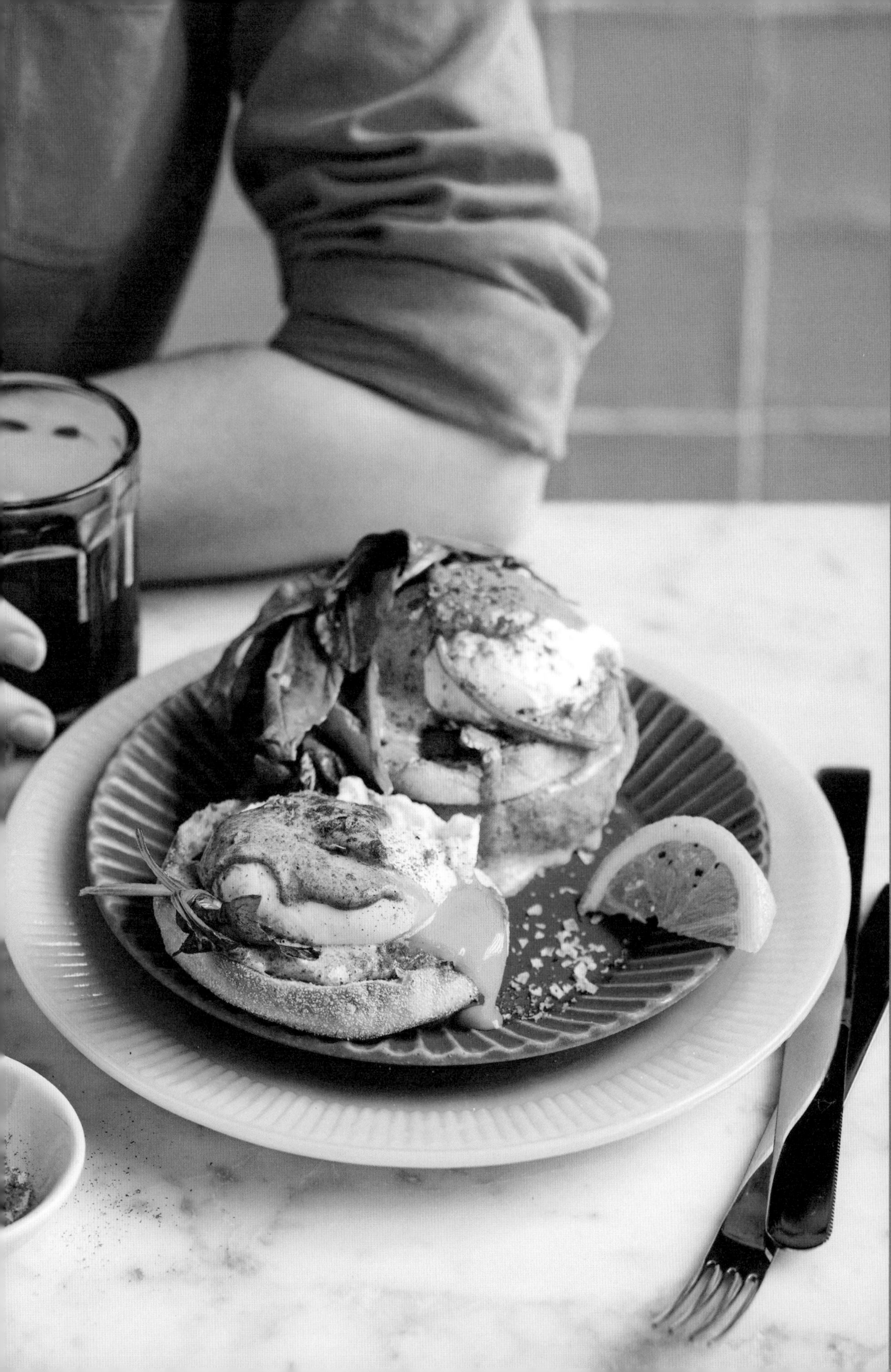

NO-WRAP SHRIMP & SPINACH DUMPLINGS

I love how easy these are to make, without the need to even attempt a single fold. I first picked up the technique years ago from chef Shaun Presland, when he was in charge of Sake restaurant in Sydney, where a version of these dumplings was an iconic menu mainstay. If you can get your hands on some water spinach, give that a whirl – both as blanched filling, and for keeping fingers clean as makeshift 'serviettes'. Instead of shrimp, you could use sliced shiitake mushrooms, or tofu blitzed up with the spinach.

MAKES 26 DUMPLINGS

45 g (1½ oz) fresh
   ginger, peeled and
   finely chopped
6 garlic cloves,
   roughly chopped
20 g (¾ oz) cilantro,
   leaves picked, plus
   extra to garnish
2 green onions (scallions),
   thinly sliced, plus
   extra to garnish
1 small red chili, roughly
   chopped, plus extra
   sliced chili to serve
1 tablespoon grated palm
   sugar (jaggery)
a good splash of soy
   sauce, plus extra
   to serve

¼ teaspoon toasted
   sesame oil
1 tablespoon salt
500 g (1 lb 2 oz) raw
   shrimp meat, roughly
   chopped
250 g (9 oz) baby spinach
   or water spinach leaves,
   blanched (see tips), plus
   extra leaves to serve
40 egg-based wonton
   wrappers (270 g/9½ oz)

Place the ginger, garlic, cilantro, green onion and chili in a food processor. Add the sugar, soy sauce, sesame oil and salt and whiz for about 10 seconds until combined. (Alternatively, use a knife to chop all the fresh ingredients together, transfer to a bowl, then stir in the liquids once you've added the chopped shrimp meat.)

Add half the shrimp meat and half the blanched spinach and whiz to combine; the mixture should still be slightly chunky. (If using a knife, chop half finely, and the rest roughly.) Fold in the remaining shrimp meat and blanched spinach to chunk the mixture up even further.

Have a bowl of warm water on stand-by. Roll up stacks of the wonton wrappers, then cut into thin strips using a sharp knife. Roll teaspoon amounts of the shrimp mixture into individual balls, then roll them around in the wonton strips, to coat them in a dumpling fashion. If your fingers get sticky, pop them into the water bowl.

Line two bamboo steamers with slashed parchment paper. Add the dumplings in a single layer. Set the steamer over a pan of simmering water and steam for 7–8 minutes, or until the dumplings are springy. (Alternatively, cook the dumplings in two batches, covering the other dumplings with a damp tea towel to stop them drying out.)

Serve immediately, garnished with extra cilantro, with extra soy sauce and chili for dipping, and fresh water spinach leaves to roll around the dumplings.

Tips Ask your fishmonger for wild shrimp meat. The shrimp will be smaller, sweeter, and often cheaper, too.

To blanch baby spinach, pop it in a heatproof bowl, pour boiling water over, then drain right away through a colander, squeezing out the excess moisture.

Shortcut Instead of slicing the wonton wrappers, pop a tablespoon of the filling in the middle of a round wrapper, then squeeze into a rough moneybag shape.

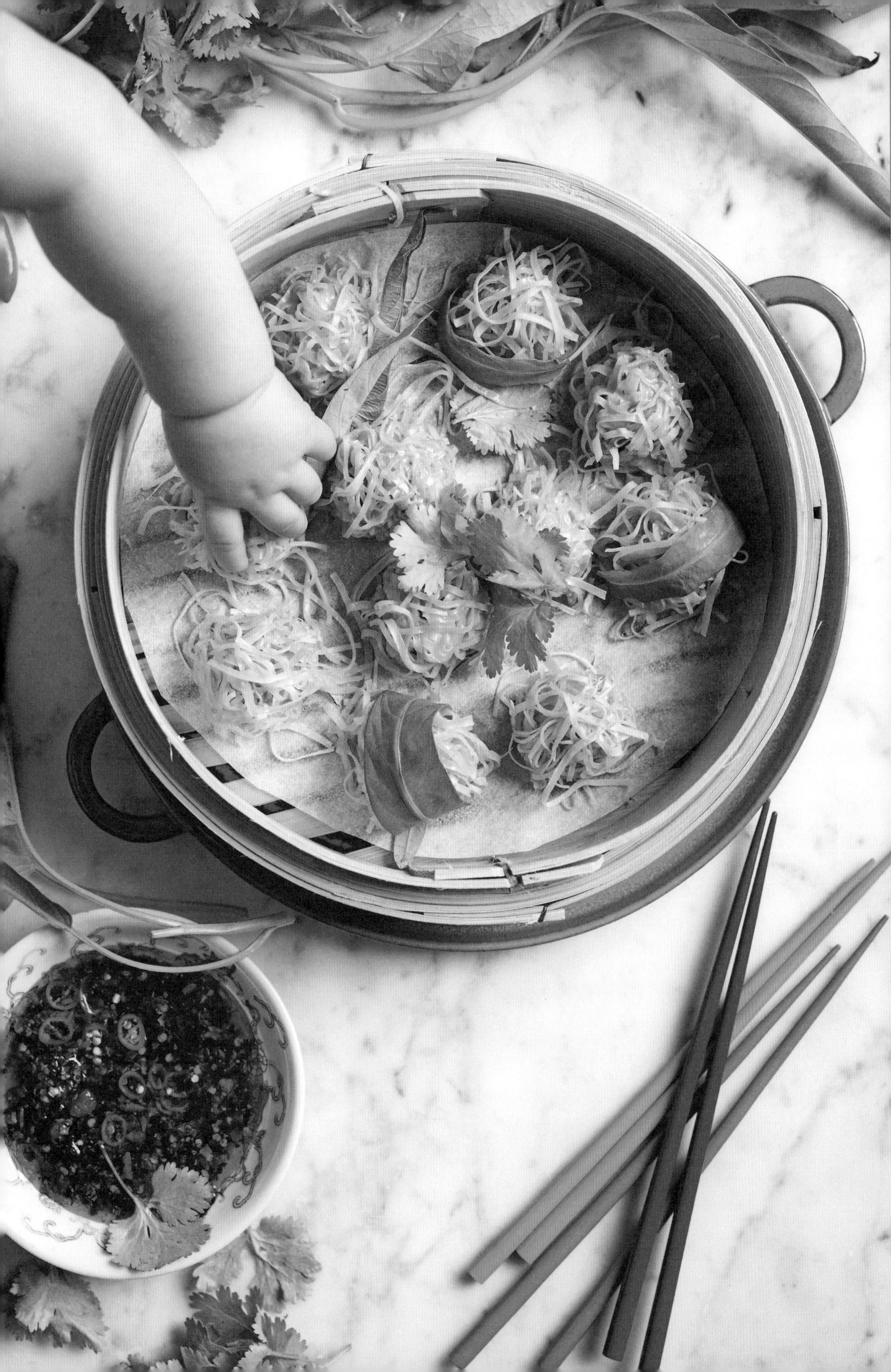

Swiss chard khachapuri
(page 336)

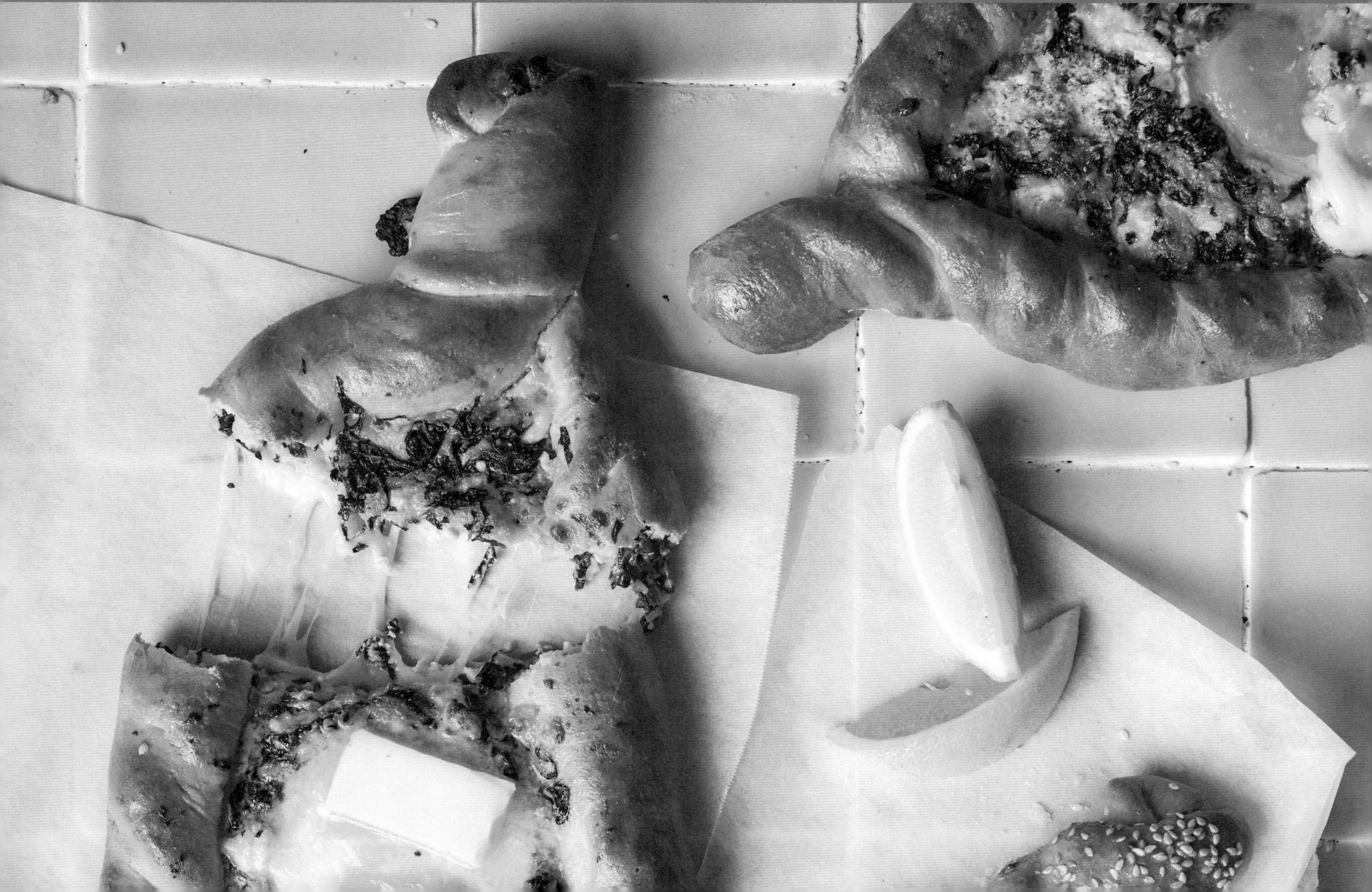

SWISS CHARD KHACHAPURI

I couldn't publish a cookbook and *not* feature this recipe – arguably, Georgia's greatest gift to the world. This cheese bread (*khacha* meaning 'cheese', *puri* meaning 'bread') has over 20 different regional iterations, across a reasonably small country, which should give you a sense of how seriously Georgians take their food. Swiss chard is usually reserved for *mkhlovana* or *pkhali* dip – so I hope they'll forgive its addition to this *adjaruli khachapuri*, which is otherwise distinguished by its gondola shape, to reflect the port city's seafaring heritage, and coddled egg in the center.

MAKES 4

1 cup (250 ml) milk, lukewarm
2 teaspoons (7 g sachet) instant dried yeast
½ teaspoon sugar
3 cups (450 g) bread flour, plus extra for dusting
2 eggs
¼ cup (60 ml) olive oil, plus extra for drizzling
½ teaspoon salt
sesame seeds, for sprinkling (optional)
40 g (1½ oz) butter, cut into 4 large slices
lemon wedges, to serve

Filling

1 tablespoon olive oil
1 onion, diced
1–2 garlic cloves, roughly chopped
1 bunch of Swiss chard, leaves picked and finely chopped, to yield about 265 g (9½ oz) chopped leaves
200 g (7 oz) cottage cheese
200 g (7 oz) mozzarella, grated
200 g (7 oz) feta
¼ teaspoon salt (optional)
½ teaspoon ground fenugreek
4 eggs

Combine the milk, yeast and sugar in a bowl and set aside to dissolve. In a saucepan, combine 25 g (1 oz) of the flour and 100 ml (3½ fl oz) water and stir over low heat for 1–2 minutes until a slurry forms. Allow to cool slightly, then add to the milk mixture, along with 1 egg and the olive oil, whisking to combine.

Sift the remaining flour into your biggest mixing bowl, or the bowl of an electric stand mixer. Sprinkle in the salt, then make a well in the center. Slowly add the milk mixture, using a spatula or your hands to combine. Knead together with your hands in the bowl, or if using an electric stand mixer, keep it whirring until a soft dough forms; this should take around 5–10 minutes. Keep kneading the dough and pulling it apart until it stops tearing when you do this. You should be able to pull the dough apart and see some elasticity as the gluten begins to activate.

When the dough comes away from the sides of the bowl, turn it out onto a floured counter and give it some more kneading if needed. You'll know you've kneaded it enough when you poke a fingertip in lightly and it springs back. More is more here – you can't overwork this dough.

Sprinkle some flour into the bottom of the bowl and use this to scoop out any left-over dough bits – if they're crumbly, discard them; otherwise, incorporate them into the dough, folding it over itself a few times to ensure the bits are fully embraced.

Wipe the bowl out with paper towel or a tea towel. Now splash a bit of extra olive oil into the bottom of the bowl and pop the dough back in, turning to coat in the oil. Cover with a tea towel and leave to prove in a warm spot for 1 hour.

Meanwhile, make the filling. Warm the olive oil in a large saucepan over medium–low heat and sweat the onion for a few minutes, until it starts to break down. Reduce the heat to low, pop a lid on and sweat the onion for another 5 minutes or so, then remove the lid and sweat for a further 2–3 minutes, until translucent and glossy.

Stir in the garlic and Swiss chard, mixing thoroughly. Pop the lid back on and leave them to get to know each other and get steamy for 5 minutes.

Tip the mixture into a fresh bowl. Add the cottage cheese and mozzarella to this bowl, then crumble in the feta and mix together well. Taste and season if need be. Divide into four equal portions and set aside.

Once the dough has doubled in size, preheat the oven to 500°F. Line two baking trays with parchment paper.

Turn the dough out onto a floured counter and knock it back, by giving the squishiest bits a few satisfying fist bumps. Divide into four equal-sized blobs and shape into balls. If you're going down the sesame seed route, here's where you sprinkle some seeds under the dough, too.

Use a rolling pin to roll out the balls into oblongs about 17 cm x 35 cm (6½ inches x 14 inches) in size. Imagine a football or rugby ball, and make a shape big enough to wrap up the sides of it.

Pop two oblongs on each baking tray. Scoop one portion of filling onto each oblong, to about 1 cm (½ inch) from the edge, then use your fingers to fold and press the pastry over to form a 'fence', folding some mixture underneath it to create a stuffed crust. Pinch, pull and twist the top and bottom of the oblong so that it forms a boat shape. Cover with a tea towel and leave to prove for a further 15 minutes.

Lightly beat the remaining egg in the reserved milk-mixture bowl from earlier (to mop up any left-over liquid from before) and brush it over to glaze the dough crusts. Sprinkle the filling with fenugreek and salt, and the edges with more sesame seeds if desired.

Pop the trays into the oven. Reduce the oven temperature to 400°F. Bake for 10–15 minutes, or until the crusts are just starting to get a glow and firm up, swapping the trays halfway through for even browning if needed.

Crank the oven temperature up to 425°F.

Use the base of a ⅓ cup (80 ml) measuring cup to create a well for the egg in the center of each khachapuri. One at a time, crack the eggs into a glass, sliding one into each well.

Bake for a final 10–15 minutes, until the eggs have just set and the crusts are golden brown. Top each hot khachapuri with a slice of butter and serve with lemon wedges, if you'd like … though my dad categorically disagrees with the lemon!

Tip The khachapuri can be baked in advance, minus the eggs. Just before serving, crack the eggs in and bake in a preheated oven at 425°F for 10–15 minutes.

Shortcut You can pop the same filling into shop-bought puff or filo pastry with equally delicious results – and leave the egg out for an even quicker zoom to the table.

Extra The just-baked khachapuri is traditionally topped with a slice of butter just before serving – but the Compound herb butter from the roasted radishes on page 190 makes an awesome alternative.

Arugula

As a green mentioned in the Old Testament, you'd think that arugula would be an uppity leaf, swinging its clout around like, say, lofty frisée. Instead, it behaves more like a humble weed, happy to grow under fairly threadbare conditions, requiring minimal water. Indeed, somewhat like Christina Aguilera, the more arugula is starved of care, the more it seems to thrive and become a 'Stronger' version of itself. You can usually tell how peppery or mustardy an arugula variety is going to be by how big and serrated its leaves are – the sharper the edges, the bitier. Think of it as being more like a herb than a lettuce. The best dish to garnish with plenty of it? Your pizza, fresh out of the oven!

'Arugula adds a natural peppery taste; blend those green leaves with some anchovy, gherkin juice, garlic and lemon, then mellow out with mayo to make a goddess sauce of sorts. This is so versatile, and highly recommended with potatoes.'
ALANNA SAPWELL, AUSTRALIA

BUYING & STORING

Available year round, but at its best in spring, good arugula is usually a matter of taste. That is to say, picking up a leaf and giving it a bite is your best bet of determining whether it has the right level of heat and, well, *bite* for you. Wilder arugula varieties are hardier, with woodier stems and firmer leaves and a mouthfeel verging on (but not quite tipping into) young kale territory. Yellowing of any leaf tips should be avoided, as should too many dark spots – however, if you feel the leaf and it's still quite firm, you'll find that those spots are mostly cosmetic and the flavor will still be fine, and often more intensified. If the arugula is encased in a container and un-tasteable, turn it over and look at the leaves towards the bottom of the box – as long as there aren't any discernibly slimy or yellowed ones, you're in business. (Do ask if you can leave the container at the register for recycling purposes.)

Arugula's leaves are sturdier than those of other leafy greens such as lettuce, which require a far more delicate touch on the storage front. However, it still benefits from being stored like a herb or leaf lettuce, wrapped in some kitchen or paper towel, then loosely bagged in the crisper. You'll find the shelf life on arugula can exceed a week – sometimes up to 10 days or so in a dry yet slightly dampened environment. Any direct moisture will see a dramatic decrease in this potential, however, so be vigilant.

BEYOND ARUGULA: NETTLE

With food as with fashion, everything old is new again. This is true of stinging nettle, a weed that has a sting to it, both in touch and taste. That 'sting' is the nettle's natural defense system; a layer of fine hairs on the underside of the leaves and on the stem that is irritating to pests (including pesky human fingers). When cooking with nettle, which you're most likely to find in specialty greengrocers in winter, be sure to wear gloves and use scissors, blanching the leaves in well-salted boiling water until the color turns bright green. Refresh in iced water to set the color and stop the cooking process, then add to starchy dishes such as pasta or risotto, and creamy ones such as soup or a cheesy spanakopita-style bake.

WITH COMPLEMENTS

Bell pepper (especially red), cheese (especially goat, parmesan), citrus (especially lemon, orange, blood orange), garlic, nuts (especially hazelnut, pine nut, walnut), pancetta, pear, radicchio, tomato, vinegar (especially balsamic, red wine vinegar).

CLASSIC CARAMELIZED BALSAMIC, ARUGULA & PEAR SALAD

Arugula, pear, parmesan: it's such a classic combination, particularly when paired with a drizzle of syrupy sweet dark vinegar. But instead of shelling out a pretty penny for aged or caramelized balsamic vinegar, try this cheat's method using regular balsamic spiked with a glug of maple syrup. It might sting your eyes while you are reducing it, but the resulting elixir is worth it.

SERVES 4 AS A SIDE DISH

½ cup (125 ml)
   balsamic vinegar
¼ cup (60 ml)
   maple syrup
2 firm pears (preferably
   Bartlett or similar),
   thinly sliced
100 g (3½ oz)
   arugula
50 g (1¾ oz) wild arugula
   – optional, but awesome

1 small red onion,
   thinly sliced
¼ cup (40 g) roasted
   hazelnuts, chopped
shaved parmesan, to serve
extra virgin olive oil,
   for drizzling

In a small saucepan, reduce the balsamic vinegar and maple syrup together over high heat until the liquid reduces by two-thirds and thickens. Pour into a clean jar (for storing any excess) and allow to cool slightly; the mixture should thicken further as it cools. It will keep in an airtight container in the fridge for up to 1 month.

Arrange the pear, arugula and onion in a bowl or on a platter. Sprinkle with the hazelnuts and season with flaked sea salt and freshly cracked black pepper. Sprinkle the parmesan on top, then drizzle with the maple balsamic and a splash of olive oil.

Serve without saying a word about where your 'caramelized' balsamic came from – your guests will think you've spent a bomb!

Tip If you're taking this salad to a party, bring the elements in separate containers and toss together when you get there.

Herbs

From bay leaves thrown into stock, to sprinkled dill on a smoked salmon bagel, good cooking starts and ends with herbs. Hard herbs – the ones with woody stems, such as rosemary, thyme, oregano, marjoram and makrut lime leaves – are hardy enough to withstand the heat; they also benefit from more time and pressure to do their best work. Soft herbs such as parsley, cilantro, basil and dill are best left out until just before the cooking's done, to protect their delicate leaves and to retain their aromas. In technical terms, the 'herb' part of a plant is the edible leafy or flowering bit, so some vegetables – especially members of the Umbelliferae family such as fennel and celery – fit into multiple camps, depending on whether you're using them for their bulbs and stems, their umbrella-like florals (hence the 'umbell'), or their seeds. I'm a big fan of layering – for instance using both the cilantro root and stalk in a curry paste, ground coriander in the sauce, and garnishing the dish with a big flourish of fresh green cilantro sprigs. Root-to-leaf, so to speak.

'One of the things Georgian cuisine has perfected over the
centuries is gathering herbs and greens in the wild, blanching
them, adding the same three spices, and getting a great result
every single time. Coriander + fenugreek + chili = magic.'

—LUKA NACHKEBIA, GEORGIA

BUYING & STORING

Regardless of the herb you're acquiring, here are a few non-negotiables. The first is no slimy bits – that's a sure-fire sign that the herbs are on their way back from whence they came. On the topic of 'earthing', flowers may seem a whimsical addition to the plate, but they also indicate that the herbs have gone to seed, and are therefore on a downward trajectory in both taste and shelf life. Gritty bits amongst the roots are okay, especially in herbs that grow close to the ground – just be sure to give them a proper soak before using. You'll notice that this can be particularly pronounced after heavy rains. Beyond the look of them, get your schnoz in. Herbs at their peak emanate enough aroma that you should be able to start smelling the good stuff instantly. Soft herbs such as basil, chervil and peppermint can be quite hit and miss, so if they smell like there's nothing doing, they likely won't give you the bang you want for your buck. Harder herbs can seem a little milder in fragrance on first whiff, so try rubbing a frond between your fingertips to gauge its true potential. Some herbs, particularly dill, can occasionally smell like wet dog or gasoline (the Dutch even call dill *stinkende vinke* or 'stinking fennel'), and no amount of washing can get rid of that funk either. I'd prefer to forgo the fronds than spoil my whole dish. If you only need a little for sprinkling into a pot to enhance flavor when cooking, consider dried herbs. Even the soft ones such as chives, mint, dill, basil, oregano, tarragon and parsley do well when dried, but it pays to check the use-by date on the back of the herb packet. To test the freshness of those dried herbs in the back of your pantry, roll them between your fingertips and sniff – if no aroma is forthcoming, they're dust. I'd choose dried herbs over a herb paste any day, particularly as most herb pastes contain less than 50 per cent actual herbs and the rest of the mix is made up of preservatives and fillers. Finally, consider going on a little expedition and finding a handy neighbor with a herb garden to make friends with. If one of these is unforthcoming, consider becoming your block's handy neighbor with a herb garden.

Herb storage is rather like a sliding scale of interventions. The more recently the herbs have been picked, the less you have to do to keep them going strong. The best way to have fresh herbs on tap is to grow them yourself – they are inexpensive to cultivate, easy enough to keep alive, and mean you don't have to feel guilty about the soggy sage stinking out the bottom of the fridge. Some pots on the windowsill, a planter on the balcony, a wicking bed, a full-blown patch – start small and work your way up. Your pocket and your palate will thank you.

If you're yet to commit to your own stash, and plan on using the herbs within a few days, store them as you would flowers – in a vase with plenty of fresh water, in a shady spot on the counter. Just make sure that none of the leaves are touching the water. Harder herbs will keep for a week or so in this way. You may also extend on this method by popping them in a jar of water and storing loosely covered in the door of your fridge. Soft herbs such as chervil, cilantro, dill, parsley and tarragon will keep like this for up to a week, though basil prefers to stay fridge-free (it's the one herb that's much easier to grow than store). If you're picking leaves for multiple dishes at once, or want to streamline your storage, pack a container with damp paper towel or cloth between layers (for the picked leaves), or wrap whole bunches in the same way and store towards the top of the crisper (so you don't forget to use them). For herbs such as oregano, rosemary and thyme, do as they do in the old country (whichever country you've just thought of will do) and dry out a whole bunch hung upside down in a well-ventilated spot, such as the inside of your pantry door – either nude, or inside a loosely tied calico bag. Harvest the tips or leaves once dry by shaking, tapping and generally agitating, then store in an airtight container with a smug sustainability-warrior look on your face.

Some herbs – particularly sturdier ones such as thyme, rosemary, pandan, and makrut lime leaves – respond well to being frozen. Wrap the sprigs in foil and keep in the door of your freezer. When freezing softer herbs such as parsley, dill and tarragon, snap-freeze them on a tray, then portion out and store in airtight containers. Alternatively, blitz up any herbs that are starting to turn with some neutral-flavored oil, scoop into an ice-cube tray and freeze, then transfer to airtight containers once they're frozen, so as not to cross-contaminate smells. Remember to label the containers, lest your industriousness discombobulate you at the other end. These frozen fronds and cubes can be added to stocks, soups, stews and the like, but I wouldn't be garnishing with them, unless you're going for an avant-garde, dystopian vibe.

COOKING WITH

If there's only one point you take away from this entire herb spread, it's that hard herbs can handle the heat, but soft herbs would prefer not to. If you're using hard herbs for roasting or braising, consider keeping the stalks whole and pulling them out once cooking is complete. They've done their job, unless you're planning on keeping things rustic, or letting your guests pull the odd thyme branch out from between their teeth as part of the experience. For ease of use, do as the French do, and create a bouquet garni by tying your herbs in a little cheesecloth (like a 'tea bag') for adding to soups and stews, or simply tie the herbs together with a bit of kitchen twine, so they're easier to pull out in one go. Alternatively, slip the herbs off their stalks by pushing in the opposite direction to the way they're growing and the leaves will zip right off. Soft herbs are better picked rather than chopped – the more you hack at them, the more bruised they get, and the more aroma and color ends up on the chopping board than in your dish. If you *must*, use a sharp knife and do a few cross-chops. For cooked dishes, pop your picked soft herbs through as soon as the heat is off, and stir. The residual heat will release more of the herbaceous aromas, without draining the leaves of color. Save a little fresh stuff for a garnish on top, too. For salads and raw dishes, garnish just before serving – once any oil touches the leaves, they'll start to wilt, just like any other leafy green.

FUNCTIONAL FOOD

Another reason for the extensive propagation of herbs worldwide is their widely documented (and occasionally disputed) homeopathic properties, with many of our most commonly accessible herbs utilized for their antiseptic, anesthetic, analgesic or anti-inflammatory properties. Some are even being synthesised and incorporated into conventional Western medicines. Here's a quick kitchen apothecary's arsenal (for steeping in tea and some such) you may like to arm yourself with.

To calm a busy head: Holy basil, lavender, lemon balm, peppermint
To settle a sore tummy: Sawtooth cilantro, dill, fennel, peppermint
To help ease period pain: Dill, fennel, thyme
To freshen your breath: Parsley, peppermint

Cilantro vs Coriander

This is one of those potato–potato situations, which really comes down to where a recipe originates from. 'Cilantro' is the Spanish word for coriander, and since it was the Spaniards who were responsible for propagating it wherever they colonized, this is what it's called in the Americas. For much of the world, a variation on 'coriander' is more common, as it's one of the oldest used herbs and spices, prized for the zing and brightness it adds to dishes, and even mentioned on the Ebers Papyrus from 1550 B.C.E. (I wonder what 'zing' looks like in hieroglyphics?). While we're here, it would be remiss of me not to mention *culantro* (nope, that's not a typo!), also known as sawtooth coriander, which is a perennial cousin of regular cilantro, with long leaves that bear a striking resemblance in flavor to cilantro (except stronger), and in appearance to a double-edged power-saw (but not quite as sharp, thankfully). This herb is often used instead of, or alongside, cilantro in South-East Asian, Indian, Caribbean and Mexican dishes.

Cilantro vs Detergent

One more note on cilantro, because my mate Sal would be livid if I left this bit out. Depending on which school of thought you subscribe to, there is between a 3–21 per cent likelihood in certain populations of an aversion to cilantro. It's still being studied, but research to date has identified specific genes that are especially sensitive to sniffing out aldehydes, molecules also found in soaps. Ethnicity seems to play a role, with people whose cuisines contain the most cilantro being least sensitive to its scent – however whether this is nature or nurture still remains to be seen. My tip is to leave the cilantro garnish as an optional extra for those that way inclined … or make new friends. Sorry, Sal.

SCRAP MEDAL

It's pretty rare that a recipe will require the full length of the herb, so there is the inevitable question of what to do with the rest. Leaves are great for garnishing and can be stored once picked and washed, as they do in restaurants, in a container with some damp paper towel or cloth. Consider blitzing stalks, which have the highest water content, into a quick pesto or marinade (such as a parsley and garlic sauce), or wrapping in foil and freezing for use in future stocks. Roots are the unsung heroes of herbs, and are sadly the first to go into the compost – even though they are full of the most intense herbaceous aromas, pungency and remedial properties. Save cilantro root for Thai curry pastes and Mexican moles, where it is prized for its intensity of flavor, and also its capacity to help preserve food for longer. If you're still at a loss as to what to do with any surplus leaves that look like they're about to cark it, try deep-frying them for a garnish, or making a herb oil, instructions for both of which you can find on the recipe overleaf (pun never not intended!).

Herbs of the world

Every country has some form of herb combination or blend that acts as a backbone to its cuisine, based on its climate and culinary history. Let me be the first to tell you that there is a lot more nuance to each of these once you start delving deeper, as each country can be further segmented by region and cultural influences, but here is a top-line selection to use as a guide to kick you off. You can pick (ha!) just one from the relevant list, or pull a couple together into a herb bouquet.

Australian native herbs Aniseed myrtle, Geraldton wax, lemon myrtle, mountain pepper leaf, river mint, strawberry gum.

Chinese Cilantro, flowering chive, garlic chive, spearmint.

French *Bouquet garni* – bay leaf, marjoram, parsley, thyme.
Fines herbes – chervil, chive, dill, lovage, tarragon.
Herbes de Provence – bay leaf, fennel, lavender, marjoram, parsley, thyme.

Greek Bay leaf, dill, fennel, marjoram, oregano, parsley, purslane, rosemary, sage, savory, spearmint, tarragon, thyme.

Indian Cilantro, curry leaf, dill, fenugreek leaf, spearmint, holy basil (tulsi).

Italian Basil, bay leaf, marjoram, oregano, parsley, rosemary, sage, thyme.

Japanese Mitsuba, negi, seaweed, shiso, wasabi leaf.

Malaysian Curry leaf, makrut lime leaf, pandan leaf, spearmint, Thai basil, Vietnamese mint.

Mexican Cilantro, epazote, marjoram, oregano, parsley.

Middle Eastern Cilantro, oregano, parsley, peppermint, savory, thyme.

Scandinavian Chives, dill, juniper, parsley.

Spanish Bay leaf, oregano, parsley, rosemary, spearmint, thyme.

Thai Cilantro, garlic chive, makrut lime, pandan leaf, spearmint, Thai basil, Vietnamese mint.

Vietnamese Betel leaf, cilantro, culantro (sawtooth coriander), garlic chive, mustard leaf, peppermint, shiso, spearmint, Thai basil, Vietnamese balm, Vietnamese mint.

FUZZY BASIL CHEESE STICKS

The return-on-investment with this dish is absolutely ridiculous, when you consider that it's basically just mozzarella on a stick, with a little flaky pastry. However, it's the basil that makes it. When basil is fried, it takes on a completely different character – like sun-drenched grass on a hot summer's day. Deep-fry some extra leaves for garnishing, then serve as swiftly as possible ... but don't forget to save a couple by the frying pot for yourself. They'll go quick!

MAKES 12

vegetable or canola oil,
    for deep-frying
250 g (9 oz) scamorza
    or hard mozzarella
300 g (10½ oz) kataifi
    pastry (see tip)

2 eggs, beaten
1 cup (50 g) basil leaves
flaked sea salt, for
    sprinkling

Have 12 bamboo skewers at the ready.

Heat 6 cm (2½ inches) of oil in a small saucepan to 400°F, or until a cube of bread dropped into the oil turns golden in 15 seconds.

Meanwhile, cut the cheese into oblongs about 1.5 cm x 4 cm (⅝ inch x 1½ inches) in size. Thread them onto the skewers – one or two per skewer.

Pull the pastry apart to the width of the cheese, then cut or tear into 50 cm (20 inch) lengths.

Dip the cheese oblongs in the egg wash, then wrap each one up in the pastry, tucking the pastry end into the top of itself to form a parcel.

Working in batches, deep-fry the parcels in the hot oil for 4 minutes, or until golden. Deep-fry the basil leaves for 1 minute, or until crisp, then briefly drain on paper towel.

Sprinkle the hot cheese sticks with flaked sea salt and the crispy basil leaves, allow to cool slightly so diners don't burn their mouths, and serve.

Tip Kataifi pastry is essentially just shredded filo, so any left-over pastry is an excellent substitute in recipes where you need filo pastry. I especially love it in custardy *galaktoboureko*. You'll find kataifi at your local Mediterranean deli or specialty grocer.

Extra Make your own basil oil to drizzle over these fuzzy frivolities. Take the stalks off a bunch of basil, then roughly chop the stalks, place in a heatproof bowl and pour boiling water over them. Strain right away and place in a blender. Add ½ cup (125 ml) grapeseed oil and ½ cup (125 ml) olive oil and blitz until combined. Leave to infuse for a few hours, then strain through cheesecloth into a sterilized jar. Use within 2–3 days, or pour into an ice-cube tray and freeze for tossing into soups and sauces.

SMASHED POTATO
& ROSEMARY FOCACCIA

This is the kind of one-pan bake that dreams are made of. Salty kalamata olives and crumbly feta, grassy rosemary with surprisingly sweet new potatoes, coddled in a soft, focaccia dough that is actually quite difficult to stop eating. Serve this with a 'cream of' something soup (like, say, the pumpkin on page 165, or the Roasted Jerusalem artichoke & tomato on page 307) and a simple green salad, and your guests will happily call it square on the substantial meal front. Begin making the dough 1 day ahead.

SERVES 8

500 g (1 lb 2 oz) new
   potatoes, washed
⅓ cup (80 ml) extra
   virgin olive oil,
   plus extra to serve
½ cup (80 g) pitted
   kalamata olives
1 bunch of rosemary,
   leaves picked, plus
   extra to serve
8 garlic cloves,
   thinly sliced
crumbly feta, to serve

Overnight dough

3 cups (450 g) bread flour
1 tablespoon honey
1 tablespoon extra
   virgin olive oil
1 teaspoon dried yeast
1½ teaspoons
   flaked sea salt
1½ cups (375 ml)
   lukewarm water

For the overnight dough, place all the ingredients in a bowl. Mix to combine until it forms a sticky wet dough. Cover with a tea towel and leave in a cool spot for at least 8 hours, or until doubled in size. If you're worried about temperature fluctuations (especially if you're in a warmer climate), leave the dough in the fridge for 12 hours, or until doubled in size.

The next day, bring the potatoes to the boil in a large saucepan of salted water, then simmer for 15 minutes, or until fork-tender. Strain the potatoes and return to the pan with the oil, olives, rosemary and garlic. Cook, roughly stirring with a wooden spoon to break up the potatoes, for 5 minutes, or until the garlic is fragrant and slightly golden. Leave to cool slightly.

Preheat the oven to 400°F.

Drain the oil from the potato mixture over a shallow lined baking tray. Transfer the dough to the tray and stretch and press it out with your fingers. Pour the potato mixture over the dough and use your fingers again to squish the flavor bombs into the dough.

Sprinkle with flaked sea salt and freshly cracked black pepper. Pour water into a heatproof mug or baking dish and sit it on the bottom of the oven to create steam (this helps the focaccia expand before forming a crust). Bake on the top shelf of the oven for 35 minutes, or until golden and cooked through.

Crumble the feta on top and sprinkle with extra rosemary. Drizzle with a little olive oil, cut into jaunty pieces and serve.

Tips This super-easy dough makes a terrific puffy pizza base; try it in the zucchini flower pizza on page 376.

   You can also pre-boil the potatoes the night before, when you're making the dough. Usually, I'll boil up a double batch, and use the rest for potato salad (page 302) or a fry-up (page 322).

Shortcuts Slice a store-bought focaccia through the middle, stuff with the potato and olive mix and crumbled feta, then squash down into a hot sandwich press to heat through.

   Or you can halve the dough (freeze the rest), then finely mandoline the potato and bake it on top.

   Quicker still, use a shop-bought pizza dough!

LOBIO
(CILANTRO KIDNEY BEAN STEW)

This is an absolute Georgian classic – and since 'lobio' translates simply to 'beans', every local version of this dish will be about as different as *ajo blanco* versions are in Spanish households. I love how much cilantro is in this, both ground and fresh. You can decide whether to make it more of a stew, or even a soup, depending on how much stock you do or don't add. It's extremely versatile, and simply delicious, particularly when served with traditional *mchadi,* Georgian cornbread.

SERVES 4–6

2 tablespoons olive oil,
    plus extra to serve
1 yellow onion,
    finely chopped
1 cup (120 g) walnuts,
    finely chopped, plus
    extra to garnish
1 teaspoon flaked sea salt
1 tablespoon ground
    fenugreek
1 teaspoon ground
    coriander
1 teaspoon curry powder
30 ml (1 fl oz) red
    wine vinegar
2 x 400 g (14 oz) cans
    kidney beans, drained
    and rinsed

3 tablespoons chopped
    cilantro stems, plus
    extra leaves to garnish
3 tablespoons chopped
    mint stems, plus extra
    leaves to garnish
2 cups (500 ml)
    vegetable stock
3–4 garlic cloves,
    finely crushed
¼ teaspoon ground white
    pepper (optional)
flatbreads or cornbread,
    to serve

Heat the olive oil in a wide saucepan over medium heat. Add the onion and wait for the sizzle, pop a lid on and sweat away over low heat for 5 minutes. Remove the lid.

Add the walnuts, salt, fenugreek, ground coriander and curry powder and stir for about 4 minutes, or until the nuts are toasted and spices aromatic. Add the vinegar and let it reduce a bit.

Stir in the beans and cook, stirring and breaking up the beans with a wooden spoon, for another 4 minutes, or until the beans have fully softened. Add the cilantro and mint stems and stir them about to soften. Pour in the stock and bring to the boil, then simmer over medium–low heat for 15 minutes.

Just before serving, stir in the garlic. Taste for seasoning, adding the white pepper and more salt and vinegar as needed.

Serve with a final drizzle of olive oil, a sprinkling of extra walnuts and mint and cilantro leaves to garnish, with flatbreads or cornbread on the side.

Tips If raw garlic is a little strong for you, add it when the walnuts and spices go in instead.

Some people like to whiz the lobio into a smooth paste, more like a dip – which is totally cool! Use an immersion blender once everything is cooked.

Shortcut Blitz the spices, crushed garlic, 100 g (3½ oz) nut butter, fresh cilantro and a 400 g (14 oz) can of rinsed and drained kidney beans together to form a simple bean dip. Season to taste.

Kale

Though it was wild and woolly on the cruciferous culinary scene through the mid 2010s, we are officially past Peak Kale. Now we can appreciate it in all its crinkly, forest-green gloriousness, without feeling like we're riding the Brassica bandwagon. Part of the winter cabbage family, yet more similar in appearance to wild cabbage, kale is mostly stalk, with most recipes requiring that the leaves be pulled off the woefully woody central stems. Tuscan kale is the slightly more bitter cousin. It's got no time for the frou-frou of 'hearting', and instead shoots straight up into straps of dark, rippled, sueded leaves on slightly less woody stalks. I cook with both varieties interchangeably when stewing, depending on whichever is freshest – except where chips are concerned, where I find the frillier leaves make for an infinitely more rewarding mouthful.

'My favorite kale is the little-known Bonanza variety, planted for years as livestock fodder, in rotation with radish, rutabaga, barley and millet. Our partner farm is growing Bonanza to save its seed – an example of how creativity in the kitchen can drive new demand for crops that might otherwise disappear.' – DAN BARBER, US

BUYING & STORING

Kale is often sold in bunches, like flowers, with frilly leaves or rounded straps beckoning. You'll also find smaller and more tender kale leaves picked and sold as 'baby kale', which still benefit from a little softening with a salt and vinegar rub-down before serving raw in a salad. As with all leafy greens, you're looking for vibrantly colored leaves – be they green, dappled white or deep purple. Any yellowing of the ends or limp stalks means that bunch has been out and about a bit too long, and may be a bargain, but will need to be used as soon as possible. Dry it completely and store in the crisper loosely bagged as a bunch, or as torn leaves washed, spun and wrapped in paper towel or cloth before bagging. If your kale is looking worse for wear, blanch and freeze on a tray or make a quick batch of kale chips (page 360).

COOKING WITH

Given it is one of the less forgiving brassicas, *you'd* be forgiven for being off kale because someone's served some up as olive-green, gassy slop and trundled off to the next table of activewearers. As with cabbage, cooking kale for too long releases sulfuric compounds, which smell eggy and drain the veg of its natural flavor and color. Kale is much better with a blast of heat – either dropped in towards the end of cooking in a soup or stew until just softened yet still bottle green, or in the oven or microwave for crispy kale. Flavor-wise, it really comes alive when you team it with something acidic such as apple cider vinegar or lemon juice, and something salty and/or spicy – flaked sea salt, soy sauce, garlic, chili. Strip each stem of leaves, either with scissors or your hands. Some people even use a special tool, but I find tearing by hand terrifically satisfying. If the leaves are on the bigger side, do a couple of cross-chops on a board to tame them into forkfuls. With Tuscan kale, check if you can easily snap the stalk at its thickest point. If that's the case, feel free to chop these leaves with stalks intact. If in doubt, blanch either of these in a big pot of boiling water until the color intensifies and the leaves just start to soften, then refresh straight away in iced water to stop the residual heat from kicking the kale into brown-green rotten egg territory.

WITH COMPLEMENTS

Butter, chili, garlic, honey, soy sauce, spices (especially bay leaf, cayenne pepper, caraway seeds, nutmeg), sweet potato, vinegar (especially apple cider).

BLONDE MINESTRONE WITH WHITE PEPPER

Tuscan kale is to my mind far easier to work with than the frilly conventional kales. It's kind of like continental parsley versus curly parsley, with the latter only ever really working in sauces such as gremolata (or butcher-shop windows). This soup is fairly set-and-forget, once you get past the chopping bit. And if you make it after a particularly frustrating work day, the chop-chop is about as meditative as a session of kick-boxing, really. The minestrone also gets better with a day or two in the fridge, as the flavors all get to know each other better. Unlike the traditional red minestrone with pasta, the heroes here (aside from the Tuscan kale) are the parmesan rinds and butter, which give everything a golden, glossy glow. Even if you're on your lonesome, make up a full batch and take a flask of it to work every day, slurp away, and you might find that suddenly nothing seems as frustrating as it once did.

SERVES 6–8

50 g (1¾ oz) butter
   (or olive oil)
1 onion, finely chopped
2–3 garlic cloves,
   roughly chopped
1 fennel bulb, about
   500 g (1 lb 2 oz),
   diced, fronds reserved
3 celery stalks, sliced
2 carrots, chopped
1 bunch of Tuscan kale,
   about 500 g (1 lb 2 oz),
   leaves torn off and
   finely shredded, thinner
   stalks finely chopped

1 teaspoon ground
   white pepper
½ teaspoon celery seeds
2 potatoes, peeled and
   chopped into 2 cm
   (¾ inch) chunks
8 cups (2 liters) vegetable
   or chicken stock
400 g (14 oz) can
   cannellini beans
parmesan rinds (optional)
lemon juice, to taste
grated parmesan, to serve
   (optional)

Melt the butter in a large soup pot, then sweat the onion, garlic, fennel, celery, carrot, Tuscan kale stalks, white pepper and celery seeds with the lid on the pot, until the vegetables have softened – this should take about 12 minutes.

Add the potato, stock, cannellini beans and parmesan rinds, if using. Bring to the boil, then reduce the heat and simmer for about 15 minutes, or until the potato is fork-tender.

Take the pot off the heat, stir in the shredded Tuscan kale leaves, season to taste with flaked sea salt and freshly cracked black pepper, then squeeze in some lemon juice to finish.

Garnish with a final twist or two of cracked black pepper and some grated parmesan, if you like.

Tip If you're after more parmesan rind than you have at your disposal, ask your local deli or cheese shop if they have any handy. You might find yourself the proud owner of a bunch of ready-rinds – a total win-win!

Dairy-free I've given the option of using olive oil instead of butter. Pop in a few sliced brown mushrooms to up the umami factor, and sprinkle nutritional yeast flakes on top instead of the crumbled parmesan.

SALT & VINEGAR KALE CHIPS

This is easily my favorite way to eat kale – either as a kitchen snack, as a garnish for something creamier, or popped in a bowl alongside other shareable starters. One complaint from aficionados is that at-home kale chips can often lose their crispiness and turn to sog within a day or so. Fear not, fellow frilly-fry lover. Flick them back into the oven at 250°F for another 5 minutes or so, and they'll crisp right back up.

SERVES 4 AS A SNACK

350 g (12 oz) curly kale
   (see tip), washed
2 tablespoons olive oil
2 teaspoons white vinegar

1 teaspoon chili flakes
finely grated zest
   of 1 lemon
1 teaspoon flaked sea salt

Preheat the oven to 325°F.

Shake the kale leaves as dry as possible. Use your hands to strip the leaves from the stalks of the kale, working from the thicker base upwards in a swift motion. If the leaves are still a little wet, feel free to give them a final pat dry with paper towel or using a salad spinner.

Tear the leaves into pieces, place in a bowl and toss with the remaining ingredients.

Spread the kale in a single layer on several wire racks set over lined baking trays. Transfer to the oven and bake for 15–20 minutes, or until the chips 'snap' between your fingertips.

Remove from the oven and leave to cool and crisp up before serving.

Tip **You can use any type of kale or other brassica leaf, but it works best with curly kale because you get all those fun, frilly edges.**

Shortcut **You can microwave the kale chips on high, between layers of paper towel – but they do have a propensity to catch on fire, thanks to something known as 'local field amplification'. That's where the sharp, uneven edges and naturally occurring metals (actual iron) in the kale can cause smoking and sparks. To avoid this, microwave in minute-long bursts and monitor carefully. Or, just bake them in the oven.**

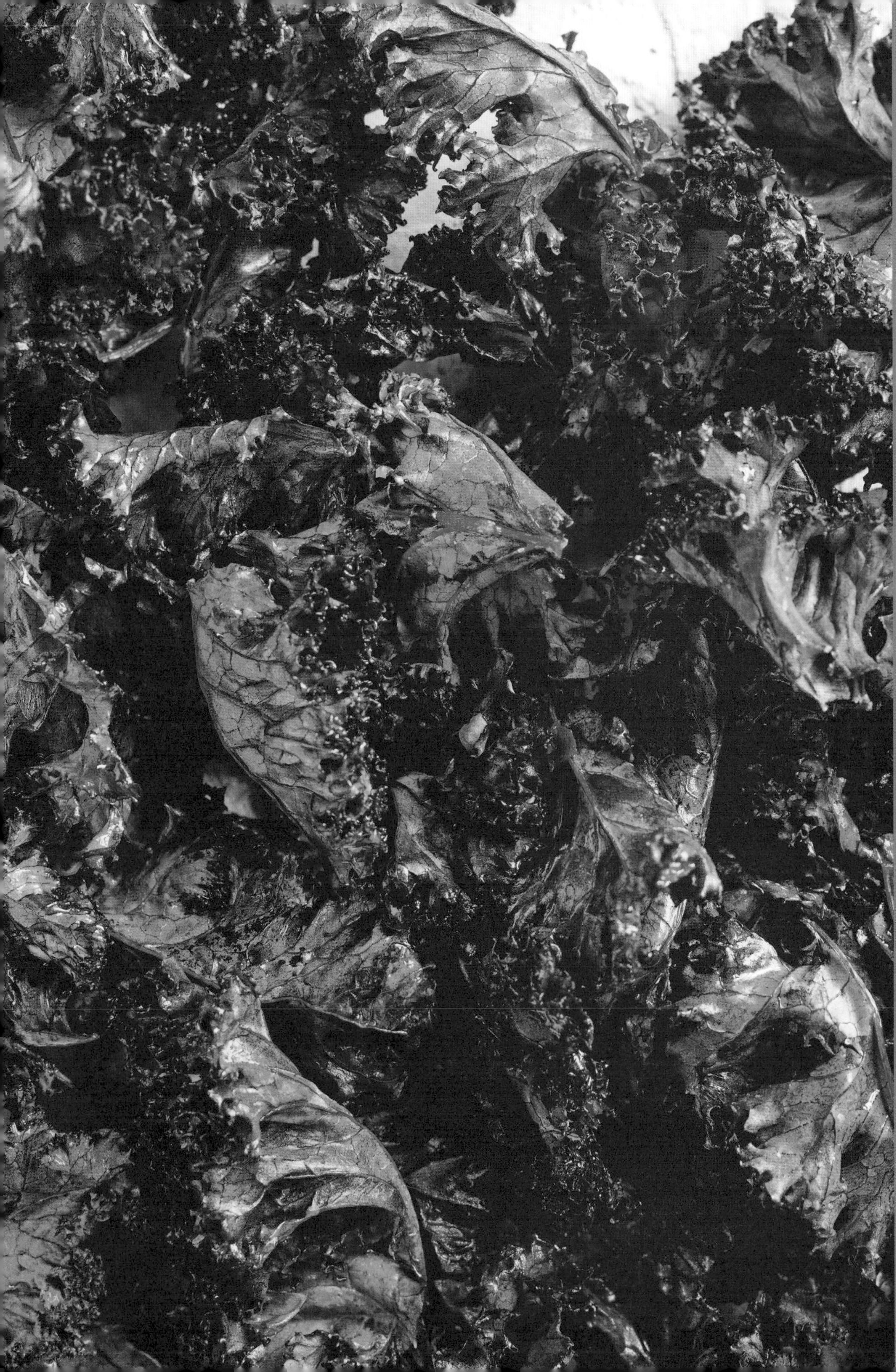

Broccoli

If there's one vegetable that gets a bad rap, it's broccoli. The butt of almost every vegetable joke, broccoli bears the brunt of criticism for being a less than desirable addition to family plates. And yet, I have it on good authority that there are parents out there who have put broccoli on a pedestal – quite literally – by turning it into the family treat. Up the broccoli goes to the top of the fridge, and only when the kids do something good do the edible 'trees' come out. It just goes to show the value of the stories that we tell when it comes to food. But you don't have to get elaborate and arrange a brocc-lolly jar for your household ... just make like Khaleesi and do what I do with all Brassicas: burn them. Broccoli's naturally bitter notes when raw bely the sweetness within. A little char from the barbecue, a blast under the broiler with a splash of soy sauce and a teaspoon or so of honey or miso paste, or tossed in a well-seasoned hot wok, and you'll have the kids (both big and small) retracting every broccoli-based retort.

'Broccoli is an easy one for the kids to enjoy. It's great for everything from salads to fillers to sides, stalks and all. Finely cross-shave the florets, place in a bowl, pour boiling water over and leave for a few minutes, then add grains such as pearl barley, couscous or quinoa, dress it with lemon zest and juice, salt and feta and you have a substantial meal. Broccoli also makes a fantastic gremolata instead of chopped herbs.' – MATT WILKINSON, UK

BUYING & STORING

When buying broccoli (or its hybrid cousin broccolini, see below), the leaves, the base of the stalk and the flower buds are a dead give-away of freshness. The leaves should be vibrant in color and firm, and the base should still be greenish, and not too parchy – some greengrocers even stock their broccoli atop ice to keep it cool. Fresh broccoli buds are tight, dark green (or occasionally purple) on top, and bright green just beyond the canopy if you press against it for a peek. If the buds have soft spots, or have started to open and flower, or are turning a jaundiced shade of yellow, the broccoli is getting on and so should you. The same rules apply for purple broccoli – whose color will, disappointingly, fade upon cooking. Occasionally, you'll chance upon romanesco broccoli, with its chartreuse fractal flesh, which looks like it's from another planet (and actually appears as space food in a scene in *Star Wars*!). These respond well to gentle cooking, and will keep their brightness if you blanch and shock judiciously. All broccoli is best stored loosely bagged in the crisper. If you're the kind of person who likes to wash their veg when they get it home from the shops, be sure to dry the broccoli well, as any moisture will kick it into mold-town.

BEYOND BROCCOLI: GAI LAN

Also known as kai lan, gai lan is characterised by its thick outer leaves and long stalk, with a central stem and flower buds hidden within. This central stem can often be quite thick and woody towards the base, so using a peeler or paring knife to peel it back to a lighter green (as you might with thicker asparagus), and pulling off any harder outer leaves is a good way to prepare for stir-frying or steaming. Pop the central stalks into the steamer for a couple of minutes before adding the outer leaves, as they'll take less time to cook through.

BEYOND BROCCOLI: BROCCOLINI

Broccolini is broccoli's love-child with gai lan. It's leggy like gai lan, but with more pronounced flowering heads like broccoli, and is sometimes known simply as 'baby broccoli', because someone literally has the 'Broccolini' name trademarked. The directions for picking, prepping and cooking the two are near-identical, and their flavor is pretty similar too, so I've chosen to whack them together for ease of reference. Just be mindful that the stalks of broccolini may take a little longer to cook than the buds, so judge doneness by testing the thickest point of the stalk.

WITH COMPLEMENTS

Butter, cauliflower, cheese (especially cheddar, goat, mozzarella, parmesan), chili, garlic, mustard, oyster sauce, soy sauce.

SCRAP MEDAL

A lot of recipes call for the broccoli florets, which is all well and good, but what to do with the stalks? As with all Brassicas, the center stalk is actually the sweetest, once you hack away its woody exterior. If the dish entails a length of time for the broccoli to cook down, consider chopping the stalk into smaller bite-sized chunks and tossing them in there too. If it's a stir-fry, hack away with paring knife or peeler and stir-fry the stalks. Just quietly, I like to save the stalk for my own personal chef-snack. It's just the right kind of mid-cook finger food that keeps me going, and if you're the designated cook in your household, then you deserve a stalk chef-snack, too.

BROCCOLINI CAESAR SALAD

Cooking broccolini is a bit like cooking fish – if you try to cook a fish fillet from skinny side to fat side in one go, you'll overcook the skinny and undercook the fat. That's why it's always a good idea to divide and conquer. Treat the florets more like their own furry entity, where the flower buds cook faster than you'd expect and the stalks are like asparagus. Here, both 'textures' of broccolini are put to good use in a classic caesar, complete with runny googs and savory rye bread crisps.

SERVES 4

⅓ cup (80 ml) extra virgin olive oil
3 oil-packed anchovy fillets, finely chopped
⅓ cup (25 g) finely grated parmesan, plus extra to serve
1 garlic clove, finely grated
150 g (5½ oz) stale rye bread, thinly sliced
3 bunches of broccolini (about 450 g/1 lb), stems thinly sliced on an angle, florets cut into 2 cm (¾ inch) pieces

2 eggs (see tip)
4 teaspoons white wine vinegar

Lemon-mayo drizzle
finely grated zest and juice of 1 lemon
2 tablespoons whole-egg mayonnaise (or Garlic aioli, page 37)
½ teaspoon freshly cracked black pepper

Heat the olive oil in a large frying pan over medium–high heat. Add the anchovies, parmesan and garlic and stir until fragrant. Pop the rye slices in the pan and cook, stirring regularly, for 5 minutes, or until the bread is golden and crispy. Set the pan aside.

Meanwhile, bring a saucepan of well-salted water to the boil. Prepare a bowl of water with ice for blanching nearby. Drop the broccolini florets into the boiling water for a minute, then add the chopped bits for another minute, or until vividly green. Scoop out with a slotted spoon and drop into the iced water to set the color. Drain, then add to the reserved frying pan and toss to coat in all the crumbly bits.

Bring the saucepan back to the boil; meanwhile, working with 1 egg at a time, crack the egg into a small bowl with 1 teaspoon of vinegar. Gently slide the eggs (and the vinegar) into the boiling water from as close to the pan as possible, then reduce the temperature and simmer for 2 minutes, until the whites have set. Scoop the eggs out with a slotted spoon, discard any gunky white bits and drain briefly on paper towel.

Pile the broccolini mixture onto a large serving platter, arranging the rye toasts on the side. Top the broccolini with the poached eggs. Combine the dressing ingredients in a small bowl, spoon over the salad, sprinkle with extra parmesan and serve.

Tip **The fresher the eggs, the better they will poach.**

Extra **A poached chicken breast makes a lovely addition. Shred it and toss through half the dressing to help it soak up maximum flavor, then finish by dressing the lot.**

Shortcut **To save some time faffing around at the stove, glug the olive oil over the rye slices, smear them with the garlic and anchovy, top with the parmesan and toast in a preheated oven at 400°F for about 8–10 minutes, until golden, while preparing the other bits. Or, fry the eggs rather than poach them.**

BROCCOLI STEAKS WITH TKEMALI

Broccoli is meaty by nature, particularly when grilled like this. If you can find smaller heads with leaves attached, they'll make an especially dramatic addition to the table – like an edible centerpiece. I love the depth of color of the plum sauce known as *tkemali*, a Georgian barbecue mainstay; be sure to use the sourest plums you can find. When I was a little girl, it was my job to go out and forage for damson plums (we called them 'alycha' – *uh-li-chah*) on nature strips in our neighborhood for Babuschka Zina's *tkemali*. I think she'd be proud of this one.

SERVES 4

2 heads of broccoli

2 tablespoons extra virgin olive oil, plus extra for drizzling

1 handful of walnuts, some grated with a microplane, some finely chopped

Tkemali plum sauce

500 g (1 lb 2 oz) Damson plums or sour equivalent, halved and pitted

1 teaspoon celery seeds

5 garlic cloves, roughly chopped

¼ teaspoon cayenne pepper

½ teaspoon ground coriander

1½ tablespoons red wine vinegar, plus a little extra if the plums aren't tart enough for your taste

Cut the broccoli heads along the side, to create a flat surface. Reserve the off-cuts, then cut the broccoli into 'steaks' about 2 cm (¾ inch) thick; you should get at least 2–3 steaks out of each broccoli. Drizzle some olive oil onto a tray, add the steaks and toss to coat. Set aside.

Preheat the oven to 400°F. Line a baking tray with parchment paper. While the oven is preheating, pop the plums for the *tkemali* on the baking tray, give them a drizzle of olive oil, then whack them into the oven. Pull them out after about 15 minutes, when they're blistered and softened, and are leaching out ruby red liquid; this should be roughly around the same time the oven is at temperature.

Pop the plums and the remaining *tkemali* ingredients in a blender and blitz to a purée. Taste for seasoning and acid, adding extra vinegar if need be.

Meanwhile, heat an ovenproof grill pan for at least 5–10 minutes, until searing hot. Working in batches, grill the oiled broccoli for 2–3 minutes, or until slightly charred. Transfer to a baking tray and repeat with the remaining broccoli, then transfer to the oven and bake for 15–20 minutes, or until a knife can go through the thickest part of the broccoli stalks.

To serve, spoon the *tkemali* sauce around a platter, then arrange the broccoli on top. Drizzle with a little more olive oil. Sprinkle with flaked sea salt, freshly cracked black pepper and the walnuts. Serve warm, or at room temperature.

Tip **If you don't have a grill, cook the broccoli in a heavy-based pan – you just won't get the char marks.**

Shortcut **Oil the broccoli well and cook in a 450°F oven until they start to burnish. Bonus points for leaving the baking tray in the oven to heat up, so that the florets really cop the heat as soon as they hit.**

Zucchini

I've purposefully put zucchini and cucumber next door to each other. The easiest way to tell them apart is by zucchini's ribbed stem – the point at which they've been detached from the mainframe. That's because zucchini (or courgette, as it's also known) is part of the gourd family, while cucumbers are a melon. If you imagine the top of a pumpkin, which has a stem, compared to the top of a watermelon, which is more of a scab, you'll never confuse the two by sight again. Cucumber's skin is glossy and often a little ridged, while zucchini's is smoother, duller and a little fleshier to the touch. There's a whole world of zucchini-like gourds or summer squash, in many colors and shapes, that behave in a similar fashion and can be served up in so many different ways. For long ones, spiralize them into 'zoodles', peel into ribbons, or slice lengthwise and grill. For squat or round ones, scoop out the seeds and flesh, then stuff with a legume and/or ground meat and bake as you might stuffed bell pepper o cabbage rolls.

'At their peak, zucchini should be not too big, with firm, glossy skins and sweet, nutty flesh. In late spring, we serve the flowers stirred through angel hair pasta with saffron and garlic. In summer, we simmer finely sliced zucchini with extra virgin olive oil, garlic and tarragon, and serve alongside braised lamb shoulder or grilled fish – or turn into gratins, pickles, purées, fritters and what the Italians call *trifolati*.'
– SKYE GYNGELL, AUSTRALIA

BUYING & STORING

Unlike many other vegetables that intensify with flavor as they ripen and grow, zucchini flavor peaks when it is around the size of a newborn's forearm, and then begins to deteriorate. As fermentation legend Sandor Katz says, 'Zucchini has a finite amount of flavor – and the bigger it gets, the less of that flavor you can taste.' You can still buy oversized zucchini, particularly when zucchini is most abundant in summertime, but at some point (probably once it's the size of a grown man's forearm) it begins to be referred to as 'marrow' – and is best treated as you might a marrow bone … scooped, stuffed, seasoned and roasted, or sliced, battered and deep-fried. For all soft-skinned summer squash, the first sign you're looking for is a nice firm stem: bright green in color, potentially furry, and never browning or slimy. No matter the shade – yellow, or varying shades of green – the color should always be vibrant and rich. Skin should be taut, with a bounce to the flesh. Any scratches or bumps are okay, as long as the flesh beneath is still firm.

Store zucchini in the crisper, in a paper bag, with some level of ventilation – trapping the zucchini in an airlock leads to sweating and an overall sense of impending doom. Zucchini freezes well, as it's so full of moisture and holds its shape when cooked; to do this, blanch it in unsalted boiling water for up to a minute (depending on the size of your chunks), then freeze on a tray with some space between the chunks, portion out when frozen, bag up, label and freeze again. As it's still quite porous, try to use within 3–4 months for the best flavor and texture, or blitz into soup beyond this point.

'My go-to vegetable would probably be zucchini. I love how versatile they are. My favorite way of cooking zucchini is to either roast them over coals or to blend them into a gazpacho with a bit of lime and olive oil.' – MONIQUE FISO, NEW ZEALAND

BEYOND ZUCCHINI: ZUCCHINI FLOWERS

If you can get your hands on them, zucchini flowers are an absolute wonder – both to look at and to cook with. What they lack in taste, they make up for both in aesthetic appeal and in their capacity to become the delivery vehicles to flavor-town. Think ricotta or goat cheese, or some form of eggy mousse (flick over to page 374 for a delightful scallop-stuffed version that will knock your socks off), tempura-battered and fried. The petals can also be torn and used as vibrant garnish for zucchini-based dishes or salads, if you're growing them and have a glut. Look for bright orange-yellow petals with no sign of sag or sog, and the same deep-green intensity of color that you'd usually expect on the young zucchini that the flowers are growing out of.

WITH COMPLEMENTS

Bell pepper, cheese (especially goat, parmesan, ricotta), chili, eggplant, garlic, herbs (especially basil, marjoram, mint, parsley), lemon, pine nuts, olive oil.

SCRAP MEDAL

There's no reason to peel zucchini when cooking with it – the vibrancy of color alone is worth preserving, as well as the natural shape of the zucchini. However, if you're spiralizing or using a julienne peeler to peel it into strips, you'll be sure to end up with awkwardly shaped scraps. Reserve the seeded middle bits or leftovers and chop into chunks to use in your next veggie dish – the flavor is so neutral that it'll go in anything, from stir-fries to casseroles.

SCALLOP-STUFFED ZUCCHINI FLOWERS

This is just about the fanciest canapé you could ever make – complete with sparkling wine in the batter. But I must say that it's also the one your guests will gush about for months, so the whole dish is pretty blue chip ... or should that be blue batter?

SERVES 8 AS A CANAPÉ

2 egg whites
1 cup (150 g)
  self-rising flour
  (page 23)
16 zucchini flowers
vegetable or canola oil,
  for deep-frying
lemon wedges, to serve

Scallop filling
150 g (5½ oz) scallop
  or shrimp meat
1 egg white, lightly beaten
finely grated zest
  of 1 lemon
1 teaspoon flaked sea salt
½ teaspoon ground
  white pepper
¼ teaspoon
  ground nutmeg
⅓ cup (80 g)
  crème fraîche
1 tablespoon thinly
  sliced chives

Sparkling wine batter
1 cup (150 g)
  self-rising flour
  (page 23)
½ teaspoon flaked sea salt
1 cup (250 ml) chilled
  sparkling white wine
  (or sparkling water)

To make the filling, place the scallop meat in a food processor, along with the egg white, lemon zest, salt, pepper and nutmeg. Whiz until finely chopped. Add the crème fraîche and pulse to combine. Stir the chives through, then transfer to a piping (icing) bag and chill until required.

Lightly whisk the egg whites in a bowl until light and frothy. Place the flour in a separate bowl.

To make the batter, combine the flour and salt in a bowl. Add the sparkling wine and whisk to a smooth batter.

Gently remove and discard the stamen from inside each zucchini flower. Pipe the scallop mixture into each flower, then gently twist the petals together to enclose the filling.

Half-fill a deep-fryer or large saucepan with oil and heat to 400°F, or until a cube of bread dropped into the oil turns golden in 15 seconds.

Dip the flowers, one at a time, in the egg white, then the flour, then the batter. Drain off the excess batter, then deep-fry each flower for 3 minutes, or until golden and crisp, turning now and then. Remove with a slotted spoon and drain on a rack set over paper towel. Cover loosely with foil to keep warm, then repeat with the remaining flowers and batter.

Serve immediately, sprinkled with flaked sea salt and cracked black pepper, with lemon wedges alongside.

Extra **If you're feeling EXTRA fancy, use chilled Champagne for the batter. It's a good excuse to open a bottle and invite some friends around! The Garlic aioli on page 37 would be terrific with these, too.**

Go fish-free **Stuff the zucchini flowers with the Mushroom tempeh 'ground' on page 428.**

TORN ZUCCHINI FLOWER PIZZA

This pizza dough is the same versatile overnight special used in the potato and rosemary focaccia on page 352. Once you get the hang of making this version, which is just sublimely pretty with the addition of torn zucchini flowers, you can add whatever toppings tickle your fancy – from truss tomatoes (or even just freshly torn basil for a plain margherita) in summer, to pumpkin and caramelized onion in autumn.

SERVES 4

200 g (7 oz) sour cream
200 g (7 oz) fior di latte
    or mozzarella cheese,
    coarsely grated, plus
    extra, torn, to serve
    (optional)
½ teaspoon
    ground nutmeg
12 baby zucchini, with
    flowers attached
120 g (4 oz) nduja,
    crumbled (or finely
    chopped chorizo)

2 tablespoons extra
    virgin olive oil
basil leaves, to serve
crispy chili oil (from
    Asian grocers), to serve
lemon wedges, to serve

Dough

1 quantity Overnight
    dough (page 352)
1 zucchini, coarsely grated
olive oil, for greasing
flour, for dusting

Make the overnight dough a day ahead.

The next day, preheat the oven to 450°F. Grease two non-stick pizza trays with oil.

Add the grated zucchini to the dough and roughly knead to combine. Divide the dough in half. On a lightly floured work surface, stretch out one piece of dough to a circle of 2 cm (¾ inch) thickness and transfer to a pizza tray. Repeat with the remaining dough, then bake for 10 minutes, or until the base is cooked.

Meanwhile, combine the sour cream, cheese and nutmeg in a bowl. Remove the flowers from the baby zucchini and tear into pretty strips. Thinly slice the baby zucchini.

Divide the creamy cheese mixture between the pizzas, using the back of a spoon to spread it out to the edges. Sprinkle the nduja over, then top with half the zucchini flowers and zucchini slices. Drizzle each pizza with 1 tablespoon of the olive oil.

Bake for 12 minutes, or until the dough is golden and moves easily from the base of the trays. Sprinkle with basil leaves, the remaining zucchini flowers and slices, and extra cheese, if using. Dollop with crispy chili oil and serve with lemon wedges alongside for squeezing over as the pizzas hit the table.

Tip This is a Roman-style pizza dough, which is quite chewy and dense. If you prefer a 'soupier' Napoli-style pizza, I'd suggest ordering a take-away margherita from your best local wood-fired pizza place, and topping with fresh zucchini and mozzarella once you get it home.

Go meat free The nduja is absolutely an optional extra. Switch it out for a tablespoon or two of chili paste, if you like.

Shortcut Some store-bought pizza doughs these days are of a pretty high quality. Look for ones where the ingredients most closely resemble those in this recipe.

SUMMER SLICE

This little slice of sunshine, inspired by a version from my mates Matt Wilkinson and Sharlee Gibb – which is literally the best we've found – is on high rotation at our house come summertime. That's because it's just as tasty fridge-cold as it is fresh from the oven. It also gets a big thumbs-up from The Nut, who delights in taking finger-lengths of the slice and turning it into mush between her fists before snuffling.

SERVES 4–6

2 medium-sized
   zucchini, coarsely
   grated
½ teaspoon salt
1 onion, finely diced
4 bacon slices, cut
   into thin strips
½ cup (75 g) gluten-free
   self-rising flour
   (page 23) (see tips)
½ cup (100 g) fresh (or
   frozen) corn kernels

½ cup (75 g) frozen peas
5 eggs
½ cup (125 ml) milk
1 cup (100 g)
   grated cheddar
4 tomatoes, sliced
   (bonus points for
   heirloom colors)

Preheat the oven to 400°F. Line a baking dish, about 20 cm x 25 cm (8 inches x 10 inches) in size, with parchment paper, letting it overhang the sides a little.

Line a bowl with a clean tea towel. Add the grated zucchini, sprinkle with the salt and mix together with your hands. Twist the tea towel into a garrotte to squeeze out the excess moisture from the zucchini, so you don't end up with a watery slice. (You could use a sieve over a bowl, but you'll have to work twice as hard.)

Wipe the bowl dry, then pop the zucchini back in, along with the onion and bacon. Using a spatula, fold the flour through.

Meanwhile, boil a kettle. Put the corn and peas in a small heatproof bowl and pour some boiling water over them. Let stand for a few minutes, then drain.

In a bowl or jug, beat the eggs with a fork until the whites and yolks are combined, then beat in the milk. Pour the mixture over the zucchini, then fold in half the cheese, as well as the corn and peas.

Pour the mixture (which will be runnier than you expect) into the baking dish. Sprinkle with the remaining cheese and arrange the tomato slices on top. Bake for 40–45 minutes, until the egg has set and the top is slightly burnished. Serve warm or cold.

Tips This slice tastes best in summer, when zucchini and tomatoes are at their peak. At other times of the year, just swap out the fresh tomatoes for a tomato chutney on the side.

I like using gluten-free flour in this slice because it's lighter than regular flour, and forms a slightly different crust set at the bottom, but you can use regular self-rising flour (page 23) if you'd prefer.

Double duty Bake the batter in a muffin pan lined with paper cases as individually portioned frittatas for work and school lunchboxes – or just wrap slices in a bit of parchment paper for on-the-go snacking.

MID-WEEK BOLOGNESE

The following recipe may seem like an affront to all that is Italian and holy, considering a proper bolognese is hours in the making, but in truth, 'bolognaise' as we know it (or however you like to spell it) didn't even exist in the first place. It was the diaspora Italians who started making a red meat sauce and calling it 'spaghetti bolognese', leaving many tourists disappointed when they visited Bologna and couldn't get a bowl of bol, so the restaurants there started making it. The ultimate chicken-and-egg scenario. The shameless sacrilege of my version is evident in every element, which is what makes it so good. From the shortcut sugo (which I came up with when I'd run out of canned tomatoes and didn't substitute) to the spiralized zucchini (lighter, greener, yum!), this is a bolshie bol that is quick to make, full of rich flavor and sure to satisfy even the greediest Italian – once they're done shaking their heads and fists.

SERVES 4

1 yellow onion, finely diced
1 tablespoon olive oil
1 tablespoon butter
1 cup (90 g) finely sliced
    mushrooms (optional)
4 beef burger patties
    (see tips)
2–3 garlic cloves, roughly
    chopped or crushed
100 g (3½ oz) tomato
    paste (see tips)
1 teaspoon aged
    balsamic vinegar

½ cup (125 ml) vegetable
    or chicken stock
    (or water, at a pinch)
6 zucchini, spiralized with
    a contraption or julienne
    peeler (see tips)
40 g (1½ oz)
    parmesan, grated

Using a large heavy-based saucepan, sweat the onion in the olive oil and butter over medium–low heat until translucent. Begin with the lid off until fragrant, then pop on the lid for about 5 minutes, giving the onion the odd stir, then finish with the lid off again. If using the mushrooms, stir them in and cook until golden.

Push the mixture to the side and carefully arrange the patties in the base of the pan, using a wooden spoon or potato masher to gently press them as thin as possible. Scoop the onion mixture on top to stop it burning, crank the heat to medium–high and leave for 2–3 minutes, until the bottom of the patties is browned.

Squash the patties into chunks and incorporate the onion mixture. Stir the garlic through, then the tomato paste, until everything is a deep shade of red.

Pour in the balsamic vinegar, sniffing until the sting in your nostrils dissipates. Pour in the stock and allow it to bubble away a little and loosen off the sauce. Simmer for 5–10 minutes, until the meat is cooked and the sauce has reduced slightly.

Add the spiralized zucchini, stirring well to combine, and simmer for another minute to soften a little. Season to taste, sprinkle with the parmesan and cracked black pepper and serve.

Tips **The closer the patties are to room temperature, the better they'll brown. Burgers are fattier than ground meat, which is why they're good here. If all you have is ground beef, add some extra butter.**

Tomato paste ingredients can vary. Look for one that literally just says '100 per cent tomatoes'.

For a wetter sauce, use 1 cup (250 ml) of stock and let it reduce a bit before stirring the zucchini through.

If you don't have a spiralizer, peel the zucchini into strips, then stack them, roll them up and cut into ribbons.

Extra **If you're not ready for The Full Zucchini, try half-n-half, subbing in some sorghum spaghetti, which is gluten free and adds extra color in its purpley-ness.**

Cucumber

As our demand for spruced-up salads increases, so too do the varieties of cucumbers available to us. Lebanese cucumbers are my pick for general salading – they're sweet, have a delightful texture that keeps their shape nicely and a finer skin that doesn't need peeling. 'Slicing' or English ones, make for good ribbons for cucumber sandwiches with the help of a peeler or mandoline, or for sautés and stir-fries. Fresh gherkins are a particularly promising proposition for those with a penchant for pickling and preserving, and most greengrocers are happy to offload these in bulk. Thicker-skinned heirloom varieties can occasionally be on the bitter side, but this is nothing that a little peeling and judicious seasoning won't fix, as it's in the dark skin where much of the astringency resides.

'Cucumber is a supporting actor in each meal – like pickles in a hamburger, *tsukemono* in Japan or Korean *oi kimchi*. I love just simply crushing cucumbers with salt, garlic, ginger, soy sauce, chopped chili, sesame oil and salted kombu.'

TETSUYA WAKUDA, JAPAN

BUYING & STORING

When they're at their peak in summer, cucumbers glisten with sunshine and emanate a sweet, fresh aroma. Look for firm cukes, with evenly dark green skin – although the odd sun-spot is to be expected and won't give you too much grief, as long as it stays put against any attempts to poke it. Avoid cucumbers that are starting to shrivel or soften – though if that's all you have access to, a good refresh in iced water overnight should breathe new life into them.

Cucumbers are full of water, and they grow in full sun, so even though they're stored in the fridge, it's best to treat them with a little more care than your average bear. Pop them in the crisper, and if you're feeling extra careful, wrap in paper towel and store in a plastic bag to help keep the moisture from escaping too rapidly, as well as protecting them from any ethylene-producing mates that happen to be farting around them.

COOKING WITH

Slice cucumbers into odd shapes for salads by rolling across the cutting board, to add more texture and interest. Season early on, to help them absorb and carry the dressing amongst the rest of the veg, like a flavor sponge. When making raita or tzatziki, be sure to salt the cucumber and leave to absorb for about 15 minutes, then squeeze out any excess moisture before adding to your yogurt base. For a quick pickle, combine equal parts sugar, salt and vinegar with any additional aromatics (such as peppercorns, dill or fennel seeds) and bring to the boil, then pour over your thinly sliced or spiralized cucumbers. Leave to cool before serving, and feel free to mix the remaining liquid with a splash of neutral oil such as peanut oil, and turn it into a dressing. For sour pickles, submerging in a 3–5 per cent salt brine works best, scraping off any blossoms and adding a few vine or oak leaves to retain the crunch.

WITH COMPLEMENTS

Cheese (especially feta, goat), chili, cilantro, dill, garlic, lemon, lime, mint, olive oil, onion (especially red), parsley, salmon, sesame (seeds and/or oil), tomatoes, vinegar (especially chardonnay), yogurt.

SESAME CUCUMBER WHACK SALAD

Often, when cucumber salad recipes get you to scrape out the seeds, they don't really tell you what to do with them. 'Pour them down the sink' is the usual assumption. But why must the seeds suffer such a fate, when they're such a delightfully textural and sweet addition to a dressing? The answer is: they shouldn't. Pop them in the dressing, or spoon them into your mouth. Whatever you choose to do, leave the sink for the dishes.

SERVES 4 AS A SIDE DISH

2 English cucumbers
¼ cup (60 ml) soy sauce
2 tablespoons apple
   cider vinegar
2 tablespoons mirin
1 tablespoon sesame oil
1 tablespoon finely
   grated fresh ginger
1 garlic clove, finely grated
1 teaspoon
   granulated sugar
3 green onions (scallions),
   thinly sliced

1 long red chili,
   thinly sliced
½ bunch of cilantro,
   leaves picked
½ bunch of mint,
   leaves picked
toasted white sesame
   seeds, to serve
crispy fried shallots,
   to serve

Halve the cucumbers lengthwise, then use a spoon to remove the seeds. Add the seeds to a mortar and use a pestle to break them up slightly. Add the soy sauce, vinegar, mirin, sesame oil, ginger, garlic and sugar to the mortar and mix together with a tablespoon or spatula, then transfer the dressing to a small bowl.

Roughly chop the cucumber into 3 cm (1¼ inch) pieces. In batches, gently pound the cucumber and green onion together using the same mortar and pestle, until the cucumber skins are slightly cracked.

Transfer to a large serving platter and toss with the chili and herbs. Spoon the dressing over, then sprinkle with toasted sesame seeds and crispy shallots to serve.

Shortcut **If you're not in the mood to cut and scoop, use Qukes or Lebanese cucumbers and keep the middles intact – just cut them on an angle and give each slice a sprinkling of salt and a squeeze to help break the cells down.**

Extra **To bulk the salad up into a main, stir some cooked soba or ramen noodles through the cucumber mixture, and perhaps top with some shredded chicken or flaked steamed fish.**

Beans

Beans have been in cultivation as a food source way back since 6000 B.C.E. – and fart jokes soon after. Their proliferation was precipitated by the fact that they were nutritious, easy to grow, bulked up a predominantly vegetarian diet and stored well when dried. These days, beans are still prized for much the same reasons, schoolyard jokes included. My pantry is full of all kinds of beans, from black to red kidney to cannellini, to use in bakes and long braises. In their fresh form, beans really shine when you don't do much to them at all – blanched green beans with a simple vinaigrette or sautéed in butter, broad beans (almost always double-podded) smashed with a crumbly feta, sliced snake beans stir-fried with garlic and chili … You'll find bean recipes from most parts of the world, with only the herbs and spices changing regionally. Once you master the basic principles of sweat, simmer, season, your repertoire really expands. Indian-style spicy green beans (*masaledar sem*) become Mexican *ejotes* with the simple addition of oregano, while French-style *haricot verts* with sautéed shallots are transformed into my mum's Georgian *lobio* with some curry powder, garlic and coriander. I suppose you could call it 'Variations on a Bean'.

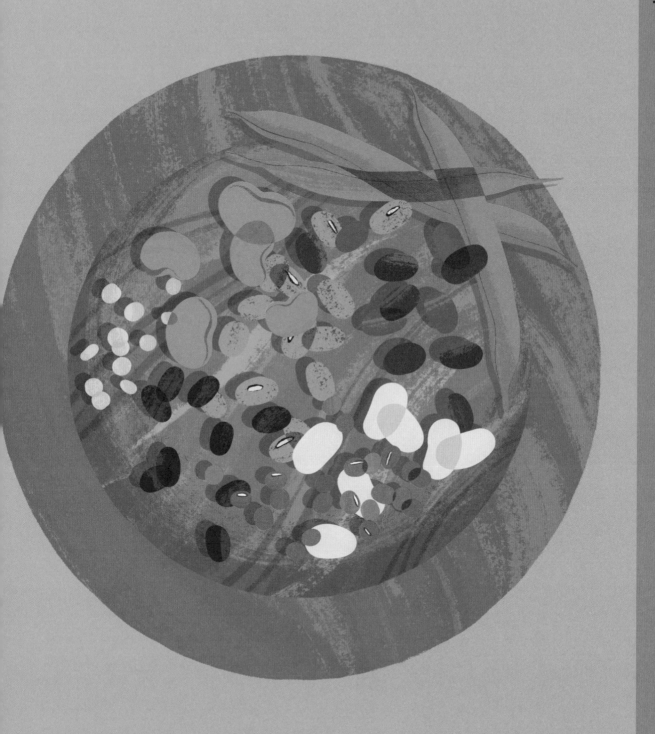

'Broad beans and baby green beans make the most scrumptious salad. I pod and quickly blanch some broad beans, then remove the little outer skin – inside is the sweet bit! Then I blanch green beans and toss them with the broad beans along with goat's milk feta, fresh basil and extra virgin olive oil. Finish with crispy fried shallots and it's the perfect salad!' – NICKY RIEMER, AUSTRALIA

BUYING & STORING

Regardless of whether you're shopping for the kind of beans you plan on podding or the ones for bunging in a pan with nary a second thought, freshness makes all the difference for beans, which are a spring sensation. The older beans get, the stringier the pod and the starchier the beans inside, which means more work to make them taste great. Beyond an obvious lack of goopiness, a glossy exterior and a crisp snap, it's not so easy to tell whether a green bean is up to scratch just by looking at it or having a cheeky feel. If no one is looking, I snap off the tip and give the beans a taste before bagging – fresh beans are really juicy and sweet to taste, kind of like an equally fresh pea. Broad beans are best selected by feeling for the size of the bean inside. The bigger the pod and bean, the older it is, and the more likely it is to be floury. Choose mid-sized pods, up to 8 cm (3¼ inches) in length, with beans no bigger than a generous thumbprint. If you chance upon smaller pods, with beans smaller than a fingernail, give one a taste – if it's sweet and tender, use them that same day and you don't even need to double-pod them (more on this below)!

Beans are pretty delicate in their natural state, so use them up as quickly as possible. Broad beans are best double-podded and used immediately, though I do enjoy an evening of steaming, blanching and podding, and find they're still okay for breakfast or lunch the next day, but by dinnertime they're kaput. 'Double podding' refers to the first 'pod' – pulling the individual beans out of their long, velvety cocoons, then blanching the beans in boiling water for 3–4 minutes (depending on size), and then podding them again by popping each bean out of its casing. My home economist Jane gave me the best explanation for why the second podding is a must – because the broad bean casing feels like blister skin. Blugh! If you do need to store them, keep them unwashed and dry, bagged up in the crisper – moisture is their nemesis. Green beans also freeze really well, and although most books will tell you to blanch, snap freeze, then freeze in earnest, I'm here to give you permission to wash, spin, chop into 2–3 cm (¾–1¼ inch) batons and freeze – the end! They'll keep for as long as you need, until the next time green beans are abundant. Along with frozen ones, dried or canned beans are always great to have on hand for a rainy day (quite literally, those days when you don't want to venture outside for fresh ingredients).

COOKING WITH

If you're cooking fresh beans, they'll either need to be topped and tailed, or strung, before blanching. Many modern varieties have been cultivated in a way that makes them stringless, but heirloom varieties require a little more work – as you tear off the tail, pull towards the bean and the string on the side should come right off. Blanching in boiling water works well for green beans and broad beans (once podded) because it helps retain their bright green color. Cook them for just long enough for the beans to turn a more vibrant shade of green, then remove and plunge into iced water to retain the color and keep the beans *al dente*. A squirt of lemon juice helps keep the color, too, and adds brightness to the flavor, but keep the beans acid free until after they've cooked, as the chemical reaction turns them yellow – which explains why tomato-based green bean braises always go a bit 'baby poop' in tone. Mind you, I don't mind a mushy bean, especially in a sugo or curry, and often prefer it to the squeak of even the mildest under-blanched ones. If you're the same, own it and serve those mushy braised beans with pride! Dried beans need to be soaked in water overnight, while canned ones are ready to go. Opt for organic canned beans where you can, and reserve the liquid they're immersed in as a plant-based alternative to egg whites and thickeners. Known as aquafaba ('bean water'), the bean liquid is perfect for fluffy desserts, mayonnaise-style emulsions and thickened soups. But do drain and rinse if the recipe calls for it, as this bean water is so thick that it can change the whole constitution of your sauce!

BEYOND BEANS: BEAN SPROUTS

Also known as bean sprouts, these are literally the sprouted shoots of mung or soy beans. Prolifically cultivated and used in Asian cuisine because of their mild flavor and crisp, juicy crunch, you can use them in Chinese and Thai stir-fries, salads and soups, blanch then dress for the Korean side-dish *kongnamul muchim*, or pop a handful on top of a Vietnamese *pho*. Store them in the fridge, nip off any discolored tails, and wash and spin well before using. You can germinate your own organic mung beans by soaking overnight, then wash morning and night for 4–7 days (depending on conditions), draining well, covering with cheesecloth or a tea towel, and storing in a cool, dark place. The same method can be applied to other microgreens and grasses such as alfalfa, too. Refrigerate once harvested.

WITH COMPLEMENTS

Butter, cheese (especially feta, goat, gruyère, parmesan), garlic, lemon, mint, nuts (especially almonds, hazelnuts, walnuts), orange (especially zest).

GEORGIAN GREEN BEANS WITH CARAMELIZED ONION

Some people like their beans squeaky, but I am *not* one of those people. I'm really into this recipe, because it makes even those who like an *al dente* bean rethink their priorities. I'd usually sprinkle in some ground fenugreek, too, which you're welcome to add, if you've any in the pantry.

SERVES 4

1 onion, finely diced

2 tablespoons olive oil

1 teaspoon flaked sea salt

1 teaspoon curry powder

1 teaspoon ground coriander

½ teaspoon ground fenugreek

500 g (1 lb 2 oz) green beans, topped

4–5 garlic cloves, crushed

1 tablespoon red wine vinegar

3 tablespoons chopped cilantro leaves and stems, plus extra to garnish

¼ cup (30 g) walnuts, chopped

Pop the onion in a large saucepan with the olive oil and salt, over medium heat. Wait until it starts sizzling, then cover the pan and reduce the heat a little. Sweat for 5 minutes, then remove the lid. Gently coax the onion to golden with regular stirring and words of encouragement for 5–10 minutes. Once the onion is colored, sprinkle in the spices and stir until fragrant.

Chop the beans in half horizontally and toss them into the pan, stirring to become glossy and coated in the spiced onion mixture. Add the garlic and stir it around, too. Splash in the vinegar and let it glaze everything in a syrupy glow, then pour in ¼ cup (60 ml) water. Close the lid for 15 minutes or so, lifting the lid every now and then to give the beans a stir.

From the 12-minute mark, check the middle of a bean with your fingernail – if it dents easily, it's cooked. Younger beans won't need as long to yield.

Once the beans are soft enough to bend and snap, stir the cilantro through. Taste and correct for seasoning Serve sprinkled with the walnuts, in a big rustic bowl in the middle of the table.

Shortcut Split the beans in half lengthwise to halve the cooking time; I use a bean splitter, but you can also use a sharp paring knife. You should have just enough time to do this while the onion caramelizes (that is one step I won't let you take a shortcut on – though you could always sprinkle in a touch of brown sugar to speed things along in this department, too).

Tip Traditionally, the garlic doesn't get scraped in until the beans are cooked, so that the heat and sulfuric sting of raw garlic is still present. I've softened this a bit, but if you're up for it, go the whole heat and only add the garlic when adding the fresh cilantro, for maximum impact.

Double duty Once you've reheated the beans in the pan, pour in some beaten egg and scramble it about to make a protein-rich, satisfying bean scramble.

JALAPEÑO FOUR BEAN SALAD

A good bean salad recipe is always handy for 'bring a plate' situations, or whenever you want to whip up something inexpensive, fresh and tasty in a jiffy. This one is particularly perfect for springtime entertaining, when broad beans are plentiful. The key here is to provide different shades of bean, but the varieties can be seasonally subbed super successfully. The dressing is sublime and will work over any beans – even canned ones! Try kidney beans, borlotti beans, butter beans, or even those four-bean-mix cans ... really puts the 'can' into 'can do'!

SERVES 4

300 g (10½ oz) green
   beans, topped
   but not tailed
100 g (3½ oz) sugar
   snap peas
150 g (5½ oz) broad bean
   pods (yielding about
   50 g/1¾ oz beans)
400 g (14 oz) can
   black beans, drained
   and rinsed
½ bunch of cilantro,
   stems finely chopped,
   leaves left whole
½ bunch of dill,
   fronds picked
1 handful of mint leaves,
   roughly chopped
100 g (3½ oz) manchego
   cheese

Lime & jalapeño dressing
½ cup (125 ml) extra
   virgin olive oil
1 French shallot,
   finely diced
1 fresh green jalapeño
   chili, finely diced
juice of 1 lime
2 tablespoons red
   wine vinegar
1 tablespoon brown sugar
½ teaspoon flaked sea salt

Slice the green beans and sugar snap peas in half lengthwise along the seams.

Blanch the green beans by adding them to a large saucepan of salted boiling water. Cook for 3 minutes exactly, then plunge into cold water to stop the cooking process and keep the color bright.

In the same pan, blanch the sugar snap peas and broad beans for 2 minutes, then plunge into cold water.

When cooled, drain off all the water from the beans and sugar snap peas. Pop them into a decent-sized mixing bowl.

Put the black beans in another bowl. Whisk all the dressing ingredients together, add the finely chopped cilantro stems and season very generously with freshly cracked black pepper. Pour the dressing over the black beans to let the flavors absorb.

When ready to serve, toss the cilantro leaves, dill and mint through the black beans, then pile over the mixed fresh beans.

Grate the cheese over the top, using a fine grater for puffy delicious clouds, then serve.

Tips We used one of those fan-dangled 'Krisk' bean slicers to slice the beans, which you can find in most kitchenware shops. It's a bit of a 'lust-have', rather than a 'must-have', but if it helps you seal the deal with yourself, you can also use it for asparagus spears.

Feel free to use edamame beans, peas or even fancy canned Spanish baby broad beans if available.

This salad is also great served while the beans are still warm, allowing the cheese to melt a little.

Shortcut Drain a 400 g (14 oz) can of four-bean mix, rinse, then toss in a bowl with the dressing. Place 1 cup (140 g) frozen peas in a heatproof bowl, pour freshly boiled hot water over, then let the water cool. Drain, then stir them through the beans and serve right away.

Okra

Okra is the quicksand of vegetables. Pick it up and you're on dry land; cook it funny and it turns into the kind of sludge Indiana Jones would be hard-pressed to survive. A relation of hibiscus, we're eating what is actually a seed pod. What makes okra so tricky and unique to cook with is the 'mucilage' it contains, which helps the plant to retain water during dry conditions, yet under moisture and heat in the kitchen transforms into something rather slimy. But from that slime comes slippery Southern gumbo (a soup thickened by okra), unctuous *bhindi masala* (fried okra in spiced tomato gravy), and viscous West African okra stew, soaked up with cassava-based *fufu*. When you've grown up with it, you'll love the goop and miss it like an old friend. If you're a fan of chia seed pudding, tapioca or those basil seed drinks, okra might just be a new texture for you that sticks.

'I usually toss okra in chickpea flour after cleaning it thoroughly and frying so that it's not slimy. It works especially well with plenty of cumin.' – SARANSH GOILA, INDIA

BUYING & STORING

Okra is best when it's on the smaller side, which you'll be mostly likely to find at the start of its season in early summer. Up to 7.5 cm (3 inches) in size is about the limit. Larger is fine if maximum mucilage is in order – just bear in mind that longer, older pods become increasingly stringy and seedy, posing another textural challenge to the cook. Fresh okra is unmistakably Kelly green, with a slightly fuzzy, occasionally spiny texture to its pods, which bruise easily; any brown or black spots may indicate mishandling, so be vigilant and feel for and avoid soft spots. Under no circumstances should okra have any moisture in or around it when purchasing – this will only exacerbate its sliminess to the point of calling in Ghostbusters.

Due to its subtropical climate preferences, take care when storing okra that its temperature doesn't dip below 45°F in the fridge. Keep it towards the front of the crisper, or, if your fridge is on the cold side, store it bagged up but with some airflow in a cool part of your pantry instead.

COOKING WITH

You know that scene in *Gremlins* where Gizmo goes from a cute little Mogwai to spawning puff balls and creating a Mogwai army, all because he got a little wet? Keep. Okra. Dry. Use a cloth to wipe the skin clean, as you might with mushrooms. The mucilage is in the membrane between skin and seed, so the less surface area you expose, the less slimy your result. Use a sharp knife, chop as little as you have to, and only right before cooking – smaller pods can even be popped in whole (just trim around the stem to help keep the seeds inside), or chopped in half horizontally to accentuate the star-shaped cross-section. Okra reacts with aluminum and cast iron, turning black, so stainless steel or enamelled cookware is best. Flash-fry pods in hot oil first, build up the flavors in your curry or stew, them pop them back in with 5–10 minutes to go. These instructions are designed to mitigate the mucilage – but if making gumbo or any other concoction where gumminess is the desired outcome, reverse pretty much everything I've said! Wash the okra – some people even soak it – chop it finely against the grain so the star shapes are the hero, and add your okra to the other ingredients earlier on in cooking. Frying it first is still a good step to take for extra flavor and texture.

WITH COMPLEMENTS

Bell pepper, chili (especially cayenne pepper, green), citrus (especially lemon, lime), corn, ginger, herbs (especially cilantro, parsley), onion, tomato.

SOUTHERN FRIED OKRA

I'm not sure how often a recipe hailing from America's Deep South calls for milk kefir, an ingredient that is far more at home on an Eastern European table, but I love how the fizz in kefir transforms any batter in much the way sparkling water does. You can always use buttermilk, if that's more readily available, but I'm also secretly trying to get you to try milk kefir as a drink, so that it finds its way to your home table, too.

SERVES 4–6

rice bran or peanut oil,
   for deep-frying
1 bunch of thyme
⅓ cup (50 g) corn flour
1 cup (150 g) all-purpose
   flour
1 teaspoon flaked sea salt
1½ teaspoons
   smoked paprika
1 teaspoon curry powder
100 ml (3½ fl oz) milk
   kefir, plus extra
   for dipping

400 g (14 oz) okra
   pods (smaller ones
   are best here)

Paprika salt
¼ cup (35 g)
   flaked sea salt
2 teaspoons smoked
   paprika

Heat 4 cm (1½ inches) of oil in a saucepan to 350°F, or until a cube of bread dropped into the oil turns golden in 15 seconds. Add the thyme leaves and cook for 1–2 minutes, or until crisp. Remove with tongs and drain on paper towel.

In a wide bowl, mix together the corn flour, all-purpose flour , salt, paprika and curry powder.

Pour the kefir into another bowl. In a third small bowl, toss together the paprika salt ingredients.

The trick to stop the okra going too gloopy is to keep the okra dry until the very last minute, and deep-fry in small batches. So, one at a time, dip the okra into the kefir, then in the flour mixture, then immediately into the hot oil. Fry for 2–3 minutes, until the batter is golden and crispy. Drain on paper towel.

Sprinkle the paprika salt over the fried okra and sprinkle with crispy thyme leaves while still hot. Serve warm, with extra kefir for dipping.

Go gluten free You can definitely go right ahead and use plain gluten-free flour here.

Go dairy free Instead of using the kefir to help this particular flour mixture adhere, you can use a tempura sparkling water or Sparkling wine batter (page 374), and serve with Garlic aioli (page 37) for dipping.

OKRA PEANUT STEW

Some recipes try to subdue the 'sliminess' that okra is best known for, while others embrace it. This one is of the latter. If you'd prefer to just dip your toe in, buy smaller okra and leave them whole to mitigate the mucilage – but if you're all about that gumbo goop, cut them into thin rounds to maximise the exposed surface area. The creamy nuttiness of peanut butter, and warming spices such as fenugreek, paprika and coriander, make this stew an absolute goer ... and stayer.

SERVES 4–6

1 tablespoon peanut oil

1 yellow onion,
   finely chopped

1 tablespoon finely
   chopped fresh ginger

2 fresh green jalapeño
   chilis, finely chopped

1 teaspoon sweet paprika

¼ teaspoon
   ground fenugreek

2 tablespoons
   coriander seeds

1 teaspoon cumin seeds

½ cup (70 g) raw peanuts

2 tablespoons
   tomato paste

2 tomatoes,
   coarsely grated

¾ cup (210 g) chunky
   peanut butter

2 teaspoons salt

4 cups (1 liter)
   vegetable stock

20 okra pods, about 250 g
   (9 oz), cut into 3 cm
   (1¼ inch) chunks (or
   kept whole, if small)

juice of 1 lime, plus lime
   wedges to serve

fresh cilantro leaves,
   to garnish

Couscous

2 tablespoons butter
   (or olive oil)

1½ cups (285 g) couscous

2 cups (500 ml)
   vegetable stock

Toasted garnish

⅓ cup (80 ml) peanut oil

250 g (9 oz) cherry
   tomatoes on the vine

1 tablespoon peanuts

1 teaspoon
   coriander seeds

Heat the peanut oil in a large saucepan over medium heat. Add the onion, ginger, chili and spices and cook, stirring, for 5–8 minutes, or until the onion has softened. Be sure to have your rangehood on (or a window open), as your eyes might sting with this one!

Stir in the peanuts and tomato paste and cook for 2 minutes to darken slightly. Add the grated tomato, peanut butter, salt and stock and bring to the boil.

Add the okra pieces, drop the heat to a low simmer, cover with a lid and cook for 30 minutes, or until the okra is tender. Stir in the lime juice and correct the seasoning if need be.

Meanwhile, prepare the couscous. Melt the butter in a saucepan. Add the couscous and mix to coat each grain, then add the stock and bring to the boil. Cover, turn the heat off and leave to cook in the residual heat for 10 minutes. Once the couscous has absorbed all the liquid, use a fork to fluff the grains up.

While you wait, toast up a snazzy garnish. Heat the peanut oil in a little pan for a minute or so over medium heat. Add the tomatoes and cook, spooning the hot oil over every so often, for 5 minutes, or until burnished slightly. Remove and set aside in a bowl. Return the pan to the heat with 1 tablespoon of the hot oil, then add the peanuts and coriander seeds. As soon as they turn golden, tip them into a bowl.

Pile the couscous into serving bowls, or onto a platter, then top with the stew. Sprinkle with the toasted nuts and seeds, garnish with the cherry tomatoes and cilantro leaves and serve with lime wedges.

Extra I like to serve this topped with Confit chili tomatoes (page 180). You could simply whack some halved fresh cherry tomatoes on top, too.

Light green

* **LEEK**
  + Green onion
* **ASPARAGUS**
* **CELERY**
  + Celtuce
* **LETTUCE**
  + Watercress
* **BOK CHOY**

* **BRUSSELS SPROUTS**
* **PEAS & SNOW PEAS**
* **CABBAGE**
* **AVOCADO**
  + Bitter melon

Leek

If you're leaving onions out of your cooking because they are too bothersome to chop or are making your eyes leak, pick up a leek. These single-bulbed members of the allium family are easier to handle, since their long stems act as a literal handle when chopping, and won't reduce you to tears. Leeks are used for sweetness and body in classic winter soups such as Scottish cock-a-leekie, where the green tops are simmered whole to draw out as much flavor as possible and then removed before serving, with the lighter parts sliced and added towards the end. Creamy leek and potato soup – or vichyssoise if you're fancy – calls for simmering the lighter parts in stock with plenty of potato, then blitzing with cream before serving hot or cold. While most recipes specify using the lighter parts of the leek, the green parts are always a worthwhile addition to stocks, providing a decidedly floral note, as well as a general feeling of smugness over not letting this part of the veg go to waste.

> 'At home, I like to add leek to my beef stir-fry with garlic, chili and lemongrass.' – RAY ADRIANSYAH, INDONESIA

BUYING & STORING

Many larger stores sell leeks already topped, so it's only the white and lightest green parts of the stalk that you're buying. At farmers' markets and greengrocers, leeks are often sold either as bunches of young leeks, or single stalks with an ombré of white through to a deeper green at the top. When whole, avoid green tops that have any yellowing or are dried out. Select stalks that have as much white and light green to them as possible, as this is what most recipes call for. Thinner stalks are younger and therefore more tender, which makes them fabulous for braising and barbecues, while thicker, more mature stems are useful for stuffing, or slicing for sweating and soups. Store unwashed leeks loosely wrapped at the bottom of the crisper, where they'll happily keep for several weeks. Surplus leeks can be sweated down in olive oil, portioned and frozen for instant flavor bombs to add to soups and stews.

PREPPING & COOKING WITH

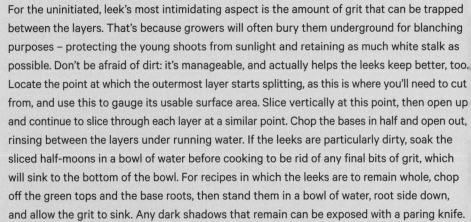

For the uninitiated, leek's most intimidating aspect is the amount of grit that can be trapped between the layers. That's because growers will often bury them underground for blanching purposes – protecting the young shoots from sunlight and retaining as much white stalk as possible. Don't be afraid of dirt: it's manageable, and actually helps the leeks keep better, too. Locate the point at which the outermost layer starts splitting, as this is where you'll need to cut from, and use this to gauge its usable surface area. Slice vertically at this point, then open up and continue to slice through each layer at a similar point. Chop the bases in half and open out, rinsing between the layers under running water. If the leeks are particularly dirty, soak the sliced half-moons in a bowl of water before cooking to be rid of any final bits of grit, which will sink to the bottom of the bowl. For recipes in which the leeks are to remain whole, chop off the green tops and the base roots, then stand them in a bowl of water, root side down, and allow the grit to sink. Any dark shadows that remain can be exposed with a paring knife.

If a dish calls for both leeks and onions, add the leeks to the pot along with the onions and sweat them in plenty of olive oil or butter. If sweating leeks alone, consider splashing in a tablespoon of water to keep them from burning, or leaving the lid on to help stop the pan drying out and burning the leeks.

Speaking of 'burning leeks', when cut in half lengthwise and placed on a hot barbecue, the leek's natural sugars are activated and begin to char, the inside cooking while the outside crusts up. The white and lighter green parts are delicious finely diced or sliced and put through anything eggy or creamy, such as quiche or cream-of soups. When quartered and subjected to sustained heat through braising or baking, the leek's layers break down from the inside out, collapsing into tender sheets like a flower opening its petals.

BEYOND LEEK: GREEN ONION

Otherwise known as scallions, or occasionally as green shallots, true green onions, with a slightly engorged white bulb and about a school ruler's length of green shoot, are actually much closer in relation to white onions than eschalots. Though true 'scallions' are a slightly different cultivar again, green onions are a very suitable replacement. Pick bunches where the tops are still as upright as possible. Wrap in damp cloth or paper towel and bag up for the crisper. To prepare, pull from the tips and let the stalks 'pop' at the point that they're still freshest (reserve these tops in the freezer for stocks), then hold the shoots together and slice from white (the most flavorsome) to green, like leeks. Chop into 3–4 cm (1½ inch) batons for stir-fries and sautés, slice the green stem vertically, thinly on a diagonal or open out flat, then roll like a carpet and cut into thin strips for garnishing. You can also regrow green onions by popping the root end into a jar with water; you'll start to see action within a week.

WITH COMPLEMENTS

Anchovies, bacon, butter, cheese (especially cheddar, gruyère, parmesan), cream, garlic, herbs (especially bay leaves, chervil, chives, oregano, parsley, tarragon, thyme), mustard, potato, spices (especially caraway, nutmeg, paprika, peppercorns), truffle, white wine.

SCRAP MEDAL

Though it's true that the lighter parts are sweeter, milder in flavor, and break down more readily during cooking, the darker green tops of leek have their own appeal – a bit like a cross between an onion and a cabbage. If making soup, consider leaving the green tops whole, simmering them with the rest of the ingredients (along with the sliced, sweated lighter parts of the leek) and then pulling out the tops at the end. The tops can also be stored either whole or roughly chopped in the freezer, for adding to stocks.

Green onions are felicitous with seafood, whether raw with oysters or sprinkled on steamed whole fish with soy sauce and garlic. When briefly blanched just enough to take away the heat, they are gloriously sweet and aromatic. A dish I love is grilled John Dory fillets, served with warm soft-boiled eggs cut in half, and green onions that have been flashed in boiling water, brushed with olive oil and briefly cooked over charcoal, then sprinkled with a mustard and olive oil vinaigrette.' – RICK STEIN, UK

MUSTARD-BUTTERED LEEKS

While it's true that leeks provide a milder, more floral alternative to onions as a base for savory dishes, they can also stand on their own as a side – or even main event – at the table. It's like the girl with the glasses and the ponytail pulling off both to reveal the glamor within. Only this one rarely shakes off her gritty side without a bit of agitation, so heed the extra soak step, friend.

SERVES 4

6 medium or 8 small leeks, about 700 g (1 lb 9 oz) in total, trimmed and rinsed well

125 g (4½ oz) unsalted butter

¼ cup (60 g) wholegrain mustard

2 garlic cloves, roughly chopped

1 tablespoon baby capers

1 teaspoon brown sugar

Cut the leeks into 5 cm (2 inch) batons, keeping as much of the lighter green bits as possible. Prick the outside layer with a fork and soak in a big bowl of water for at least 10 minutes. Riffle through each layer of the leeks like a deck of cards as you rinse again under running water.

Meanwhile, three-quarters fill a saucepan with well-salted water and bring to the boil over medium heat, popping the dark bits of the leek in to add extra flavor to the simmering liquid (or freeze them in your 'stock-up' bag). Drop in the light leek batons and simmer for 10–12 minutes, until soft. Refresh the batons in iced water for 5 minutes to keep the color vibrant.

While the leeks are chilling, melt the butter in a saucepan. Stir in the mustard, garlic, capers and sugar and taste for seasoning. If the capers aren't already salted, pop in a pinch of salt.

Toss the leek in the mustard butter for 3–4 minutes to soften further and suck up the sauce, ensuring they're nice and coated. Taste for seasoning and serve.

Tip The outer layers of the leek are the most fibrous, and the grittiest. Pricking through them with a fork or paring knife tip gives grit a chance to escape during soaking. Just be sure not to poke all the way through, so that the layers don't start to fall apart in the pot.

Shortcut Refreshing the leek in iced water helps keep its vibrant color, but if you're strapped for time, skip this step and toss the simmered leeks straight into the pan of mustard butter, toss through the sauce for a minute or so, then serve right away.

Double duty The softened leeks are one blitz and a splash of good stock away from being soup, or an easy addition to your next frittata or quiche – just add eggs.

GREEN ONION QUICHE

Think of this as a classic quiche lorraine, except easier to prepare. That's because the oftentimes sandy leeks are replaced by conveniently clean green onions, which also require far less effort to slice and soften. I also like that it uses every part of the green onion in a slightly different way, taking full advantage of the whites as you might leeks, the main green body behaving like a leafy green through the mix, and the very tops thinly sliced and sprinkled as a garnish. If you're feeling particularly cheffy, you might like to try frying the (well-cleaned) fuzzy roots until they crisp and frizzle, and laying these on top of the quiche, too. Get creative with seasonal additions by popping in a handful of asparagus in spring, or cherry tomatoes in summer.

SERVES 12

15 green onions (scallions)
50 g (1¾ oz) butter
125 g (4½ oz) speck, chopped into 1 cm (½ inch) pieces
200 ml (7 fl oz) heavy cream
8 eggs
3 tablespoons roughly chopped dill, plus extra to serve
½ teaspoon ground nutmeg (or a few good scrapes of fresh nutmeg)
100 g (3½ oz) gruyère (or cheddar), grated

chopped baby parsley, to garnish (optional)

Shortcrust pastry
1⅔ cups (250 g) all-purpose flour, plus extra for dusting
100 g (3½ oz) cold salted butter, chopped
½ teaspoon flaked sea salt
½ teaspoon ground white pepper
1 egg yolk
1 tablespoon apple cider vinegar

To make the pastry, place the flour, butter, salt and pepper in a food processor and blitz to breadcrumb consistency. Add the egg yolk and vinegar and pulse until the dough forms a ball, adding water 1 teaspoon at a time if needed to bring it together. Shape into a disc and cover with plastic wrap. Chill for 1 hour, or overnight.

Preheat the oven to 450°F. Line the base of a 5 cup (1.25 liter) baking dish with parchment paper.

On a lightly floured work surface, roll out the pastry to a 5 mm (¼ inch) thickness. Use the pastry to line your baking dish, patting it into the sides of the dish, leaving the overhang. Chill for 15 minutes. Dock the base with a fork (in other words, just 'poke' it) and trim the overhang.

Pop a sheet of parchment paper on top of the pastry, fill the dish with baking weights (or dried rice or beans) and blind-bake for 20 minutes. Remove the parchment paper and weights, then bake for a further 10 minutes, or until golden and crisp.

Meanwhile, finely slice the white ends of the green onions, chop the green stems into 1 cm (½ inch) pieces, and reserve the tops, leaving them whole. Melt the butter in a frying pan and sauté the white green onion bits with the speck over medium heat for 3–4 minutes. Transfer to a bowl and chill slightly.

Add the cream, eggs, dill, nutmeg, cheese and green green onion stems to the speck mixture and whisk to combine. Season with sea salt and freshly ground black pepper. Pour the mixture into the pastry shell.

Turn the oven temperature down to 350°F. Bake the quiche for 40 minutes, or until the egg has set. Thinly slice the remaining green onion and sprinkle over the baked quiche, along with the parsley, if using, and the extra dill. Serve warm.

Shortcut **Use shop-bought pastry, speedster. Shortcrust, puff or even filo pastry will hold this filling. The fewer ingredients listed on the packet, the closer it will taste (and feel) to the pastry you'd make at home.**

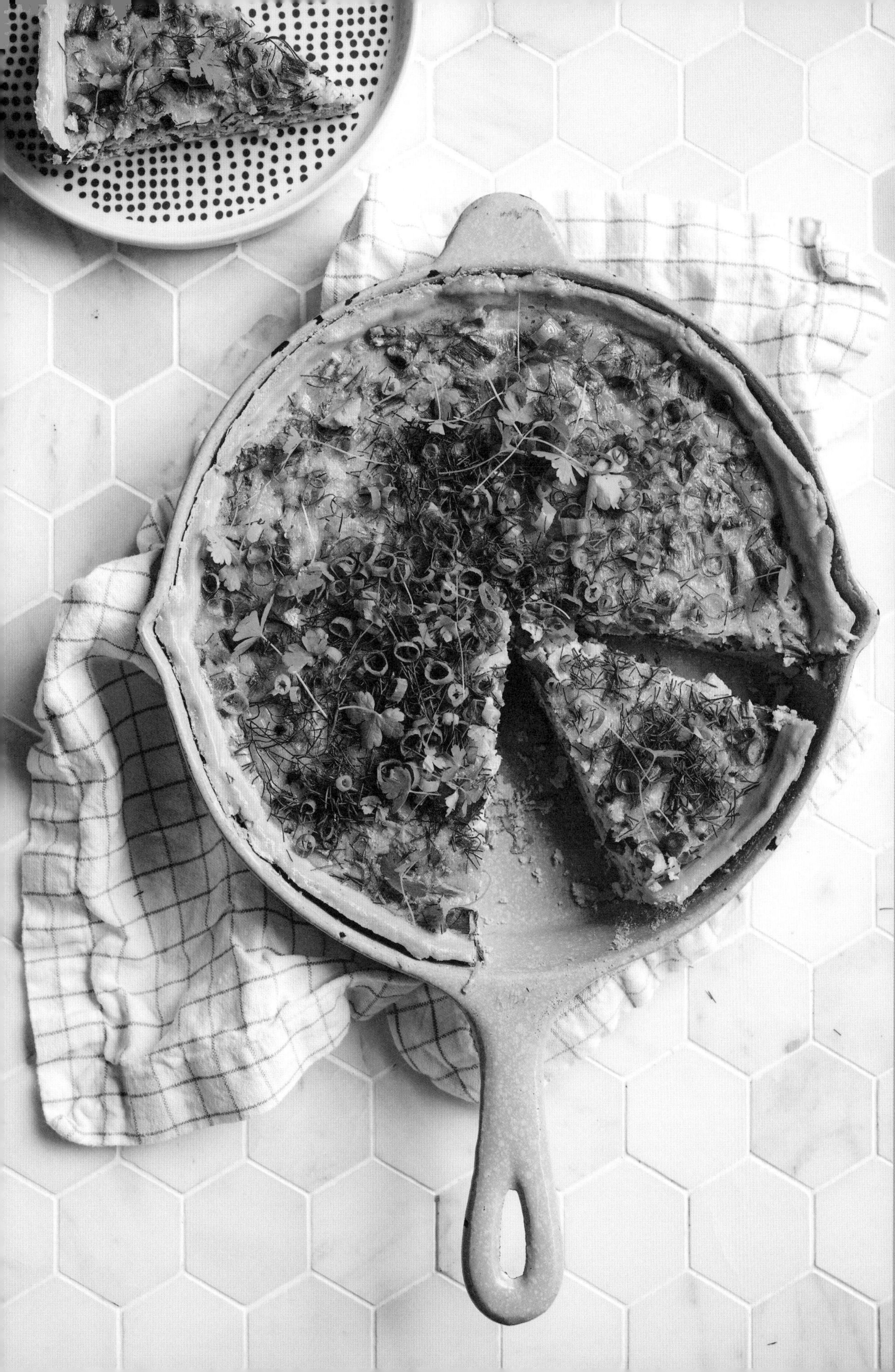

Asparagus

Nothing screams 'SPRING!' like asparagus, and it's more of a staccato outburst than a sustained shout, because blink, and you'll miss it. Your standard spears are usually bright green and the girth of a pencil, but there are plenty of other variations on this theme. Thicker spears early in the season can be tossed through salads raw. White asparagus is prized by chefs for its unusual appearance and tenderness – cultivated by being grown in the dark. Being rarer and more expensive, this is often simply tossed through butter, particularly the tender tips. Speaking of rare, if you ever come across purple asparagus, grab some: it's highest in antioxidants and is often sweeter in flavor. It's still bright green on the inside, so shaving it into ribbons makes for an especially dramatic garnish.

Here's one of my favorite ways to cook asparagus, from the first chef I worked for. Make a garlic butter and drizzle over blanched asparagus. Sprinkle with lemon juice and grated parmesan, bake in a hot oven for 6–8 minutes, spoon a little more garlic butter over and serve. My kids love it!' – ASHLEY PALMER-WATTS, UK

BUYING & STORING

I judge my spears by their tips – buds should be tight and bright, with not a droop or gloop in sight. The woodier the ends, the longer your asparagus has been out of the ground (which means less nutrient value and less flavor), so look for ends that don't appear too parchy; clever greengrocers will even store their spears in iced boxes to retain maximum crunch. If you're hoping to hold onto those spears until the end of the week or beyond, especially if you plan on serving them raw, store them as you would herbs or a bunch of flowers. Trim off the very end of the tips (don't 'snap' the ends off until just before cooking) and store the spears upright in a jar of water, with a plastic bag or damp paper towel over the tips. For shorter storage, the crisper drawer is quite alright.

COOKING WITH

The biggest pitfall with asparagus is chopping too much usable product off the stems. Rather than hacking at an arbitrary point, allow me to recommend the 'bend-n-snap'. That's where you bend the asparagus towards the base and let it snap at a point it's comfortable with. Save these woody bottoms in your 'stock-up' bag as a sweet, nutty addition to vegetable stocks during spear season and beyond. And when it comes to cooking asparagus, the less you do to it, the better. In fact, early-harvest asparagus is incredibly delicious sliced raw through salads, with a taste similar to fresh snow peas (mangetout). The stems are so tender that you don't even need to get rid of the stringy last bit. But you'll have to get in quick, as asparagus is only around for a short few weeks. If you're going to cook your spears, all they need is a simple blanch in boiling well-salted water until bright green (1–2 minutes, depending on thickness). I blanch the asparagus to just before perfect, and let the residual heat cook it through – an approach I use for cooking seafood, too.

WITH COMPLEMENTS

Butter, cheese (especially goat, ricotta, parmesan), cured meats, eggs, garlic, lemon, olive oil, pepper, shallot.

ASPARAGUS CRUMB & SOLDIERS WITH SOFT-BOILED EGG

If you've ever snapped off the woody ends of asparagus and flicked them into the compost with a sigh, fear not! Applications like this, where the woodiness is incorporated into the crunchy crumb, are just a reframe ahead – just think of the ends as aromatic roughage.

SERVES 4

2 bunches of asparagus, about 600 g (1 lb 5 oz)

250 g (9 oz) sourdough bread, roughly chopped

25 g (1 oz) parmesan, roughly chopped

1 teaspoon flaked sea salt

1 teaspoon freshly cracked black pepper

1 tablespoon capers, drained

2 tablespoons extra virgin olive oil, plus extra for drizzling

8 eggs

4 lemon wedges

Preheat the oven broiler to high. Line a baking tray with foil. Bring a saucepan of water to the boil.

Snap the ends off the asparagus spears at their natural bend-point, then place the woody ends in a small food processor, along with the bread, parmesan, salt and pepper. Whiz until fine breadcrumbs form. Transfer to the baking tray and sprinkle with the capers. Broil for 5 minutes, or until beginning to turn golden.

Cut the asparagus spears in half lengthwise, toss with the olive oil and place on the tray with the crumbs. Broil for another 3 minutes, or until the asparagus is just cooked.

Meanwhile, add the eggs to the boiling water. Cook for 6 minutes, then immediately strain into the sink. Run a cold tap over the eggs for 30 seconds, or until cool enough to handle. Peel the eggs under the running tap (this helps to achieve a smooth egg).

To serve, divide the crumbs and eggs among shallow serving bowls or plates. Cut the eggs in half. Place the asparagus spears alongside, with a lemon wedge for squirting more acid into the rich mix. Drizzle with a little extra olive oil, season with salt and pepper and serve.

Shortcut **Blanch the asparagus with the eggs for 2–3 minutes, depending on the width of the spears.**

Scrap medal **If you're not in the mood to make no crumb, save the asparagus ends in the freezer for your next stock.**

THREE-INGREDIENT PUFFY ASPARAGUS & PERSIAN FETA OMELET

Believe it or not, Persians never even made feta. Well, not the marinated kind, at any rate. In fact, the very notion of a 'Persian feta' came about in the Yarra Valley, in the Australian state of Victoria – the same state responsible for over 90 per cent of the country's asparagus production! Dairy scientist Richard Thomas, often referred to as 'The Godfather of Cheese', had come upon an all-new preservation technique on his travels through Iran, which rendered feta silkier and creamier than ever before. These days, this style of feta is far more readily available around the world – perhaps even in Iran.

MAKES 2 OMELETS

6 eggs
50 g (1¾ oz) Persian feta, crumbled, plus 2 tablespoons of the marinating oil

1 bunch of asparagus, thicker spears halved lengthwise
parsley leaves, to serve

Preheat the oven to 425°F.

Separate 4 of the eggs, placing the egg whites in a large bowl, and the yolks with the remaining 2 eggs in another bowl.

Whisk the yolks and eggs until creamy. Wash the whisk well, then whisk the egg whites to soft peaks.

Fold a little of the beaten egg white through the yolky mixture, then swirl the rest through using a flexible spatula and a figure-eight motion until combined.

Working in two batches, heat 1 tablespoon of the marinating oil in an ovenproof 18 cm (7 inch) non-stick frying pan over high heat. Add half the asparagus and cook for 30 seconds to soften slightly. Remove to a plate. Pour half the egg mixture into the hot pan. It'll be fluffier than you think, so treat it more like a pancake, waiting until the top has set a little, before popping in the asparagus mixture and a bit of the feta on the outer corner, folding over gently and whacking into the oven for 2 minutes, or until the egg is just set.

Carefully transfer to a plate. Drizzle with more marinated feta and a little more of the oil. Season with flaked sea salt and freshly ground black pepper and serve immediately, sprinkled with parsley.

Shortcut **If you're whisking off somewhere and can't be bothered whisking a thing, crack 3 eggs into a bowl and fork them together until the whites and yolks are broken up and mostly uniform in color. Use the oil to cook skinny discs of asparagus until just tender (or keep it raw if it's super fresh), then pour the eggs over, like a crêpe batter, stir about a bit, flip over and onto a plate.**

Double duty **Marinated goat cheese is a wonder ingredient – first it's a mezze board marvel, then it's a salad dressing dahhhling, and finally, it even blitzes into a whipped cheese dip with the magical addition of soy milk. That's a tip from my chef mate Mark Best.**

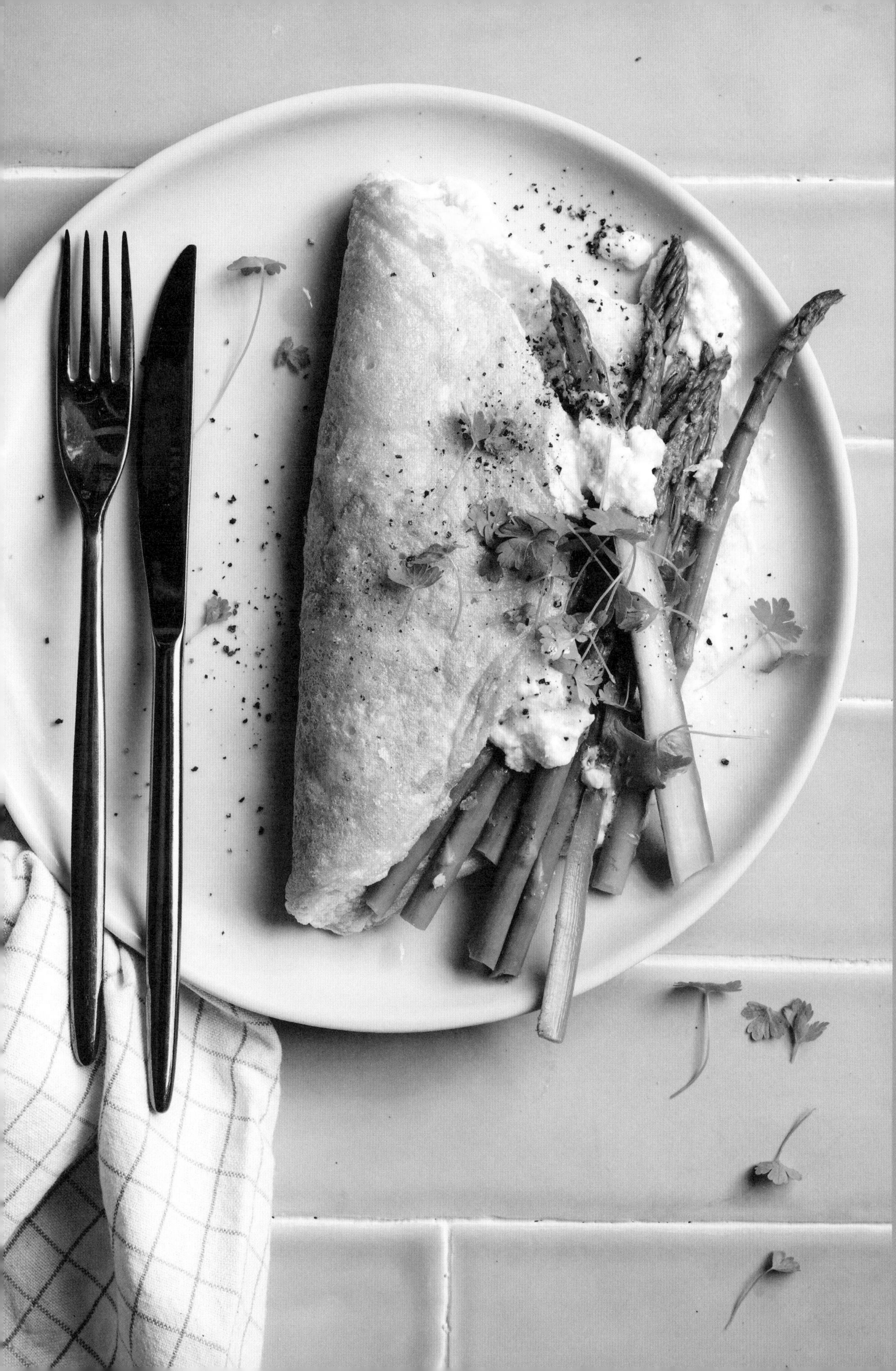

Celery

The best way to get the most out of celery is to think of it as separate vegetables: a leafy herb garnish with a bitter kick, crunchy stalky 'ribs' as dippers for nut butters, and an earthy aromatic stalk base to be sweated down with onion and carrot in soups and stews. Even the seeds of celery are culinarily useful, and are to my mind the true heroes of a proper Bloody Mary – as is the whole stalk stirrer that accompanies it. Celery's bitterness and nuttiness sits on a spectrum, from the occasionally bitey pale yellow leaves and stalks, celery hearts that taste mild and sweet with a hint of walnut, all the way through to deep green stalks that require de-stringing and have a flintiness that smacks you in the nostrils. All serve important purposes for a cook. The deeper greens are fantastic for stewing and braising, while the paler stalks – particularly the hearts – are sublime steamed, buttered, or chopped raw through salads and sandwiches. Don't forget to save the leaves from the heart, for a dainty garnish with gentle bite.

'I love using celery raw for its crunch and flavor in my favorite sandwich – chicken with mayonnaise and diced celery between fresh sourdough slices.' – GUILLAUME BRAHIMI, FRANCE

BUYING & STORING

Fresh celery is vibrantly green, with minimal bumps, bruises and browning. Greengrocers will often slice bunches in half down the middle to sell, which gives you a strong indicator of what yours will look like inside if you plan on buying a whole bunch. Buying ready-cut celery ribs is fine, as long as you plan on using them right away; if not, store them submerged in water in an airtight container in the fridge. If you use only part of your celery bunch and have a heap of stalks left over, cover them completely in foil or beeswax wrap to retain moisture, and store them in the crisper away from ethylene-producing vegetables and fruit, such as apples, pears and bananas (the biggest culprit of them all).

COOKING WITH

Almost every braise, casserole, soup and stew will be made better with a handful of chopped celery added once some onion has sweated down a little. Finely sliced into half-moons, celery is an invaluable source of color, crunch and subtle acidity in sandwiches and salads. Chop some stalks into hand-sized sticks to use as edible dippers. Roast similarly sized sticks with herbs such as thyme or tarragon to bring out a creamy sweetness. When in doubt, add walnuts; the two ingredients share the same distinct aromatic compounds known as phthalides, and bring out the best in each other.

BEYOND CELERY: CELTUCE

You can probably guess what this is a cross between? A mutant celery–lettuce that's more stem than leaf. When cooking with celtuce (or *wo sun*, or *woo chu*, as it's also known), peel off the woody outer layer of the stem, to reveal a crisp heart that is delicately sweet and mildly nutty in flavor. It can be used as you might the inside of a broccoli stalk, so you might like to try it steamed, stir-fried, or perhaps sliced or grated and served raw in salads. The leaves can be used, too, but are quite bitter, so put the smaller ones through a much sweeter mesclun mix or cook the larger leaves as you might radicchio, with plenty of black vinegar and soy sauce.

WITH COMPLEMENTS

Apple, butter, carrot, cream, cheese (especially blue, cheddar), peanut butter, vinegar (especially red wine vinegar), walnuts.

BLEND & SNAP CELERY SOUP

If you're wondering where the 'snap' element of this soup comes in, it's well before any 'blending' takes place, where fresh celery is 'snapped' of its heart and leaves for use as garnish. These bits often fall by the wayside and are left to wilt before they can really shine. Here, the hearts take center stage, where they belong. I heart this soup like Elle Woods loves Bruiser. And if that movie reference went over your head, then you're probably still shaking your head at the name of the recipe and hoping this obscure introduction ends soon.

SERVES 4; MAKES 1.5 LITERS (6 CUPS)

1 bunch of celery, about 500 g (1 lb 2 oz)
1 leek, white part only, chopped
1 liter (4 cups) chicken or vegetable stock
½ bunch of marjoram, leaves picked (or use oregano)
¾ teaspoon celery salt
1 teaspoon ground white pepper

1 cup (250 ml) half and half cream
2 bay leaves
2 tablespoons pine nuts, toasted (see tip)
2 tablespoons chopped dried cranberries
1 tablespoon white wine vinegar
extra virgin olive oil, for drizzling

Remove and reserve the heart and young leaves of the celery.

Roughly chop the celery stalks and place in a blender, along with the leek, stock, marjoram, celery salt and white pepper. Whiz until the mixture is finely chopped and your desired level of smoothness. I prefer to leave some chunky bits for texture – but you could pass the mixture through a sieve, if so inclined.

Transfer to a saucepan, along with the cream and bay leaves, and place over medium heat. Bring to a simmer, then cover and cook over low heat for 25 minutes, or until the soup is smooth and the celery fibers have softened in texture. Season to taste.

Finely chop the celery heart and combine in a bowl with the celery leaves, pine nuts, cranberries and vinegar.

Ladle the soup into serving bowls, spoon the pine nut mixture over and finish with a drizzle of olive oil.

Tip **For burn-free pine nuts, heat a frying pan for 5–10 minutes over medium heat. Turn the heat off and add the pine nuts, giving them the odd toss to color through.**

Double duty **Use dinner rolls as bowls and turn this soup into mini cobs! Preheat the oven to 400°F. Cut the tops off the rolls and use your fingers to remove the insides, leaving a shell. Place both the rolls and inners on a baking tray and toast in the oven for 10 minutes. Divide the hot soup between the rolls, add the toasted inners to the soup as croutons, and garnish as directed.**

CUCUMBER, CELERY & APPLE GRANITA WITH JUNIPER SUGAR

Cucumber and celery are two vegetables that are mainstays of juices because they're choc-full of water and refreshing flavor. Let's take total advantage of this by freezing said juice and creating a crunchy, cooling granita that is just perfection on hot summer evenings. The juniper sugar will immediately make you think of G&Ts.

SERVES 4–6

2 English cucumbers, peeled and cut into chunks (to yield about 4 cups)

2 celery stalks, cut into chunks

1 green apple, cored and cut into chunks

2 tablespoons lime juice (reserve the spent lime innards for rimming your serving glasses)

6 mint leaves

¼ cup (55 g) granulated sugar

Juniper sugar

1 tablespoon dried juniper berries

⅓ cup (75 g) granulated sugar

finely grated zest of 1 lime

Put the cucumber, celery and apple in a food processor or blender. Add the lime juice, mint, sugar and 400 ml (14 fl oz) cold water and blitz until the sugar has dissolved (pop a little out between your fingertips and feel for any grainy bits). Strain.

Pour the mixture into a 6 cup (1.2 liter) container and place in the freezer.

Every 30 minutes for the next 1½ hours, scrape down the frozen granita with a fork, using a raking action. You'll start to see large ice crystals to begin with, then the icy crystals will get smaller and smaller until you have what looks like pale green snow.

To make the juniper sugar, blitz the juniper berries into a fine dust, then toss with the sugar and lime zest and sprinkle onto a tray or saucer.

Use the spent lime innards to rim the tops of your chilled serving glasses with 'glue', then dip them into the juniper sugar. Spoon the granita into the chilled glasses and serve immediately.

Tip Use this granita ratio of 100 ml (3½ fl oz) liquid to 20 ml (¾ fl oz) simple sugar syrup (made from equal parts sugar and water) to have a play with your own veggie juice flavor combinations. Try carrot and orange, beet and chili, or whatever whacky combo you can come up with.

Double duty Go ahead and splosh in a little gin, and you've got yourself a frozen cocktail slushie. Look out!

Lettuce

There's a lot more to lettuce than salad. Whenever you need freshness and crunch in a recipe, or an edible plate that isn't bread, lettuce remember that this leafy green might be just what you're after. Butter lettuce, with its billowing green or red-tipped leaves and slightly waxy texture, is terrific in sandwiches because it takes longer to wilt when dressed, while being soft enough to collapse between bread slices and filling. Iceberg lettuce's rounded leaves create an ideal cup shape for san choy bau, and for wrapping around Vietnamese spring rolls with plenty of fresh herbs. Romaine lettuce, also known as cos lettuce, has a slight bitterness that is terrific for cutting through rich salad dressings – hence its popularity in caesar salads – and holds its shape well when charred on the barbecue. Any lettuce that is starting to look a little limp can always be added to juices and soups, too.

'Nothing better than grabbing a beautiful romaine lettuce and barbecuing it over charcoal.' – MATT MORAN, AUSTRALIA

BUYING & STORING

You'll likely find lettuce sold in one of two ways: as whole heads or loose leaves. Whole heads are more cost-effective, while loose leaves – most often sold as mixes of different varieties of sweet and bitter greens (mesclun) – are a little more convenient, but dearer. When picking whole heads, turn them over and inspect the stem end. Unless they're a non-pinking variety, a discolored stem signifies that the lettuce has spent some time in storage – and the same can be said of the exposed pinked edges of any mesclun leaves. Don't look too hard at the outer leaves – these are more akin to a protective casing and will likely be headed for compost, or shredded into soup, if you're up for a Scrap Medal. Instead, give the lettuce a gentle pat on its sides; is there a discernible hollow crunch? If the lettuce is one of the frilly varieties, such as frisée, check that the tips of the leaves are still nice and sharp. The presence of dirt is also a decent indicator of freshness – the older the lettuce, the likelier it is for the dirt to have fallen off; any dirt will get washed away once you're ready to use the lettuce anyway. For mesclun, unless it's pre-boxed or bagged, pick the leaves in handfuls (with tongs, you monster!), making some effort to avoid slimy hangers on (you know what they say about 'bad apples'). If pre-packed is the only option, turn a packet upside down and check for the aforementioned slimies and pinked edges. There's no need to get attached to one variety, either – just keep the texture (some are more robust and crisper than others) and level of bitterness in consideration when subbing in and out.

Lettuce is 95 per cent water, so the leaves are quite susceptible to moisture loss and degradation. The two most important storage considerations are maintaining high humidity (but not 'wetness') and some level of airflow. If you've bought a whole head, leave it whole and unwashed, loosely bagged with a little paper towel or cloth in the crisper, where it'll keep for up to a week. For loose leaves, pick out any slimy stragglers straight away, then wash and spin until reasonably dry, lay out a clean tea towel and arrange the leaves across it, then roll up loosely and ease a bag over the top. The towel will absorb any remaining moisture, giving the leaves a slightly damp environment and enough airflow to last a good week.

PREPARING

However you're serving them, you'll want to give the leaves a thorough wash. If using a whole head, start by tearing off any mangy outer leaves (check Scrap Medal over the page for ideas for these leaves), then turn the whole head upside down and give it a good whack against the kitchen counter. This will help to dislodge the leaves, so that when you twist out the stem and core, they'll all come away. For a salad, tear the leaves into fork-friendly bits; for sandwiches or lettuce cups, keep the leaves whole. You'll notice I haven't once mentioned a knife, and that's for very good reason. Lettuce is extremely prone to bruising, and unless you're using a supremely sharp knife to create a very fine lettuce chiffonade (highly unlikely, but quite nice stirred through buttered peas) or to cut distinct wedges, use your hands. Soak the leaves in a large bowl of water for at least 20 minutes (if you have a salad spinner, use the bowl of the spinner for this purpose, and the insert as a colander to drain). This will not only help dislodge any dirt amongst the leaves (and potential *E. coli* in 'pre-washed' leaves), it'll also reinvigorate them with extra moisture and crunch. If you don't have a salad spinner (and I highly recommend getting one if your salad bowl is on heavy rotation), drain the leaves in a colander, then pop them into a clean tea towel, twist into a swag and spin your linen mace around, avoiding any heirloom pieces of kitchen china by heading out onto the balcony or garden. If you're making a salad to take somewhere, keep the lettuce separate from the other ingredients until the very last minute, as the dressing will weigh down the leaves and make them wilt. If you simply *must* dress before departure, make an oil-free vinaigrette.

BEYOND LETTUCE: WATERCRESS

Known to grow wild across rivers and streams – hence the name – watercress is a leafy green to seek out if you're a lettuce fan. The ideal way to buy it is with the roots still attached, which does wonders for its shelf life and for its taste, which can best be described as a milder version of arugula. Its pepperiness dissipates immensely with the application of heat, which you should use sparingly, as its fine, floppy leaves wilt even more easily than comparable leaves such as baby spinach or arugula. The whole tangle of watercress can be consumed, so trim as close to the root as possible, soak and spin well, then serve bunched into sandwiches, through salads and as a grassy garnish on fancy fish dishes. Watercress also has impressive health-promoting properties, so if you're looking to up your iron and calcium with one easy-to-consume leafy green, this one should rocket to the top of the list.

WITH COMPLEMENTS

Avocado, bacon, cheese (cheddar, feta, parmesan, ricotta salata), citrus (lemon, orange), mustard, olive oil, shallot, soft herbs, vinegar (especially balsamic, white wine vinegar).

SCRAP MEDAL

Lettuce's lank outer leaves often end up in the compost, but they can be braised and blitzed with broth, or finely shredded and popped through another soup as you might soft herbs, for extra texture, color and mild bitterness – which is particularly complementary to 'cream of' versions. If using a whole head of lettuce, consider steaming the stem, or popping it in a glass of water on the windowsill to regrow. The small leaves that shoot up are delightful as a garnish, and make for a fantastic little science experiment for school holidays, too.

San choy bau
(page 428)

Mushroom
tempeh 'ground'
(page 428)

Veggie spring roll
lettuce wraps
(page 429)

Vietnamese
green nuoc cham
(page 221)

LETTUCE CUPS TWO WAYS

MUSHROOM TEMPEH 'GROUND'

MAKES 3 CUPS (750 G)

If tofu and tempeh were on *The Brady Bunch*, tempeh is the Jan to tofu's Marcia. Tempeh hardly ever gets a look-in, with cooks choosing the fairer and more familiar version of wobbly soy beans. But tofu's dimply, broody sister has a nuttiness to it, with a great chew and distinctive tang that keeps you wanting more. My favorite kind is darker and ready-marinated, which I fry up as slabs or slices for meat-free stir-fries. It also crumbles into a ground-like texture, and fries up a treat, which means it's a great option for dietaries, particularly when you're making shareable stuff like san choy bau and spring rolls.

250 g (9 oz) tempeh, roughly chopped (or chopped firm tofu, if need be)

⅔ cup (100 g) roasted cashews

150 g (5½ oz) mixed mushrooms (we used oyster, button and portobello), roughly chopped

100 g (3½ oz) fresh shiitake mushrooms, roughly chopped

½ cup (40 g) crispy fried shallots

3 garlic cloves, finely grated

1½ tablespoons finely grated fresh ginger

2 tablespoons soy sauce

2 teaspoons sesame oil

Place the tempeh and cashews in a food processor and whiz until finely chopped. Add the remaining ingredients and whiz until finely chopped.

The mixture can be used straight away, or frozen in an airtight container for up to 3 months, then thawed overnight in the fridge before using.

SAN CHOY BAU

SERVES 4

A yum cha classic with a twist. I love the way the water chestnut crunches in the mouth with every bite, with the crisp lettuce holding it all together.

1 iceberg lettuce, leaves separated, core reserved

¼ cup (60 ml) peanut oil

¼ cup (35 g) raw peanuts

2 green onions (scallions), white part finely chopped, green part thinly sliced

1 long red chili, thinly sliced

2 cups (500 g) Mushroom tempeh 'ground' (see left)

225 g (8 oz) canned water chestnuts, finely chopped

¼ cup (60 ml) shaoxing rice wine

1 tablespoon oyster sauce

1 tablespoon hoisin sauce

juice of 1 lemon

lime wedges, to serve

Finely chop the lettuce core and 1–2 of the larger leaves and set aside.

Heat the peanut oil in a large frying pan or wok over high heat. Add the peanuts, white green onion bits and half the chili and cook for 10 seconds, or until slightly golden.

Add the mushroom tempeh 'ground' and cook, stirring constantly and scraping the bottom of the pan, for 4 minutes, or until the mixture is catching and beginning to crisp.

Stir the water chestnuts, rice wine and chopped lettuce through, then add the oyster and hoisin sauce. Cook for 1–2 minutes, or until the mixture is coated and beginning to caramelize. Stir in the lemon juice and remaining chili.

Transfer to bowls, sprinkle over the green green onion bits and serve with the lettuce cups and lime wedges.

VEGGIE SPRING ROLL LETTUCE WRAPS

MAKES 14 SMALL SPRING ROLLS

The hot, flaky spring roll pastry against the cool crisp lettuce and zingy herbs is a killer combination. You'll find it hard to stop at your allocated quota.

cup (250 g) Mushroom
 tempeh 'ground' (see left)
2 tablespoons
 kecap manis
½ bunch of cilantro, leaves
 picked, roots and stems
 finely chopped
14 square spring roll
 pastry sheets (see tip),
 measuring 12.5 cm
 (4½ inches)
rice bran oil, for
 shallow-frying

1 butter lettuce,
 leaves separated
1 carrot, peeled into
 long thin strips
½ bunch of
 Vietnamese mint
 or regular mint
1 quantity Vietnamese
 green nuoc cham
 (page 221), to serve

In a bowl, combine the mushroom tempeh 'ground', kecap manis, and the cilantro roots and stems.

Place the spring roll sheets on a tray and cover with a damp tea towel. Place one spring roll sheet on a work surface, with a corner facing you, and brush the edges with a little water. Pop a tablespoon of the mushroom tempeh mixture 3 cm (1¼ inch) from the bottom corner, then roll away from you, bringing the corners in halfway as you go. Brush the final corner with water to seal, then repeat with the remaining sheets.

Heat 3 cm (1¼ inches) of oil in a large heavy-based frying pan or wok over medium–high heat and heat to 400°F, or until a cube of bread dropped into the oil turns golden in 15 seconds.

Working in three batches, cook the spring rolls for 3 minutes, or until the pastry is golden, turning frequently to prevent sticking. Drain on paper towel.

Serve the spring rolls with lettuce leaves for wrapping, and the carrot, mint and nuoc cham alongside, to be dished up and dipped as your diners deem fit.

Tip You can find spring roll pastry sheets at all Asian grocers. Alternatively, you can use filo pastry, too.

Shortcut Try using some left-over chow mein (page 446) in the spring rolls instead.

Bok choy

A juicier, looser-leafed member of the Brassica family that's available for much of the year, but peaks in winter along with the rest of them, bok choy behaves more like Swiss chard stalks than what you might expect from other traditional cabbage varieties. That's because originally, these greens were actually derived from turnips, which also explains the hint of pepperiness to their flavor. Transliterations of its name can get a little confusing – pak choy, pak choi and even just straight up 'Chinese white cabbage' – as can its various iterations, which range from longer, white-stalked and crinkly-leafed, all the way through to the squat stalks of baby bok choy. ('Baby' can either refer to it being picked young, or just a small breed, such as the Shanghai bok choy, which is characterised by its jade-green stalks and soup-spoon shaped leaves.) On the Brassica bitterness scale, bok choy sits squarely at the opposite end of the spectrum to something like Tuscan kale, and is more sweet and crisp than astringent and fibrous – particularly baby bok choy.

'Chinese vegetables are often coated in a sauce thickened with starch. Before thickening a ginger/garlic/oyster sauce, give veggies such as bok choy just enough time in the boiling sauce to allow the flavors and moisture to penetrate through osmosis.' – ANDREW WONG, UK

BUYING & STORING

Bok choy's leaves are a bit like herbs in terms of sensitivity to moisture loss and temperature fluctuation. Any wilting is a no-no. Rub a leaf and it shouldn't yield to your touch, remaining unruffled and waxy. Look out for brown spots, yellowing or tell-tale caterpillar holes. Stems can be pale green or white for mature heads, and should stand up in the way a succulent plant might. Give the bunch a squeeze – it should squeak audibly with crispness. When recipes call for 'bok choy' with no picture and no specificity around whether it's the larger or smaller variety that you're after, it's best to err on the side of smaller if you can find them, as these are the most forgiving in flavor (almost like celery), while the larger ones can be more bitter, with a distinctive minerality. Bok choy tolerates far less time in the fridge than regular cabbage, so wrap in paper towel or cloth and then bag loosely, but leave towards the top of your vegetable pile so you remember to use it first, and so it doesn't get squashed and bruised.

PREPARING & COOKING WITH

Wash bok choy judiciously, as grit is wont to get stuck between the leaf layers, and rear its head as undesirable shadows as the stems cook and become translucent. I like to wash them under running water, soak in a salad spinner, then rinse and spin a couple of times, just in case. The outer layer is especially prone to stowing soil, so peel this layer away with your fingers and give it a proper going over, being careful not to tear it away from the stem. If it's a particularly dirty bunch, it might be worth chopping at the stem so that the leaves come away completely, then rubbing each leaf individually to agitate any remaining soil away.

Baby bok choy are often cooked whole, their tender leaves and crisp stems gaining still more character through heat, while larger ones benefit from being quartered, or even picked stalk for stalk, before being steamed. With such elegant, soft leaves and crisp, fine-fleshed stalks, bok choy loves being steamed and then served with lashings of sesame oil, garlic and ginger, or tossed through oyster sauce. If stir-frying, consider chopping the leaves away from the stalks and cooking the stalks through first, then popping the leaves in for the last minute or so. Some adventurous cooks have also been known to halve and grill smaller bok choy, too.

WITH COMPLEMENTS

Chili, Chinese five-spice, garlic, ginger, oyster sauce, sesame oil, shaoxing rice wine, shallot, soy sauce, green onion (scallion).

MISO SOUP WITH BOK CHOY, POTATO & RADISH

Here you've got three options: a long-ways broth that gives kombu an overnight soaking and treats every ingredient with care and attention in a way only Japanese cooking can; a medium-ways version that is a bit like an 'assemble your own' meal kit; and a short-ways packet version that you can access by skipping straight to the shortcut at the end of the recipe. That's because the hero here isn't the broth – it's the bok choy, its leaves softened without falling to pieces by staying poolside most of the time, just before taking a final dip in hot broth, while the stems cook away until they're tender enough to bite through, but are still bright with flavor.

SERVES 4–6

2–3 potatoes (not too
   big!), peeled and cut
   into bite-sized pieces
30 g (1 oz) bonito flakes
2–3 dried shiitake
   mushrooms (optional)
2 bunches of baby
   bok choy
12 small radishes, left
   whole, or baby turnips,
   quartered
3–4 tablespoons red
   miso paste (or
   powdered equivalent)
1 green onion (scallion),
   finely sliced into rings
½ teaspoon sesame oil

Long-ways dashi broth
20 g (¾ oz) kombu
   (2–3 sheets, depending
   on the brand; see tip)
8 cups (2 liters)
   filtered water

**Medium-ways
dashi broth**
8 cups (2 liters)
   filtered water
1 teaspoon dashi powder

If making the long-ways dashi broth, gently brush the kombu sheets with a very mildly dampened cloth, just to shoo off any grit (too much water or friction will wipe off the umami flavor you're going for). Pop the kombu in an airtight container, pour in your filtered water and leave to soak for at least 4 hours; real diehards leave it overnight.

When ready to cook, warm the kombu water in a large saucepan over medium heat, removing the kombu just before the water comes to the boil.

If making the medium-ways dashi broth, bring the filtered water to a gentle boil and mix in the dashi powder.

Pop the potato, bonito flakes and dried shiitake, if using, into the saucepan and simmer for about 10 minutes, until the potato is almost fork-tender.

Meanwhile, slice the bok choy vertically into quarters or sixths; you want to be able to fish them out of your bowl and eat with company without making too much of a mess. Soak in a big bowl of water until needed.

Plop the radish into the broth. Shake the bok choy dry, then arrange them in the saucepan so that the 'soup spoon' leaves hang over the rim of the pan and the stalk ends simmer away in the liquid. Simmer for 10 minutes, or until the midpoint of the stalk turns a bit translucent. Now tuck the leaves into the broth and remove from the heat.

Ladle 1 cup (250 ml) of the soup broth into a small heatproof bowl, then mix in the miso paste until dissolved. Pour the mixture back into the pot and sprinkle in the green onion. Taste for seasoning.

Arrange the vegetables in the bottom of your serving bowls, ladle the soup over and finish with a drop or two of sesame oil.

Tip You'll find kombu at Asian grocers and health food shops, or you can order some good ones online.

Shortcut Miso soup is such an easy 'just add hot water' lunch; simply follow the packet instructions. Go miso soup paste over powder – it's fresher, and often 'purer'

GRILLED BOK CHOY
WITH PEANUT SAUCE

If you're a fan of celery with peanut butter, or satay skewers with the butane-laced tang of a street-food barbecue, then you'll probably want to get a load of this dish. The key here is to leave the bok choy oil-free, allowing a dry heat to permeate and steam through the center while the leaves crisp a little, rather than wilt.

SERVES 2-4

- 4 small–medium baby bok choy, split lengthwise
- ¾ cup (170 ml) vegetable stock (or water)
- ⅓ cup (90 g) peanut butter
- 1 tablespoon oyster sauce
- 1 tablespoon soy sauce
- 1 teaspoon rice wine vinegar
- ¼ cup (35 g) raw or roasted peanuts
- 2 tablespoons crispy fried shallots
- 1 teaspoon finely sliced long red chili (optional)

Heat a grill pan or barbecue grill plate until smoking. (Alternatively, you can use a large frying pan.)

Meanwhile, soak the bok choy in a big bowl of water, agitating to help dislodge any grit, paying particular attention to the outer layers. Run under cold water, using your thumbs to push the leaves apart for one more gander.

Once the pan is smoking, shake off the bok choy and press it face down into the pan. Leave over medium–high heat for 10 minutes, then flip face-side-up for another 3 minutes or so, until the stalks are mildly translucent.

Meanwhile, pop the stock, peanut butter, oyster sauce, soy sauce and vinegar in a saucepan and mix to combine. Place over medium heat and bring to a simmer, stirring, and adding more stock if the sauce needs to be thinned slightly.

If using raw peanuts, toast these in a pan until golden, then roughly chop.

Arrange the bok choy across a platter. Pour over plenty of the sauce, then garnish with the peanuts, shallots and chili, if using. Serve hot.

Tip This method also works with other Brassicas, particularly leafy Asian veggies such as choy sum. Try it with celery, lettuce and even cucumber, too.

Shortcuts If you don't have time to make the sauce, drizzle a little oyster sauce across the grilled bok choy, and sprinkle with the crispy fried shallots.

If you're in the mood for high-heat, high-stakes, heat a few tablespoons of peanut oil in a hot wok, then add your bok choy bits, cut into sixths, until colored, soft and wilted. Toss in the combined sauce ingredients and serve.

Brussels sprouts

The brussels sprout may well have been the earliest example of influencer marketing, when in the early 19th century a greengrocer in America employed a circus performer, Tom Thumb, to help advertise this newly arrived crop. The sell was that these 'Tom Thumb Cabbages' were a shrunken version of a familiar favorite. And, like whitening strips and diet tea, it worked. The campaign, that is. Unfortunately, what didn't seem to be conveyed was how to cook those sprouts so they tasted great, leading to a compounding sentiment over the years that these were the embodiment of all that is yuck about veg. And it's true: boil the bejeezus out of sprouts (as people are wont to do when they're merely doing what they've seen done before) and you will have yourself an actual fart bomb. Thumbs down to that.

'Brussels sprouts roasted with smoky bacon, garlic and thyme usually bring any non-believers around. I also like to thinly shave small sprouts, dress simply with a lemon vinaigrette and top with parmesan shavings.' – ANDREW McCONNELL, AUSTRALIA

BUYING & STORING

Brussels sprouts grow on one central stalk, and occasionally you'll even see them sold this way at farmers' markets, at the peak of sprout season in winter. With loose sprouts, check their bases for oxidation and dehydration. Also check the leaf tips for yellowing, as well as any mangy gnaw marks. (As long as it doesn't look like a small family of green caterpillars have taken out a six-month lease on the condo of their dreams inside your sprout, you're in business.) Pull off any yellowed leaves before storing, but don't wash, as any moisture will accelerate decomposition. Sometimes sprouts are sold pre-packaged, and though it's tempting to just stash these into the fridge as is – which is fine if using them within a day or so – they will last much longer if you unpack them, sort for mange, dry off any condensation, then store loosely bagged in the crisper, with some airflow. Sprouts turn from sweet to sulfuric the longer they sit, so aim to use them within 3–4 days of purchasing.

PREPARING & COOKING WITH

I use the 'willingness to give sprouts a chance' as my Myers–Briggs of friendships test: if someone is closed off to brussels sprouts, how are they going to go with aerial yoga, or arthouse cinema, or cat memes? The key is to treat them right. Some recipes say to cut an 'X' in the top of the sprout to help it cook through, but I don't find it's necessary, unless they're particularly large. Trim off the dried-out bit of the base and any scungy leaf tips, leaving them whole, halved or quartered, depending on size. Let them bob around in a bowl of water for 20 minutes or so to encourage any squirmy squatters to have a dip in the pool.

Whether you're hitting them with heat or serving raw, be liberal with acid, sweetness and salt to mitigate any bitterness. Halve them, toss with olive oil, add something sweet (honey, maple syrup, brown sugar) to aid caramelization and sprinkle generously with flaked sea salt or soy sauce. Pop them on a tray that's been heating in a hot oven, then bake for 15–20 minutes, until the faces turn crispy brown. Suddenly, they'll be tender and sweet through the middle like braised cabbage, and crunchy through the tops like kale chips. Smaller sprouts are sweeter and can be steamed or roasted whole, the mid-sized ones are best for the halve and bake approach, and larger ones are perfect for finely slicing and turning raw into sprout slaw.

WITH COMPLEMENTS

Butter, cheese (parmesan, ricotta), cream, cured meats (bacon, pancetta), garlic, herbs (chives, parsley, thyme), lemon, nuts (almonds, chestnuts), vinegar (balsamic, apple cider vinegar).

BRUSSELS SPROUT SLAW WITH CHIVES, PARMESAN & CHARDONNAY VINEGAR

Is it possible to have too many slaw recipes? I doubt it. What sets this one apart are the shapes and colors of Brassicas at your disposal. Baby kale is a thing of beauty, a frilly fop of kale, as though shrunk to miniature. If you can't find these, or purple sprouts, just stick with the regular green ones. Thinly slicing with the shape of your chosen cabbages and sprouts will create a gorgeously spacious salad to pop on the table, with plenty of 'wow' factor and minimal energy. Just do me a favor and watch those fingers on the mandoline.

Place the vinegar, olive oil, mustard and chives in a bowl and whisk to combine. Add the brussels sprouts, cabbage and apple and toss to coat. Stand for 5 minutes to soften slightly.

Sprinkle with the parmesan, hazelnuts and chosen garnishes and serve.

SERVES 4–6 AS A SIDE DISH

2 tablespoons chardonnay vinegar

¼ cup (60 ml) extra virgin olive oil

1½ tablespoons wholegrain mustard

1 bunch of chives, finely sliced

300 g (10½ oz) purple or red brussels sprouts, or baby kale, thinly sliced using a mandoline

100 g (3½ oz) red cabbage, thinly sliced

1 red apple, cut into matchsticks

30 g (1 oz) parmesan, finely grated

¼ cup (35 g) roasted hazelnuts, finely chopped

dill sprigs, sunflower sprouts or micro herbs, to garnish

For vegans Shave enough fresh macadamia nuts with a fine microplane and they'll turn into a fluffy cloud of parmesan cheese-like proportions. Your vegan friends will love you.

Shortcut Shred the cabbage using a food processor, mandoline or sharp knife. Toss with some Kewpie mayo, snipped chives or green onion (scallion), and season to taste. This quick version works best with napa cabbage.

SEVENTIES DINNER PARTY SPROUTS

The title of this dish is codswallop, actually – these sprouts are extremely unlikely to have featured at a 1970s dinner party, seeing as this era still saw green stuff boiled into oblivion, and because these parties were about showcasing flavors and ingredients that weren't your run of the mill weeknight meat-n-three – like, say, soy sauce and caraway seeds. The ultimate compliment was a request for The Recipe, which would oft-times be handed over handwritten, and is how my in-laws (*ergo*, me, and *ergo*, you) came to be in possession of Rob's rump marinade. It's originally for lamb fillet (and delicious, if you're that way inclined), but brussels sprouts are so savory and, well, meaty that this marinade works equally as well with them. Indeed, you can serve it alongside any main you like, and it still feels like a party.

SERVES 4

500 g (1 lb 2 oz)
   brussels sprouts,
   trimmed and halved
1 tablespoon peanut oil
roasted peanuts,
   roughly chopped,
   to garnish (optional)
chopped red chili, to
   garnish (optional)

Rob's rump marinade
2 tablespoons honey
   (preferably runny)
2 tablespoons light
   soy sauce
2 tablespoons peanut oil
1 teaspoon ground
   coriander
1 teaspoon caraway seeds
¼ teaspoon
   cayenne pepper
2–3 garlic cloves, crushed

Preheat the oven to 450°F, with a heavy baking tray or roasting pan inside.

Meanwhile, in a shallow dish, stir all the marinade ingredients together until combined. Arrange the brussels sprouts, cut side down, in the marinade to help it soak in.

When the oven has heated up, give the brussels sprouts one last stir through the marinade. Wearing an oven mitt, take the hot tray from the oven, line it with parchment paper, then pop the brussels sprouts onto the hot tray, from outside in, using a pair of tongs in your other hand to turn them cut side down again; reserve the remaining marinade in the bowl.

Roast the sprouts for 10 minutes, or until the top leaves are basically burnt.

Pour the peanut oil into your left-over marinade to loosen it off, then drizzle over the roasted sprouts.

Toss them into a bowl and smugly serve, sprinkled with peanuts and chopped red chili if you like. These sprouts are sure to turn even the most bullish Brassica denier into a believer.

Tips **Preheating the tray helps give more of a golden crust on the sprouts. Feel free to skip lining the tray before using if you like to live dangerously – it'll give you more color on the sprouts, but will take some cleaning. Soaking the stains in vinegar and baking soda followed by a good scrub should do it.**

I like to use an appropriately sized storage vessel for marinading purposes, so that I can pop the leftovers in there and save on washing up!

If you decide to give the marinade a whirl with lamb, try using lamb eye fillet rather than rump, and pull back on the honey; 1 tablespoon should suffice.

Dietaries **Sub in maple syrup instead of honey to turn this one fully plant-based.**

Peas & snow peas

Podding peas in the garden on a spring afternoon used to be a favorite, if fleeting, pastime of the kitchen gardener. However, thanks to advances in snap freezing, peas are one of the easiest green meal additions any time of year. But you'll be peased – er, *pleased* – to know that the rest of the pea family, from sugar snaps to snow peas (mangetout), are just as easy to cook with. One of the simpler crops to grow, peas pop up in cuisines worldwide, all the way back to antiquity – from verdant bursts of tender sweetness in risotto, to rich split-pea curries and hammy soups. For the Egyptians of the Nile Delta, whose diets were primarily plant-based, peas provided a valuable source of protein, as they continue to do in modern-day *dal bhat* dishes and pea protein smoothies.

'I think Indians have a natural instinct to cook with vegetables. By using traditional Indian techniques at the restaurant, we try to make everyday vegetables the hero, and this always surprises our guests. For me it's a big score to make guests eat an almost all-vegetarian menu and not have them miss meat.' – GARIMA ARORA, INDIA

BUYING & STORING

The natural sweetness of peas is most pronounced when freshly picked or shelled, which is why spring peas continue to be prized for the most delicate, morning-dew-in-a-pod taste. When buying fresh, don't get greedy with size: smaller peas – about the size of a pinkie fingernail – are best, as the bigger ones start to get starchy and bland. I would choose a pack of organic frozen peas over mature ones with no flavor, especially in the colder months. When it comes to snow peas and sugar snaps, size is a slightly less important indicator of flavor and freshness than color. You're looking for a bright, grassy green, with no inklings of yellowing or ashiness, withering or soft spots. Tops and leaves should be spritely.

Fresh peas don't store particularly well, so try not to exceed a couple of days, bagged up in the crisper. No need to blanch for freezing – just be sure that they're frozen unwashed and dry, to avoid ending up with a pea-encrusted clump of water crystals.

COOKING WITH

Like all good green stuff, peas love herbs and cheese. Team them with mint and grated pecorino in a rich risotto, or give them a blanch and toss together with a softer cheese for a fresh spring side dish. Snow peas benefit from having their leafy hats topped, and if you pull towards the pod, you can take any stringy bits from the sides with it. Occasionally, you'll chance upon a golden or even purple variety of garden pea or snow pea, which are rarer than hen's teeth, and can be treated in the same way as green ones; the peas inside are still green, and much of the anthocyanin that turns the pods purple ends up in your cooking water, so to preserve their color it's best to simply flash-fry these or keep them raw for salads. My favorite method for cooking frozen peas is to pour a kettleful of boiling water over them and let stand for 5–6 minutes, then toss them into a pan with butter, or straight into another dish for serving. With stews and braises, you can simply stir in the frozen peas towards the end of cooking. Chuck a mugful into the boiling pasta water with a minute to go.

WITH COMPLEMENTS

Butter, carrot, cheese (especially feta, goat, pecorino, ricotta), cream, cured meats (especially bacon, ham, lardon, prosciutto), garlic, herbs (especially basil, bay leaves, chives, mint, parsley, tarragon, thyme), lemon, lettuce, onion, shallot, green onion (scallion).

GENTLEMAN'S SALAD

There's a pretty obvious reason this is called a gentleman's salad, and it isn't because it is reserved for some sort of 'gentlemen only' club. It's because this is the pasta salad you already know and love, with the delightfully kitschy addition of farfalle – 'bow tie' pasta. You can use any short pasta you have in the pantry, but I love the way the peas occasionally overlap the bow ties to form patterns, and the mint blooms forth like mini corsages.

SERVES 4

500 g (1 lb 2 oz) fresh
   or frozen broad beans
400 g (14 oz) farfalle
4 cups (560 g)
   frozen peas
100 g (3½ oz) snow
   peas (mangetout)
100 g (3½ oz)
   crumbly feta

finely grated zest
   and juice of 1 lemon
2–3 garlic cloves, crushed
⅓ cup (80 ml) olive oil
1 large handful of
   mint leaves

Put the broad beans in a heatproof bowl. Pour boiling water over them and let them stand for 5 minutes. Pop them out of their skins and set aside.

Meanwhile, bring a big saucepan of well-salted water to the boil. Add the pasta and cook according to the packet instructions, adding the peas and snow peas during the final 2 minutes. Drain.

Crumble the feta into a small bowl, then mix in the lemon zest and juice, garlic and olive oil, to make a dressing. Season with plenty of cracked black pepper.

While still warm, toss the pasta, broad beans, peas and half the dressing together to allow the flavors to get to know each other.

At the very last minute, drizzle with the remaining dressing, add the mint and serve.

Tips Leafy herbs such as mint need very little heat to help infuse their fragrance and flavor into starchy stuff like pasta. Popping the mint in at the very last minute will keep it vibrant while giving the salad an overall brightness, too.

To get extra life out of your pasta salad, store it in a colander over a mixing bowl, or in the colander part of your salad spinner, in the fridge. This'll help stop the bottom pasta getting soggy, and means you can just plonk it all back into the mixing bowl to serve up the next day, adding extra mint for another fresh kick. Pull it out of the fridge at least 15 minutes or so before serving, to keep it from feeling fridge-cold on the teeth.

Shortcut This is a great pasta salad to make with left-over pasta. It works best with any short pasta shape – from penne to macaroni, and even orecchiette. Just pour a little boiling water over the cooked pasta to give it a new lease on life, leave to warm through a little, then proceed with the rest of the recipe.

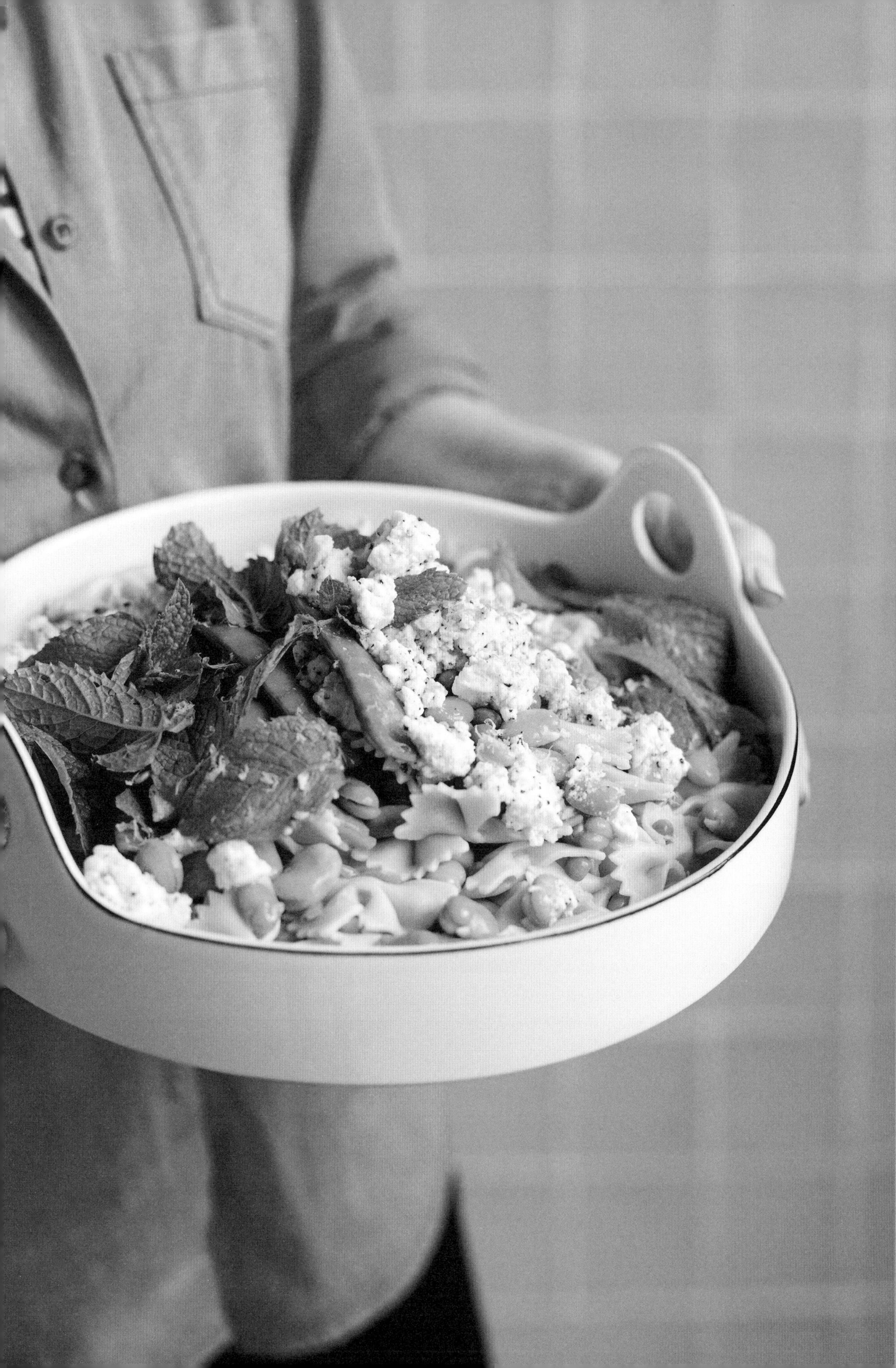

SNOW PEA & CABBAGE CHOW MEIN

As far as kitschy dishes go, chow mein is enjoying somewhat of a 'so uncool it's cool' resurgence, so I'm not about to let you miss out. The best part about this dish is how quickly it all comes together – and even quicker still if you use 400 g (14 oz) fresh noodles instead of boiling up the dried noodles, and if you use the more tender napa cabbage. This will work with conventional cabbages, mind you – even purple, if you're that way inclined. I love how the snow peas flash green through the shades of browns and taupes. Feel free to add whatever other veg you have left in your crisper. Treat this like an end-of-the-week meal. Cool.

SERVES 4–6

200 g (7 oz) dried
 thin egg noodles
⅓ cup (80 ml) shaoxing
 rice wine
⅓ cup (80 ml)
 vegetable stock
¼ cup (60 ml) soy sauce
2 tablespoons
 oyster sauce
2 teaspoons sesame oil
2 teaspoons mild
 curry powder
1 teaspoon cornstarch
¼ teaspoon ground
 white pepper
⅓ cup (80 ml) vegetable
 or canola oil

4 green onions (scallions),
 white part finely
 chopped, green part
 sliced on an angle
1 garlic clove,
 finely chopped
100 g (3½ oz) enoki
 mushrooms, trimmed
2 carrots, shredded
200 g (7 oz) snow peas
 (mangetout), topped
400 g (14 oz)
 cabbage, shredded
1 cup (250 g) mushroom
 tempeh 'ground'
 (optional, see page 428)
sesame seeds, to serve

Boil the egg noodles as per the packet instructions. Drain and rinse under cold water, then drizzle a little oil over them to keep them from sticking.

Meanwhile, in a small bowl combine the shaoxing, stock, soy sauce, oyster sauce, sesame oil, curry powder, cornstarch and white pepper, using a fork to whisk it all together until smooth. Set aside.

Heat a wok over high heat for at least 5 minutes, then add 2 tablespoons of the oil to coat the wok. Add the white green onion bits and garlic and cook for 20–30 seconds, or until fragrant. Add the mushrooms, carrot, snow peas, cabbage and tempeh, if using. If your pan doesn't seem to be coloring the mixture fast enough, batch-cook each ingredient, then transfer to a bowl to wait for the others. Cook, stirring constantly, for 3–4 minutes, or until softened. Add half the soy mixture and cook, tossing constantly, for 1 minute, or until coated. Transfer to a large bowl.

Heat the remaining 2 tablespoons oil in the wok. Add the noodles, spreading them in a thin, even layer, and cook for 2–3 minutes without disturbing. Flip the noodles over and cook, stirring frequently, for a further 3–4 minutes, or until golden. Add the remaining soy mixture and stir through to coat. Return the vegetables to the wok and stir to warm through.

Sprinkle with the green onion greens and sesame seeds and serve immediately.

Tip **The key with any stir-fry is to batch-cook each vegetable separately, popping the burnished bits off into a big bowl, before returning all the stir-fried bits to the wok at the very end, to heat through and bring it all together.**

Double duty **Any left-over chow mein makes a great spring roll filling (see page 429).**

PEA PILAF

You know those recipes that just roll off on auto-pilot when you're home late and absolutely pooped? This is one of them. I love the way that each grain of rice becomes fluffy and ridged, absorbing whatever fat and/or spice I've reached for with my eyes half-shut. The peas popped in at the end add fantastically juicy bursts of sweetness – and are my excuse to slip this recipe (which I know you'll love as a midweek stayer) into the book.

SERVES 4

1 yellow onion,
  finely chopped
2 tablespoons ghee
  or olive oil
2–3 garlic cloves,
  roughly chopped
400 g (14 oz) basmati rice

1 tablespoon
  flaked sea salt
½ teaspoon curry powder
2 cups (500 ml)
  vegetable or chicken
  stock (or water)
1 cup (140 g) frozen peas

Sweat the onion in the pan with your chosen fat until translucent. Start with the lid off for a few minutes, pop the lid on for 5 minutes or so, then finish with the lid off.

Toss in the garlic, rice, salt and curry powder, stirring for 5 minutes or so to get the rice nice and coated in spice and fat.

Pour in your liquid of choice, then bring to the boil. Reduce the heat to low, pop the lid on and let the rice cook away for 20 minutes.

Turn off the heat. Working quickly, to let minimal heat escape, throw in the frozen peas and put the lid back on.

Leave for 10 minutes before serving to heat the peas through. Stir the peas in, season to taste and serve.

Tips **Instead of ghee and stock, I like to use the *schmaltz* and juices left behind in a roast chicken pan as the base for this recipe. It's a great way of using up what I've got, and adds so many bonus layers of savory flavor.**

Jasmine rice will work, too. It cooks in only about 15 minutes, and requires only 400 ml (14 fl oz) liquid.

Double duty **The next day, pop more vegetables into the rice and heat it through for a bulked-out veg pilaf.**

Extra **Sometimes I'll shred left-over meat into the pan alongside the rice, garlic and spices, and then let it cook into the rice, turning the dish into more of a biryani. You could do the same with firmer root vegetables, too.**

Cabbage

Just like the rest of its Brassica relations, cabbage is a winter wonder, growing effortlessly in conditions of bitter chill. You'll also find wild cabbage growing quite happily along train tracks, in open fields and as bright-yellow blooming weeds in your garden. Considering cabbages have been around since Neolithic days, there has been plenty of time for cultivation of different varieties. My favorites are napa cabbage, which is fresh, crisp and fine enough to be eaten raw, and perfect for kimchi (and scores its own chapter in White; see pages 90–95), and red cabbage, which I love turning into sauerkraut, or sautéing with plenty of butter and a splash of red wine vinegar. Savoy cabbage is great for braising because it has a robust texture and its flavor doesn't turn too farty under sustained heat, and white cabbage for blanching, then wrapping around pulses and/or ground meat to turn into cabbage rolls. Sugarloaf cabbage, which is elongated with a tapered tip, is great for cutting in half (or even quartering) and charring in a smoking hot pan or on the barbecue, which enhances its natural sweetness and looks incredibly impressive coming to the table.

'I like spring cabbage or pointed cabbage best – especially grilled, with a nam jim dipping sauce. It has a wonderful peanut-like taste when charred. Don't blanch it first – cook it straight from raw and char the cut side. It wants to be a bit crunchy in the center.' – JACK STEIN, UK

BUYING & STORING

Cabbages come in many shapes, colors and sizes, with hardier varieties sweetest in the colder months, but common to all are their luscious layers of leaves. Fear not if you see a few bug bites on the outer leaves – what's good for bugs to eat is good for us, too! There should be no strong odor emanating from your cabbage (which may suggest it has begun rotting from the inside), and the bottom stem should be light in color (the darker it is, the more time it has had to oxidize off the stem). Whole cabbages are very forgiving in the storage department. Keep them in a bag in the crisper section of your fridge, but try not to fully seal the bag – the gases cabbages emit will make them deteriorate more quickly if they can't escape a little. If you're slicing off a bit at a time, try to leave as little surface area exposed as possible, and your cabbage should last for up to 2 weeks. Don't bother trying to freeze cabbage – it denatures disappointingly quickly. Instead, try fermenting your own sauerkraut (see opposite) and you'll have delicious (and nutritious!) cabbage 'on tap' for months.

COOKING WITH

Cabbage leaves are perfect for stuffing with rice and ground meat (or chopped veggies) and braising until softened. To help encourage the leaves to 'leave' the central stalk, use a small knife to carefully make a 5 cm (2 inch) deep incision around the core of the cabbage. Remove the core and mangy outer leaves, and save these for snacking or chopping through a stir-fry (such as the chow mein on page 446). Place the cabbage in a large saucepan, cover with cold water and bring to the boil over high heat. Cook for 5 minutes, or until the leaves have a bend to them and are pliable, making sure the cabbage is always submerged. Drain, then transfer the cabbage to a bowl of iced water to cool, before peeling the layers away. You can also slice leaves finely into a broth for 'instant' noodles, or keep the slices thicker and cook in your soup until the cabbage softens (but not into mush), which should take about 20–25 minutes. Or, slice a white cabbage into quarters, lightly coat with peanut oil and sear each side in a hot pan as you might steak, then drizzle with soy sauce or tamari and bake at 350°F for about 10 minutes, until cooked through. And don't forget about the cabbage heart – my favorite bit – which can be accessed by shaving off the woody externals of the stalk, and slicing finely or chomping on whole like a carrot. I like to reserve this bit to share with any young cooks assisting me, as I find it's a just reward for a job well done and tends to turn the tide if they're Brassica hesitant.

Kraut it out

Fermentation revivalist Sandor Katz calls kraut 'The Gateway', because it's so easy, and tasty! Shred cabbage leaves finely with a food processor or sharp knife, then add 1.5 per cent of their weight in salt (or 2.5 per cent in warmer weather). Massage the cabbage and salt together in a large bowl for a few minutes to start breaking down the cell walls; you'll have done enough when you can pick up a handful and squeeze liquid out like you're wringing out a sponge. Pack the cabbage into a crock or jars, use the extracted juice to cover to not quite the top, then cover with one of the large outer leaves and weigh down with something heavy to stop any shredded bits floating to the top. Check on your kraut daily, especially at the start when fermentation will be at its most vigorous. It'll be ready for eating after 5 days, and will keep developing its funk over the coming weeks. Refrigerate when you're happy with the flavor.

FUNCTIONAL FOOD

Considering it is over 90 per cent water, cabbage has a fascinating relationship with it. On the one hand, salt helps draw excess moisture out of the cabbage, which is why making a coleslaw is always improved by first salting the cabbage for an hour or so, squeezing out the excess moisture, then adding the rest of the ingredients. But cabbage also has the capacity to draw moisture back into itself, as can be attested to by anyone who has ever applied a cabbage poultice to swelling. For nursing mothers, chilled cabbage leaves from the freezer offer a natural salve for engorged breasts (though it should be noted that prolonged use can also have an adverse effect on milk supply). For swollen hands, feet and ankles, applying cabbage leaves directly helps to draw out excess moisture, as well as cooling the area.

WITH COMPLEMENTS

Apple, apple cider vinegar, bacon, butter, caraway seeds, cheese (cheddar, feta, goat), chili, cream, curry powder, garlic, ginger, juniper berries, lemon (juice, zest), mustard, onion, pepper.

BLACK & WHITE CABBAGE

What I like most about this recipe is that it is literally two ingredients, which, with the wonders of heat and moisture control, become far more than the sum of their parts. The saltiness of the soy sauce brings out even more of the cabbage's natural sweetness, particularly when steamed. Burning the exposed cabbage faces in a hot pan adds bitterness and dimension to the flavor, for quite a delicious burnt-toffee vibe.

SERVES 4 AS A SIDE DISH

1 x 700 g (1 lb 9 oz) chunk of white cabbage (about ¼ of a medium cabbage)

¼ cup (60 ml) soy sauce, plus extra to serve

Preheat the oven to 400°F.

Heat a dry, heavy-based ovenproof pan until smoking.

Pop the cabbage onto one flat cut side, pressing it into the pan with your hand or with another heavy pan on top, for maximum contact. Leave to char and blacken over high heat for 8 minutes, then carefully flip and leave to blacken for another 8 minutes on the other exposed side, too.

Splash the soy sauce over the cabbage, encouraging it to trickle between the layers.

Use an oven mitt to carefully shape some foil around the cabbage.

Transfer the pan to the oven and steam the cabbage in the foil for 20 minutes. Remove the foil, then bake for at least another 5 minutes, until the cabbage has softened and turned quite a pale shade of green, rather than white.

If you're after some extra burnished bits, place the pan back over high heat for a few minutes on each side.

Serve warm, with an extra splash of soy sauce.

Tip **Depending on the shape of your cabbage, it might benefit from some extra weight from another heavy-based pan or some other weight, to help gain as much surface contact with the hot pan as possible.**

Shortcut **Slice the cabbage into thinner wedges and scorch several at a time in the hot pan, then roast in the foil for 10–15 minutes, until softened through.**

SINGED CABBAGE ROLLS

I'm not too proud to admit that the first time these rolls caught in the oven, it was a distracted accident. Yet the flavor intensified, and the drama of the singed cabbage poking out of the crimson tide of sauce was just too irresistible to leave out of this book. Every Jewish mother will have a conniption about this suggestion, but using half pork and half veal would be ideal in these rolls. Turkey and chicken, or just rice and raisins, would work, too.

SERVES 4–6

12 large leaves from
   1 large cabbage
2 tablespoons olive oil
1 yellow onion,
   finely chopped
3 garlic cloves,
   finely chopped
½ bunch of parsley, stems
   finely chopped, leaves
   picked and chopped
½ bunch of thyme, leaves
   picked and chopped
2 teaspoons
   smoked paprika
⅓ cup (65 g) basmati
   rice, rinsed
250 g (9 oz) ground
   pork or beef
1 egg
finely grated zest
   of 1 lemon
1 teaspoon flaked sea salt
1 teaspoon ground
   white pepper

Greek-style yogurt,
   to serve
finely chopped chives,
   to serve

Braising sauce

1 red onion, chopped
1 red bell pepper, chopped
1 garlic clove, chopped
½ bunch of thyme,
   leaves picked
1 teaspoon ground
   white pepper
1 teaspoon smoked paprika
1 teaspoon ground allspice
½ teaspoon
   cayenne pepper
700 g (1 lb 9 oz) tomato
   passata (strained
   tomatoes)
1 cup (250 ml)
   chicken stock

Plunge the cabbage leaves into a large pot of salted boiling water for 2–3 minutes, until soft and malleable, making sure they are always submerged. Drain, then transfer to a bowl of iced water and leave to cool.

Heat the olive oil in a frying pan over medium–high heat. Sweat the onion with the lid on for 5 minutes, then the lid off for a further 3–4 minutes, giving the odd stir. Add the garlic, parsley stems, thyme, paprika and rice and stir to coat, then cook for a minute or two, until aromatic.

Stir in ¼ cup (60 ml) water, remove from the heat and cover with a lid. Stand for 15 minutes to partially cook the rice. Transfer to a bowl and leave to cool.

Meanwhile, preheat the oven to 375°F.

Whiz all the braising sauce ingredients in a blender, then pour half into a large baking or casserole dish.

Add the meat, egg, lemon zest, salt and pepper to the cooled rice mixture, then use your hands to work it all together. Place about ⅓ cup of the mixture in the center of each cabbage leaf. Fold the cabbage leaf over the mixture, fold in the ends, then tightly roll up, giving it all one last squeeze to keep everything in place.

Repeat to make 12 rolls, placing them seam side down in the dish in a single layer. Spoon the remaining sauce over, to submerge them as much as possible. Cover with foil and bake for 1 hour, or until the cabbage is tender.

Remove the foil and cook for a further 1 hour, or until the rolls are beginning to char and the sauce has thickened to your liking. If you're impatient (like me), crank the broiler on for the last 5–10 minutes, to really encourage some theatrical tips.

Dollop with yogurt, sprinkle with the parsley leaves and chives and serve.

Shortcut **Cook the rice separately. Shred the cabbage and fry in batches in a large pan with the other filling ingredients over high heat. Combine with the rice, tip into a baking dish, add 400 g (14 oz) crushed tomatoes or passata, then bubble away in a moderate oven for 20–30 minutes, until the sauce thickens slightly.**

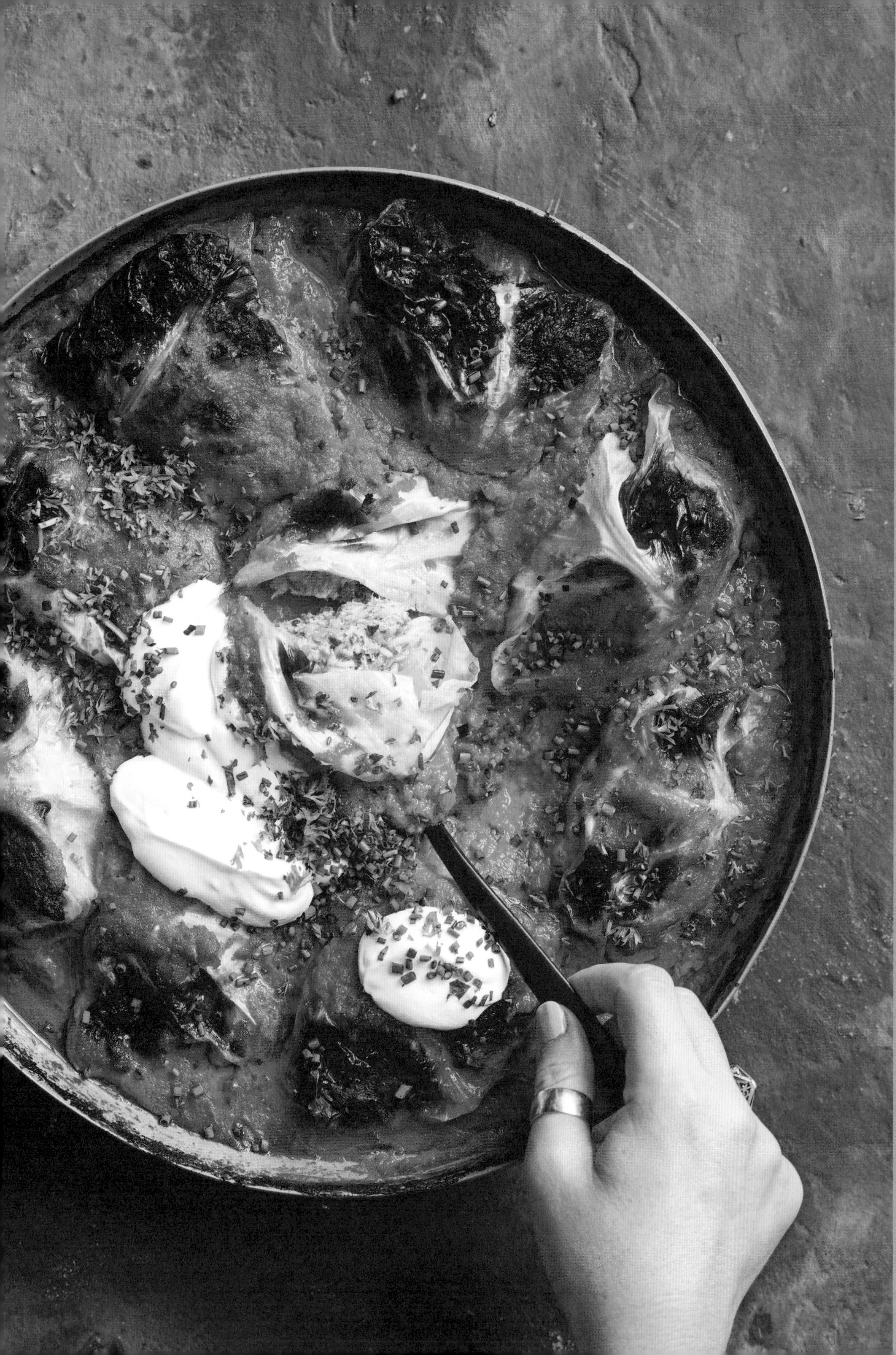

CAREFREE CABBAGE CURRY

Often, when cabbage gets braised, it is shredded, grated or chopped in some way where you lose the beauty of its folds and undulations. Here, the rich golden marinade and equally shimmering gravy only serves to emphasise the majestic grandeur of this brilliant Brassica. This dish is fully plant-based, too, which means it's a perfect plan-ahead for when people come round and you're not quite sure of their dietaries.

SERVES 4

1 teaspoon
   ground turmeric
⅓ cup (80 g)
   coconut yogurt
1 teaspoon flaked sea salt
750 g (1 lb 10 oz) savoy
   or white cabbage
   (about ½ cabbage)
1 tablespoon coconut oil
3 curry leaf branches
1 yellow onion,
   thickly sliced
1 long green chili, split,
   plus extra sliced green
   chili to serve
250 g (9 oz) white-fleshed
   potatoes, cleaned and
   chopped into 2 cm
   (¾ inch) pieces
400 ml (14 fl oz) can
   coconut milk
1 tablespoon
   granulated sugar
juice of 1 lemon
1 cup (140 g) frozen peas

nigella seeds,
   for sprinkling
steamed basmati rice
   and flatbreads, to
   serve (optional)

Curry paste
1 tablespoon coconut oil
4 garlic cloves, bruised
   and peeled
3 cm (1¼ inch) knob
   of fresh ginger,
   peeled and sliced
2 teaspoons mild chili
   powder (we used
   Kashmiri)
1½ teaspoons
   coriander seeds
1 teaspoon fennel seeds
1 teaspoon
   ground cinnamon
1 teaspoon
   ground cardamom
½ teaspoon freshly
   cracked black pepper

Mix the turmeric, yogurt and salt together in a medium-sized bowl. If you'd like the cabbage as 'steaks', cut the cabbage into four thick wedges, including the core. For a 'pulled cabbage' curry, remove the core and separate the leaves. Add the cabbage leaves or wedges to the turmeric mixture and stir to coat well.

For the curry paste, heat the coconut oil in a wide heavy-based frying pan over medium–low heat. Add the garlic and ginger and gently fry, stirring, for 2–3 minutes, or until a light golden brown. Add the remaining curry paste ingredients and cook for another 1–2 minutes, until aromatic and darkened slightly. Transfer to a blender with ⅓ cup (80 ml) water and whiz until smooth.

Place the pan back over medium heat and add the coconut oil. When the oil is hot, add the curry leaf branches and cook for 1–2 minutes, or until crisp. Remove using tongs and drain on paper towel.

Add the curry paste to the pan, along with the onion, green chili and potato and cook, stirring frequently, for 4 minutes, until caramelized. Stir in most of the coconut milk (reserving a drizzle for serving), along with the sugar and 1 cup (250 ml) water. Bring to a gentle simmer and cook for 10 minutes, or until the potato is half-cooked.

Add the cabbage, with the marinade. Cover and cook, stirring or turning the cabbage halfway through, for 15 minutes, or until the cabbage has softened and the potato is cooked through.

Stir in the lemon juice and peas, then remove from the heat. Cover and leave to stand for 5 minutes to warm through.

To serve, sprinkle the curry with the crispy curry leaves, nigella seeds and extra chili, and a final drizzle of coconut milk. This curry yields quite a bit of gravy, so you may like to serve with basmati rice and flatbreads, or on its own as more of a soup.

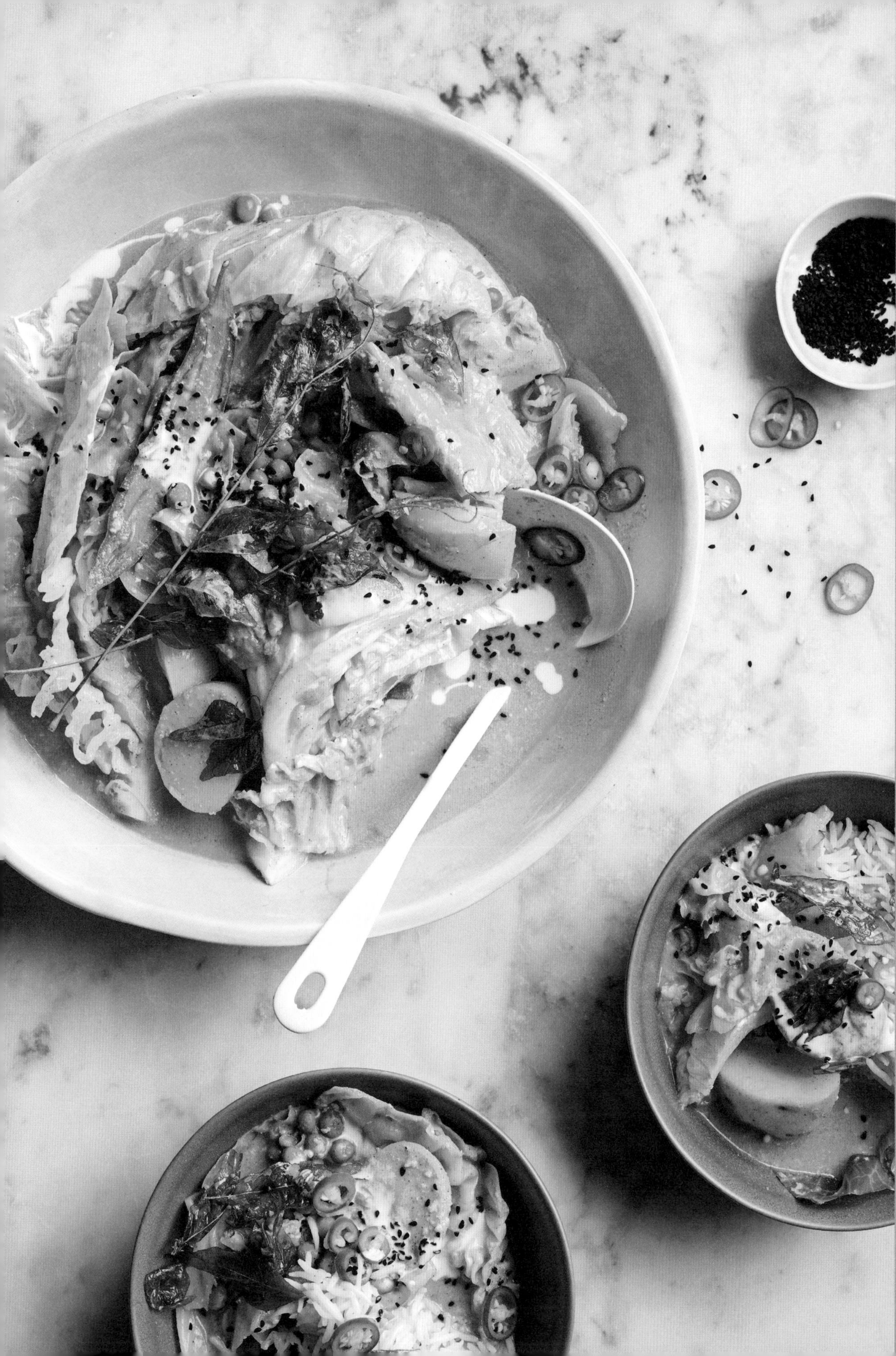

PURPLE NOODLE RICE PAPER ROLLS

This one's great to make with kids for so many reasons – not least of which is because the addition of red cabbage turns it into an edible science experiment. Watch their delight as the anthocyanins leach out of the cabbage and color the noodles a delightful shade of violet.

MAKES 12

12 red cabbage leaves (avoid any thick stems, or cut these out of the leaves)

50 g (1¾ oz) vermicelli noodles

2 cups (200 g) shredded cooked chicken (see tips) or fried firm tofu

2 green onions (scallions), thinly sliced

1 tablespoon Vietnamese green or red nuoc cham (page 221) or sweet chili sauce, plus extra to serve

2 tablespoons crispy fried shallots

12 round rice paper sheets, 22 cm (8½ inch) in diameter

1 bunch of Thai basil, leaves picked

1 Lebanese cucumber, cut into matchsticks

1 carrot, shredded

lime wedges, to serve

Place the cabbage and noodles in a heatproof bowl. Cover with boiling water and stand for 4 minutes to soften; this will also turn your noodles purple. Fun!

Drain the noodles and place in a bowl. Place the cabbage sheets on a tray lined with paper towel to drain.

In a bowl, combine the chicken, green onion, nuoc cham and fried shallots.

Working with one sheet at a time, soak the rice paper in a bowl of warm water for 10–20 seconds, or until just softened. Pop on a clean tea towel to absorb the excess water. Place a Thai basil leaf and then a cabbage leaf over the top. Add 2 tablespoons of the chicken mixture, then some noodles, cucumber and carrot.

First, roll up just the cabbage to create a small cabbage parcel, similar in size to what will be the rice paper roll. Then place it towards the bottom of the rice paper sheet. Bring the bottom edge of rice paper up and over the cabbage roll, bring the sides in, then roll up to enclose the filling.

Place the roll on a serving plate and cover with a slightly damp cloth to stop it drying out. Repeat to make 12 rolls.

Cut in half and serve with lime wedges, extra nuoc cham and any remaining Thai basil leaves.

Tips Rice paper can be tricky to work with, so if you're just starting out or working with little helpers, try layering two sheets on top of each other for insurance purposes. It might be a little chewier on the ends with the extra layers and folds, but if it helps to build roll-rolling confidence, it's worth it.

Left-over roasted or poached chicken is best for this recipe, but if you don't happen to have any, grab a roasted barbecue chook from the shops.

Shortcut Shred the cabbage before soaking with the noodles for a couple of minutes, then toss everything together into a simple cabbage-noodle salad, drizzling with nuoc cham and a little oil to dress.

Avocado

Long before they were turned into a symbol of affluence the world over – from 'extra guac' in North America to the Australian Millennial–Boomer divide – avocados were a symbol of an abundance of an entirely different flavor. Their shape, and the way they hang low in pairs on trees as they grow, led the Aztecs to name them *āhuacatl* – erm, testicle – and they soon became a fertility charm, with husbands bringing pairs of ripe avocados home as a token of their affection, and hey, if you've ever tried to pick two perfectly ripe avocados in one go, you'll know this is no mean feat. Avocados also require a second avocado tree close by to help pollinate and bear fruit – just like any successful interdependent relationship. I'll often acquire a handful at a time, a few firm, several squishier, so I have some that are ready to enjoy straight away, and some for later. I guess you could say I have an interdependent relationship with avocado!

'Which "team avo" are you on – sliced, smashed or diced?
We serve it sliced in restaurants, but at home I usually dice it
into a salsa. A few newspapers have flatteringly described me
as the "inventor of avocado toast". Fake news? I suspect it might
be. It was just always something I ate. But who would turn down
such an accolade?' – BILL GRANGER, AUSTRALIA

BUYING & STORING

Even though they're available almost year round, avocados are supposed to be a summer
fling, so I always go heaviest on them in the warmer months. The best way to check if your
avocado is ripe is to gently press the knobbly bit on top. If it pops into the green flesh with
ease, you're good to go. Unfortunately, many avocados sold in supermarkets lose their stems
in transit, so the next best way to check is to squeeze the narrow end ever so gently – a little
give tells you the avocado will be ripe the next day. In fact, think about using the old steak-
grip for avocado ripeness.

Why is it so important to tread lightly when it comes to picking the right avocado for
you? Because just like any *āhuacatl*, overhandling can have dire consequences. Have you
ever brought home an avocado that you assumed was just right, only to discover that it had
been prematurely tenderised by too much touchy touchy? I advocate a strict 'one stroke, one
strike' policy nowadays. If I'm at the shop and see someone fondling the whole pile like a bull
in a china shop, I give them the sort of side-eye reserved for this purpose only. It's enough
that we have to save our pennies for smashed avocado – the least we can do is make sure
it only gets smashed when it's supposed to. If bruised avocados get you down, practice some
patience and buy them green. Waiting for them to ripen can feel like watching cement dry,
but at least you know that path's going to dry without paw prints trampled through it.

Storage depends on the state of your avocados, and your menu plans. Store ripe avos in
the fridge door. If firm and green, store them in the fruit bowl, away from apples and bananas
(unless you're after an accelerated ripening path, in which case, the closer the better). Once
you've hacked into an avocado, be sure to cover it, and try to keep the stone in to minimise
the exposed surface area. If you cut into an avocado only to discover that it is disappointingly
under-ripe, cover it with beeswax wrap or a tight-lidded container and leave it out of the fridge.
The other option is to peel it, blitz with a little lemon juice and freeze for up to 6 months.
Once properly thawed, it will sneak into a guacamole or creamy salad dressing just fine.

COOKING WITH

The creamy nature of this multipurpose ingredient means it's like a natural butter and
makes a super-simple condiment for spreading and dipping ... G'day guacamole! The basis of
guacamole is mashed avo, plus some form of acid such as lime or lemon juice to complement

the richness of the avocado, and to help keep the color bright against the threat of oxidation. Indeed, any time you're working with avocado – particularly if it will be sitting around exposed for some time – squeezing in a little citrus juice or a splash of clear vinegar will help keep the greige away. The ubiquitous smashed avocado is simply another guacamole of sorts; I like to add freshly sliced chili and a little goat cheese or feta through the smash for added flavor. You can also use avocado as a plant-based alternative for creamy desserts. Melt a block or two of dark chocolate and blitz with an avocado to create a simple creamy chocolate ganache that can either be served as is like a mousse, or set firmer with a little time in the fridge. There are few things that set me off like hot avocado. Some people recommend ripening an avocado by popping it into the oven at a low heat until it softens. I am not one of those people. Heat generates a bitter compound in its flesh that tastes positively putrid – like rotten egg. Don't do it.

FUNCTIONAL FOOD

Not only is avocado a fantastic source of monounsaturated fats, which have proven benefits for cardiovascular function and heart health, it also helps to improve the bioavailability of other phytochemicals such as carotenoids, which means tossing half an avocado into a salad seems like a good idea for tasting great and feeling great all at once. Good fats like those contained in avocado also increase our feeling of satiety, giving you a satisfied tum even at the desk on a Monday. In the tradition of Ayurvedic medicine, avocado is considered a cooling food, which is why it's particularly beneficial when the mercury climbs.

WITH COMPLEMENTS

Chili, cheese (feta, goat), citrus (grapefruit, lemon, lime), corn, cucumber, herbs (chives, cilantro, mint), mango, seafood (shrimp, lobster), green onion (scallion).

BEYOND AVOCADO: BITTER MELON

While we're on the topic of veg with an alligator skin, meet bitter melon. Looking like a knobbly (and occasionally spiky) light green cucumber, this gourd is best known for its challenging bitter taste. If you enjoy the odd gin and tonic, however, it's the quinine in both that gives them their trademark astringency, and just like a G&T, it leaves your palate curious for more. Buy smaller gourds (less than 10 cm/4 inches), as their bitterness has less of a sting, with skin that is less waxy and thick, meaning you don't have to peel and lose the unique patterns. Bitterness is best met with saltiness, so salting them for half an hour or so before cooking (as you might with eggplant) is effective – as is teaming it with saltier flavors such as fermented black bean or miso paste. They also respond well to heat, so try stir-frying or baking. Halve lengthwise, scoop out the seeds, cut into half-moons and add to your next beef and black bean stir-fry, or stuff and roast as you might butternut squash.

BLT SALAD WITH AVO-LI

Let's call this one a 'sandwich salad', where the bread is, let's face it, entirely optional. Although it may seem like the avocado – or even tomato – is the hero here, I think it's the lettuce that brings it all together. Bacon is definitely an optional extra; the 'B' could just as easily become an 'M' for 'marinated tempeh', which you can fry in a pan until golden and crispy. This is going to sound like an audacious statement, but Avo-li may just usurp 'green goddess' as the go-to green salad dressing. Feel free to make a double batch of it and serve it as a dip for any manner of things – most likely just your fingers.

SERVES 4

500 g (1 lb 2 oz)
   mixed tomatoes
   (I like a mix of heirloom
   and cherry), halved
   or quartered if large
1 green onion (scallion),
   finely chopped
2 tablespoons apple
   cider vinegar
100 g (3½ oz) bacon slices
½ head lettuce (butter
   or romaine work best),
   leaves separated,
   washed and dried
½ head frisee, leaves
   separated, washed and
   dried (optional)

½ avocado, sliced
   into wedges
lemon wedges, to serve
crusty bread, to serve
   (optional)

Avo-li
½ cup (120 g) mayonnaise
   (home-made, or whole-
   egg store-bought)
3 tablespoons roughly
   chopped parsley
1 garlic clove, grated
   or crushed
1 ripe avocado, skin and
   stone discarded

Preheat the oven to 500°F. Line a baking tray with foil.

Toss the tomatoes, green onion and vinegar together in a bowl and set aside to pickle slightly.

Drape the bacon over a wire rack and place on the lined baking tray. Transfer to the oven and bake for 10 minutes, or until the bacon is golden. Remove from the oven and leave to cool slightly. If you like, use scissors to cut the bacon into bite-sized pieces.

Meanwhile, put the Avo-li ingredients in a food processor, add the pickling liquid from the tomatoes and blend until creamy and combined. (Alternatively, you can use an immersion blender.) If your Avo-li splits, add a dash of warm water and use a whisk to bring it back together. Season to taste with sea salt and freshly cracked black pepper.

Spoon the Avo-li into a serving dish, smearing it around to the edge, as you might butter on toast. Top with the lettuce leaves, frisee (if using), avocado, tomato mixture and bacon pieces. Serve immediately, with lemon wedges and crusty bread, if you like.

Tip **No wire rack? Create a make-shift air-fryer! Cut a piece of foil twice the length of your baking tray, then fold it in half to create a stronger piece of foil. Crimp the short ends of the foil, in 2.5 cm (1 inch) intervals, folding back into itself, like you would a fan, until you reach the end. Open the fan out to create a 'rack', then use it to line your baking tray. Once you're finished cooking, harvest the bacon fat trapped in the foil for making pasta carbonara or pea and ham soup.**

Shortcut **No time to make the Avo-li? Serve the avocado as wedges, and squirt some Kewpie mayo across the top of your salad.**

Double duty **Turn any leftovers into an actual BLT for lunch the next day.**

FEEL-GOOD NACHOS

I've written this recipe 'for two' because it's the sort of thing you'll want to whip up for a night on the couch with your significant other. And, unlike traditional nachos, which can leave you feeling gassy and gross, the fresh tomatoes, plain yogurt and zesty guacamole will give you the right kind of sustenance to stream and chill all night long. However, you can easily double (or triple) the quantities as needed.

SERVES 2

1 red onion, thinly sliced

4 ripe tomatoes, chopped

400 g (14 oz) can whole peeled tomatoes

2 tablespoons olive oil, plus extra for drizzling

½ teaspoon salt

¼ teaspoon Mexican oregano (see tip)

200 g (7 oz) corn chips (preferably unsalted)

120 g (4 oz) cheddar, grated

2 tablespoons plain yogurt

3 cilantro stems, leaves picked

finely sliced red chili, to serve (optional)

Guacamole

2–3 avocados

juice of ½ lime

2 tablespoons plain yogurt

3 cilantro stems, finely chopped

2 garlic cloves, crushed

Preheat the oven to 425°F.

In a large shallow baking dish, toss together the onion, fresh and canned tomatoes, olive oil, salt and oregano. Bake for 25 minutes, or until the tomato and onion are completely soft and a little burnished.

Meanwhile, make the guacamole. Scoop the avocado flesh into a bowl and squeeze the lime juice over. Add the remaining ingredients and roughly mash together. Season with salt, pepper and/or more lime juice.

Pull the dish out of the oven and sprinkle half the corn chips on top, swirling them through the sauce until they sag and collapse. Add another handful on top and do the same again. Sprinkle with half the cheese and drizzle with olive oil. Arrange the remaining corn chips in some jaunty way, then sprinkle with the rest of the cheese and one more glug of oil for good measure.

Bake for a further 8–10 minutes, or until the cheese has melted and the corn chip tips have colored a little.

Top with the yogurt, cilantro and chili, if using. Serve the guacamole in a separate bowl, or blobbed around the dish.

Tip Mexican oregano is a totally different plant to the Mediterranean variety we're used to, and is closer in flavor to lemon verbena – quite citrusy, with a hint of anise. If you're making Mexican dishes quite often, it's worth hunting down from a specialty spice store. Greek oregano, the kind often sold dried in bunches, is an acceptable alternative. Regular oregano is fine, too – just be a little more sparing with it.

Take stock, make stock

There isn't a savory recipe around that wouldn't benefit from some extra dimension in the form of stock. Light stocks are ideal for delicate dishes, while dark ones give body and depth to robust soups and stews.

Having some pantry packs of stock, or a jar or two in the fridge, is a simple cheat for building quick and easy flavor, taking you one step closer to a satisfying meal. However, it can get pricey buying stock as you go, and nothing beats the taste of home-made stock. If you have to nip out for a store-bought one, check the ingredients for hidden extras, and taste before you pour – some brands add an inordinate amount of salt, which means you should consider diluting theirs with water, and hold the seasoning until you've tasted the final product. When making your own stock, it's a good idea to skip the salt entirely, so that even if you're using it in a sauce that will be significantly reduced, you won't be drinking seawater on the other end.

I like to keep a 'stock up' calico bag in the freezer for any veggie scraps that are bound for the pot, and make up batches of stock whenever the bag gets full enough, at a ratio of 1 cup (250 ml) filtered water to 1 cup roughly chopped veg for a brighter flavor, or 2 cups (500 ml) water to 1 cup chopped veg if I'm scraping the bottom of the scrap barrel. Anything that's deserving of a Scrap Medal can probably end up in your stock bag – right down to corn cobs, which add a deliciously sweet note to a light stock. The only thing I'd avoid are too many Brassicas, bitter scraps or onion skins in the one pot – try to balance this with sweetness from leek tops and parsnip or carrot peelings, or even by adding an extra onion. Asparagus ends, herb stalks, mushroom stems, tomato scraps – even the scooped-out seeds and stringy bits of pumpkin and butternut squash – are welcome in your freezer and your stock. I specify 'filtered water' because tap water is notoriously variable in chemical composition, so even if it's via the tediousness of filling and refilling a countertop filter jug, it's well worth the effort.

For chicken or beef stock, consider using offcuts such as wingtips, wingettes, drumettes or chicken carcasses, or marrow and chuck bones, as these are inexpensive and offer great bang for buck in the flavor and richness stakes. Beef bones are best roasted in a hot oven until golden brown before adding to a stock.

Before adding any veg, bring meat to the boil, then simmer for at least 30 minutes, skimming off the scum occasionally but judiciously. I also like to pour off a smaller pot-full of home-made stock (chicken works especially well) and reduce it until it's more of a concentrate, then let it cool and freeze in one of those novelty oversized silicon ice-cube trays, to pop into everything from rice to stir-fries. I measure this out as the weight of the frozen stock cube + filtered water being equivalent to a 500 ml (2 cup) packet of stock.

And if you're reading this thinking, 'This all just seems too hard', then let's meet halfway: invest in some quality shop-bought stocks until you're ready to commit to making your own. As American cook Michael Ruhlman says, 'It's not just that everything tastes better when you use fresh stock ... it's hard to make anything that's *not* delicious when you have good stock on hand.'

A light stock

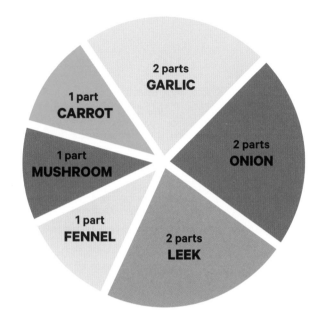

2 parts
GARLIC

1 part
CARROT

1 part
MUSHROOM

2 parts
ONION

1 part
FENNEL

2 parts
LEEK

1. Start with 1 cup chopped veg : 2 cups (500 ml) filtered water.
2. Sweat the veggies in olive oil until golden and glossy, but not colored.
3. Add water, bay leaf, peppercorns + optional parsley stems.
4. Simmer at just below the boil for 1 hour.
5. Strain.

A dark stock

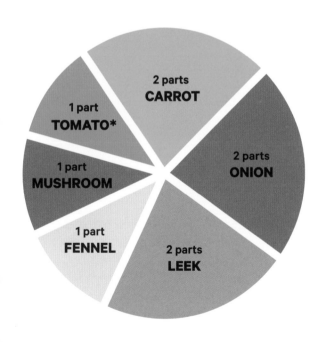

2 parts
CARROT

1 part
TOMATO*

2 parts
ONION

1 part
MUSHROOM

1 part
FENNEL

2 parts
LEEK

1. Start with 1 cup chopped veg : 2 cups (500 ml) filtered water.
2. Toss the veggies with olive oil.
3. Roast veggies at 425°F for 30–40 minutes.
4. Add water, bay leaf, peppercorns, garlic cloves + optional parsley stems.
5. Simmer at just below the boil for 1 hour.
6. Strain.

*or paste/purée

Tip The smaller you chop your veggies, the more flavor you can extract from them. Use this time to practice your knife skills, or even try making a version with a quick, rough blitz in the food processor and see how you like that intensity.

Shortcut If you have a pressure cooker, try using it to make stock. Bring the ingredients to the boil, close the lid, and 15 minutes under pressure is all it takes for vegetable stock (or 1 hour if making chicken or beef stock).

Epilogue

On chefs & vegetables

I've had the opportunity to spend a heck of a lot of time with chefs from across the globe. And they'll be the first to tell you that, contrary to the pedestal that the media often clambers to put them on, chefs are not rock stars. Some chefs are, in a sense, scientists – always experimenting and learning. Some are philosophers, conveying big-picture thoughts and concepts through the lens of gastronomy. Others chefs are artists, and the plate is their canvas. Most importantly, chefs are at the front line of trying out new ideas, and seeing what direction techniques, ingredients and flavors might go.

When I was a restaurant critic, I was always far more interested in what chefs were doing with vegetables than anything else on their menus. I believe that the skill of a cook can best be gauged by their ability to transform an everyday thing, like a carrot, into something greater than the sum of its parts. I wanted to include their thoughts in this book, because it is a chef's greatest talent to bring out the best in an ingredient, and that's something that we're capable of achieving at home, too.

Chefs move around a lot, which is why I've chosen to include their country of origin rather than where they're at in this moment in time. (And this isn't necessarily where they were born, but the country they have the most affinity with.) It's also interesting to explore how a chef's background or country of origin informs the way in which they handle a vegetable – someone born in Mumbai may take okra and think entirely differently about it than someone from Accra, for example. It's unsurprising that for many, the flavors of their childhood are still the most evocative. If you've met a chef amongst these pages whose ethos or ideas resonate with you and you wish to learn more about them or connect – and better yet, taste their food in situ – I encourage you to go for a dig online.

On kids & vegetables

Before helping people learn to love veg, I helped middle-school students learn to love English, history and geography. The topics and ideas were often new for my students and sometimes took a little getting used to, but eventually, their understanding and appreciation grew. I'd offer them delectable 'food for thought', then back it up with genuine enthusiasm. I would never walk into the room and say, 'The Plague … you're not going to like it, but let's begin …' I didn't always get it right, mind you, but the best classes were those that came from a place of optimism and exploration; because kids, by nature, love learning – as long as it's made fun for them.

This attitude has informed my philosophy around kids and vegetables, too. For generations, we've been spoon-fed a narrative regarding children's disdain for vegetables, and our need to sweeten the deal somehow. But in perpetuating this story and feeding into it – the 'chocolate-covered broccoli' mindset, we inadvertently vilify veggies and glorify dessert. The usual media tropes of parents pushing and kids pushing back at the dinner table only serve to reinforce the stereotypes. We make kids believe that vegetables are something they shouldn't like, before they even get a chance to form their own opinion.

That's not to say that children won't have their own likes and dislikes – it's perfectly natural for toddlers to go through a phase of exploring the word 'No', as agency over personal choice and preference is explored and gained. Food flinging and familiarisation is at the heart of a small human learning to feed themselves. That healthy scepticism your toddler is showing when it comes to new foods is totally normal, and proved a biological imperative when curious chubby knuckles considered reaching towards potentially poisonous plants. This hesitation in trying new things even has a name – 'neophobia' – though it's more of a reservation than a fear. Spitting out and slapping down may look to adult eyes like rejection, but it's all part of the process of learning to eat. Often, it's really just as simple as wanting to see what happens when something is dropped. According to experts, the best thing we can do is keep offering, and let them be the decision-makers in what they pick up and eat – a 'division of responsibility'. With patience and time, the slaps and spits become squishes, squashes and eventual swallows. The less fuss we make – the fewer 'special meals' and negotiations – the more likely that this period, which peaks between 2–4 years of age, will be breezed through with egos and relationships unscathed.

The groundwork can start well before that, too. Studies have shown the importance of eating vegetables throughout pregnancy as not only nutritionally beneficial, but as the optimum time to begin shaping your child's palate. Earthy foods such as mushrooms and beets and bitter leafy greens eaten during breastfeeding can also contribute to increased acceptance, particularly when paired with tasty morsels of those foods on the plate, too.

For older kids, trying to explain the health benefits of fresh foods as a driver is about as effective as trying to teach them about superannuation. Indeed, the more we do, the less they seem to respond in a positive way. However, the kids' food space continues to be saturated with well-meaning nutrition-based parenting advice, none of which sticks, because as a general rule, kids don't care about 'health'. In fact, studies have shown that telling anyone (child or adult) a food is 'healthy' for them actually has the opposite effect to what's desired – the expectation of flavor goes down, and people are less likely to want to give it a go.

However, there are three key factors that actually do contribute to positive results: exposure, positive role-modeling and an implicit (rather than explicit) reward structure. That is to say, offer a little of it often (some studies have shown that around 15 times may be the sweet spot for many kids), get excited about it yourself, and don't get caught up in sticker charts or 'eat this or no dessert' messaging. Most importantly, the ultimate implicit reward is the surprising revelation that, 'Hey wait, this is actually delicious … what else have I been missing out on?'

To me, a 'Kids' Meal' is just a smaller version of a grown-up's. The recipes in this book are delicious first, nutritious by nature and easily adaptable for cooking with and for your brood. The more they get into the kitchen to connect with food, the more we connect with them by cooking and eating together with enthusiasm and joy, and the less we subscribe to the fallacy that kids are supposed to dislike vegetables, the further we can move the needle on a back-rod of our own making.

Books you'll love

It's nigh-on impossible for a cook-bookworm to narrow down a reading list to a single page, but here's a starting point to offer you some direction.

In a hurry

For a culinary question answered

Cuisine & Culture, Linda Civitello

Lateral Cooking, Niki Segnit

On Food & Cooking, Harold McGee

Ratio, Michael Ruhlman

Salt, Fat, Acid, Heat, Samin Nosrat

The Book of Jewish Food, Claudia Roden
   (her books on Middle Eastern and Mediterranean
   cuisine are also top notch)

The Cook's Book, Jill Norman *et al.*

The Cook's Companion, Stephanie Alexander

The Flavor Bible, Karen A. Page, Andrew Dornenburg

Vegetable Book, Jane Grigson

Light & bright

Fresh cooking, quick & easy

Essentials of Classic Italian Cooking, Marcella Hazan

A Modern Way to Cook, Anna Jones

Community; Neighborhood; Family, Hetty McKinnon

The River Cottage Cookbook, Hugh Fearnley-Whittingstall

The Zuni Café Cookbook, Judy Rodgers

Mr Wilkinson's Favourite Vegetables, Matt Wilkinson

The entire *Barefoot Contessa* back catalogue, Ina Garten

Simple, Diana Henry (all of her cookbooks are
   just brill!)

Tender, Nigel Slater (anything from him, really!)

Meatless, Martha Stewart (her baking books work
   great, too!)

Well Seasoned, Mary Berg

Low & slow

For languishing in the language of food

A. A. Gill	Dorie Greenspan
Anthony Bourdain	Elizabeth David
Barbara Kafka	Jeffrey Steingarten
Calvin Trillin	Jonathan Gold
Darra Goldstein	Nigella Lawson

Flavor bombs

Cheffy books that will blow your mind

Best Kitchen Basics, Mark Best

Zahav, Michael Solomonov

The Food Lab, J. Kenji Lopez-Alt

Momofuku, David Chang

Thai Street Food, David Thompson

The Noma Guide to Fermentation, David Zilber,
   René Redzepi

The Whole Fish Cookbook, Josh Niland

On Vegetables, Jeremy Fox

Plenty, Yotam Ottolenghi (*Plenty More* and the
   others deserve honorable mentions, too!)

Six Seasons, Joshua McFadden

Vegetables Unleashed, José Andrés

On babies & food

**I'm often asked for recommendations on this front,
and there are two I'd recommend**

For theory: *Child of Mine*, Ellyn Satter

For practice: *Food to Grow On*, Sarah Remmer, RD
   & Cara Rosenbloom, RD

Acknowledgements

This book is dedicated to The Nut, for multiple reasons. Firstly, because it took our human baby being born to make room for the inspiration for this book baby. Secondly, because I hope that Hazel Wren can look at this in years to come and use it like a treasure map for her own culinary discovery. Finally, because without her patient coos at our feet and general vibe-bringing around the study and on set, these pages would not be so bursting with life and luster. Speaking of 'patience', to my husband Nick, who happily holds the fort while I tappily forge the words, my gratitude is immeasurable. Prompting you to nod and chuckle as I read aloud is my greatest content quality control.

To Frada and Arkady, thank you for continuing to support my creative culinary endeavors; it's no accident that 'Patrons' is only one letter and a few jumbles off 'Parents'. To my brother Stan, thanks for walking me home.

To Jackie and Razmo, thank you for growing the vegetables, baking the cakes, and raising a truly magnificent groom.

To all the mavericks at Murdoch who let me loose on this project, especially to Jane Morrow, Virginia Birch and Megan Pigott, whose expertise, foresight and infinite enthusiasm kept me buoyed throughout this mammoth task, and to Carol Warwick, Sarah Hatton and team for the hypothetical (and actual) hype. To Vera Babida, you are remarkably talented – your way with colors, with shapes and textures, the witticisms in your brush strokes and asides – if Mother Nature had an iPad and a stylus, she would wish to have your hand. To *IPOV*'s word editor, Katri Hilden, who gets to read this all in advance, the writer within me honors and respects the writer within you. To *IPOV*'s food editor, Samantha Parish, working with you is a maximum of fun, minimum of fuss – thank you for throwing your whole self into this project. And to Helena Holmgren, for taking on the huge task of indexing this beast into submission. To my American publishing fam, Robert, Lindsay, Colin and everyone at Appetite and PRHC, thank you for helping bring all of the colORs (!) to your shores.

To the studio dream-team that is Lucy Tweed and Ben Dearnley, the imagery in this book is a testament to the love and light that you bring to your work. To the photo-chefs, Kay, Lauren and to my home-economist-for-ever, Grylltown, your fingerprints are all over this food, in the best possible way. To the ceramicists, Batch Ceramics, Hayden Youlley, LouiseM Studio, Mud Australia, and to Sift Produce for sourcing many of the sublime vegetables you see in these pages. To Jacqui Porter who, like any good cook (and designer), took these raw ingredients and whipped them into something greater still than the sum of its parts.

To Alec and Christian for our Hours of Power and your hours of passion, insights and care. To my friends in food who helped connect me with the people who knew the people, especially to Dani Valent, Monica Brown, Kylie Millar and Tawnya Bahr. To the chef-wranglers and to the chefs themselves, I asked for only a few sentences, sometimes in the very shoddiest French, Spanish, Italian, and Russian, and you delivered paragraphs of prose; your passion is palpable.

Finally, to the agronomists, breeders, growers, pickers, packers, wholesalers, suppliers and retailers of vegetables around the world, you are the ones who deserve the highest praise of all.

Seasonal index

A general guide; veggies in **bold** are at their peak.

Spring

artichoke	cauliflower	**onion**
arugula	celery	parsnip
asparagus	chili	**peas**
beans	ginger	potato
beets	herbs	**radicchio**
bell pepper	kohlrabi	**radish**
bok choy	**leek**	rhubarb
broccoli	lemongrass	spinach
butternut	**lettuce**	sweet potato
squash	mushrooms	tomato
carrot	napa cabbage	**zucchini flower**

Summer

arugula	cucumber	parsnip
avocado	eggplant	patty pan
beans	fennel	squash
beets	garlic	potato
bell pepper	ginger (young)	radish
broccoli	herbs	rhubarb
butternut	leek	spinach
squash	**lemongrass**	sweet potato
carrot	lettuce	**tomato**
cauliflower	mushrooms	turnip
celery	napa cabbage	**zucchini**
chili	okra	zucchini flower
corn	**onion**	

Autumn

arugula	chili	mushrooms
avocado	corn	napa cabbage
beets	daikon	onion
bell pepper	eggplant	parsnip
bok choy	fennel	potato
broccoli	ginger (young)	pumpkin
butternut	herbs	spinach
squash	horseradish	**sweet potato**
carrot	kohlrabi	tomato
cauliflower	leek	turnip
celeriac	lemongrass	yams & tubers
celery	lettuce	zucchini

Winter

arugula	daikon	napa cabbage
beets	fennel	onion
bok choy	ginger	parsnip
broccoli	herbs	potato
brussels sprouts	horseradish	pumpkin
butternut	Jerusalem	rhubarb
squash	artichoke	spinach
cabbage	**kale**	sweet potato
carrot	kohlrabi	tomato
cauliflower	**leek**	turnip
celeriac	lemongrass	**Tuscan kale**
celery	**lettuce**	yams & tubers
chili	mushrooms	

Index

h

i

quiche

Library and Archives Canada Cataloguing in Publication is available upon request.

ISBN: 978-0-525-61212-4
eBook ISBN: 978-0-525-61213-1

Interior designer: Northwood Green
Cover designer: Trish Garner
Photographer: Ben Dearnley
Illustrator: Vera Babida
Stylist: Lucy Tweed

Printed in China

Originally published in Australia by Murdoch Books, an imprint of Allen & Unwin.

Published in Canada by Appetite by Random House®, a division of Penguin Random House Canada Limited.

www.penguinrandomhouse.ca

10 9 8 7 6 5 4 3 2 1

appetite
by RANDOM HOUSE | Penguin
Random House
Canada

My family treads lightly on the lands of the Boon Wurrung (Bunurong) people of the Kulin Nation.

We recognize their continuing connection to land, waters and culture, and pay our respects to their Elders – past, present and emerging.

Alice Zaslavsky

TABLESPOON MEASURES: Teaspoon and tablespoon measurements vary by country. In this book, 1 tsp = 5ml, and 1 tbsp = 20ml.

OVEN GUIDE: All recipes were tested in a fan-assisted oven using Celsius temperatures; for this edition of the book, temperatures were converted to the equivalent Fahrenheit temperature for a regular oven. Ovens vary (mine is hot!) so look for visual descriptions in the recipes, rather than just timing, to get the best results.

MORE IN PRAISE OF VEG: Scan the QR code with the camera of your smartphone or tablet for a nifty guide to getting the most out of this book! Or come visit me at www.inpraiseofveg.com.